Mastering the C

Make full use of the standard library components in C++17

Arthur O'Dwyer

BIRMINGHAM - MUMBAI

Mastering the C++17 STL

Copyright © 2017 Packt Publishing

All rights reserved. No part of this book may be reproduced, stored in a retrieval system, or transmitted in any form or by any means, without the prior written permission of the publisher, except in the case of brief quotations embedded in critical articles or reviews.

Every effort has been made in the preparation of this book to ensure the accuracy of the information presented. However, the information contained in this book is sold without warranty, either express or implied. Neither the author, nor Packt Publishing, and its dealers and distributors will be held liable for any damages caused or alleged to be caused directly or indirectly by this book.

Packt Publishing has endeavored to provide trademark information about all of the companies and products mentioned in this book by the appropriate use of capitals. However, Packt Publishing cannot guarantee the accuracy of this information.

First published: September 2017

Production reference: 1250917

Published by Packt Publishing Ltd.
Livery Place
35 Livery Street
Birmingham
B3 2PB, UK.

ISBN 978-1-78712-682-4

www.packtpub.com

Credits

Author
Arthur O'Dwyer

Reviewer
Will Brennan

Commissioning Editor
Merint Thomas Matthew

Acquisition Editor
Sandeep Mishra

Content Development Editor
Lawrence Veigas

Technical Editor
Dhiraj Chandanshive

Copy Editor
Safis Editing

Project Coordinator
Prajakta Naik

Proofreader
Safis Editing

Indexer
Mariammal Chettiyar

Production Coordinator
Nilesh Mohite

About the Author

Arthur O'Dwyer has used modern C++ in his day job for about ten years--since the days when "modern C++" meant "classic C++." Between 2006 and 2011 he worked on the Green Hills C++ compiler. Since 2014 he has organized a weekly C++ meetup in the San Francisco Bay Area, and he speaks regularly on topics such as those to be found in this book. Later this year, he will attend an ISO C++ committee meeting for the second time.

This is his first book.

About the Reviewer

Will Brennan is a C++/Python developer based in London with experience working on high performance image processing and machine learning applications. You can visit his GitHub link at `https://github.com/WillBrennan`.

www.PacktPub.com

For support files and downloads related to your book, please visit www.PacktPub.com.

Did you know that Packt offers eBook versions of every book published, with PDF and ePub files available? You can upgrade to the eBook version at www.PacktPub.com and as a print book customer, you are entitled to a discount on the eBook copy. Get in touch with us at service@packtpub.com for more details.

At www.PacktPub.com, you can also read a collection of free technical articles, sign up for a range of free newsletters and receive exclusive discounts and offers on Packt books and eBooks.

https://www.packtpub.com/mapt

Get the most in-demand software skills with Mapt. Mapt gives you full access to all Packt books and video courses, as well as industry-leading tools to help you plan your personal development and advance your career.

Why subscribe?

- Fully searchable across every book published by Packt
- Copy and paste, print, and bookmark content
- On demand and accessible via a web browser

Customer Feedback

Thanks for purchasing this Packt book. At Packt, quality is at the heart of our editorial process. To help us improve, please leave us an honest review on this book's Amazon page at https://www.amazon.com/dp/178712682X. If you'd like to join our team of regular reviewers, you can email us at customerreviews@packtpub.com. We award our regular reviewers with free eBooks and videos in exchange for their valuable feedback. Help us be relentless in improving our products!

Table of Contents

Preface	1
Chapter 1: Classical Polymorphism and Generic Programming	7
Concrete monomorphic functions	8
Classically polymorphic functions	8
Generic programming with templates	10
Summary	14
Chapter 2: Iterators and Ranges	15
The problem with integer indices	15
On beyond pointers	17
Const iterators	19
A pair of iterators defines a range	21
Iterator categories	22
Input and output iterators	25
Putting it all together	28
The deprecated std::iterator	31
Summary	35
Chapter 3: The Iterator-Pair Algorithms	37
A note about headers	37
Read-only range algorithms	38
Shunting data with std::copy	44
Variations on a theme - std::move and std::move_iterator	47
Complicated copying with std::transform	51
Write-only range algorithms	53
Algorithms that affect object lifetime	55
Our first permutative algorithm: std::sort	56
Swapping, reversing, and partitioning	57
Rotation and permutation	62
Heaps and heapsort	63
Merges and mergesort	66
Searching and inserting in a sorted array with std::lower_bound	67
Deleting from a sorted array with std::remove_if	69
Summary	73
Chapter 4: The Container Zoo	75

The notion of ownership	76
The simplest container: std::array<T, N>	78
The workhorse: std::vector<T>	81
Resizing a std::vector	83
Inserting and erasing in a std::vector	86
Pitfalls with vector<bool>	88
Pitfalls with non-noexcept move constructors	89
The speedy hybrid: std::deque<T>	91
A particular set of skills: std::list<T>	92
What are the special skills of std::list?	93
Roughing it with std::forward_list<T>	95
Abstracting with std::stack<T> and std::queue<T>	96
The useful adaptor: std::priority_queue<T>	97
The trees: std::set<T> and std::map<K, V>	99
A note about transparent comparators	103
Oddballs: std::multiset<T> and std::multimap<K, V>	104
The hashes: std::unordered_set<T> and std::unordered_map<K, V>	108
Load factor and bucket lists	110
Where does the memory come from?	111
Summary	111
Chapter 5: Vocabulary Types	113
The story of std::string	114
Tagging reference types with reference_wrapper	115
C++11 and algebraic types	116
Working with std::tuple	117
Manipulating tuple values	120
A note about named classes	121
Expressing alternatives with std::variant	121
Visiting variants	123
What about make_variant? and a note on value semantics	125
Delaying initialization with std::optional	127
Revisiting variant	131
Infinite alternatives with std::any	132
std::any versus polymorphic class types	134
Type erasure in a nutshell	135
std::any and copyability	137
Again with the type erasure: std::function	138
std::function, copyability, and allocation	140
Summary	141

Chapter 6: Smart Pointers — 143
- **The origins of smart pointers** — 143
- **Smart pointers never forget** — 145
- **Automatically managing memory with std::unique_ptr<T>** — 145
  - Why C++ doesn't have the finally keyword — 149
  - Customizing the deletion callback — 150
  - Managing arrays with std::unique_ptr<T[]> — 151
- **Reference counting with std::shared_ptr<T>** — 152
  - Don't double-manage! — 155
  - Holding nullable handles with weak_ptr — 156
  - Talking about oneself with std::enable_shared_from_this — 159
  - The Curiously Recurring Template Pattern — 162
  - A final warning — 163
- **Denoting un-special-ness with observer_ptr<T>** — 163
- **Summary** — 165

Chapter 7: Concurrency — 167
- **The problem with volatile** — 168
- **Using std::atomic<T> for thread-safe accesses** — 171
  - Doing complicated operations atomically — 173
  - Big atomics — 175
- **Taking turns with std::mutex** — 175
  - "Taking locks" the right way — 178
- **Always associate a mutex with its controlled data** — 181
- **Special-purpose mutex types** — 185
  - Upgrading a read-write lock — 188
  - Downgrading a read-write lock — 188
- **Waiting for a condition** — 189
- **Promises about futures** — 193
- **Packaging up tasks for later** — 197
- **The future of futures** — 198
- **Speaking of threads...** — 201
  - Identifying individual threads and the current thread — 202
- **Thread exhaustion and std::async** — 205
- **Building your own thread pool** — 207
  - Improving our thread pool's performance — 212
- **Summary** — 214

Chapter 8: Allocators — 215
- **An allocator is a handle to a memory resource** — 217

[iii]

Refresher - Interfaces versus concepts	218
Defining a heap with memory_resource	219
Using the standard memory resources	222
Allocating from a pool resource	224
The 500 hats of the standard allocator	226
Carrying metadata with fancy pointers	230
Sticking a container to a single memory resource	235
Using the standard allocator types	237
Setting the default memory resource	238
Making a container allocator-aware	240
Propagating downwards with scoped_allocator_adaptor	246
Propagating different allocators	249
Summary	251

Chapter 9: Iostreams — 253

The trouble with I/O in C++	254
Buffering versus formatting	255
Using the POSIX API	256
Using the standard C API	260
Buffering in the standard C API	262
Formatting with printf and snprintf	267
The classical iostreams hierarchy	270
Streaming and manipulators	275
Streaming and wrappers	278
Solving the sticky-manipulator problem	280
Formatting with ostringstream	282
A note on locales	283
Converting numbers to strings	284
Converting strings to numbers	287
Reading a line or word at a time	291
Summary	293

Chapter 10: Regular Expressions — 295

What are regular expressions?	296
A note on backslash-escaping	297
Reifying regular expressions into std::regex objects	299
Matching and searching	301
Pulling submatches out of a match	302
Converting submatches to data values	306
Iterating over multiple matches	307

[iv]

Using regular expressions for string replacement	311
A primer on the ECMAScript regex grammar	**314**
Non-consuming constructs	317
Obscure ECMAScript features and pitfalls	318
Summary	**319**

Chapter 11: Random Numbers — 321

Random numbers versus pseudo-random numbers	**322**
The problem with rand()	**324**
Solving problems with <random>	**325**
Dealing with generators	**326**
Truly random bits with std::random_device	326
Pseudo-random bits with std::mt19937	327
Filtering generator outputs with adaptors	329
Dealing with distributions	**331**
Rolling dice with uniform_int_distribution	332
Generating populations with normal_distribution	334
Making weighted choices with discrete_distribution	335
Shuffling cards with std::shuffle	337
Summary	**338**

Chapter 12: Filesystem — 339

A note about namespaces	**339**
A very long note on error-reporting	**341**
Using <system_error>	344
Error codes and error conditions	348
Throwing errors with std::system_error	351
Filesystems and paths	**353**
Representing paths in C++	355
Operations on paths	358
Statting files with directory_entry	**359**
Walking directories with directory_iterator	**360**
Recursive directory walking	361
Modifying the filesystem	**362**
Reporting disk usage	**363**
Summary	**363**

Index — 365

Preface

The C++ language has a long history, dating back to the 1980s. Recently it has undergone a renaissance, with major new features being introduced in 2011 and 2014. At press time, the C++17 standard is just around the corner.

C++11 practically doubled the size of the standard library, adding such headers as `<tuple>`, `<type_traits>`, and `<regex>`. C++17 doubles the library again, with additions such as `<optional>`, `<any>`, and `<filesystem>`. A programmer who's been spending time writing code instead of watching the standardization process might fairly feel that the standard library has gotten away from him--that there's so many new things in the library that he'll never be able to master the whole thing, or even to sort the wheat from the chaff. After all, who wants to spend a month reading technical documentation on `std::locale` and `std::ratio`, just to find out that they aren't useful in your daily work?

In this book, I'll teach you the most important features of the C++17 standard library. In the interest of brevity, I omit some parts, such as the aforementioned `<type_traits>`; but we'll cover the entire modern STL (every standard container and every standard algorithm), plus such important topics as smart pointers, random numbers, regular expressions, and the new-in-C++17 `<filesystem>` library.

I'll teach by example. You'll learn to build your own iterator type; your own memory allocator using `std::pmr::memory_resource`; your own thread pool using `std::future`.

I'll teach concepts beyond what you'd find in a reference manual. You'll learn the difference between monomorphic, polymorphic, and generic algorithms (Chapter 1, *Classical Polymorphism and Generic Programming*); what it means for `std::string` or `std::any` to be termed a "vocabulary type" (Chapter 5, *Vocabulary Types*); and what we might expect from future C++ standards in 2020 and beyond.

I assume that you are already reasonably familiar with the core language of C++11; for example, that you already understand how to write class and function templates, the difference between lvalue and rvalue references, and so on.

What this book covers

Chapter 1, *Classical Polymorphism and Generic Programming*, covers classical polymorphism (virtual member functions) and generic programming (templates).

Chapter 2, *Iterators and Ranges*, explains the concept of *iterator* as a generalization of pointer, and the utility of half-open ranges expressed as a pair of iterators.

Chapter 3, *The Iterator-Pair Algorithms*, explores the vast variety of standard generic algorithms that operate on ranges expressed as iterator-pairs.

Chapter 4, *The Container Zoo*, explores the almost equally vast variety of standard container class templates, and which containers are suitable for which jobs.

Chapter 5, *Vocabulary Types*, walks you through algebraic types such as `std::optional`. and ABI-friendly type-erased types such as `std::function`.

Chapter 6, *Smart Pointers*, teaches the purpose and use of smart pointers.

Chapter 7, *Concurrency*, covers atomics, mutexes, condition variables, threads, futures, and promises.

Chapter 8, *Allocators*, explains the new features of C++17's `<memory_resource>` header.

Chapter 9, *Iostreams*, explores the evolution of the C++ I/O model, from `<unistd.h>` to `<stdio.h>` to `<iostream>`.

Chapter 10, *Regular Expressions*, teaches regular expressions in C++.

Chapter 11, *Random Numbers*, walks you through C++'s support for pseudo-random number generation.

Chapter 12, *Filesystem*, covers the new-in-C++17 `<filesystem>` library.

What you need for this book

As this book is not a reference manual, it might be useful for you to have a reference manual, such as cppreference (en.cppreference.com/w/cpp), at your side to clarify any confusing points. It will definitely help to have a C++17 compiler handy. At press time, there are several more or less feature-complete C++17 implementations, including GCC, Clang, and Microsoft Visual Studio. You can run them locally or via many free online compiler services, such as Wandbox (wandbox.org), Godbolt (gcc.godbolt.org), and Rextester (rextester.com).

Who this book is for

This book is for developers who would like to master the C++17 STL and make full use of its components. Prior C++ knowledge is assumed.

Conventions

In this book, you will find a number of text styles that distinguish between different kinds of information. Here are some examples of these styles and an explanation of their meaning.

Code words in text, database table names, folder names, filenames, file extensions, pathnames, dummy URLs, user input, and Twitter handles are shown as follows: "The `buffer()` function accepts arguments of type `int`."

A block of code is set as follows:

```
try {
    none.get();
} catch (const std::future_error& ex) {
    assert(ex.code() == std::future_errc::broken_promise);
}
```

New terms and **important words** are shown in bold.

Warnings or important notes appear like this.

Tips and notes appear like this.

Reader feedback

Feedback from our readers is always welcome. Let us know what you think about this book--what you liked or disliked. Reader feedback is important for us as it helps us develop titles that you will really get the most out of. To send us general feedback, simply e-mail `feedback@packtpub.com`, and mention the book's title in the subject of your message. If there is a topic that you have expertise in and you are interested in either writing or contributing to a book, see our author guide at www.packtpub.com/authors.

Preface

Customer support

Now that you are the proud owner of a Packt book, we have a number of things to help you to get the most from your purchase.

Downloading the example code

You can download the example code files for this book from your account at `http://www.packtpub.com`. If you purchased this book elsewhere, you can visit `http://www.packtpub.com/support` and register to have the files e-mailed directly to you. You can download the code files by following these steps:

1. Log in or register to our website using your e-mail address and password.
2. Hover the mouse pointer on the **SUPPORT** tab at the top.
3. Click on **Code Downloads & Errata**.
4. Enter the name of the book in the **Search** box.
5. Select the book for which you're looking to download the code files.
6. Choose from the drop-down menu where you purchased this book from.
7. Click on **Code Download**.

Once the file is downloaded, please make sure that you unzip or extract the folder using the latest version of:

- WinRAR / 7-Zip for Windows
- Zipeg / iZip / UnRarX for Mac
- 7-Zip / PeaZip for Linux

The code bundle for the book is also hosted on GitHub at `https://github.com/PacktPublishing/Mastering-the-Cpp17-STL`. We also have other code bundles from our rich catalog of books and videos available at `https://github.com/PacktPublishing/`. Check them out!

Errata

Although we have taken every care to ensure the accuracy of our content, mistakes do happen. If you find a mistake in one of our books--maybe a mistake in the text or the code-- we would be grateful if you could report this to us. By doing so, you can save other readers from frustration and help us improve subsequent versions of this book. If you find any errata, please report them by visiting http://www.packtpub.com/submit-errata, selecting your book, clicking on the **Errata Submission Form** link, and entering the details of your errata. Once your errata are verified, your submission will be accepted and the errata will be uploaded to our website or added to any list of existing errata under the Errata section of that title. To view the previously submitted errata, go to https://www.packtpub.com/books/content/support and enter the name of the book in the search field. The required information will appear under the **Errata** section.

Piracy

Piracy of copyrighted material on the Internet is an ongoing problem across all media. At Packt, we take the protection of our copyright and licenses very seriously. If you come across any illegal copies of our works in any form on the Internet, please provide us with the location address or website name immediately so that we can pursue a remedy. Please contact us at copyright@packtpub.com with a link to the suspected pirated material. We appreciate your help in protecting our authors and our ability to bring you valuable content.

Questions

If you have a problem with any aspect of this book, you can contact us at questions@packtpub.com, and we will do our best to address the problem.

1
Classical Polymorphism and Generic Programming

The C++ standard library has two distinct, yet equally important, missions. One of these missions is to provide rock-solid implementations of certain concrete data types or functions that have tended to be useful in many different programs, yet aren't built into the core language syntax. This is why the standard library contains `std::string`, `std::regex`, `std::filesystem::exists`, and so on. The other mission of the standard library is to provide rock-solid implementations of widely used *abstract algorithms* such as sorting, searching, reversing, collating, and so on. In this first chapter, we will nail down exactly what we mean when we say that a particular piece of code is "abstract," and describe the two approaches that the standard library uses to provide abstraction: *classical polymorphism* and *generic programming*.

We will look at the following topics in this chapter:

- Concrete (monomorphic) functions, whose behavior is not parameterizable
- Classical polymorphism by means of base classes, virtual member functions, and inheritance
- Generic programming by means of concepts, requirements, and models
- The practical advantages and disadvantages of each approach

Concrete monomorphic functions

What distinguishes an abstract algorithm from a concrete function? This is best shown by example. Let's write a function to multiply each of the elements in an array by 2:

```
class array_of_ints {
  int data[10] = {};
public:
    int size() const { return 10; }
    int& at(int i) { return data[i]; }
};

void double_each_element(array_of_ints& arr)
{
  for (int i=0; i < arr.size(); ++i) {
    arr.at(i) *= 2;
  }
}
```

Our function `double_each_element` works *only* with objects of type `array_of_int`; passing in an object of a different type won't work (nor even compile). We refer to functions like this version of `double_each_element` as *concrete* or *monomorphic* functions. We call them *concrete* because they are insufficiently *abstract* for our purposes. Just imagine how painful it would be if the C++ standard library provided a concrete `sort` routine that worked only on one specific data type!

Classically polymorphic functions

We can increase the abstraction level of our algorithms via the techniques of classical **object-oriented** (**OO**) programming, as seen in languages such as Java and C#. The OO approach is to decide exactly which behaviors we'd like to be customizable, and then declare them as the public virtual member functions of an *abstract base class*:

```
class container_of_ints {
public:
    virtual int size() const = 0;
    virtual int& at(int) = 0;
};

class array_of_ints : public container_of_ints {
  int data[10] = {};
public:
    int size() const override { return 10; }
    int& at(int i) override { return data[i]; }
```

```cpp
};

class list_of_ints : public container_of_ints {
  struct node {
    int data;
    node *next;
  };
  node *head_ = nullptr;
  int size_ = 0;
 public:
   int size() const override { return size_; }
   int& at(int i) override {
     if (i >= size_) throw std::out_of_range("at");
     node *p = head_;
     for (int j=0; j < i; ++j) {
        p = p->next;
     }
     return p->data;
   }
   ~list_of_ints();
};

void double_each_element(container_of_ints& arr)
{
  for (int i=0; i < arr.size(); ++i) {
    arr.at(i) *= 2;
  }
}

void test()
{
  array_of_ints arr;
  double_each_element(arr);

  list_of_ints lst;
  double_each_element(lst);
}
```

Classical Polymorphism and Generic Programming

Inside `test`, the two different calls to `double_each_element` compile because in classical OO terminology, an `array_of_ints` **IS-A** `container_of_ints` (that is, it inherits from `container_of_ints` and implements the relevant virtual member functions), and a `list_of_ints` **IS-A** `container_of_ints` as well. However, the behavior of any given `container_of_ints` object is parameterized by its *dynamic type*; that is, by the table of function pointers associated with this particular object.

Since we can now parameterize the behavior of the `double_each_element` function without editing its source code directly--simply by passing in objects of different dynamic types--we say that the function has become *polymorphic*.

But still, this polymorphic function can handle only those types which are descendants of the base class `container_of_ints`. For example, you couldn't pass a `std::vector<int>` to this function; you'd get a compile error if you tried. Classical polymorphism is useful, but it does not get us all the way to full genericity.

An advantage of classical (object-oriented) polymorphism is that the source code still bears a one-to-one correspondence with the machine code that is generated by the compiler. At the machine-code level, we still have just one `double_each_element` function, with one signature and one well-defined entry point. For example, we can take the address of `double_each_element` as a function pointer.

Generic programming with templates

In modern C++, the typical way to write a fully generic algorithm is to implement the algorithm as a *template*. We're still going to implement the function template in terms of the public member functions `.size()` and `.at()`, but we're no longer going to require that the argument `arr` be of any particular type. Because our new function will be a template, we'll be telling the compiler "I don't care what type `arr` is. Whatever type it is, just generate a brand-new function (that is, a template instantiation) with that type as its parameter type."

```
template<class ContainerModel>
void double_each_element(ContainerModel& arr)
{
  for (int i=0; i < arr.size(); ++i) {
    arr.at(i) *= 2;
  }
}

void test()
{
  array_of_ints arr;
```

[10]

```
    double_each_element(arr);

    list_of_ints lst;
    double_each_element(lst);

    std::vector<int> vec = {1, 2, 3};
    double_each_element(vec);
}
```

In most cases, it helps us design better programs if we can put down in words exactly what operations must be supported by our template type parameter `ContainerModel`. That set of operations, taken together, constitutes what's known in C++ as a *concept*; in this example we might say that the concept `Container` consists of "having a member function named `size` that returns the size of the container as an `int` (or something comparable to `int`); and having a member function named `at` that takes an `int` index (or something implicitly convertible from `int`) and produces a non-const reference to the *index*'th element of the container." Whenever some class `array_of_ints` correctly supplies the operations required by the concept `Container`, such that `array_of_ints` is usable with `double_each_element`, we say that the concrete class `array_of_ints` *is a model of* the `Container` concept. This is why I gave the name `ContainerModel` to the template type parameter in the preceding example.

It would be more traditional to use the name `Container` for the template type parameter itself, and I will do that from now on; I just didn't want to start us off on the wrong foot by muddying the distinction between the `Container` concept and the particular template type parameter to this particular function template that happens to desire as its argument a concrete class that models the `Container` concept.

When we implement an abstract algorithm using templates, so that the behavior of the algorithm can be parameterized at compile time by any types modeling the appropriate concepts, we say we are doing generic programming.

Notice that our description of the `Container` concept didn't mention that we expect the type of the contained elements to be `int`; and not coincidentally, we find that we can now use our generic `double_each_element` function even with containers that don't hold `int`!

```
    std::vector<double> vecd = {1.0, 2.0, 3.0};
    double_each_element(vecd);
```

This extra level of genericity is one of the big benefits of using C++ templates for generic programming, as opposed to classical polymorphism. Classical polymorphism hides the varying behavior of different classes behind a stable *interface signature* (for example, `.at(i)` always returns `int&`), but once you start messing with varying signatures, classical polymorphism is no longer a good tool for the job.

Another advantage of generic programming is that it offers blazing speed through increased opportunities for inlining. The classically polymorphic example must repeatedly query the `container_of_int` object's virtual table to find the address of its particular virtual `at` method, and generally cannot see through the virtual dispatch at compile time. The template function `double_each_element<array_of_int>` can compile in a direct call to `array_of_int::at` or even inline the call completely.

Because generic programming with templates can so easily deal with complicated requirements and is so flexible in dealing with types--even primitive types like `int`, where classical polymorphism fails--the standard library uses templates for all its algorithms and the containers on which they operate. For this reason, the algorithms-and-containers part of the standard library is often referred to as the **Standard Template Library** or **STL**.

That's right--technically, the STL is only a small part of the C++ standard library! However, in this book, as in real life, we may occasionally slip up and use the term STL when we mean standard library, or vice versa.

Let's look at a couple more hand-written generic algorithms, before we dive into the standard generic algorithms provided by the STL. Here is a function template `count`, returning the total number of elements in a container:

```
template<class Container>
int count(const Container& container)
{
  int sum = 0;
  for (auto&& elt : container) {
    sum += 1;
  }
  return sum;
}
```

And here is `count_if`, which returns the number of elements satisfying a user-supplied *predicate* function:

```
template<class Container, class Predicate>
int count_if(const Container& container, Predicate pred)
{
  int sum = 0;
  for (auto&& elt : container) {
    if (pred(elt)) {
        sum += 1;
    }
  }
  return sum;
}
```

These functions would be used like this:

```
std::vector<int> v = {3, 1, 4, 1, 5, 9, 2, 6};

assert(count(v) == 8);

int number_above =
   count_if(v, [](int e) { return e > 5; });
int number_below =
   count_if(v, [](int e) { return e < 5; });

assert(number_above == 2);
assert(number_below == 5);
```

There is so much power packed into that little expression `pred(elt)`! I encourage you to try re-implementing the `count_if` function in terms of classical polymorphism, just to get a sense of where the whole thing breaks down. There are a lot of varying signatures hidden under the syntactic sugar of modern C++. For example, the ranged for-loop syntax in our `count_if` function is converted (or lowered") by the compiler into a for-loop in terms of `container.begin()` and `container.end()`, each of which needs to return an iterator whose type is dependent on the type of `container` itself. For another example, in the generic-programming version, we never specify--we never *need* to specify--whether `pred` takes its parameter `elt` by value or by reference. Try doing *that* with a `virtual bool operator()`!

Classical Polymorphism and Generic Programming

Speaking of iterators: you may have noticed that all of our example functions in this chapter (no matter whether they were monomorphic, polymorphic, or generic) have been expressed in terms of containers. When we wrote `count`, we counted the elements in the entire container. When we wrote `count_if`, we counted the matching elements in the entire container. This turns out to be a very natural way to write, especially in modern C++; so much so that we can expect to see container-based algorithms (or their close cousin, range-based algorithms) arriving in C++20 or C++23. However, the STL dates back to the 1990s and pre-modern C++. So, the STL's authors assumed that dealing primarily in containers would be very expensive (due to all those expensive copy-constructions--remember that move semantics and move-construction did not arrive until C++11); and so they designed the STL to deal primarily in a much lighter-weight concept: the *iterator*. This will be the subject of our next chapter.

Summary

Both classical polymorphism and generic programming deal with the essential problem of parameterizing the behavior of an algorithm: for example, writing a search function that works with any arbitrary matching operation.

Classical polymorphism tackles that problem by specifying an *abstract base class* with a closed set of *virtual member functions*, and writing *polymorphic functions* that accept pointers or references to instances of concrete classes *inheriting from* that base class.

Generic programming tackles the same problem by specifying a *concept* with a closed set of *requirements*, and instantiating *function templates* with concrete classes *modeling* that concept.

Classical polymorphism has trouble with higher-level parameterizations (for example, manipulating function objects of any signature) and with relationships between types (for example, manipulating the elements of an arbitrary container). Therefore, the Standard Template Library uses a great deal of template-based generic programming, and hardly any classical polymorphism.

When you use generic programming, it will help if you keep in mind the conceptual requirements of your types, or even write them down explicitly; but as of C++17, the compiler cannot directly help you check those requirements.

2
Iterators and Ranges

In the previous chapter, we implemented several generic algorithms that operated on containers, but in an inefficient manner. In this chapter, you'll learn:

- How and why C++ generalizes the idea of pointers to create the *iterator* concept
- The importance of *ranges* in C++, and the standard way to express a half-open range as a pair of iterators
- How to write your own rock-solid, const-correct iterator types
- How to write generic algorithms that operate on iterator pairs
- The standard iterator hierarchy and its algorithmic importance

The problem with integer indices

In the previous chapter, we implemented several generic algorithms that operated on containers. Consider one of those algorithms again:

```
template<typename Container>
void double_each_element(Container& arr)
{
  for (int i=0; i < arr.size(); ++i) {
    arr.at(i) *= 2;
  }
}
```

Iterators and Ranges

This algorithm is defined in terms of the lower-level operations `.size()` and `.at()`. This works reasonably well for a container type such as `array_of_ints` or `std::vector`, but it doesn't work nearly so well for, say, a linked list such as the previous chapter's `list_of_ints`:

```
class list_of_ints {
  struct node {
    int data;
    node *next;
  };
  node *head_ = nullptr;
  node *tail_ = nullptr;
  int size_ = 0;
public:
  int size() const { return size_; }
  int& at(int i) {
    if (i >= size_) throw std::out_of_range("at");
    node *p = head_;
    for (int j=0; j < i; ++j) {
      p = p->next;
    }
    return p->data;
  }
  void push_back(int value) {
    node *new_tail = new node{value, nullptr};
    if (tail_) {
      tail_->next = new_tail;
    } else {
      head_ = new_tail;
    }
    tail_ = new_tail;
    size_ += 1;
  }
  ~list_of_ints() {
    for (node *next, *p = head_; p != nullptr; p = next) {
      next = p->next;
      delete p;
    }
  }
};
```

The implementation of `list_of_ints::at()` is O(n) in the length of the list--the longer our list gets, the slower `at()` gets. And particularly, when our `count_if` function loops over each element of the list, it's calling that `at()` function n times, which makes the runtime of our generic algorithm $O(n^2)$--for a simple counting operation that ought to be $O(n)$!

It turns out that integer indexing with .at() isn't a very good foundation on which to build algorithmic castles. We ought to pick a primitive operation that's closer to how computers actually manipulate data.

On beyond pointers

In the absence of any abstraction, how does one normally identify an element of an array, an element of a linked list, or an element of a tree? The most straightforward way would be to use a *pointer* to the element's address in memory. Here are some examples of pointers to elements of various data structures:

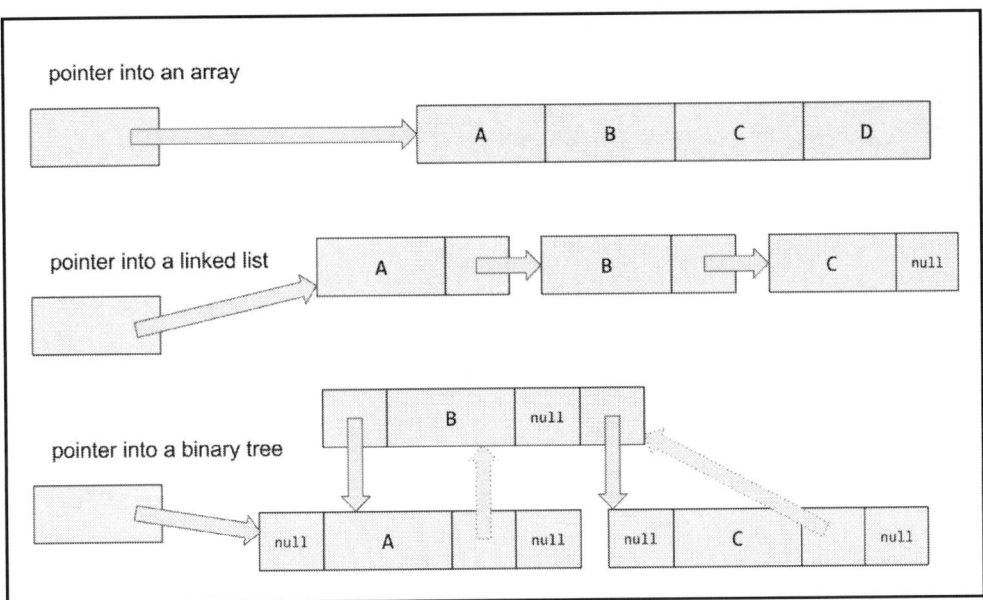

To iterate over an *array*, all we need is that pointer; we can handle all the elements in the array by starting with a pointer to the first element and simply incrementing that pointer until it reaches the last element. In C:

```
for (node *p = lst.head_; p != nullptr; p = p->next) {
  if (pred(p->data)) {
    sum += 1;
  }
}
```

Iterators and Ranges

But in order to efficiently iterate over a *linked list*, we need more than just a raw pointer; incrementing a pointer of type `node*` is highly unlikely to produce a pointer to the next node in the list! In that case, we need something that acts like a pointer--in particular, we should be able to dereference it to retrieve or modify the pointed-to element--but has special, container-specific behavior associated with the abstract concept of incrementing.

In C++, given that we have operator overloading built into the language, when I say "associate special behavior with the concept of incrementing", you should be thinking "let's overload the ++ operator." And indeed, that's what we'll do:

```
struct list_node {
  int data;
  list_node *next;
};

class list_of_ints_iterator {
  list_node *ptr_;

  friend class list_of_ints;
  explicit list_of_ints_iterator(list_node *p) : ptr_(p) {}
public:
  int& operator*() const { return ptr_->data; }
  list_of_ints_iterator& operator++() { ptr_ = ptr_->next; return *this; }
  list_of_ints_iterator operator++(int) { auto it = *this; ++*this; return it; }
  bool operator==(const list_of_ints_iterator& rhs) const
    { return ptr_ == rhs.ptr_; }
  bool operator!=(const list_of_ints_iterator& rhs) const
    { return ptr_ != rhs.ptr_; }
};

class list_of_ints {
  list_node *head_ = nullptr;
  list_node *tail_ = nullptr;
  // ...
public:
  using iterator = list_of_ints_iterator;
  iterator begin() { return iterator{head_}; }
  iterator end() { return iterator{nullptr}; }
};

template<class Container, class Predicate>
int count_if(Container& ctr, Predicate pred)
{
  int sum = 0;
  for (auto it = ctr.begin(); it != ctr.end(); ++it) {
```

```
            if (pred(*it)) {
                sum += 1;
            }
        }
        return sum;
    }
```

Notice that we also overload the unary `*` operator (for dereferencing) and the `==` and `!=` operators; our `count_if` template requires all of these operations be valid for the loop control variable `it`. (Well, okay, technically our `count_if` doesn't require the `==` operation; but if you're going to overload one of the comparison operators, you should overload the other as well.)

Const iterators

There's just one more complication to consider, before we abandon this list iterator example. Notice that I quietly changed our `count_if` function template so that it takes `Container&` instead of `const Container&`! That's because the `begin()` and `end()` member functions we provided are non-const member functions; and that's because they return iterators whose `operator*` returns non-const references to the elements of the list. We'd like to make our list type (and its iterators) completely const-correct--that is, we'd like you to be able to define and use variables of type `const list_of_ints`, but prevent you from modifying the elements of a `const` list.

The standard library generally deals with this issue by giving each standard container two different kinds of iterator: `bag::iterator` and `bag::const_iterator`. The non-const member function `bag::begin()` returns an `iterator` and the `bag::begin() const` member function returns a `const_iterator`. The underscore is all-important! Notice that `bag::begin() const` does not return a mere `const iterator`; if the returned object were `const`, we wouldn't be allowed to `++` it. (Which, in turn, would make it darn difficult to iterate over a `const bag`!) No, `bag::begin() const` returns something more subtle: a non-const `const_iterator` object whose `operator*` simply happens to yield a *const* reference to its element.

Maybe an example would help. Let's go ahead and implement `const_iterator` for our `list_of_ints` container.

Iterators and Ranges

Since most of the code for the `const_iterator` type is going to be exactly the same as the code for the `iterator` type, our first instinct might be to cut and paste. But this is C++! When I say "most of this code is going to be exactly the same as this other code," you should be thinking "let's make the common parts into a template." And indeed, that's what we'll do:

```
struct list_node {
  int data;
  list_node *next;
};

template<bool Const>
class list_of_ints_iterator {
  friend class list_of_ints;
  friend class list_of_ints_iterator<!Const>;

  using node_pointer = std::conditional_t<Const, const list_node*, list_node*>;
  using reference = std::conditional_t<Const, const int&, int&>;

  node_pointer ptr_;

  explicit list_of_ints_iterator(node_pointer p) : ptr_(p) {}
public:
  reference operator*() const { return ptr_->data; }
  auto& operator++() { ptr_ = ptr_->next; return *this; }
  auto operator++(int) { auto result = *this; ++*this; return result; }

  // Support comparison between iterator and const_iterator types
  template<bool R>
  bool operator==(const list_of_ints_iterator<R>& rhs) const
    { return ptr_ == rhs.ptr_; }

  template<bool R>
  bool operator!=(const list_of_ints_iterator<R>& rhs) const
    { return ptr_ != rhs.ptr_; }

  // Support implicit conversion of iterator to const_iterator
  // (but not vice versa)
  operator list_of_ints_iterator<true>() const
    { return list_of_ints_iterator<true>{ptr_}; }
};

class list_of_ints {
  list_node *head_ = nullptr;
  list_node *tail_ = nullptr;
  // ...
public:
```

```
            using const_iterator = list_of_ints_iterator<true>;
            using iterator = list_of_ints_iterator<false>;

            iterator begin() { return iterator{head_}; }
            iterator end() { return iterator{nullptr}; }
            const_iterator begin() const { return const_iterator{head_}; }
            const_iterator end() const { return const_iterator{nullptr}; }
        };
```

The preceding code implements fully const-correct iterator types for our `list_of_ints`.

A pair of iterators defines a range

Now that we understand the fundamental concept of an iterator, let's put it to some practical use. We've already seen that if you have a pair of iterators as returned from `begin()` and `end()`, you can use a for-loop to iterate over all the elements of the underlying container. But more powerfully, you can use some pair of iterators to iterate over any sub-range of the container's elements! Let's say you only wanted to view the first half of a vector:

```
        template<class Iterator>
        void double_each_element(Iterator begin, Iterator end)
        {
          for (auto it = begin; it != end; ++it) {
            *it *= 2;
          }
        }

        int main()
        {
          std::vector<int> v {1, 2, 3, 4, 5, 6};
          double_each_element(v.begin(), v.end());
            // double each element in the entire vector
          double_each_element(v.begin(), v.begin()+3);
            // double each element in the first half of the vector
          double_each_element(&v[0], &v[3]);
            // double each element in the first half of the vector
        }
```

Notice that in the first and second test cases in `main()` we pass in a pair of iterators derived from `v.begin()`; that is, two values of type `std::vector::iterator`. In the third test case, we pass in two values of type `int*`. Since `int*` satisfies all the requirements of an iterator type in this case--namely: it is incrementable, comparable, and dereferenceable--our code works fine even with pointers! This example demonstrates the flexibility of the iterator-pair model. (However, in general you should avoid messing around with raw pointers, if you're using a container such as `std::vector` that offers a proper `iterator` type. Use iterators derived from `begin()` and `end()` instead.)

We can say that a pair of iterators implicitly defines a *range* of data elements. And for a surprisingly large family of algorithms, that's good enough! We don't need to have access to the *container* in order to perform certain searches or transformations; we only need access to the particular *range* of elements being searched or transformed. Going further down this line of thought will eventually lead us to the concept of a *non-owning view* (which is to a data sequence as a C++ reference is to a single variable), but views and ranges are still more modern concepts, and we ought to finish up with the 1998-vintage STL before we talk about those things.

In the previous code sample, we saw the first example of a real STL-style generic algorithm. Admittedly, `double_each_element` is not a terribly generic algorithm in the sense of implementing a behavior that we might want to reuse in other programs; but this version of the function is now perfectly generic in the sense of operating only on pairs of `Iterators`, where `Iterator` can be any type in the world that implements incrementability, comparability, and dereferenceability. (We'll see a version of this algorithm that is more generic in that first sense in this book's next chapter, when we talk about `std::transform`.)

Iterator categories

Let's revisit the `count` and `count_if` functions that we introduced in Chapter 1, *Classical Polymorphism and Generic Programming*. Compare the function template definition in this next example to the similar code from that chapter; you'll see that it's identical except for the substitution of a pair of `Iterators` (that is, an implicitly defined *range*) for the `Container&` parameter--and except that I've changed the name of the first function from `count` to `distance`. That's because you can find this function, almost exactly as described here, in the Standard Template Library under the name `std::distance` and you can find the second function under the name `std::count_if`:

```
template<typename Iterator>
int distance(Iterator begin, Iterator end)
```

```
{
  int sum = 0;
  for (auto it = begin; it != end; ++it) {
    sum += 1;
  }
  return sum;
}

template<typename Iterator, typename Predicate>
int count_if(Iterator begin, Iterator end, Predicate pred)
{
  int sum = 0;
  for (auto it = begin; it != end; ++it) {
    if (pred(*it)) {
        sum += 1;
    }
  }
  return sum;
}

void test()
{
   std::vector<int> v = {3, 1, 4, 1, 5, 9, 2, 6};

   int number_above = count_if(v.begin(), v.end(), [](int e) { return e > 5; });
   int number_below = count_if(v.begin(), v.end(), [](int e) { return e < 5; });

   int total = distance(v.begin(), v.end()); // DUBIOUS

   assert(number_above == 2);
   assert(number_below == 5);
   assert(total == 8);
}
```

But let's consider the line marked DUBIOUS in that example. Here we're computing the distance between two Iterators by repeatedly incrementing the one until it reaches the other. How performant is this approach? For certain kinds of iterators--for example, list_of_ints::iterator--we're not going to be able to do better than this. But for vector::iterator or int*, which iterate over contiguous data, it's a little silly of us to be using a loop and an O(n) algorithm when we could accomplish the same thing in O(1) time by simple pointer subtraction. That is, we'd like the standard library version of std::distance to include a template specialization something like this:

```
template<typename Iterator>
int distance(Iterator begin, Iterator end)
```

Iterators and Ranges

```
{
  int sum = 0;
  for (auto it = begin; it != end; ++it) {
    sum += 1;
  }
  return sum;
}

template<>
int distance(int *begin, int *end)
{
  return end - begin;
}
```

But we don't want the specialization to exist only for `int*` and `std::vector::iterator`. We want the standard library's `std::distance` to be efficient for all the iterator types that support this particular operation. That is, we're starting to develop an intuition that there are (at least) two different kinds of iterators: there are those that are incrementable, comparable, and dereferenceable; and then there are those that are incrementable, comparable, dereferenceable, *and also subtractable!* It turns out that for any iterator type where the operation `i = p - q` makes sense, its inverse operation `q = p + i` also makes sense. Iterators that support subtraction and addition are called *random-access iterators*.

So, the standard library's `std::distance` ought to be efficient for both random-access iterators and other kinds of iterators. To make it easier to supply the partial specializations for these templates, the standard library introduced the idea of a hierarchy of iterator kinds. Iterators such as `int*`, which support addition and subtraction, are known as random-access iterators. We'll say that they satisfy the concept `RandomAccessIterator`.

Iterators slightly less powerful than random-access iterators might not support addition or subtraction of arbitrary distances, but they at least support incrementing and decrementing with `++p` and `--p`. Iterators of this nature are called `BidirectionalIterator`. All `RandomAccessIterator` are `BidirectionalIterator`, but not necessarily vice versa. In some sense, we can imagine `RandomAccessIterator` to be a sub-class or sub-concept relative to `BidirectionalIterator`; and we can say that `BidirectionalIterator` is a *weaker concept*, imposing fewer requirements, than `RandomAccessIterator`.

An even weaker concept is the kind of iterators that don't even support decrementing. For example, our `list_of_ints::iterator` type doesn't support decrementing, because our linked list has no previous pointers; once you've got an iterator pointing at a given element of the list, you can only move forward to later elements, never backward to previous ones. Iterators that support `++p` but not `--p` are called `ForwardIterator`. `ForwardIterator` is a weaker concept than `BidirectionalIterator`.

Input and output iterators

We can imagine even weaker concepts than `ForwardIterator`! For example, one useful thing you can do with a `ForwardIterator` is to make a copy of it, save the copy, and use it to iterate twice over the same data. Manipulating the iterator (or copies of it) doesn't affect the underlying range of data at all. But we could invent an iterator like the one in the following snippet, where there is no underlying data at all, and it's not even meaningful to make a copy of the iterator:

```cpp
class getc_iterator {
  char ch;
public:
  getc_iterator() : ch(getc(stdin)) {}
  char operator*() const { return ch; }
  auto& operator++() { ch = getc(stdin); return *this; }
  auto operator++(int) { auto result(*this); ++*this; return result; }
  bool operator==(const getc_iterator&) const { return false; }
  bool operator!=(const getc_iterator&) const { return true; }
};
```

(In fact, the standard library contains some iterator types very similar to this one; we'll discuss one such type, `std::istream_iterator`, in Chapter 9, *Iostreams*.) Such iterators, which are not meaningfully copyable, and do not point to data elements in any meaningful sense, are called `InputIterator` types.

The mirror-image case is also possible. Consider the following invented iterator type:

```cpp
class putc_iterator {
  struct proxy {
    void operator= (char ch) { putc(ch, stdout); }
  };
public:
  proxy operator*() const { return proxy{}; }
  auto& operator++() { return *this; }
  auto& operator++(int) { return *this; }
  bool operator==(const putc_iterator&) const { return false; }
  bool operator!=(const putc_iterator&) const { return true; }
};

void test()
{
  putc_iterator it;
  for (char ch : {'h', 'e', 'l', 'l', 'o', '\n'}) {
    *it++ = ch;
  }
}
```

[25]

Iterators and Ranges

(Again, the standard library contains some iterator types very similar to this one; we'll discuss `std::back_insert_iterator` in Chapter 3, *The Iterator-Pair Algorithms,* and `std::ostream_iterator` in Chapter 9, *Iostreams.*) Such iterators, which are not meaningfully copyable, and are writeable-into but not readable-out-of, are called `OutputIterator` types.

Every iterator type in C++ falls into at least one of the following five categories:

- `InputIterator`
- `OutputIterator`
- `ForwardIterator`
- `BidirectionalIterator`, and/or
- `RandomAccessIterator`

Notice that while it's easy to figure out at compile time whether a particular iterator type conforms to the `BidirectionalIterator` or `RandomAccessIterator` requirements, it's impossible to figure out (purely from the syntactic operations it supports) whether we're dealing with an `InputIterator`, an `OutputIterator`, or a `ForwardIterator`. In our examples just a moment ago, consider: `getc_iterator`, `putc_iterator`, and `list_of_ints::iterator` support exactly the same syntactic operations--dereferencing with `*it`, incrementing with `++it`, and comparison with `it != it`. These three classes differ only at the semantic level. So how can the standard library distinguish between them?

It turns out that the standard library needs a bit of help from the implementor of each new iterator type. The standard library's algorithms will work only with iterator classes which define a *member typedef* named `iterator_category`. That is:

```
class getc_iterator {
  char ch;
public:
  using iterator_category = std::input_iterator_tag;

  // ...
};

class putc_iterator {
  struct proxy {
    void operator= (char ch) { putc(ch, stdout); }
  };
public:
  using iterator_category = std::output_iterator_tag;

  // ...
```

```
};

template<bool Const>
class list_of_ints_iterator {
  using node_pointer = std::conditional_t<Const, const list_node*,
    list_node*>;
  node_pointer ptr_;

public:
  using iterator_category = std::forward_iterator_tag;

  // ...
};
```

Then any standard (or heck, non-standard) algorithm that wants to customize its behavior based on the iterator categories of its template type parameters can do that customization simply by inspecting those types' `iterator_category`.

The iterator categories described in the preceding paragraph, correspond to the following five standard tag types defined in the `<iterator>` header:

```
struct input_iterator_tag { };
struct output_iterator_tag { };
struct forward_iterator_tag : public input_iterator_tag { };
struct bidirectional_iterator_tag : public forward_iterator_tag { };
struct random_access_iterator_tag : public bidirectional_iterator_tag
  { };
```

Notice that `random_access_iterator_tag` actually derives (in the classical-OO, polymorphic-class-hierarchy sense) from `bidirectional_iterator_tag`, and so on: the *conceptual hierarchy* of iterator kinds is reflected in the *class hierarchy* of `iterator_category` tag classes. This turns out to be useful in template metaprogramming when you're doing tag dispatch; but all you need to know about it for the purposes of using the standard library is that if you ever want to pass an `iterator_category` to a function, a tag of type `random_access_iterator_tag` will be a match for a function expecting an argument of type `bidirectional_iterator_tag`:

```
void foo(std::bidirectional_iterator_tag t [[maybe_unused]])
{
  puts("std::vector's iterators are indeed bidirectional...");
}

void bar(std::random_access_iterator_tag)
{
  puts("...and random-access, too!");
}
```

Iterators and Ranges

```
void bar(std::forward_iterator_tag)
{
  puts("forward_iterator_tag is not as good a match");
}

void test()
{
  using It = std::vector<int>::iterator;
  foo(It::iterator_category{});
  bar(It::iterator_category{});
}
```

At this point I expect you're wondering: "But what about `int*`? How can we provide a member typedef to something that isn't a class type at all, but rather a primitive scalar type? Scalar types can't have member typedefs." Well, as with most problems in software engineering, this problem can be solved by adding a layer of indirection. Rather than referring directly to `T::iterator_category`, the standard algorithms are careful always to refer to `std::iterator_traits<T>::iterator_category`. The class template `std::iterator_traits<T>` is appropriately specialized for the case where `T` is a pointer type.

Furthermore, `std::iterator_traits<T>` proved to be a convenient place to hang other member typedefs. It provides the following five member typedefs, if and only if `T` itself provides all five of them (or if `T` is a pointer type): `iterator_category`, `difference_type`, `value_type`, `pointer`, and `reference`.

Putting it all together

Putting together everything we've learned in this chapter, we can now write code like the following example. In this example, we're implementing our own `list_of_ints` with our own iterator class (including a const-correct `const_iterator` version); and we're enabling it to work with the standard library by providing the five all-important member typedefs.

```
struct list_node {
  int data;
  list_node *next;
};

template<bool Const>
class list_of_ints_iterator {
  friend class list_of_ints;
  friend class list_of_ints_iterator<!Const>;
```

```cpp
    using node_pointer = std::conditional_t<Const, const list_node*,
      list_node*>;
    node_pointer ptr_;

    explicit list_of_ints_iterator(node_pointer p) : ptr_(p) {}
  public:
    // Member typedefs required by std::iterator_traits
    using difference_type = std::ptrdiff_t;
    using value_type = int;
    using pointer = std::conditional_t<Const, const int*, int*>;
    using reference = std::conditional_t<Const, const int&, int&>;
    using iterator_category = std::forward_iterator_tag;

    reference operator*() const { return ptr_->data; }
    auto& operator++() { ptr_ = ptr_->next; return *this; }
    auto operator++(int) { auto result = *this; ++*this; return result; }

    // Support comparison between iterator and const_iterator types
    template<bool R>
    bool operator==(const list_of_ints_iterator<R>& rhs) const
      { return ptr_ == rhs.ptr_; }

    template<bool R>
    bool operator!=(const list_of_ints_iterator<R>& rhs) const
      { return ptr_ != rhs.ptr_; }

    // Support implicit conversion of iterator to const_iterator
    // (but not vice versa)
    operator list_of_ints_iterator<true>() const { return
      list_of_ints_iterator<true>{ptr_}; }
};

class list_of_ints {
  list_node *head_ = nullptr;
  list_node *tail_ = nullptr;
  int size_ = 0;
public:
  using const_iterator = list_of_ints_iterator<true>;
  using iterator = list_of_ints_iterator<false>;

  // Begin and end member functions
  iterator begin() { return iterator{head_}; }
  iterator end() { return iterator{nullptr}; }
  const_iterator begin() const { return const_iterator{head_}; }
  const_iterator end() const { return const_iterator{nullptr}; }

  // Other member operations
  int size() const { return size_; }
```

Iterators and Ranges

```
    void push_back(int value) {
      list_node *new_tail = new list_node{value, nullptr};
      if (tail_) {
        tail_->next = new_tail;
      } else {
        head_ = new_tail;
      }
      tail_ = new_tail;
      size_ += 1;
    }
    ~list_of_ints() {
      for (list_node *next, *p = head_; p != nullptr; p = next) {
        next = p->next;
        delete p;
      }
    }
};
```

Then, to show that we understand how the standard library implements generic algorithms, we'll implement the function templates `distance` and `count_if` exactly as the C++17 standard library would implement them.

> **TIP**: Notice the use of C++17's new `if constexpr` syntax in `distance`. We won't talk about C++17 core language features very much in this book, but suffice it to say, you can use `if constexpr` to eliminate a lot of awkward boilerplate compared to what you'd have had to write in C++14.

```
template<typename Iterator>
auto distance(Iterator begin, Iterator end)
{
  using Traits = std::iterator_traits<Iterator>;
  if constexpr (std::is_base_of_v<std::random_access_iterator_tag,
      typename Traits::iterator_category>) {
    return (end - begin);
  } else {
    auto result = typename Traits::difference_type{};
    for (auto it = begin; it != end; ++it) {
      ++result;
    }
    return result;
  }
}

template<typename Iterator, typename Predicate>
auto count_if(Iterator begin, Iterator end, Predicate pred)
{
  using Traits = std::iterator_traits<Iterator>;
```

```
    auto sum = typename Traits::difference_type{};
    for (auto it = begin; it != end; ++it) {
      if (pred(*it)) {
        ++sum;
      }
    }
    return sum;
}

void test()
{
    list_of_ints lst;
    lst.push_back(1);
    lst.push_back(2);
    lst.push_back(3);
    int s = count_if(lst.begin(), lst.end(), [](int i){
        return i >= 2;
    });
    assert(s == 2);
    int d = distance(lst.begin(), lst.end());
    assert(d == 3);
}
```

In the next chapter we'll stop implementing so many of our own function templates from scratch, and start marching through the function templates provided by the Standard Template Library. But before we leave this deep discussion of iterators, there's one more thing I'd like to talk about.

The deprecated std::iterator

You might be wondering: "Every iterator class I implement needs to provide the same five member typedefs. That's a lot of boilerplate--a lot of typing that I'd like to factor out, if I could." Is there no way to eliminate all that boilerplate?

Well, in C++98, and up until C++17, the standard library included a helper class template to do exactly that. Its name was `std::iterator`, and it took five template type parameters that corresponded to the five member typedefs required by `std::iterator_traits`. Three of these parameters had "sensible defaults," meaning that the simplest use-case was pretty well covered:

```
namespace std {
  template<
    class Category,
    class T,
```

```
        class Distance = std::ptrdiff_t,
        class Pointer = T*,
        class Reference = T&
    > struct iterator {
        using iterator_category = Category;
        using value_type = T;
        using difference_type = Distance;
        using pointer = Pointer;
        using reference = Reference;
    };
}

class list_of_ints_iterator :
    public std::iterator<std::forward_iterator_tag, int>
{
    // ...
};
```

Unfortunately for `std::iterator`, real life wasn't that simple; and `std::iterator` was deprecated in C++17 for several reasons that we're about to discuss.

As we saw in the section *Const iterators,* const-correctness requires us to provide a const iterator type along with every "non-const iterator" type. So what we really end up with, following that example, is code like this:

```
template<
    bool Const,
    class Base = std::iterator<
        std::forward_iterator_tag,
        int,
        std::ptrdiff_t,
        std::conditional_t<Const, const int*, int*>,
        std::conditional_t<Const, const int&, int&>
    >
>
class list_of_ints_iterator : public Base
{
    using typename Base::reference; // Awkward!

    using node_pointer = std::conditional_t<Const, const list_node*,
        list_node*>;
    node_pointer ptr_;

public:
    reference operator*() const { return ptr_->data; }
    // ...
};
```

[32]

The preceding code isn't any easier to read or write than the version that didn't use `std::iterator`; and furthermore, using `std::iterator` in the intended fashion complicates our code with *public inheritance,* which is to say, something that looks an awful lot like the classical object-oriented class hierarchy. A beginner might well be tempted to use that class hierarchy in writing functions like this one:

```
template<typename... Ts, typename Predicate>
int count_if(const std::iterator<Ts...>& begin,
             const std::iterator<Ts...>& end,
             Predicate pred);
```

This looks superficially similar to our examples of "polymorphic programming" from Chapter 1, *Classical Polymorphism and Generic Programming,* a function that implements different behaviors by taking parameters of type reference-to-base-class. But in the case of `std::iterator` this similarity is purely accidental and misleading; inheriting from `std::iterator` does *not* give us a polymorphic class hierarchy, and referring to that "base class" from our own functions is never the correct thing to do!

So, the C++17 standard deprecates `std::iterator` with an eye toward removing it completely in 2020 or some later standard. You shouldn't use `std::iterator` in code you write.

However, if you use Boost in your codebase, you might want to check out the Boost equivalent of `std::iterator`, which is spelled `boost::iterator_facade`. Unlike `std::iterator`, the `boost::iterator_facade` base class provides default functionality for pesky member functions such as `operator++(int)` and `operator!=` that would otherwise be tedious boilerplate. To use `iterator_facade`, simply inherit from it and define a few primitive member functions such as `dereference`, `increment`, and `equal`. (Since our list iterator is a `ForwardIterator`, that's all we need. For a `BidirectionalIterator` you would also need to provide a `decrement` member function, and so on.)

Since these primitive member functions are `private`, we grant Boost access to them via the declaration `friend class boost::iterator_core_access;`:

```
#include <boost/iterator/iterator_facade.hpp>

template<bool Const>
class list_of_ints_iterator : public boost::iterator_facade<
  list_of_ints_iterator<Const>,
  std::conditional_t<Const, const int, int>,
  std::forward_iterator_tag
>
{
```

```
        friend class boost::iterator_core_access;
        friend class list_of_ints;
        friend class list_of_ints_iterator<!Const>;

        using node_pointer = std::conditional_t<Const, const list_node*,
          list_node*>;
        node_pointer ptr_;

        explicit list_of_ints_iterator(node_pointer p) : ptr_(p) {}

        auto& dereference() const { return ptr_->data; }
        void increment() { ptr_ = ptr_->next; }

        // Support comparison between iterator and const_iterator types
        template<bool R>
        bool equal(const list_of_ints_iterator<R>& rhs) const {
          return ptr_ == rhs.ptr_; }
    public:
        // Support implicit conversion of iterator to const_iterator
        // (but not vice versa)
        operator list_of_ints_iterator<true>() const { return
          list_of_ints_iterator<true>{ptr_}; }
    };
```

Notice that the first template type argument to `boost::iterator_facade` is always the class whose definition you're writing: this is the Curiously Recurring Template Pattern, which we'll see again in Chapter 6, *Smart Pointers*.

This list-iterator code using `boost::iterator_facade` is significantly shorter than the same code in the previous section; the savings comes mainly from not having to repeat the relational operators. Because our list iterator is a `ForwardIterator`, we only had two relational operators; but if it were a `RandomAccessIterator`, then `iterator_facade` would generate default implementations of operators -, <, >, <=, and >= all based on the single primitive member function `distance_to`.

Summary

In this chapter, we've learned that traversal is one of the most fundamental things you can do with a data structure. However, raw pointers alone are insufficient for traversing complicated structures: applying ++ to a raw pointer often doesn't "go on to the next item" in the intended way.

The C++ Standard Template Library provides the concept of *iterator* as a generalization of raw pointers. Two iterators define a *range* of data. That range might be only part of the contents of a container; or it might be unbacked by any memory at all, as we saw with `getc_iterator` and `putc_iterator`. Some of the properties of an iterator type are encoded in its iterator category--input, output, forward, bidirectional, or random-access--for the benefit of function templates that can use faster algorithms on certain categories of iterators.

If you're defining your own container type, you'll need to define your own iterator types as well--both const and non-const versions. Templates are a handy way to do that. When implementing your own iterator types, avoid the deprecated `std::iterator`, but consider `boost::iterator_facade`.

3
The Iterator-Pair Algorithms

Now that you've been introduced to iterator types--both standard-provided and user-defined--it's time to look at some of the things you can *do* with iterators.

In this chapter you'll learn:

- The notion of a "half-open range," which nails down the exact manner in which two iterators can be said to define a *range*
- How to classify each standard algorithm as "read-only," "write-only", "transformative", or "permutative"; and as "one-range", "two-range", or "one-and-a-half range"
- That some standard algorithms, such as `merge` and `make_heap`, are merely the necessary building blocks out of which we make higher-level entities such as `stable_sort` and `priority_queue`
- How to sort a range based on a comparator other than `operator<`
- How to manipulate sorted arrays using the *erase-remove idiom*

A note about headers

Most function templates discussed in this chapter are defined in the standard header `<algorithm>`. The special iterator types, on the other hand, are generally defined in `<iterator>`. If you're wondering where to find a specific entity, I strongly recommend that you consult an online reference such as `cppreference.com` for the authoritative answer; don't just guess!

The Iterator-Pair Algorithms

Read-only range algorithms

In the preceding chapters, we built up an algorithm that we called `distance` and another called `count_if`. Both of these algorithms appear in the standard library.

`std::count_if(a,b,p)` returns the number of elements between a and b that satisfy the predicate function p--that is, the number of elements e for which `p(e)` is `true`.

Notice that, whenever we say "between a and b", we're talking about the range that includes `*a` but does not include `*b`--what mathematicians call a "half-open range" and represented by the asymmetrical notation `[a,b)`. Why should we not include `*b`? Well, for one thing, if b is the `end()` of some vector, then it doesn't point to an element of that vector at all! So in general, dereferencing the *end point* of a range is a dangerous thing to do. For another thing, using half-open ranges conveniently allows us to represent *empty* ranges; for example, the range "from x to x" is an empty range consisting of zero data elements.

Half-open ranges are quite natural in C++ just as they are in C. For decades, we've been writing for-loops that range from a lower bound (inclusive) to an upper bound (exclusive); this idiom is so common that deviation from the idiom often indicates a bug:

```
constexpr int N = 10;
int a[N];

// A correct for-loop.
for (int i=0; i < N; ++i) {
  // ...
}

// One variety of "smelly" for-loop.
for (int i=0; i <= N; ++i) {
  // ...
}

// A correct invocation of a standard algorithm.
std::count_if(std::begin(a), std::end(a), [](int){ return true; });

// A "smelly" invocation.
std::count_if(std::begin(a), std::end(a) - 1, [](int){ return true; });

// A "trivial" invocation: counting a range of length zero.
std::count_if(std::begin(a), std::begin(a), [](int){ return true; });
```

`std::distance(a,b)` returns the number of elements between `a` and `b`--that is, the number of times you'd have to apply `++` to `a` in order to reach `b`. You could think of this function as being equivalent in its effects to `std::count_if(a,b,[](auto&&){return true;})`.

As we saw in Chapter 2, *Iterators and Ranges*, if the iterators in question are random-access iterators, this number can be quickly computed as `(b - a)`, and so the standard `std::distance` will do so. Notice that `(b - a)` might be a negative number, if you gave the arguments in the "wrong" order!

```
int a[] {1, 2, 3, 4, 5};
std::list<int> lst {1, 2, 3, 4, 5};
std::forward_list<int> flst {1, 2, 3, 4, 5};

assert(std::distance(std::begin(a), std::end(a)) == 5);
assert(std::distance(std::begin(lst), std::end(lst)) == 5);
assert(std::distance(std::begin(lst), std::end(lst)) == 5);

assert(std::distance(std::end(a), std::begin(a)) == -5);
```

When the iterators are random-access iterators, `std::distance` does nothing more than subtract them; so passing in "wrongly ordered" arguments is explicitly supported and blessed by the C++ standard. However, if the iterators in question are merely bidirectional iterators (such as `std::list<int>::iterator`--see Chapter 4, *The Container Zoo*), "wrongly ordered" iterators are *not* supported. You might expect that `std::distance(b,a) == -std::distance(a,b)` should be true of all iterator types; but consider, how would the `std::distance` algorithm itself have any idea whether the iterators you gave it were "wrongly ordered" or not? The only thing it *can* do (in the absence of an `operator-`) is to keep incrementing `a`--perhaps past the end of the container and off into space--in the vain hope that it'll eventually reach `b`:

```
// The following line gives an "incorrect" answer!
// assert(std::distance(std::end(lst), std::begin(lst)) == 1);
// And this one just segfaults!
// std::distance(std::end(flst), std::begin(flst));
```

> **TIP** Consult the diagrams of `std::list` and `std::forward_list` in Chapter 4, *The Container Zoo*, to understand this code sample's odd behavior.

The Iterator-Pair Algorithms

`std::count(a,b,v)` returns the number of elements between `a` and `b` that are equal to `v`—that is, the number of elements `e` for which `e == v` is true. You can think of this function as being equivalent in its effects to `std::count_if(a,b, [&v](auto&& e){return e == v;})`, and in fact both versions should give the same assembly code. If C++ had had lambda-expressions in 1998, they probably wouldn't have put the `std::count` algorithm in the standard library.

Notice that `std::count(a,b,v)` necessarily loops over *all* of the elements in the range between `a` and `b`. It can't take advantage of special information you might have about the arrangement of the data in the range. For example, suppose I want to count the instances of 42 in a `std::set<int>`? I could write the code in either of the following ways:

```
std::set<int> s { 1, 2, 3, 10, 42, 99 };
bool present;

// O(n): compare each element with 42
present = std::count(s.begin(), s.end(), 42);

// O(log n): ask the container to look up 42 itself
present = s.count(42);
```

The raw algorithm `std::count` is outperformed by the second approach, which simply asks the `set` itself for the answer. This turns a O(*n*) traversal of the whole set into a O(log *n*) tree lookup. Similarly, `std::unordered_set` provides a `count` method that is roughly O(1).

For more about these containers, see Chapter 4, *The Container Zoo*; the takeaway point here right now is that, Q sometimes there is important structure in your data that can be exploited by choosing the proper tool for the job. Even though I'm pointing to cases where the standard algorithms seem to "magically" do the right thing (as with `std::distance` delegating to `(b - a)`), you should not imagine that this "magic" stretches farther than it does. The standard algorithms know only as much as they're told, which is to say, only about the properties of the *iterator types* you pass them. They'll never change their behavior based on the relationships of the *underlying data elements* to each other. Arranging your code to exploit relationships in the underlying data (for example, "this data is sorted," "this range spans the entire container") is part of your job as the programmer.

Here are some more algorithms similar to `std::count` and `std::count_if`.

`std::find(a,b,v)` and `std::find_if(a,b,p)` work just like `std::count(a,b,v)` and `std::count_if(a,b,p)` respectively, except that, rather than looping over the entire range and returning the *count* of matching elements, the `find` variants loop only until they've found the first match, and then return an iterator to the data element that matched. There is also a variant `find_if_not` that is just like `find_if` but with the sense of the predicate negated; this variant also probably wouldn't have needed to exist if we'd gotten lambdas earlier in the history of C++:

```
template<class InputIterator, class UnaryPredicate>
InputIterator find_if(InputIterator first, InputIterator last,
  UnaryPredicate p)
{
  for (; first != last; ++first) {
    if (p(*first)) {
      return first;
    }
  }
  return last;
}

template<class It, class U>
It find_if_not(It first, It last, U p) {
  return std::find_if(first, last, [&](auto&& e){ return !p(e); });
}

template<class It, class T>
It find(It first, It last, T value) {
  return std::find_if(first, last, [&](auto&& e)
    { return e == value; });
}
```

Notice that because `find` returns *immediately* upon finding the first match, it's faster on average than the `count` algorithm (which scans the whole range no matter what). This kind of "return immediately" behavior is often referred to as "short-circuiting".

`std::all_of(a,b,p)`, `std::any_of(a,b,p)`, and `std::none_of(a,b,p)` return either `true` or `false`, depending on how often the provided predicate function p is true of the elements in the range. They can all be built on top of the `find` algorithms, thus picking up the short-circuiting behavior for free:

```
template<class It, class UnaryPredicate>
bool all_of(It first, It last, UnaryPredicate p)
{
  return std::find_if_not(first, last, p) == last;
}
```

The Iterator-Pair Algorithms

```
template <class It, class U>
bool any_of(It first, It last, U p)
{
    return std::find_if(first, last, p) != last;
}

template <class It, class U>
bool none_of(It first, It last, U p)
{
    return std::find_if(first, last, p) == last;
}
```

There is one more `find`-related algorithm I should mention: `find_first_of`. It implements the operation of "looking in a sequence for the first occurrence of any of a fixed set of target elements"--that is, just like `strcspn` in the C standard library, but for any type, not just `char`. Abstractly speaking, `find_first_of` takes two conceptual parameters: the range to search in, and the set of target elements. This being the STL, they're both passed in as ranges, which is to say, pairs of iterators. So a call to this algorithm looks like `find_first_of(haystack, haystack, needle, needle)`: two pairs of iterators side by side. This can get confusing--beware of algorithms taking multiple similar parameters!

```
template <class It, class FwdIt>
It find_first_of(It first, It last, FwdIt targetfirst,
    FwdIt targetlast)
{
    return std::find_if(first, last, [&](auto&& e) {
        return std::any_of(targetfirst, targetlast, [&](auto&& t) {
            return e == t;
        });
    });
}

template <class It, class FwdIt, class BinaryPredicate>
It find_first_of(It first, It last, FwdIt targetfirst,
    FwdIt targetlast, BinaryPredicate p)
{
    return std::find_if(first, last, [&](auto&& e) {
        return std::any_of(targetfirst, targetlast, [&](auto&& t) {
            return p(e, t);
        });
    });
}
```

Notice that the "haystack" iterators are expected to be of any old `InputIterator` type, but the "needle" iterators are required to be at least `ForwardIterator`. Recall from Chapter 2, *Iterators and Ranges*, that the big thing about `ForwardIterator` types is that they can be meaningfully *copied*, letting the same range be traversed multiple times. This is exactly what `find_first_of` needs! It traverses the "needle" range once per character in the "haystack"; so the "needle" must be re-traversable--and incidentally, must be finite in size! Contrariwise, there's nothing particularly requiring that the "haystack" be finite; it might be pulling its elements from a potentially unbounded input stream:

```
std::istream_iterator<char> ii(std::cin);
std::istream_iterator<char> iend{};
std::string s = "hello";

// Chomp characters from std::cin until finding an 'h', 'e', 'l', or 'o'.
std::find_first_of(ii, iend, s.begin(), s.end());
```

Speaking of multiple similar parameters, let's finish our look at simple read-only algorithms with these two: `std::equal` and `std::mismatch`.

`std::equal(a,b,c,d)` takes two iterator-pairs: the range `[a,b)` and the range `[c,d)`. It returns `true` if the two ranges are element-for-element equal, and `false` otherwise.

`std::mismatch(a,b,c,d)` is sort of like `find`: it'll tell you exactly which pair of elements was the one that torpedoed the match:

```
template<class T> constexpr bool is_random_access_iterator_v =
    std::is_base_of_v<std::random_access_iterator_tag, typename
    std::iterator_traits<T>::iterator_category>;

template<class It1, class It2, class B>
auto mismatch(It1 first1, It1 last1, It2 first2, It2 last2, B p)
{
    while (first1 != last1 && first2 != last2 && p(*first1, *first2)) {
        ++first1;
        ++first2;
    }
    return std::make_pair(first1, first2);
}

template<class It1, class It2>
auto mismatch(It1 first1, It1 last1, It2 first2, It2 last2)
{
    return std::mismatch(first1, last1, first2, last2,
std::equal_to<>{});
}
```

The Iterator-Pair Algorithms

```
template<class It1, class It2, class B>
bool equal(It1 first1, It1 last1, It2 first2, It2 last2, B p)
{
  if constexpr (is_random_access_iterator_v<It1> &&
    is_random_access_iterator_v<It2>) {
    // Ranges of different lengths can never be equal.
    if ((last2 - first2) != (last1 - first1)) {
      return false;
    }
  }
  return std::mismatch(first1, last1, first2, last2, p) ==
    std::make_pair(last1, last2);
}

template<class It1, class It2>
bool equal(It1 first1, It1 last1, It2 first2, It2 last2)
{
  return std::equal(first1, last1, first2, last2, std::equal_to<>{});
}
```

Notice the use of `std::equal_to<>{}` as a predicate object; we won't cover the built-in predicates in depth in this book, so just take it for granted that `std::equal_to<>{}` is an object whose behavior is similar to `[](auto a, auto b){ return a == b; }` but with more *perfect forwarding* involved.

Finally, watch out again! Many of the two-range algorithms in the C++17 standard library also have variant forms colloquially known as one-and-a-half-range algorithms. For example, in addition to `std::mismatch(a,b,c,d)` you'll find `std::mismatch(a,b,c)` -- the second range's "end" point is simply assumed to be at `c + std::distance(a, b)`. If c actually points into a container where `c + std::distance(a, b)` would be "off the end," then, tough luck!

Because "tough luck" is never a really *great* answer to a technical question, the C++17 standard added safe two-range variants for many of the one-and-a-half-range algorithms that had existed in C++14.

Shunting data with std::copy

We've just seen our first few two-range algorithms. The `<algorithm>` header is full of two-range algorithms and their siblings, the one-and-a-half-range algorithms. What's the simplest possible such algorithm?

A reasonable answer would be: "Copy each data element from the first range into the second range." Indeed, the STL provides that algorithm, under the name `std::copy`:

```
template<class InIt, class OutIt>
OutIt copy(InIt first1, InIt last1, OutIt destination)
{
  while (first1 != last1) {
    *destination = *first1;
    ++first1;
    ++destination;
  }
  return destination;
}
```

Notice that this is a one-and-a-half-range algorithm. The standard library actually does not provide a two-range version of `std::copy`; the assumption is that if you are actually trying to write into a buffer, then you must have checked its size already, so checking "are we at the end of the buffer yet" inside the loop would be both redundant and inefficient.

Now I can practically hear you exclaiming: "Horrors! This is the same crude logic that brought us `strcpy`, `sprintf`, and `gets`! This is an invitation to buffer overflows!" Well, *if* you were to exclaim thusly, you'd be right about the bad behavior of `gets`--in fact, the `gets` function has been officially removed from the C++17 standard library. And you'd be right about `sprintf`--anyone who needs that functionality is better of using the range-checked version `snprintf`, which is analogous to a "two-range algorithm" in this context. But about `strcpy` I'd disagree. With `gets` it is *impossible* to know the correct size for the output buffer; with `sprintf` it is *difficult*; but with `strcpy` it is *trivial*: you just measure the `strlen` of the input buffer and that's your answer. Likewise with `std::copy`, the relationship between "input elements consumed" and "output elements produced" is exactly one-to-one, so sizing the output buffer doesn't present a technical challenge.

Notice that the parameter we called `destination` is an *output iterator*. This means that we can use `std::copy`, not merely to shunt data around in memory, but even to feed data to an arbitrary "sink" function. For example:

```
class putc_iterator : public boost::iterator_facade<
    putc_iterator, // T
    const putc_iterator, // value_type
    std::output_iterator_tag
  >
{
  friend class boost::iterator_core_access;

  auto& dereference() const { return *this; }
  void increment() {}
```

The Iterator-Pair Algorithms

```
      bool equal(const putc_iterator&) const { return false; }
      public:
      // This iterator is its own proxy object!
      void operator= (char ch) const { putc(ch, stdout); }
};

void test()
{
  std::string s = "hello";
  std::copy(s.begin(), s.end(), putc_iterator{});
}
```

You may find it instructive to compare this version of our `putc_iterator` to the version from Chapter 2, *Iterators and Ranges*; this version is using `boost::iterator_facade` as introduced at the end of Chapter 2, *Iterators and Ranges* and also using a common trick to return `*this` instead of a new proxy object.

Now we can use the flexibility of `destination` to solve our concerns about buffer overflow! Suppose that, instead of writing into a fixed-size array, we were to write into a resizable `std::vector` (see Chapter 4, *The Container Zoo*). Then "writing an element" corresponds to "pushing an element back" on the vector. So we could write an output iterator very similar to `putc_iterator`, that would `push_back` instead of `putc`, and then we'd have an overflow-proof way of filling up a vector. Indeed, the standard library provides just such an output iterator, in the `<iterator>` header:

```
namespace std {
  template<class Container>
  class back_insert_iterator {
    using CtrValueType = typename Container::value_type;
    Container *c;
  public:
    using iterator_category = output_iterator_tag;
    using difference_type = void;
    using value_type = void;
    using pointer = void;
    using reference = void;

    explicit back_insert_iterator(Container& ctr) : c(&ctr) {}

    auto& operator*() { return *this; }
    auto& operator++() { return *this; }
    auto& operator++(int) { return *this; }

    auto& operator= (const CtrValueType& v) {
        c->push_back(v);
        return *this;
```

```cpp
            }
            auto& operator= (CtrValueType&& v) {
                c->push_back(std::move(v));
                return *this;
            }
        };
        template<class Container>
        auto back_inserter(Container& c)
        {
            return back_insert_iterator<Container>(c);
        }
    }

    void test()
    {
      std::string s = "hello";
      std::vector<char> dest;
      std::copy(s.begin(), s.end(), std::back_inserter(dest));
      assert(dest.size() == 5);
    }
```

The function call `std::back_inserter(dest)` simply returns a `back_insert_iterator` object. In C++17, we could rely on template type deduction for constructors and write the body of that function as simply `return std::back_insert_iterator(dest);` or dispense with the function entirely and just write `std::back_insert_iterator(dest)` directly in our code--where C++14 code would have to "make do" with `std::back_inserter(dest)`. However, why would we want all that extra typing? The name `back_inserter` was deliberately chosen to be easy to remember, since it's the one that we were expected to use most often. Although C++17 allows us to write `std::pair` in place of `std::make_pair`, and `std::tuple` in place of `std::make_tuple`, it would be silly to write the cumbersome `std::back_insert_iterator` in place of `std::back_inserter`. You should prefer `std::back_inserter(dest)` even in C++17.

Variations on a theme - std::move and std::move_iterator

As you might guess from the name, or you might have noticed in the preceding implementation, the `std::copy` algorithm works by copying elements from the input range to the output. As of C++11, you might wonder: What if instead of *copying* the elements, we used move semantics to *move* them from the input to the output?

The Iterator-Pair Algorithms

The STL provides two different approaches to this problem. The first one is the most straightforward: there is a `std::move` algorithm (defined in the `<algorithm>` header) with the following definition:

```
template<class InIt, class OutIt>
OutIt move(InIt first1, InIt last1, OutIt destination)
{
  while (first1 != last1) {
    *destination = std::move(*first1);
    ++first1;
    ++destination;
  }
  return destination;
}
```

It's exactly the same as the `std::copy` algorithm except for the addition of a single `std::move` on the input element (be careful--this inner `std::move`, with *one* argument, defined in the `<utility>` header, is a completely different beast from the outer, three-argument `std::move` defined in `<algorithm>`! The fact that they share a name is unfortunate. Ironically, one of the few other STL functions to suffer a similar situation is `std::remove`; see the *Deleting from a sorted array* section, and also Chapter 12, *Filesystem*).

The other approach is a variation of what we saw previously with `back_inserter`. Rather than switching out the core *algorithm*, we can continue using `std::copy` but parameterize it differently. Suppose we passed in a new type of iterator, which (like `back_inserter`) wrapped around our original object and changed its behavior? In particular, we need an input iterator whose `operator*` returns an rvalue. We can do that!

```
template<class It>
class move_iterator {
  using OriginalRefType = typename std::iterator_traits<It>::reference;
  It iter;
public:
  using iterator_category = typename
    std::iterator_traits<It>::iterator_category;
  using difference_type = typename
    std::iterator_traits<It>::difference_type;
  using value_type = typename std::iterator_traits<It>::value_type;
  using pointer = It;
  using reference = std::conditional_t<
    std::is_reference_v<OriginalRefType>,
    std::remove_reference_t<OriginalRefType>&&,
    OriginalRefType
    >;

  move_iterator() = default;
```

```
    explicit move_iterator(It it) : iter(std::move(it)) {}

    // Allow constructing or assigning from any kind of move-iterator.
    // These templates also serve as our own type's copy constructor
    // and assignment operator, respectively.
    template<class U>
    move_iterator(const move_iterator<U>& m) : iter(m.base()) {}
    template<class U>
    auto& operator=(const move_iterator<U>& m)
      { iter = m.base(); return *this; }

    It base() const { return iter; }

    reference operator*() { return static_cast<reference>(*iter); }
    It operator->() { return iter; }
    decltype(auto) operator[](difference_type n) const
      { return *std::move(iter[n]); }

  auto& operator++() { ++iter; return *this; }
  auto& operator++(int)
    { auto result = *this; ++*this; return result; }
  auto& operator--() { --iter; return *this; }
  auto& operator--(int)
    { auto result = *this; --*this; return result; }

  auto& operator+=(difference_type n) const
    { iter += n; return *this; }
  auto& operator-=(difference_type n) const
    { iter -= n; return *this; }
};

// I've omitted the definitions of non-member operators
// == != < <= > >= + - ; can you fill them in?

template<class InputIterator>
auto make_move_iterator(InputIterator& c)
{
  return move_iterator(c);
}
```

The Iterator-Pair Algorithms

Sorry for the density of that code; trust me that you can safely skip over the details. For those who like this kind of thing, you might notice that we're providing a templated constructor from `move_iterator<U>` that happens to double as our copy constructor (when `U` is the same type as `It`); and that we're providing a lot of member functions (such as `operator[]` and `operator--`) whose bodies will error out for a lot of possible types of `It` (for example, when `It` is a forward iterator--see Chapter 2, *Iterators and Ranges*), but this is fine because their bodies won't get instantiated unless the user actually tries to call those functions at compile time (if the user actually *does* try to -- a `move_iterator<list_of_ints::iterator>`, then of course that'll yield a compile-time error).

Just as with `back_inserter`, notice that the STL provides a helper function `make_move_iterator` for the benefit of pre-C++17 compilers that don't have constructor template type deduction. In this case, as with `make_pair` and `make_tuple`, the "helper" name is uglier than the actual class name, and so I tentatively recommend using the C++17 feature in your code; why type an extra five characters and instantiate an extra function template if you don't have to?

Now we have two different ways of moving data from one container or range to another: the `std::move` algorithm and the `std::move_iterator` adaptor class. Here are examples of both idioms:

```
std::vector<std::string> input = {"hello", "world"};
std::vector<std::string> output(2);

// First approach: use the std::move algorithm
std::move(input.begin(), input.end(), output.begin());

// Second approach: use move_iterator
std::copy(
  std::move_iterator(input.begin()),
  std::move_iterator(input.end()),
  output.begin()
);
```

The first approach, using `std::move`, is obviously much cleaner if moving data is all you're doing. So why did the standard library bother to provide this "messier" approach with `move_iterator`? To answer that question, we'll have to explore yet another algorithm that is fundamentally related to `std::copy`.

Complicated copying with std::transform

You might have noticed, way back when we presented the implementation of `std::copy`, that the `value_type` of the two iterator type parameters were not constrained to be the same. This is a feature, not a bug! It means that we can write code that relies on implicit conversions and it will just Do The Right Thing:

```
std::vector<const char *> input = {"hello", "world"};
std::vector<std::string> output(2);

std::copy(input.begin(), input.end(), output.begin());

assert(output[0] == "hello");
assert(output[1] == "world");
```

Looks trivial, right? Look closely! Deep within our instantiation of `std::copy` is a call to the implicit constructor that converts `const char *` (the type of `*input.begin()`) to `std::string` (the type of `*output.begin()`). So for the umpteenth time, we're seeing an example of generic code that does surprisingly complicated operations simply by virtue of being given certain iterator types.

But sometimes you want to apply a complicated transformation function during the copying operation--something more complicated than implicit conversions can handle. The standard library has got you covered!

```
template<class InIt, class OutIt, class Unary>
OutIt transform(InIt first1, InIt last1, OutIt destination, Unary op)
{
  while (first1 != last1) {
    *destination = op(*first1);
    ++first1;
    ++destination;
  }
  return destination;
}

void test()
{
  std::vector<std::string> input = {"hello", "world"};
```

The Iterator-Pair Algorithms

```
    std::vector<std::string> output(2);

    std::transform(
      input.begin(),
      input.end(),
      output.begin(),
      [](std::string s) {
        // It works for transforming in-place, too!
        std::transform(s.begin(), s.end(), s.begin(), ::toupper);
        return s;
      }
    );

    assert(input[0] == "hello");
    assert(output[0] == "HELLO");
}
```

Sometimes you even need to do a transformation using a function that takes *two* arguments. Again the library has you covered:

```
    template<class InIt1, class InIt2, class OutIt, class Binary>
    OutIt transform(InIt1 first1, InIt1 last1, InIt2 first2, OutIt destination,
        Binary op)
    {
      while (first1 != last1) {
        *destination = op(*first1, *first2);
        ++first1;
        ++first2;
        ++destination;
      }
      return destination;
    }
```

This version of `std::transform` might be humorously described as a one-and-two-halves-range algorithm!

(What about functions of three arguments? Four arguments? Unfortunately there's no fully variadic version of `std::transform`; variadic templates weren't introduced to C++ until C++11. You might try implementing a variadic version and see what kinds of problems you run into--they're surmountable but certainly not trivial.)

The existence of `std::transform` gives us yet a third way to move data elements from one place to another:

```
    std::vector<std::string> input = {"hello", "world"};
    std::vector<std::string> output(2);
```

```
// Third approach: use std::transform
std::transform(
  input.begin(),
  input.end(),
  output.begin(),
  std::move<std::string&>
);
```

I certainly don't recommend this approach, though! The biggest and reddest of its red flags is that it contains explicit specialization of the `std::move` template. Whenever you see an explicit specialization--those angle brackets after the template's name--that's an almost sure sign of very subtle and fragile code. Advanced readers might enjoy figuring out how the compiler deduces which of the two `std::move`s I meant; remember, there's one in `<utility>` and one in `<algorithm>`.

Write-only range algorithms

We began this chapter looking at algorithms such as `std::find` that march through a range reading its elements in order without modification. You might be surprised to learn that the inverse operation also makes sense: there is a family of standard algorithms that march through a range *modifying* each element without reading it!

`std::fill(a,b,v)` does what its name implies: fill each element of the given range `[a,b)` with a copy of the provided value v.

`std::iota(a,b,v)` is slightly more interesting: it fills the elements of the given range with copies of ++v. That is, `std::iota(a,b,42)` will set `a[0]` equal to 42, `a[1]` equal to 43, `a[2]` equal to 44, and so on all the way up to b. This algorithm's funny name comes from the APL programming language, where a function named ι (that's the Greek letter *iota*) performed this operation. Another funny thing about this algorithm is that, for whatever reason, its definition is found in the standard `<numeric>` header instead of in `<algorithm>`. It's just an oddball that way.

`std::generate(a,b,g)` is even more interesting: it fills the elements of the given range with the successive results of `g()`, whatever it is:

```
template<class FwdIt, class T>
void fill(FwdIt first, FwdIt last, T value) {
  while (first != last) {
    *first = value;
    ++first;
  }
}
```

The Iterator-Pair Algorithms

```
template<class FwdIt, class T>
void iota(FwdIt first, FwdIt last, T value) {
  while (first != last) {
    *first = value;
    ++value;
    ++first;
  }
}

template<class FwdIt, class G>
void generate(FwdIt first, FwdIt last, G generator) {
  while (first != last) {
    *first = generator();
    ++first;
  }
}
```

Here's an example of using each of these standard algorithms to fill a vector of strings with different contents. Test your understanding: do you understand why each call produces the output that it does? The example I picked for `std::iota` is particularly interesting (yet unlikely to be helpful in real-world code):

```
std::vector<std::string> v(4);

std::fill(v.begin(), v.end(), "hello");
assert(v[0] == "hello");
assert(v[1] == "hello");
assert(v[2] == "hello");
assert(v[3] == "hello");

std::iota(v.begin(), v.end(), "hello");
assert(v[0] == "hello");
assert(v[1] == "ello");
assert(v[2] == "llo");
assert(v[3] == "lo");

std::generate(v.begin(), v.end(), [i=0]() mutable {
  return ++i % 2 ? "hello" : "world";
});
assert(v[0] == "hello");
assert(v[1] == "world");
assert(v[2] == "hello");
assert(v[3] == "world");
```

Algorithms that affect object lifetime

The <memory> header provides an obscure family of algorithms with names such as std::uninitialized_copy, std::uninitialized_default_construct, and std::destroy (for the full list, consult an online reference such as cppreference.com). Consider the following algorithm that uses explicit destructor calls to destroy the elements of a range:

```
template<class T>
void destroy_at(T *p)
{
  p->~T();
}

template<class FwdIt>
void destroy(FwdIt first, FwdIt last)
{
  for ( ; first != last; ++first) {
    std::destroy_at(std::addressof(*first));
  }
}
```

Notice that std::addressof(x) is a convenient little helper function that returns the address of its parameter; it's exactly the same thing as &x except in the rare case that x is of some class type that sadistically overloads its own operator&.

And consider this algorithm that uses explicit placement-new syntax to "copy-construct into" the elements of a range (notice how it neatly cleans up after itself if an exception is thrown during the copying). This algorithm clearly shouldn't be used on any range whose elements already exist; so the following example looks very contrived:

```
template<class It, class FwdIt>
FwdIt uninitialized_copy(It first, It last, FwdIt out)
{
  using T = typename std::iterator_traits<FwdIt>::value_type;
  FwdIt old_out = out;
  try {
    while (first != last) {
      ::new (static_cast<void*>(std::addressof(*out))) T(*first);
      ++first;
      ++out;
    }
    return out;
  } catch (...) {
    std::destroy(old_out, out);
    throw;
```

```
        }
    }

    void test()
    {
        alignas(std::string) char b[5 * sizeof (std::string)];
        std::string *sb = reinterpret_cast<std::string *>(b);

        std::vector<const char *> vec = {"quick", "brown", "fox"};

        // Construct three std::strings.
        auto end = std::uninitialized_copy(vec.begin(), vec.end(), sb);

        assert(end == sb + 3);

        // Destroy three std::strings.
        std::destroy(sb, end);
    }
```

We'll see more about how these algorithms are *meant* to be used in Chapter 4, *The Container Zoo*, when we talk about std::vector.

Our first permutative algorithm: std::sort

So far all the algorithms we've covered simply walk through their given ranges in order, linearly, from one element to the next. Our next family of algorithms doesn't behave that way. Instead, it takes the values of the elements in the given range and shuffles them around so that the same values still appear, but in a different order. The mathematical name for this operation is a *permutation*.

The simplest permutative algorithm to describe is std::sort(a,b). It does what the name implies: sort the given range so that the smallest elements appear at the front and the biggest elements at the back. To figure out which elements are "smallest," std::sort(a,b) uses operator<.

If you want a different order, you could try to overload `operator<` to return `true` under different conditions--but probably what you should do is use the three-argument version of the algorithm, `std::sort(a,b,cmp)`. The third argument should be a *comparator*; that is, a function, functor, or lambda that returns `true` whenever its first argument is "smaller" than its second argument. For example:

```
std::vector<int> v = {3, 1, 4, 1, 5, 9};
std::sort(v.begin(), v.end(), [](auto&& a, auto&& b) {
  return a % 7 < b % 7;
});
assert((v == std::vector{1, 1, 9, 3, 4, 5}));
```

Notice that I carefully chose my lambda in this example so that it would sort the array in a deterministic way. If I'd chosen the function (a % 6 < b % 6) instead, then there would have been two possible outputs: either {1, 1, 3, 9, 4, 5} or {1, 1, 9, 3, 4, 5}. The standard `sort` algorithm doesn't guarantee anything about the relative position of elements that happen to be *equal* under the given comparison function!

To fix this problem (if it *is* a problem), you should replace your use of `std::sort` with `std::stable_sort`. The latter might be a little slower, but it will guarantee that in the case of equal elements the original order is preserved--that is, in this case we'll get {1, 1, 3, 9, 4, 5} because in the original (unsorted) vector, element 3 came in front of element 9.

There's an even worse thing that can happen with `sort` and `stable_sort`--what if I had chosen the comparison function (a % 6 < b)? Then I would have had certain pairs of elements x, y where x < y and simultaneously y < x! (One such pair of elements in the original vector is 5 and 9.) In this case, there's nothing that can save us; we've passed in a "comparison function" that simply *isn't* a comparison function! This is a violation of the preconditions of `std::sort`, just as if we'd passed it a null pointer. When sorting an array, make sure you're sorting it based on a comparison function that makes sense!

Swapping, reversing, and partitioning

The STL contains a surprisingly large number of permutative algorithms besides `std::sort`. Many of these algorithms can be seen as "building blocks" that implement just a small part of the overall sorting algorithm.

The Iterator-Pair Algorithms

`std::swap(a,b)` is the most basic building block; it just takes its two arguments and "swaps" them--which is to say, it exchanges their values. This is implemented in terms of the given type's move constructor and move assignment operator. `swap` is actually a little special among the standard algorithms because it is *such* a primitive operation, and because there is *almost always* a faster way to swap two arbitrary objects than by performing the equivalent of `temp = a; a = b; b = temp;`. The usual idiom for standard library types (such as `std::vector`) is for the type itself to implement a `swap` member function (as in `a.swap(b)`), and then to add a function overload of `swap` in the same namespace as the type--that is, if we're implementing `my::obj`, we'd add the overload in namespace `my`--such that `swap(a,b)` for that particular type, will call `a.swap(b)` instead of doing the three move operations. Here's an example:

```
namespace my {
  class obj {
    int v;
  public:
    obj(int value) : v(value) {}

    void swap(obj& other) {
      using std::swap;
      swap(this->v, other.v);
    }
  };

  void swap(obj& a, obj& b) {
    a.swap(b);
  }
} // namespace my

void test()
{
  int i1 = 1, i2 = 2;
  std::vector<int> v1 = {1}, v2 = {2};
  my::obj m1 = 1, m2 = 2;
  using std::swap;
  swap(i1, i2); // calls std::swap<int>(int&, int&)
  swap(v1, v2); // calls std::swap(vector&, vector&)
  swap(m1, m2); // calls my::swap(obj&, obj&)
}
```

The Iterator-Pair Algorithms

Now that we have `swap` and bidirectional iterators, we can build `std::reverse(a,b)`, a permutative algorithm that simply reverses the order of a range of elements by swapping the first item with the last item, the second item with the penultimate item, and so on. One common application of `std::reverse` is to reverse the order of larger chunks of a string-- for example, to reverse the order of the words in a sentence:

```
void reverse_words_in_place(std::string& s)
{
  // First, reverse the whole string.
  std::reverse(s.begin(), s.end());

  // Next, un-reverse each individual word.
  for (auto it = s.begin(); true; ++it) {
    auto next = std::find(it, s.end(), ' ');
    // Reverse the order of letters in this word.
    std::reverse(it, next);
    if (next == s.end()) {
      break;
    }
    it = next;
  }
}

void test()
{
  std::string s = "the quick brown fox jumps over the lazy dog";
  reverse_words_in_place(s);
  assert(s == "dog lazy the over jumps fox brown quick the");
}
```

A small tweak to the implementation of `std::reverse` gives us another building block of sort, namely `std::partition`. Whereas `std::reverse` walks through the range from both ends swapping each pair of elements unconditionally, `std::partition` swaps them only if they are "out of order" with respect to a certain predicate function. In the following example, we're partitioning all *even* elements to the front of our range and all *odd* elements to the back. If we were using `std::partition` to build a Quicksort sorting routine, we'd be partitioning elements *less than the pivot element* to the front of the range and elements *greater than the pivot element* to the back:

```
template<class BidirIt>
void reverse(BidirIt first, BidirIt last)
{
  while (first != last) {
    --last;
    if (first == last) break;
    using std::swap;
```

[59]

The Iterator-Pair Algorithms

```cpp
      swap(*first, *last);
      ++first;
    }
  }

  template<class BidirIt, class Unary>
  auto partition(BidirIt first, BidirIt last, Unary p)
  {
    while (first != last && p(*first)) {
      ++first;
    }

    while (first != last) {
      do {
        --last;
      } while (last != first && !p(*last));
      if (first == last) break;
      using std::swap;
      swap(*first, *last);
      do {
        ++first;
      } while (first != last && p(*first));
    }
    return first;
  }

  void test()
  {
    std::vector<int> v = {3, 1, 4, 1, 5, 9, 2, 6, 5};
    auto it = std::partition(v.begin(), v.end(), [](int x) {
      return x % 2 == 0;
    });
    assert(it == v.begin() + 3);
    assert((v == std::vector{6, 2, 4, 1, 5, 9, 1, 3, 5}));
  }
```

You might notice something interesting about the preceding code: The code for `reverse` and the code for `partition` are almost identical! The only difference is that `partition` contains an awkward do-while loop where `reverse` has just a simple increment or decrement.

You might also have noticed that the first do-while loop in `partition` is equivalent to a standard algorithm we've already seen; namely, `std::find_if_not`. And the second do-while loop is sort of equivalent to `std::find_if`... except that it needs to run *backwards*, not forwards! Unfortunately for us, there is no such algorithm as `std::rfind_if`. But--as you might have suspected by now--the standard library isn't going to leave us in the lurch.

We need something that behaves just like an iterator for the purposes of `std::find_if`, but iterates "backwards." The standard library provides this exact thing in the form of the `std::reverse_iterator` adaptor. We won't show the code for it; revisit Chapter 2, *Iterators and Ranges*, if you need a refresher on how it might be implemented. Suffice it to say, a `std::reverse_iterator<FwdIt>` object wraps and behaves just like a `FwdIt` object, except that when you increment the wrapper, it decrements the wrapped object, and vice versa. So we can write `partition` in terms of `reverse_iterator` as follows:

```
// Shorthands for "reversing" and "unreversing".
template<class It>
auto rev(It it) {
  return std::reverse_iterator(it);
};

template<class InnerIt>
auto unrev(std::reverse_iterator<InnerIt> it) {
  return it.base();
}

template<class BidirIt, class Unary>
auto partition(BidirIt first, BidirIt last, Unary p)
{
  first = std::find_if_not(first, last, p);

  while (first != last) {
    last = unrev(std::find_if(rev(last), rev(first), p));
    if (first == last) break;
    using std::swap;
    swap(*first++, *--last);
    first = std::find_if_not(first, last, p);
  }
  return first;
}
```

Of course, sometimes it's useful to partition a range without changing the relative order of the elements in either partition. For those times, there's `std::stable_partition(a,b,p)` (but see the section *Merges and mergesort* for a caveat about `stable_partition`: It may allocate memory using `operator new`).

There are a few non-permutative algorithms that also deal with partitions:

`std::is_partitioned(a,b,p)` returns `true` if the given range is already partitioned by the predicate p (so that all the elements satisfying p come at the front and all the ones not satisfying p come at the back).

The Iterator-Pair Algorithms

`std::partition_point(a,b,p)` uses binary search to find the first element in an already partitioned range that doesn't satisfy p.

`std::partition_copy(a,b,ot,of,p)` copies each of the elements in the range [a,b) to one or the other of the output iterators: `*ot++ = e` for elements where `p(e)` is `true`, and `*of++ = e` for elements where `p(e)` is `false`.

Incidentally, if you only want one output sequence or the other, then you can use `std::copy_if(a,b,ot,p)` or `std::remove_copy_if(a,b,of,p)` respectively.

Rotation and permutation

Remember our code from *Swapping, reversing, and partitioning* to reverse the order of words in a sentence? When the "sentence" contains only two words, there is another way to look at the reversal: you could consider it a *cyclic rotation* of the elements in the underlying range. `std::rotate(a,mid,b)` rotates the elements of the range [a,b) so that the element formerly addressed by `mid` is now at `a` (and returns an iterator pointing to the element whose value was formerly at `a`):

```cpp
template<class FwdIt>
FwdIt rotate(FwdIt a, FwdIt mid, FwdIt b)
{
  auto result = a + (b - mid);

  // First, reverse the whole range.
  std::reverse(a, b);

  // Next, un-reverse each individual segment.
  std::reverse(a, result);
  std::reverse(result, b);

  return result;
}

void test()
{
  std::vector<int> v = {1, 2, 3, 4, 5, 6};
  auto five = std::find(v.begin(), v.end(), 5);
  auto one = std::rotate(v.begin(), five, v.end());
  assert((v == std::vector{5, 6, 1, 2, 3, 4}));
  assert(*one == 1);
}
```

Another miscellaneous but sometimes useful permutative algorithm is `std::next_permutation(a,b)`. Calling this function in a loop runs through all the possible permutations of *n* elements, which might be useful if you're trying to brute-force a solution to a (small) instance of the Traveling Salesman Problem:

```
std::vector<int> p = {10, 20, 30};
std::vector<std::vector<int>> results;

// Collect the permutations of these three elements.
for (int i=0; i < 6; ++i) {
  results.push_back(p);
  std::next_permutation(p.begin(), p.end());
}

assert((results == std::vector<std::vector<int>>{
  {10, 20, 30},
  {10, 30, 20},
  {20, 10, 30},
  {20, 30, 10},
  {30, 10, 20},
  {30, 20, 10},
}));
```

Notice that `next_permutation` uses the idea of a "less-than relationship" to determine that one permutation is lexicographically "less than" another; for example, {20, 10, 30} is "less than" {20, 30, 10} because 10 is less than 30. Therefore, `next_permutation` also has a comparator-based version: `std::next_permutation(a,b,cmp)`. There are also `std::prev_permutation(a,b)` and `std::prev_permutation(a,b,cmp)`, which count lexicographically "downward" instead of "upward."

By the way, to compare two sequences lexicographically in this way, you could use `std::mismatch` from section *Read-only range algorithms*, or you could just use the standard-provided `std::lexicographical_compare(a,b,c,d)`.

Heaps and heapsort

`std::make_heap(a,b)` (or its comparator-based version, `std::make_heap(a,b,cmp)`) takes a range of unsorted elements and rearranges them into an order that satisfies the *max-heap property*: in an array with the max-heap property, each element of the range at index *i* will be at least as great as either of the elements at indices 2*i*+1 and 2*i*+2. This implies that the greatest element of all will be at index 0.

The Iterator-Pair Algorithms

`std::push_heap(a,b)` (or its comparator-based version) assumes that the range `[a,b-1)` is already a max-heap. It takes the element currently at `b[-1]` and "bubbles it up," by swapping with its parent in the heap, until the max-heap property is restored for the whole range `[a,b)`. Notice that `make_heap` can be implemented as a simple loop repeatedly calling `std::push_heap(a,++b)`.

`std::pop_heap(a,b)` (or its comparator-based version) assumes that the range `[a,b)` is already a max-heap. It swaps `a[0]` with `b[-1]`, so that the greatest element is now at the *back* of the range instead of at the front; and then it swaps `a[0]` with one of its children in the heap, and so on, "bubbling it down" until the max-heap property is restored. After a call to `pop_heap(a,b)`, the greatest element will be at `b[-1]` and the range `[a, b-1)` will have the max-heap property.

`std::sort_heap(a,b)` (or its comparator-based version) takes a range with the max-heap property and permutes it into sorted order by repeatedly calling `std::pop_heap(a, b--)`.

Using these building blocks, we can implement the classic "heapsort" algorithm. The standard library's `std::sort` function might reasonably be implemented like this (but in practice it is typically implemented as a hybrid algorithm, such as "introsort"):

```
template<class RandomIt>
void push_heap(RandomIt a, RandomIt b)
{
  auto child = ((b-1) - a);
  while (child != 0) {
    auto parent = (child - 1) / 2;
    if (a[child] < a[parent]) {
      return; // max-heap property has been restored
    }
    std::iter_swap(a+child, a+parent);
    child = parent;
  }
}

template<class RandomIt>
void pop_heap(RandomIt a, RandomIt b)
{
  using DistanceT = decltype(b - a);

  std::iter_swap(a, b-1);

  DistanceT parent = 0;
  DistanceT new_heap_size = ((b-1) - a);
```

```
    while (true) {
      auto leftchild = 2 * parent + 1;
      auto rightchild = 2 * parent + 2;
      if (leftchild >= new_heap_size) {
        return;
      }
      auto biggerchild = leftchild;
      if (rightchild < new_heap_size && a[leftchild] < a[rightchild]) {
        biggerchild = rightchild;
      }
      if (a[biggerchild] < a[parent]) {
        return;  // max-heap property has been restored
      }
      std::iter_swap(a+parent, a+biggerchild);
      parent = biggerchild;
    }
}

template<class RandomIt>
void make_heap(RandomIt a, RandomIt b)
{
  for (auto it = a; it != b; ) {
    push_heap(a, ++it);
  }
}

template<class RandomIt>
void sort_heap(RandomIt a, RandomIt b)
{
  for (auto it = b; it != a; --it) {
    pop_heap(a, it);
  }
}

template<class RandomIt>
void sort(RandomIt a, RandomIt b)
{
  make_heap(a, b);
  sort_heap(a, b);
}
```

We'll see another application of push_heap and pop_heap in Chapter 4, *The Container Zoo*, when we talk about std::priority_queue.

Merges and mergesort

As long as we're on the topic of sorting algorithms, let's write `sort` a different way!

`std::inplace_merge(a,mid,b)` takes a single range `[a,b)` which has already been sorted with the equivalent of `std::sort(a,mid)` and `std::sort(mid,b)`, and merges the two subranges together into a single sorted range. We can use this building block to implement the classic mergesort algorithm:

```
template<class RandomIt>
void sort(RandomIt a, RandomIt b)
{
  auto n = std::distance(a, b);
  if (n >= 2) {
    auto mid = a + n/2;
    std::sort(a, mid);
    std::sort(mid, b);
    std::inplace_merge(a, mid, b);
  }
}
```

However, beware! The name `inplace_merge` seems to imply that the merging is happening "in-place" without the need for any additional buffer space; but this is not what happens in fact. In actuality, the `inplace_merge` function allocates a buffer for its own use, typically by calling `operator new`. If you are programming in an environment where heap allocation is problematic, then you should *avoid* `inplace_merge` *like the plague*.

The other standard algorithms that may allocate temporary buffers on the heap are `std::stable_sort` and `std::stable_partition`.

`std::merge(a,b,c,d,o)` is the non-allocating merge algorithm; it takes two iterator-pairs representing the ranges `[a,b)` and `[c,d)` and merges them into the output range defined by `o`.

Searching and inserting in a sorted array with std::lower_bound

Once a range of data has been sorted, it becomes possible to search within that data using binary search, as opposed to the slower linear search. The standard algorithm that implements binary search is called `std::lower_bound(a,b,v)`:

```
template<class FwdIt, class T, class C>
FwdIt lower_bound(FwdIt first, FwdIt last, const T& value, C lessthan)
{
  using DiffT = typename std::iterator_traits<FwdIt>::difference_type;
  FwdIt it;
  DiffT count = std::distance(first, last);

  while (count > 0) {
    DiffT step = count / 2;
    it = first;
    std::advance(it, step);
    if (lessthan(*it, value)) {
      ++it;
      first = it;
      count -= step + 1;
    } else {
      count = step;
    }
  }
  return first;
}

template<class FwdIt, class T>
FwdIt lower_bound(FwdIt first, FwdIt last, const T& value)
{
  return std::lower_bound(first, last, value, std::less<>{});
}
```

This function returns an iterator to the first element in the range that is *not less than* the given value v. If there is an instance of the value v already in the range, then the returned iterator will point at it (in fact, it will point at the *first* such value in the range). If there's no instance already in the range, then the returned iterator will point at the place where v should go.

The Iterator-Pair Algorithms

We can use the return value of `lower_bound` as the input to `vector::insert` in order to insert v into the proper place in a sorted vector while preserving its sorted order:

```
std::vector<int> vec = {3, 7};
for (int value : {1, 5, 9}) {
  // Find the appropriate insertion point...
  auto it = std::lower_bound(vec.begin(), vec.end(), value);
  // ...and insert our value there.
  vec.insert(it, value);
}
// The vector has remained sorted.
assert((vec == std::vector{1, 3, 5, 7, 9}));
```

The similar function `std::upper_bound(a,b,v)` returns an iterator to the first element in the range that is *greater than* the given value v. If v is not in the given range, then `std::lower_bound` and `std::upper_bound` will have the same return value. But if v is present in the range, then `lower_bound` will return an iterator pointing to the first instance of v in the range and `upper_bound` will return an iterator pointing "one past" the last instance of v in the range. In other words, using the two functions together will give you a half-open range `[lower, upper)` containing nothing but instances of the value v:

```
std::vector<int> vec = {2, 3, 3, 3, 4};
auto lower = std::lower_bound(vec.begin(), vec.end(), 3);

// First approach:
// upper_bound's interface is identical to lower_bound's.
auto upper = std::upper_bound(vec.begin(), vec.end(), 3);

// Second approach:
// We don't need to binary-search the whole array the second time.
auto upper2 = std::upper_bound(lower, vec.end(), 3);
assert(upper2 == upper);

// Third approach:
// Linear scan from the lower bound might well be faster
// than binary search if our total range is really big.
auto upper3 = std::find_if(lower, vec.end(), [](int v) {
  return v != 3;
});
assert(upper3 == upper);

// No matter which approach we take, this is what we end up with.
assert(*lower >= 3);
assert(*upper > 3);
assert(std::all_of(lower, upper, [](int v) { return v == 3; }));
```

This handles searching and inserting values in a sorted array. But what about deletion?

Deleting from a sorted array with std::remove_if

In all our discussion of standard generic algorithms up to this point, we haven't covered the question of how to remove items from a range. This is because the concept of "a range" is fundamentally read-only: we might change the *values* of the elements of a given range, but we can never use a standard algorithm to shorten or lengthen *the range itself*. When, in the *Shunting data with std::copy* section, we used `std::copy` to "insert into" a vector named `dest`, it wasn't the `std::copy` algorithm that was doing the inserting; it was the `std::back_insert_iterator` object itself that held a reference to the underlying container and was able to insert into the container. `std::copy` didn't take `dest.begin()` and `dest.end()` as parameters; instead it took the special object `std::back_inserter(dest)`.

So how do we erase items from a range? Well, we can't. All we can do is erase items from a *container*; and the algorithms of the STL do not deal in containers. So what we ought to be looking for is a way to rearrange the values of a range so that the "removed" items will wind up somewhere predictable, so that we can quickly erase them all from the underlying container (using some means other than an STL algorithm).

We've seen one possible approach already:

```
std::vector<int> vec = {1, 3, 3, 4, 6, 8};

// Partition our vector so that all the non-3s are at the front
// and all the 3s are at the end.
auto first_3 = std::stable_partition(
  vec.begin(), vec.end(), [](int v){ return v != 3; }
);

assert((vec == std::vector{1, 4, 6, 8, 3, 3}));

// Now erase the "tail" of our vector.
vec.erase(first_3, vec.end());

assert((vec == std::vector{1, 4, 6, 8}));
```

The Iterator-Pair Algorithms

But this is much more wasteful than it needs to be (notice that `stable_partition` is one of those few STL algorithms that allocates a temporary buffer on the heap!). The algorithm we want is actually much simpler:

```
template<class FwdIt, class T>
FwdIt remove(FwdIt first, FwdIt last, const T& value)
{
  auto out = std::find(first, last, value);
  if (out != last) {
    auto in = out;
    while (++in != last) {
      if (*in == value) {
        // don't bother with this item
      } else {
        *out++ = std::move(*in);
      }
    }
  }
  return out;
}

void test()
{
  std::vector<int> vec = {1, 3, 3, 4, 6, 8};

  // Partition our vector so that all the non-3s are at the front.
  auto new_end = std::remove(
    vec.begin(), vec.end(), 3
  );

  // std::remove_if doesn't preserve the "removed" elements.
  assert((vec == std::vector{1, 4, 6, 8, 6, 8}));

  // Now erase the "tail" of our vector.
  vec.erase(new_end, vec.end());

  assert((vec == std::vector{1, 4, 6, 8}));

  // Or, do both steps together in a single line.
  // This is the "erase-remove idiom":
  vec.erase(
    std::remove(vec.begin(), vec.end(), 3),
    vec.end()
  );

  // But if the array is very long, and we know it's sorted,
  // then perhaps it would be better to binary-search for
  // the elements to erase.
```

```cpp
        // Here the "shifting-down" is still happening, but it's
        // happening inside vector::erase instead of inside std::remove.
        auto first = std::lower_bound(vec.begin(), vec.end(), 3);
        auto last = std::upper_bound(first, vec.end(), 3);
        vec.erase(first, last);
    }
```

`std::remove(a,b,v)` removes all values equal to v from a range `[a,b)`. Notice that the range does *not* have to be sorted--but `remove` will preserve whatever order was there before, by "shifting down" the non-removed elements to fill in the gaps in the range. If `remove` removes *k* elements from the range, then when the `remove` function returns, there will be *k* elements at the end of the range whose values are in the moved-from state, and return value of `remove` will be an iterator pointing to the first such moved-from element.

`std::remove_if(a,b,p)` removes all elements satisfying the given predicate; that is, it removes all elements e such that `p(e)` is true. Just like `remove`, `remove_if` shifts elements down to fill in the range and returns an iterator to the first "moved-from" element.

The common idiom for removing items from a sequence container is what's known as the *erase-remove idiom*, because it involves passing that return value straight into the container's own `.erase()` member function.

Another standard library algorithm that works with the erase-remove idiom is `std::unique(a,b)`, which takes a range and, for each set of consecutive equivalent items, removes all but the first of them. Like `std::remove`, the input range doesn't need to be sorted; the algorithm will preserve whatever ordering was there to begin with:

```cpp
        std::vector<int> vec = {1, 2, 2, 3, 3, 3, 1, 3, 3};

        vec.erase(
          std::unique(vec.begin(), vec.end()),
          vec.end()
        );

        assert((vec == std::vector{1, 2, 3, 1, 3}));
```

The Iterator-Pair Algorithms

Finally, notice that we can often do better than `std::remove` in general, either by using the `erase` member function of whatever our underlying container is (for example, we'll see in the next chapter how `std::list::erase` can be much faster than the erase-remove idiom on a `std::list`)--and even if we're removing from a vector whose order happens *not* to be significant, we'll still usually be better off with something like the following generic algorithm `unstable_remove`, which has been proposed for future standardization but (at the time of writing) not yet adopted into the STL:

```cpp
namespace my {
  template<class BidirIt, class T>
  BidirIt unstable_remove(BidirIt first, BidirIt last, const T& value)
  {
    while (true) {
      // Find the first instance of "value"...
      first = std::find(first, last, value);
      // ...and the last instance of "not value"...
      do {
        if (first == last) {
          return last;
        }
        --last;
      } while (*last == value);
      // ...and move the latter over top of the former.
      *first = std::move(*last);
      // Rinse and repeat.
      ++first;
    }
  }
} // namespace my

void test()
{
  std::vector<int> vec = {4, 1, 3, 6, 3, 8};

  vec.erase(
    my::unstable_remove(vec.begin(), vec.end(), 3),
    vec.end()
  );

  assert((vec == std::vector{4, 1, 8, 6}));
}
```

In the next chapter, we'll look at *containers*--the STL's answer to the question, "Where are all these elements being stored, anyway?"

[72]

Summary

The Standard Template Library has a generic algorithm for (almost) every desire. If you're doing something algorithmic, check the STL first!

STL algorithms deal in the half-open ranges defined by pairs of iterators. Be careful when dealing with any of the one-and-a-half-range algorithms.

STL algorithms that deal with comparison and sorting will use `operator<` by default, but you can always pass a two-argument "comparator" instead. If you want to perform a non-trivial operation on a whole range of data, remember that the STL might support it directly (`std::move`, `std::transform`) or indirectly via a special iterator type (`std::back_inserter`, `std::istream_iterator`).

You should know what a "permutation" is, and how the standard permutative algorithms (`swap`, `reverse`, `rotate`, `partition`, `sort`) are implemented in terms of one another. Just three STL algorithms (`stable_sort`, `stable_partition`, `inplace_merge`) may quietly allocate memory from the heap; if you can't afford heap allocation, avoid these three algorithms like the plague.

Use the erase-remove idiom to maintain the sort order of a sequence container even as you delete items from it. Use something like `my::unstable_remove` if you don't care about the sort order. Use `.erase()` for containers that support it.

4
The Container Zoo

In the previous two chapters, we introduced the ideas of *iterators* and *ranges* (Chapter 2, *Iterators and Ranges*) and the vast library of standard *generic algorithms* that operate on ranges of data elements defined by pairs of those iterators (Chapter 3, *The Iterator-Pair Algorithms*). In this chapter, we'll look at where those data elements themselves are allocated and stored. That is, now that we know all about how to iterate, the question gains urgency: what is it that we are iterating *over*?

In the Standard Template Library, the answer to that question is generally: We are iterating over some sub-range of the elements contained in a *container*. A container is simply a C++ class (or class template) which, by its nature, *contains* (or *owns*) a homogeneous range of data elements, and exposes that range for iteration by generic algorithms.

Topics we will cover in this chapter are:

- The notion of one object *owning* another (this being the essential difference between a *container* and a *range*)
- The sequence containers (`array`, `vector`, `list`, and `forward_list`)
- The pitfalls of iterator invalidation and reference invalidation
- The container adaptors (`stack`, `queue`, and `priority_queue`)
- The associative containers (`set`, `map`, and friends)
- When it is appropriate to provide a *comparator*, *hash function*, *equality comparator*, or *allocator* as additional template type parameters

The notion of ownership

When we say that object A *owns* object B, what we mean is that object A manages the lifetime of object B--that A controls the construction, copying, moving, and destruction of object B. The user of object A can (and should) "forget about" managing B (for example, via explicit calls to `delete B`, `fclose(B)`, and so on).

The simplest way for an object A to "own" an object B is for B to be a member variable of A. For example:

```
struct owning_A {
  B b_;
};

struct non_owning_A {
  B& b_;
};

void test()
{
  B b;

  // a1 takes ownership of [a copy of] b.
  owning_A a1 { b };

  // a2 merely holds a reference to b;
  // a2 doesn't own b.
  non_owning_A a2 { b };
}
```

Another way is for A to hold a pointer to B, with the appropriate code in `~A()` (and, if necessary, in the copy and move operations of A) to clean up the resources associated with that pointer:

```
struct owning_A {
  B *b_;

  explicit owning_A(B *b) : b_(b) {}

  owning_A(owning_A&& other) : b_(other.b_) {
    other.b_ = nullptr;
  }

  owning_A& operator= (owning_A&& other) {
    delete b_;
    b_ = other.b_;
```

```
    other.b_ = nullptr;
    return *this;
  }

  ~owning_A() {
    delete b_;
  }
};

struct non_owning_A {
  B *b_;
};

void test()
{
  B *b = new B;

  // a1 takes ownership of *b.
  owning_A a1 { b };

  // a2 merely holds a pointer to *b;
  // a2 doesn't own *b.
  non_owning_A a2 { b };
}
```

The notion of *ownership* is tightly bound up with the C++-specific catchphrase **Resource Allocation Is Initialization**, which you will often see abbreviated as **RAII**. (That cumbersome abbreviation should properly have been more like "Resource Freeing Is Destruction", but that acronym was taken.)

The goal of the standard *container classes* is to provide access to a particular bunch of data objects B, while making sure that the *ownership* of those objects is always clear--namely, a container always has ownership of its data elements. (Contrariwise, an *iterator*, or a pair of iterators defining a *range*, never owns its data elements; we saw in Chapter 3, *The Iterator-Pair Algorithms*, that the standard iterator-based algorithms such as std::remove_if never actually deallocate any elements, but instead simply permute the values of the elements in various ways.)

In the remainder of this chapter, we'll explore the various standard container classes.

The Container Zoo

The simplest container: std::array<T, N>

The simplest standard container class is `std::array<T, N>`, which behaves just like a built-in ("C-style") array. The first template parameter to `std::array` indicates the type of the array's elements, and the second template parameter indicates the number of elements in the array. This is one of the very few places in the standard library where a template parameter is an integer value instead of the name of a type.

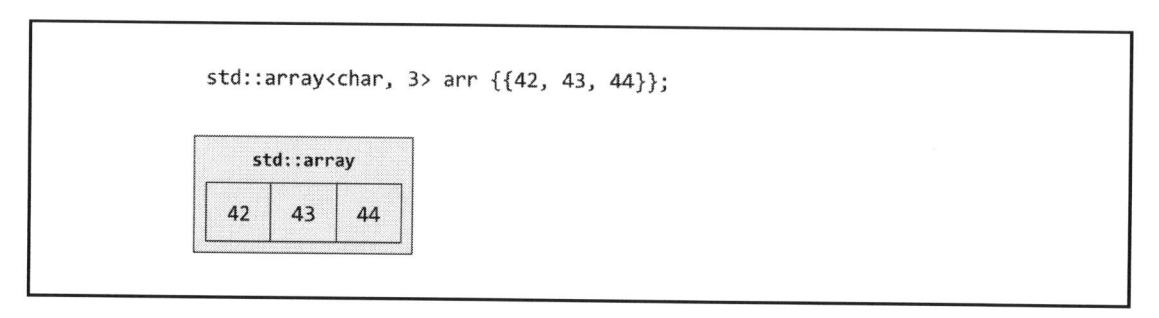

```
std::array<char, 3> arr {{42, 43, 44}};
```

```
std::array
| 42 | 43 | 44 |
```

Normal C-style arrays, being part of the core language (and a part that dates back to the 1970s, at that!), do not provide any built-in operations that would take linear time to run. C-style arrays let you index into them with `operator[]`, and compare their addresses, since those operations can be done in constant time; but if you want to assign the entire contents of one C-style array to another, or compare the contents of two arrays, you'll find that you can't do it straightforwardly. You'll have to use some of the standard algorithms we discussed in Chapter 3, *The Iterator-Pair Algorithms*, such as `std::copy` or `std::equal` (the function template `std::swap`, being an "algorithm" already, *does* work for C-style arrays. It would be a shame if it didn't work.):

```
std::string c_style[4] = {
  "the", "quick", "brown", "fox"
};
assert(c_style[2] == "brown");
assert(std::size(c_style) == 4);
assert(std::distance(std::begin(c_style), std::end(c_style)) == 4);

// Copying via operator= isn't supported.
std::string other[4];
std::copy(std::begin(c_style), std::end(c_style), std::begin(other));

// Swapping IS supported... in linear time, of course.
using std::swap;
swap(c_style, other);

// Comparison isn't supported; you have to use a standard algorithm.
```

```
    // Worse, operator== does the "wrong" thing: address comparison!
    assert(c_style != other);
    assert(std::equal(
      c_style, c_style + 4,
      other, other + 4
    ));
    assert(!std::lexicographical_compare(
      c_style, c_style + 4,
      other, other + 4
    ));
```

`std::array` behaves just like a C-style array, but with more syntactic sugar. It offers `.begin()` and `.end()` member functions; and it overloads the operators =, ==, and < to do the natural things. All of these operations still take time linear in the size of the array, because they have to walk through the array copying (or swapping or comparing) each individual element one at a time.

One gripe about `std::array`, which you'll see recurring for a few of these standard container classes, is that when you construct a `std::array` with an initializer list inside a set of curly braces, you actually need to write *two* sets of curly braces. That's one set for the "outer object" of type `std::array<T, N>`, and another set for the "inner data member" of type `T[N]`. This is a bit annoying at first, but the double-brace syntax will quickly become second nature once you have used it a few times:

```
    std::array<std::string, 4> arr = {{
      "the", "quick", "brown", "fox"
    }};
    assert(arr[2] == "brown");

    // .begin(), .end(), and .size() are all provided.
    assert(arr.size() == 4);
    assert(std::distance(arr.begin(), arr.end()) == 4);

    // Copying via operator= is supported... in linear time.
    std::array<std::string, 4> other;
    other = arr;

    // Swapping is also supported... in linear time.
    using std::swap;
    swap(arr, other);

    // operator== does the natural thing: value comparison!
    assert(&arr != &other); // The arrays have different addresses...
    assert(arr == other); // ...but still compare lexicographically equal.
    assert(arr >= other); // Relational operators are also supported.
```

One other benefit of `std::array` is that you can return one from a function, which you can't do with C-style arrays:

```
// You can't return a C-style array from a function.
// auto cross_product(const int (&a)[3], const int (&b)[3]) -> int[3];

// But you can return a std::array.
auto cross_product(const std::array<int, 3>& a,
 const std::array<int, 3>& b) -> std::array<int, 3>
{
  return {{
    a[1] * b[2] - a[2] * b[1],
    a[2] * b[0] - a[0] * b[2],
    a[0] * b[1] - a[1] * b[0],
  }};
}
```

Because `std::array` has a copy constructor and a copy assignment operator, you can also store them in containers: for example, `std::vector<std::array<int, 3>>` is fine whereas `std::vector<int[3]>` wouldn't work.

However, if you find yourself returning arrays from functions or storing arrays in containers very often, you should consider whether "array" is really the right abstraction for your purposes. Would it be more appropriate to wrap that array up into some kind of class type?

In the case of our `cross_product` example, it turns out to be an extremely good idea to encapsulate our "array of three integers" in a class type. Not only does this allow us to name the members (x, y, and z), but we can also initialize objects of the `Vec3` class type more easily (no second pair of curly braces!) and perhaps most importantly for our future sanity, we can avoid defining the comparison operators such as `operator<` which don't actually make sense for our mathematical domain. Using `std::array`, we have to deal with the fact that the array `{1, 2, 3}` compares "less than" the array `{1, 3, -9}`--but when we define our own `class Vec3`, we can simply omit any mention of `operator<` and thus ensure that nobody will ever accidentally misuse it in a mathematical context:

```
struct Vec3 {
  int x, y, z;
  Vec3(int x, int y, int z) : x(x), y(y), z(z) {}
};

bool operator==(const Vec3& a, const Vec3& b) {
  return std::tie(a.x, a.y, a.z) ==
    std::tie(b.x, b.y, b.z);
}
```

```
bool operator!=(const Vec3& a, const Vec3& b) {
  return !(a == b);
}

// Operators < <= > >= don't make sense for Vec3

Vec3 cross_product(const Vec3& a, const Vec3& b) {
  return {
    a.y * b.z - a.z * b.y,
    a.z * b.x - a.x * b.z,
    a.x * b.y - a.y * b.x,
  };
}
```

`std::array` holds its elements inside itself. Therefore, `sizeof (std::array<int, 100>)` is equal to `sizeof (int[100])`, which is equal to `100 * sizeof (int)`. Don't make the mistake of trying to place a gigantic array on the stack as a local variable!

```
void dont_do_this()
{
  // This variable takes up 4 megabytes of stack space ---
  // enough to blow your stack and cause a segmentation fault!
  int arr[1'000'000];
}

void dont_do_this_either()
{
  // Changing it into a C++ std::array doesn't fix the problem.
  std::array<int, 1'000'000> arr;
}
```

Working with "gigantic arrays" is a job for the next container on our list: `std::vector`.

The workhorse: std::vector<T>

`std::vector` represents a contiguous array of data elements, but allocated on the heap instead of on the stack. This improves on `std::array` in two ways: First, it allows us to create a really gigantic array without blowing our stack. Second, it allows us to resize the underlying array dynamically--unlike `std::array<int, 3>` where the size of the array is an immutable part of the type, a `std::vector<int>` has no intrinsic size. A vector's `.size()` method actually yields useful information about the current state of the vector.

A `std::vector` has one other salient attribute: its *capacity*. The capacity of a vector is always at least as large as its size, and represents the number of elements that the vector currently *could* hold, before it would need to reallocate its underlying array:

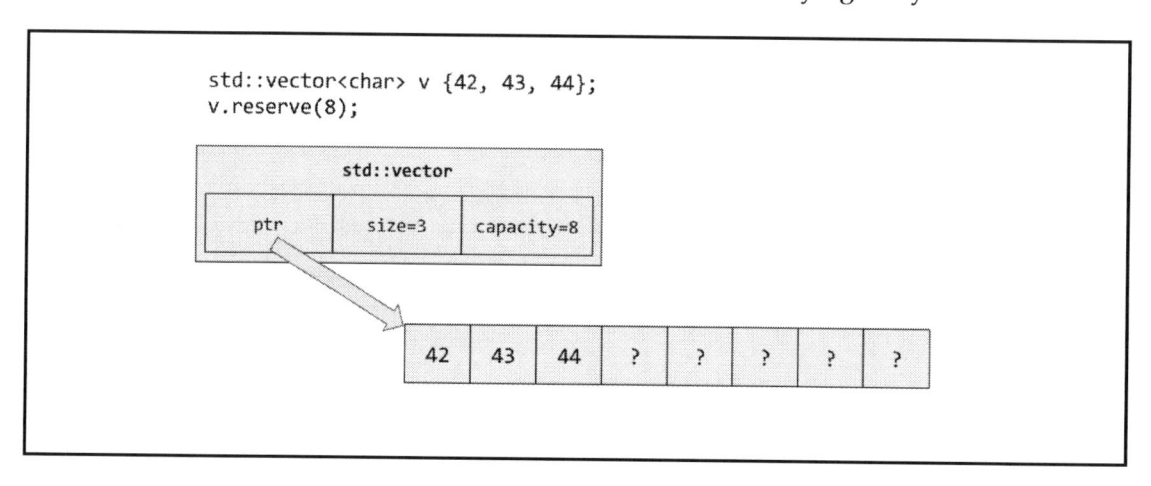

```
std::vector<char> v {42, 43, 44};
v.reserve(8);
```

```
std::vector
┌─────┬────────┬──────────┐
│ ptr │ size=3 │ capacity=8│
└──┬──┴────────┴──────────┘
   │
   ▼
┌────┬────┬────┬───┬───┬───┬───┬───┐
│ 42 │ 43 │ 44 │ ? │ ? │ ? │ ? │ ? │
└────┴────┴────┴───┴───┴───┴───┴───┘
```

Other than its resizeability, `vector` behaves similarly to `array`. Like arrays, vectors are copyable (copying all their data elements, in linear time) and comparable (`std::vector<T>::operator<` will report the lexicographical order of the operands by delegating to `T::operator<`).

Generally speaking, `std::vector` is the most commonly used container in the entire standard library. Any time you need to store a "lot" of elements (or "I'm not sure how many elements I have"), your first thought should always be to use a `vector`. Why? Because `vector` gives you all the flexibility of a resizeable container, with all the simplicity and efficiency of a contiguous array.

Contiguous arrays are the most efficient data structures (on typical hardware) because they provide good *locality*, also known as `cache-friendliness`. When you're traversing a vector in order from its `.begin()` to its `.end()`, you're also traversing *memory* in order, which means that the computer's hardware can predict with very high accuracy the next piece of memory you're going to look at. Compare this to a linked list, in which traversing from `.begin()` to `.end()` might well involve following pointers all over the address space, and accessing memory locations in no sensible order. With a linked list, pretty much every address you hit will be unrelated to the previous one, and so none of them will be in the CPU's cache. With a vector (or array), the opposite is true: every address you hit will be related to the previous one by a simple linear relationship, and the CPU will be able to have the values all ready and waiting for you by the time you need them.

Even if your data is "more structured" than a simple list of values, you can often get away with using a vector to store it. We'll see near the end of this chapter how you can use vector to simulate a stack or a priority queue.

Resizing a std::vector

std::vector has a whole family of member functions concerned with adding and deleting elements. These member functions aren't present in std::array because std::array isn't resizable; but they *are* present in most of the other containers we're going to be talking about in this chapter. So it's a good idea to get familiar with them now.

Let's start with the two primitive operations specific to vector itself: .resize() and .reserve().

vec.reserve(c) updates the capacity of the vector--it "reserves" space for as many as c elements (total) in the underlying array. If c <= vec.capacity() then nothing happens; but if c > vec.capacity() then the vector will have to reallocate its underlying array. Reallocation follows an algorithm equivalent to the following:

```cpp
template<typename T>
inline void destroy_n_elements(T *p, size_t n)
{
  for (size_t i = 0; i < n; ++i) {
    p[i].~T();
  }
}

template<typename T>
class vector {
  T *ptr_ = nullptr;
  size_t size_ = 0;
  size_t capacity_ = 0;

public:
// ...

  void reserve(size_t c) {
    if (capacity_ >= c) {
      // do nothing
      return;
    }

    // For now, we'll ignore the problem of
    // "What if malloc fails?"
```

The Container Zoo

```
            T *new_ptr = (T *)malloc(c * sizeof (T));

            for (size_t i=0; i < size_; ++i) {
              if constexpr (std::is_nothrow_move_constructible_v<T>) {
                // If the elements can be moved without risking
                // an exception, then we'll move the elements.
                ::new (&new_ptr[i]) T(std::move(ptr_[i]));
              } else {
                // If moving the elements might throw an exception,
                // then moving isn't safe. Make a copy of the elements
                // until we're sure that we've succeeded; then destroy
                // the old elements.
                try {
                  ::new (&new_ptr[i]) T(ptr_[i]);
                } catch (...) {
                  destroy_n_elements(new_ptr, i);
                  free(new_ptr);
                  throw;
                }
              }
            }
            // Having successfully moved or copied the elements,
            // destroy the old array and point ptr_ at the new one.
            destroy_n_elements(ptr_, size_);
            free(ptr_);
            ptr_ = new_ptr;
            capacity_ = c;
          }

          ~vector() {
            destroy_n_elements(ptr_, size_);
            free(ptr_);
          }
        };
```

If you've been reading this book in order, you might recognize that the crucial for-loop in this `.reserve()` function closely resembles the implementation of `std::uninitialized_copy(a,b,c)` from Chapter 3, *The Iterator-Pair Algorithms*. Indeed, if you were implementing `.reserve()` on a container that was not allocator-aware (see Chapter 8, *Allocators*), you might reuse that standard algorithm:

```
            // If the elements can be moved without risking
            // an exception, then we'll move the elements.
            std::conditional_t<
              std::is_nothrow_move_constructible_v<T>,
              std::move_iterator<T*>,
              T*
```

```
        > first(ptr_);

    try {
      // Move or copy the elements via a standard algorithm.
        std::uninitialized_copy(first, first + size_, new_ptr);
    } catch (...) {
      free(new_ptr);
      throw;
    }

    // Having successfully moved or copied the elements,
    // destroy the old array and point ptr_ at the new one.
    std::destroy(ptr_, ptr_ + size_);
    free(ptr_);
    ptr_ = new_ptr;
    capacity_ = c;
```

`vec.resize(s)` changes the size of the vector--it chops elements off the end of the vector (calling their destructors in the process), or adds additional elements to the vector (default-constructing them), until the size of the vector is equal to s. If s > `vec.capacity()`, then the vector will have to reallocate its underlying array, just as in the `.reserve()` case.

You may have noticed that when a vector reallocates its underlying array, the elements change addresses: the address of `vec[0]` before the reallocation is different from the address of `vec[0]` after the reallocation. Any pointers that pointed to the vector's old elements become "dangling pointers." And since `std::vector::iterator` is essentially just a pointer as well, any *iterators* that pointed to the vector's old elements become invalid as well. This phenomenon is called *iterator invalidation,* and it is a major source of bugs in C++ code. Watch out when you're dealing with iterators and resizing vectors at the same time!

Here are some classic cases of iterator invalidation:

```
    std::vector<int> v = {3, 1, 4};

    auto iter = v.begin();
    v.reserve(6);  // iter is invalidated!

    // This might look like a way to produce the result
    // {3, 1, 4, 3, 1, 4}; but if the first insertion
    // triggers reallocation, then the next insertion
    // will be reading garbage from a dangling iterator!
    v = std::vector{3, 1, 4};
    std::copy(
      v.begin(),
      v.end(),
```

```
    std::back_inserter(v)
);
```

And here's another case, familiar from many other programming languages as well, in which erasing elements from a container while iterating over it produces subtle bugs:

```
auto end = v.end();
for (auto it = v.begin(); it != end; ++it) {
  if (*it == 4) {
    v.erase(it); // WRONG!
  }
}

// Asking the vector for its .end() each time
// through the loop does fix the bug...
for (auto it = v.begin(); it != v.end(); ) {
  if (*it == 4) {
    it = v.erase(it);
  } else {
    ++it;
  }
}

// ...But it's much more efficient to use the
// erase-remove idiom.
v.erase(
  std::remove_if(v.begin(), v.end(), [](auto&& elt) {
    return elt == 4;
  }),
  v.end()
);
```

Inserting and erasing in a std::vector

`vec.push_back(t)` adds an item to the end of the vector. There is no corresponding `.push_front()` member function, because as you can see from the diagram at the start of this section, there's no efficient way to push anything onto the *front* of a vector.

`vec.emplace_back(args...)` is a perfect-forwarding variadic function template that acts just like `.push_back(t)`, except that, instead of placing a copy of `t` at the end of the vector, it places a `T` object constructed as if by `T(args...)`.

Both `push_back` and `emplace_back` have what is called "amortized constant time" performance. To see what this means, consider what would happen to a naive vector if you call `v.emplace_back()` a hundred times in a row. With each call, the vector needs to get just a little bit bigger; so it reallocates its underlying array and moves all `v.size()` elements from the old array to the new one. Soon you'd be spending more time copying old data from place to place than you're spending actually "pushing back" new data! Fortunately, `std::vector` is smart enough to avoid this trap. Whenever an operation such as `v.emplace_back()` causes reallocation, the vector won't make room for just `capacity() + 1` elements in the new array; it will make room for `k * capacity()` elements (where k is 2 for libc++ and libstdc++, and approximately 1.5 for Visual Studio). So, although reallocation gets more and more expensive as the vector grows, you do fewer and fewer reallocations per `push_back`--and so the cost of a single `push_back` is constant, *on average*. This trick is known as *geometric resizing*.

`vec.insert(it, t)` adds an item into the middle of the vector, at the position indicated by the iterator `it`. If `it == vec.end()`, then this is equivalent to `push_back`; if `it == vec.begin()`, then this is a poor man's version of `push_front`. Notice that, if you insert anywhere but the end of the vector, all the elements after the insertion point in the underlying array will get shifted over to make room; this can be expensive.

There are several different overloads of `.insert()`. Generally speaking, none of these will be useful to you, but you might want to be aware of them in order to interpret the cryptic error messages (or cryptic runtime bugs) that will show up if you accidentally provide the wrong arguments to `.insert()` and overload resolution ends up picking one of these instead of the one you expected:

```cpp
std::vector<int> v = {1, 2};
std::vector<int> w = {5, 6};

// Insert a single element.
v.insert(v.begin() + 1, 3);
assert((v == std::vector{1, 3, 2}));

// Insert n copies of a single element.
v.insert(v.end() - 1, 3, 4);
assert((v == std::vector{1, 3, 4, 4, 4, 2}));

// Insert a whole range of elements.
v.insert(v.begin() + 3, w.begin(), w.end());
assert((v == std::vector{1, 3, 4, 5, 6, 4, 4, 2}));

// Insert a braced list of elements.
v.insert(v.begin(), {7, 8});
assert((v == std::vector{7, 8, 1, 3, 4, 5, 6, 4, 4, 2}));
```

The Container Zoo

`vec.emplace(it, args...)` is to `insert` as `emplace_back` is to `push_back`: it's a perfect-forwarding version of the C++03 function. Prefer `emplace` and `emplace_back` over `insert` and `push_back`, when possible.

`vec.erase(it)` erases a single item from the middle of a vector, at the position indicated by the iterator `it`. There's also a two-iterator version, `vec.erase(it, it)`, which erases a contiguous range of items. Notice that this two-iterator version is the same one we used in the *erase-remove idiom* in the previous chapter.

To delete just the last element from the vector, you could use either `vec.erase(vec.end()-1)` or `vec.erase(vec.end()-1, vec.end())`; but since this is a common operation, the standard library provides a synonym in the form of `vec.pop_back()`. You can implement a dynamically growable *stack* using nothing more than the `push_back()` and `pop_back()` methods of `std::vector`.

Pitfalls with vector<bool>

The `std::vector` template has one special case: `std::vector<bool>`. Since the `bool` datatype has only two possible values, the values of eight bools can be packed into a single byte. `std::vector<bool>` uses this optimization, which means that it uses eight times less heap-allocated memory than you might naturally expect.

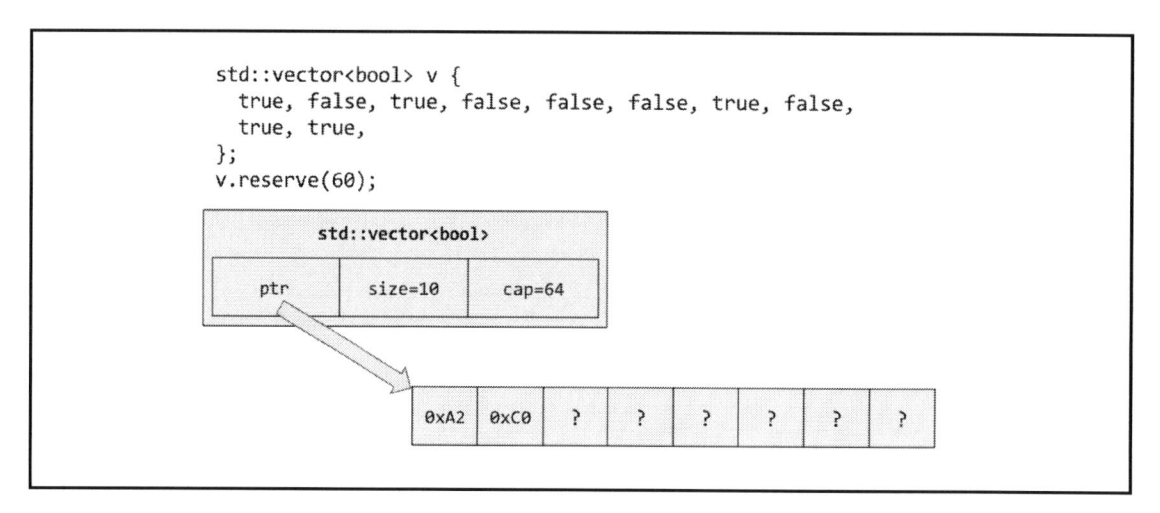

```
std::vector<bool> v {
    true, false, true, false, false, false, true, false,
    true, true,
};
v.reserve(60);
```

```
           std::vector<bool>
    ┌──────┬─────────┬────────┐
    │ ptr  │ size=10 │ cap=64 │
    └──────┴─────────┴────────┘

    ┌──────┬──────┬───┬───┬───┬───┬───┬───┐
    │ 0xA2 │ 0xC0 │ ? │ ? │ ? │ ? │ ? │ ? │
    └──────┴──────┴───┴───┴───┴───┴───┴───┘
```

The downside of this packing is that the return type of vector<bool>::operator[] cannot be bool&, because the vector doesn't store actual bool objects anywhere. Therefore, operator[] returns a customized class type, std::vector<bool>::reference, which is convertible to bool but which is not, itself, a bool (types like this are often called "proxy types" or "proxy references").

The result type of operator[] const is "officially" bool, but in practice, some libraries (notably libc++) return a proxy type for operator[] const. This means that code using vector<bool> is not only subtle but sometimes non-portable as well; I advise avoiding vector<bool> if you can:

```
std::vector<bool> vb = {true, false, true, false};

// vector<bool>::reference has one public member function:
vb[3].flip();
assert(vb[3] == true);

// The following line won't compile!
// bool& oops = vb[0];

auto ref = vb[0];
assert((!std::is_same_v<decltype(ref), bool>));
assert(sizeof vb[0] > sizeof (bool));

if (sizeof std::as_const(vb)[0] == sizeof (bool)) {
  puts("Your library vendor is libstdc++ or Visual Studio");
} else {
  puts("Your library vendor is libc++");
}
```

Pitfalls with non-noexcept move constructors

Recall the implementation of vector::resize() from section *Resizing a std::vector*. When the vector resizes, it reallocates its underlying array and moves its elements into the new array--unless the element type is not "nothrow move-constructible," in which case it *copies* its elements! What this means is that resizing a vector of your own class type will be unnecessarily "pessimized" unless you go out of your way to specify that your move constructor is noexcept.

Consider the following class definitions:

```
struct Bad {
  int x = 0;
  Bad() = default;
```

```
    Bad(const Bad&) { puts("copy Bad"); }
    Bad(Bad&&) { puts("move Bad"); }
};

struct Good {
    int x = 0;
    Good() = default;
    Good(const Good&) { puts("copy Good"); }
    Good(Good&&) noexcept { puts("move Good"); }
};

class ImplicitlyGood {
    std::string x;
    Good y;
};

class ImplicitlyBad {
    std::string x;
    Bad y;
};
```

We can test the behavior of these classes in isolation using a test harness such as the following. Running `test()` will print "copy Bad--move Good--copy Bad--move Good." What an appropriate mantra!

```
template<class T>
void test_resizing()
{
    std::vector<T> vec(1);
    // Force a reallocation on the vector.
    vec.resize(vec.capacity() + 1);
}

void test()
{
    test_resizing<Good>();
    test_resizing<Bad>();
    test_resizing<ImplicitlyGood>();
    test_resizing<ImplicitlyBad>();
}
```

This is a subtle and arcane point, but it can have a major effect on the efficiency of your C++ code in practice. A good rule of thumb is: Whenever you declare your own move constructor or swap function, make sure you declare it `noexcept`.

The speedy hybrid: std::deque<T>

Like `std::vector`, `std::deque` presents the interface of a contiguous array--it is random-access, and its elements are stored in contiguous blocks for cache-friendliness. But unlike `vector`, its elements are only "chunkwise" contiguous. A single deque is made up of an arbitrary number of "chunks," each containing a fixed number of elements. To insert more elements on either end of the container is cheap; to insert elements in the middle is still expensive. In memory it looks something like this:

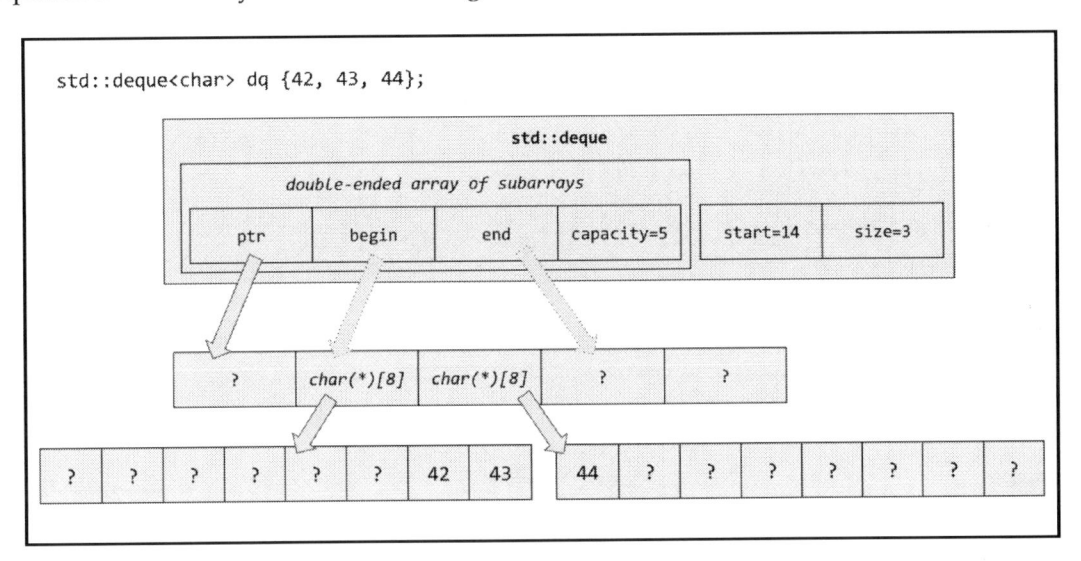

```
std::deque<char> dq {42, 43, 44};
```

```
                         std::deque
              double-ended array of subarrays
        ptr      begin       end    capacity=5    start=14   size=3

              ?       char(*)[8]  char(*)[8]    ?         ?

    ?  ?  ?  ?  ?  ?  42  43  44  ?  ?  ?  ?  ?  ?
```

`std::deque<T>` exposes all the same member functions as `std::vector<T>`, including an overloaded `operator[]`. In addition to vector's `push_back` and `pop_back` methods, deque exposes an efficient `push_front` and `pop_front`.

Notice that, when you repeatedly `push_back` into a vector, you eventually trigger a reallocation of the underlying array and invalidate all your iterators and all your pointers and references to elements within the container. With `deque`, iterator invalidation still happens, but individual elements never change their addresses unless you insert or erase elements in the middle of the deque (in which case one end of the deque or the other will have to shift outward to make room, or shift inward to fill the gap):

```
std::vector<int> vec = {1, 2, 3, 4};
std::deque<int> deq = {1, 2, 3, 4};
int *vec_p = &vec[2];
int *deq_p = &deq[2];
for (int i=0; i < 1000; ++i) {
  vec.push_back(i);
```

The Container Zoo

```
        deq.push_back(i);
    }
    assert(vec_p != &vec[2]);
    assert(deq_p == &deq[2]);
```

Another advantage of `std::deque<T>` is that there is no specialization for `std::deque<bool>`; the container presents a uniform public interface no matter what `T` is.

The disadvantage of `std::deque<T>` is that its iterators are significantly more expensive to increment and dereference, since they have to navigate the array of pointers depicted in the following diagram. This is a significant enough disadvantage that it makes sense to stick with `vector`, unless you happen to need quick insertion and deletion at both ends of the container.

A particular set of skills: std::list<T>

The container `std::list<T>` represents a linked list in memory. Schematically, it looks like this:

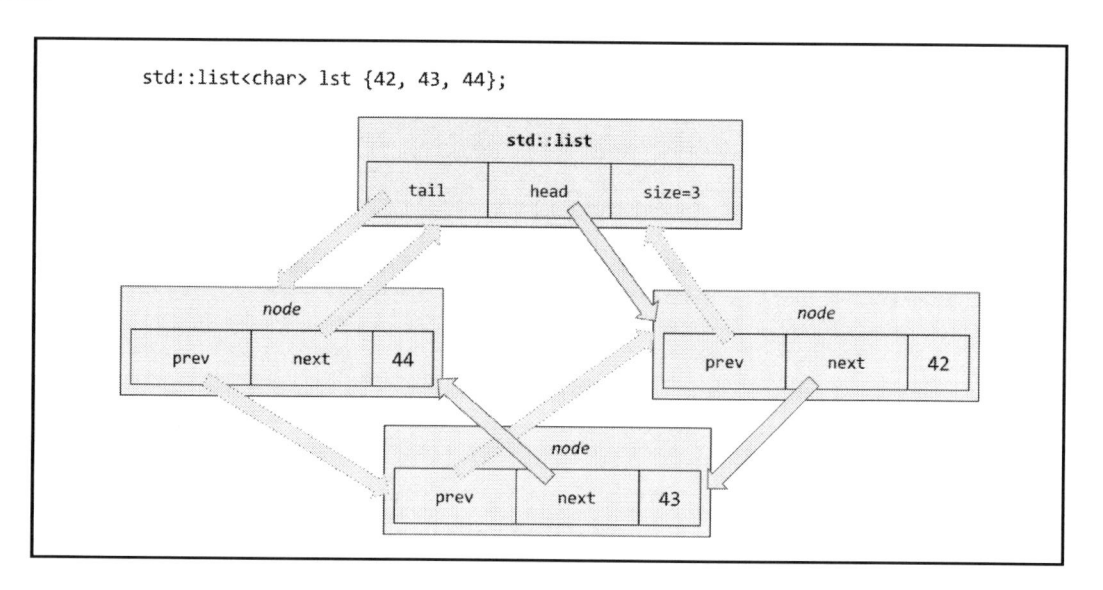

Notice that each node in the list contains pointers to its "next" and "previous" nodes, so this is a doubly linked list. The benefit of a doubly linked list is that its iterators can move both forwards and backwards through the list--that is, `std::list<T>::iterator` is a *bidirectional iterator* (but it is not *random-access*; getting to the *n*th element of the list still requires O(*n*) time).

`std::list` supports many of the same operations as `std::vector`, except for those operations that require random access (such as `operator[]`). It can afford to add member functions for pushing and popping from the front of the list, since pushing and popping from a `list` doesn't require expensive move operations.

In general, `std::list` is much less performant than a contiguous data structure such as `std::vector` or `std::deque`, because following pointers to "randomly" allocated addresses is much harder on the cache than following pointers into a contiguous block of memory. Therefore, you should treat `std::list` as a generally *undesirable* container; you should only pull it out of your toolbox when you absolutely need one of the things it does *better* than `vector`.

What are the special skills of std::list?

First, there's no *iterator invalidation* for lists! `lst.push_back(v)` and `lst.push_front(v)` always operate in constant time, and don't ever need to "resize" or "move" any data.

Second, many mutating operations that would be expensive on `vector` or require out-of-line storage ("scratch space") become cheap for linked lists. Here are some examples:

`lst.splice(it, otherlst)` "splices" the entirety of `otherlst` into `lst`, as if by repeated calls to `lst.insert(it++, other_elt);` except that the "inserted" nodes are actually stolen from the right-hand `otherlst`. The entire splicing operation can be done with just a couple of pointer swaps. After this operation, `otherlst.size() == 0`.

`lst.merge(otherlst)` similarly empties out `otherlst` into `lst` using only pointer swaps, but has the effect of "merging sorted lists." For example:

```
std::list<int> a = {3, 6};
std::list<int> b = {1, 2, 3, 5, 6};

a.merge(b);
assert(b.empty());
assert((a == std::list{1, 2, 3, 3, 5, 6, 6}));
```

As always with STL operations that involve comparison, there is a version taking a comparator: `lst.merge(otherlst, less)`.

The Container Zoo

Another operation that can be done only with pointer swaps is reversing the list in place: `lst.reverse()` switches all the "next" and "previous" links so that the head of the list is now the tail, and vice versa.

Notice that all of these operations *mutate the list in place,* and generally return `void`.

Another kind of operation that is cheap on linked lists (but not on contiguous containers) is removal of elements. Recall from Chapter 3, *The Iterator-Pair Algorithms,* that the STL provides algorithms such as `std::remove_if` and `std::unique` for use with contiguous containers; these algorithms shuffle the "removed" elements to the end of the container so that they can be picked off in a single `erase()`. With `std::list`, shuffling elements is more expensive than simply erasing them in-place. So, `std::list` provides the following member functions, with names that are unfortunately similar to the non-erasing STL algorithms:

- `lst.remove(v)` removes *and erases* all elements equal to v.
- `lst.remove_if(p)` removes *and erases* all elements e which satisfy the unary predicate p(e).
- `lst.unique()` removes *and erases* all but the first element of each "run" of consecutive equal elements. As always with STL operations that involve comparison, there is a version taking a comparator: `lst.unique(eq)` removes and erases e2 whenever p(e1, e2).
- `lst.sort()` sorts the list in-place. This is particularly helpful because the permutative algorithm `std::sort(ctr.begin(), ctr.end())` does not work on the non-random-access `std::list::iterator`.

It's strange that `lst.sort()` can only sort the entire container, instead of taking a sub-range the way `std::sort` does. But if you want to sort just a sub-range of `lst`, you can do it with--say it with me--just a couple of pointer swaps!

```
std::list<int> lst = {3, 1, 4, 1, 5, 9, 2, 6, 5};
auto begin = std::next(lst.begin(), 2);
auto end = std::next(lst.end(), -2);

// Sort just the range [begin, end)
std::list<int> sub;
sub.splice(sub.begin(), lst, begin, end);
sub.sort();
lst.splice(end, sub);
assert(sub.empty());

assert((lst == std::list{3, 1, 1, 2, 4, 5, 9, 6, 5}));
```

Roughing it with std::forward_list<T>

The standard container `std::forward_list<T>` is a linked list like `std::list`, but with fewer amenities--no way to get its size, no way to iterate backward. In memory it looks similar to `std::list<T>`, but with smaller nodes:

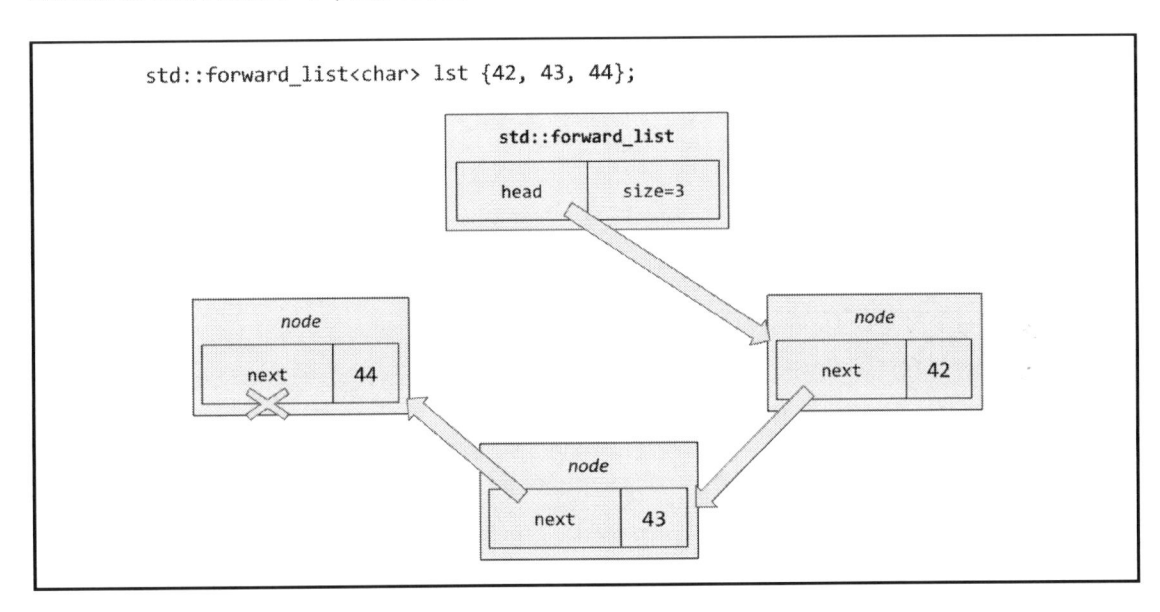

```
std::forward_list<char> lst {42, 43, 44};
```

[Diagram: std::forward_list with head and size=3, pointing to node (next, 42) → node (next, 43) → node (next, 44)]

Nevertheless, `std::forward_list` retains almost all of the "special skills" of `std::list`. The only operations that it can't do are `splice` (because that involves inserting "before" the given iterator) and `push_back` (because that involves finding the end of the list in constant time).

`forward_list` replaces these missing member functions with `_after` versions:

- `flst.erase_after(it)` to erase the element *after* the given position
- `flst.insert_after(it, v)` to insert a new element *after* the given position
- `flst.splice_after(it, otherflst)` to insert the elements of `otherflst` *after* the given position

As with `std::list`, you should avoid using `forward_list` at all unless you are in need of its particular set of skills.

Abstracting with std::stack<T> and std::queue<T>

We've now seen three different standard containers with the member functions `push_back()` and `pop_back()` (and, although we didn't mention it, `back()` to retrieve a reference to the last element of the container). These are the operations we'd need if we wanted to implement a stack data structure.

The standard library provides a convenient way to abstract the idea of a stack, with the container known as (what else?) `std::stack`. Unlike the containers we've seen so far, though, `std::stack` takes an extra template parameter.

`std::stack<T, Ctr>` represents a stack of elements of type `T`, where the underlying storage is managed by an instance of the container type `Ctr`. For example, `stack<T, vector<T>>` uses a vector to manage its elements; `stack<T, list<T>>` uses a list; and so on. The default value for the template parameter `Ctr` is actually `std::deque<T>`; you may recall that `deque` takes up more memory than `vector` but has the benefit of never needing to reallocate its underlying array or move elements post-insertion.

To interact with a `std::stack<T, Ctr>`, you must restrict yourself to only the operations push (corresponding to `push_back` on the underlying container), pop (corresponding to `pop_back`), top (corresponding to `back`), and a few other accessors such as `size` and `empty`:

```
std::stack<int> stk;
stk.push(3); stk.push(1); stk.push(4);
assert(stk.top() == 4);
stk.pop();
assert(stk.top() == 1);
stk.pop();
assert(stk.top() == 3);
```

One bizarre feature of `std::stack` is that it supports the comparison operators ==, !=, <, <=, >, and >=; and that these operators work by comparing the underlying containers (using whatever semantics the underlying container type has defined). Since the underlying container type generally compares via lexicographical order, the result is that comparing two stacks compares them "lexicographically bottom up."

```
std::stack<int> a, b;
a.push(3); a.push(1); a.push(4);
b.push(2); b.push(7);
assert(a != b);
```

```
assert(a.top() < b.top()); // that is, 4 < 7
assert(a > b); // because 3 > 2
```

This is fine if you're using only `==` and `!=`, or if you're relying on `operator<` to produce a consistent ordering for `std::set` or `std::map`; but it's certainly surprising the first time you see it!

The standard library also provides an abstraction for "queue." `std::queue<T, Ctr>` exposes the methods `push_back` and `pop_front` (corresponding to `push_back` and `pop_front` on the underlying container), as well as a few other accessors such as `front`, `back`, `size`, and `empty`.

Knowing that the container must support these primitive operations as efficiently as possible, you should be able to guess the *default* value of `Ctr`. Yes, it's `std::deque<T>`, the low-overhead double-ended queue.

Notice that, if you were implementing a queue from scratch using `std::deque<T>`, you could choose whether to push on the front of the deque and pop from the back, or to push on the back of the deque and pop from the front. The standard `std::queue<T, std::deque<T>>` chooses specifically to push on the back and pop from the front, which is easy to remember if you think about a "queue" in the real world. When you're queueing up at a ticket counter or a lunch line, you join the queue at the back and are served when you get to the front--never vice versa! It is a useful art to choose technical terms (such as `queue`, `front`, and `back`) whose technical meanings are an accurate mirror of their real-world counterparts.

The useful adaptor: std::priority_queue<T>

In `Chapter 3`, *The Iterator-Pair Algorithms*, we introduced the family of "heap" algorithms: `make_heap`, `push_heap`, and `pop_heap`. You can use these algorithms to give a range of elements the max-heap property. If you maintain the max-heap property on your data as an invariant, you get a data structure commonly known as a *priority queue*. In data-structure textbooks, a priority queue is often depicted as a kind of *binary tree*, but as we saw in `Chapter 3`, *The Iterator-Pair Algorithms*, there's nothing about the max-heap property that requires an explicitly pointer-based tree structure.

The standard container `std::priority_queue<T, Ctr, Cmp>` represents a priority queue, represented internally as an instance of `Ctr` where the elements of the `Ctr` are invariably in max-heap order (as determined by an instance of the comparator type `Cmp`).

The Container Zoo

The default value of `Ctr` in this case is `std::vector<T>`. Remember that `vector` is the most efficient container; the only reason `std::stack` and `std::queue` chose `deque` as their default is that they didn't want to move elements after they'd been inserted. But with a priority queue, the elements are moving all the time, moving up and down in the max-heap as other elements are inserted or erased. So there's no particular benefit to using `deque` as the underlying container; therefore, the standard library followed the same rule I've been repeating like a drumbeat--use `std::vector` unless you have a specific reason to need something else!

The default value of `Cmp` is the standard library type `std::less<T>`, which represents `operator<`. In other words, the `std::priority_queue` container uses the same comparator by default as the `std::push_heap` and `std::pop_heap` algorithms from Chapter 3, *The Iterator-Pair Algorithms*.

The member functions exposed by `std::priority_queue<T, Ctr>` are `push`, `pop`, and `top`. Conceptually, the item at the front of the underlying container is at the "top" of the heap. One thing to remember is that in a max-heap, the item at the "top" of the heap is the *greatest* item--think of the items as playing King of the Hill, so that the biggest one wins and ends up on the top of the heap.

- `pq.push(v)` inserts a new item into the priority queue, as if by `std::push_heap()` on the underlying container
- `pq.top()` returns a reference to the element currently on top of the priority queue, as if by calling `ctr.front()` on the underlying container
- `pq.pop()` pops off the maximum element and updates the heap, as if by `std::pop_heap()` on the underlying container

To get a *min-heap* instead of a max-heap, simply reverse the sense of the comparator you provide to the `priority_queue` template:

```
std::priority_queue<int> pq1;
std::priority_queue<int, std::vector<int>, std::greater<>> pq2;

for (int v : {3, 1, 4, 1, 5, 9}) {
  pq1.push(v);
  pq2.push(v);
}

assert(pq1.top() == 9); // max-heap by default
assert(pq2.top() == 1); // min-heap by choice
```

The trees: std::set<T> and std::map<K, V>

The class template `std::set<T>` provides the interface of a "unique set" for any `T` that implements `operator<`. As always with STL operations that involve comparison, there is a version taking a comparator: `std::set<T, Cmp>` provides "unique set" functionality using `Cmp(a,b)` instead of `(a < b)` to sort the data elements.

A `std::set` is conceptually a binary search tree, analogous to Java's `TreeSet`. In all popular implementations it's specifically a *red-black tree*, which is a particular kind of self-balancing binary search tree: even if you are constantly inserting and removing items from the tree, it will never get *too* unbalanced, which means that `insert` and `find` will always run in O(log *n*) time on average. Notice the number of pointers involved in its memory layout:

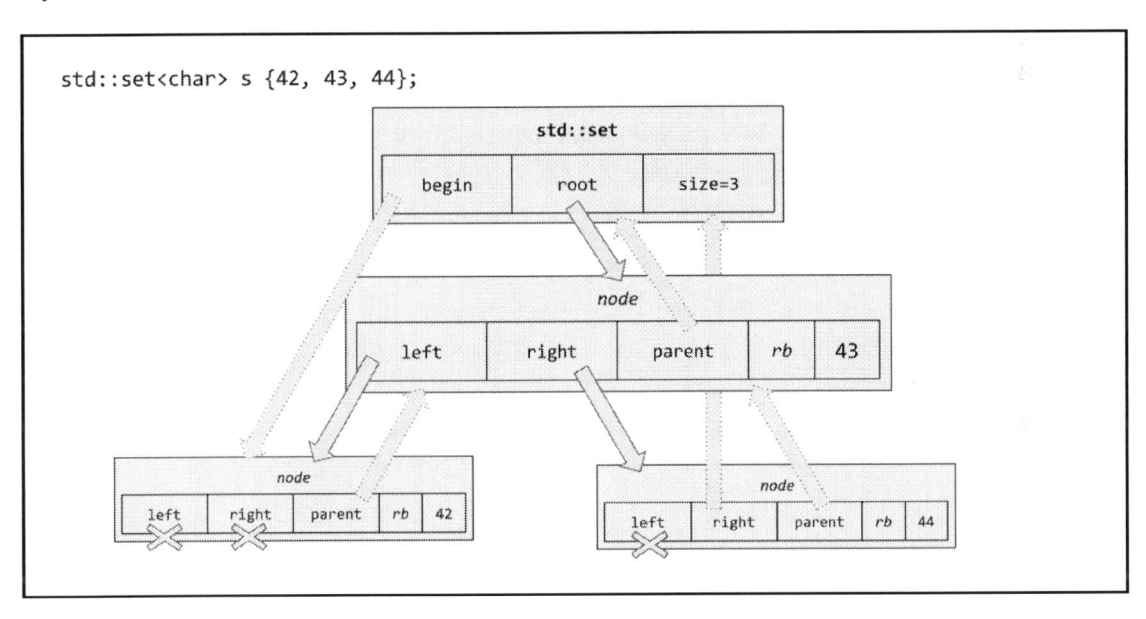

Since, by definition, a binary search tree's elements are stored in their sort order (least to greatest), it would not be meaningful for `std::set` to provide member functions `push_front` or `push_back`. Instead, to add an element v to the set, you use `s.insert(v);` and to delete an element, you use `s.erase(v)` or `s.erase(it)`:

```
std::set<int> s;
for (int i : {3, 1, 4, 1, 5}) {
  s.insert(i);
}
```

```
// A set's items are stored sorted and deduplicated.
assert((s == std::set{1, 3, 4, 5}));

auto it = s.begin();
assert(*it == 1);
s.erase(4);
s.erase(it);  // erase *it, which is 1

assert((s == std::set{3, 5}));
```

The return value of s.insert(v) is interesting. When we insert into a vector, there are only two possible outcomes: either the value is successfully added to the vector (and we get back an iterator to the newly inserted element), or else the insertion fails and an exception is thrown. When we insert into a set, there is a third possible outcome: maybe the insertion doesn't happen because there is already a copy of v in the set! That's not a "failure" worthy of exceptional control flow, but it's still something that the caller might want to know about. So s.insert(v) always returns a pair of return values: ret.first is the usual iterator to the copy of v now in the data structure (no matter whether it was just now inserted), and ret.second is true if the pointed-to v was just inserted and false if the pointed-to v was already in the set to begin with:

```
std::set<int> s;
auto [it1, b1] = s.insert(1);
assert(*it1 == 1 && b1 == true);

auto [it2, b2] = s.insert(2);
assert(*it2 == 2 && b2 == true);

auto [it3, b3] = s.insert(1);  // again
assert(*it3 == 1 && b3 == false);
```

> The square-bracketed variable definitions in the preceding snippet are using C++17 *structured bindings*.

As the example just prior to this one shows, the elements of a set are stored in order--not just conceptually but visibly, in that *s.begin() is going to be the least element in the set and *std::prev(s.end()) is going to be the greatest element. Iterating over the set using a standard algorithm or a ranged for loop will give you the set's elements in ascending order (remember, what "ascending" means is dictated by your choice of comparator--the Cmp parameter to the class template set).

The tree-based structure of a `set` implies that some standard algorithms such as `std::find` and `std::lower_bound` (Chapter 3, *The Iterator-Pair Algorithms*) will still work, but only inefficiently--the algorithm's iterators will spend a lot of time climbing up and down in the foothills of the tree, whereas if we had access to the tree structure itself, we could descend directly from the root of the tree and find a given element's position very quickly. Therefore, `std::set` provides member functions that can be used as replacements for the inefficient algorithms:

- For `std::find(s.begin(), s.end(), v)`, use `s.find(v)`
- For `std::lower_bound(s.begin(), s.end(), v)`, use `s.lower_bound(v)`
- For `std::upper_bound(s.begin(), s.end(), v)`, use `s.upper_bound(v)`
- For `std::count(s.begin(), s.end(), v)`, use `s.count(v)`
- For `std::equal_range(s.begin(), s.end(), v)`, use `s.equal_range(v)`

Notice that `s.count(v)` will only ever return 0 or 1, because the set's elements are deduplicated. This makes `s.count(v)` a handy synonym for the set-membership operation--what Python would call `v in s` or what Java would call `s.contains(v)`.

`std::map<K, V>` is just like `std::set<K>`, except that each key `K` is allowed to have a value `V` associated with it; this makes a data structure analogous to Java's `TreeMap` or Python's `dict`. As always, there's `std::map<K, V, Cmp>` if you need a sorting order on your keys that's different from the natural `K::operator<`. Although you won't often think of `std::map` as "just a thin wrapper around a `std::set` of pairs," that's exactly how it looks in memory:

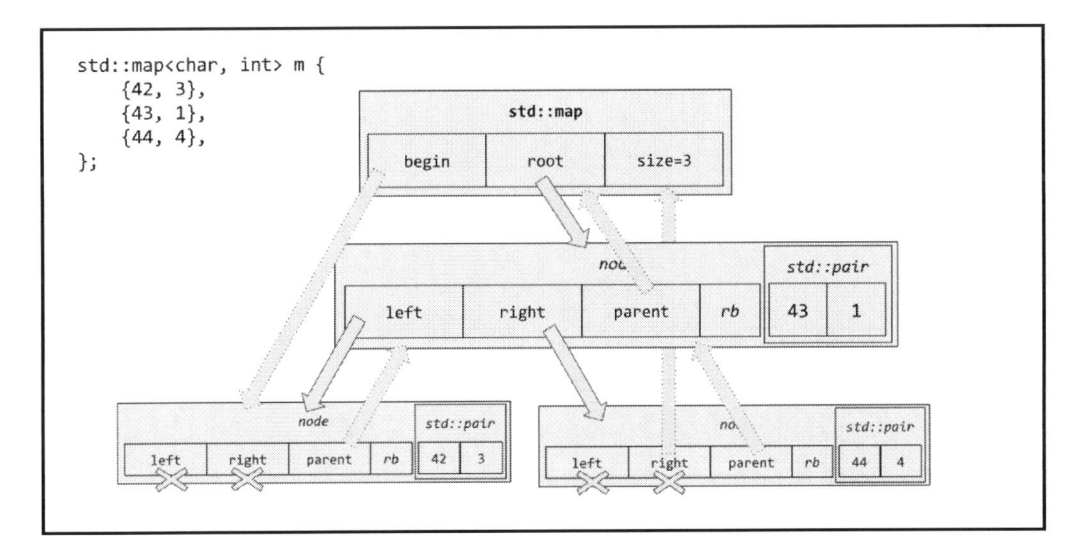

```
std::map<char, int> m {
    {42, 3},
    {43, 1},
    {44, 4},
};
```

[Diagram showing std::map structure with begin, root, size=3 pointing to tree nodes containing std::pair values {42,3}, {43,1}, {44,4} with left, right, parent, rb fields] `std::map` supports indexing with `operator[]`, but with a surprising twist. When you index into a size-zero vector with `vec[42]`, you get undefined behavior. When you index into a size-zero *map* with `m[42]`, the map helpfully inserts the key-value pair `{42, {}}` into itself and returns a reference to the second element of that pair!

This quirky behavior is actually helpful for writing code that's easy on the eyes:

```
std::map<std::string, std::string> m;
m["hello"] = "world";
m["quick"] = "brown";
m["hello"] = "dolly";
assert(m.size() == 2);
```

But it can lead to confusion if you don't pay attention:

```
assert(m["literally"] == "");
assert(m.size() == 3);
```

You'll notice that there is no `operator[] const` for maps, because `operator[]` always reserves the potential to insert a new key-value pair into `*this`. If you have a const map--or just a map that you really don't want to insert into right now--then the appropriate way to query it non-mutatively is with `m.find(k)`. Another reason to avoid `operator[]` is if your map's value type V is not default-constructible, in which case `operator[]` simply won't compile. In that case (real talk: in *any* case) you should use `m.insert(kv)` or `m.emplace(k, v)` to insert the new key-value pair exactly as you want it, instead of default-constructing a value just to assign over it again. Here's an example:

```
// Confusingly, "value_type" refers to a whole key-value pair.
// The types K and V are called "key_type" and "mapped_type",
// respectively.
using Pair = decltype(m)::value_type;

if (m.find("hello") == m.end()) {
  m.insert(Pair{"hello", "dolly"});

  // ...or equivalently...
  m.emplace("hello", "dolly");
}
```

Received wisdom in the post–C++11 world is that `std::map` and `std::set`, being based on trees of pointers, are so cache-unfriendly that you should avoid them by default and prefer to use `std::unordered_map` and `std::unordered_set` instead.

A note about transparent comparators

In the last code example, I wrote `m.find("hello")`. Notice that `"hello"` is a value of type `const char[6]`, whereas `decltype(m)::key_type` is `std::string`, and (since we didn't specify anything special) `decltype(m)::key_compare` is `std::less<std::string>`. This means that when we call `m.find("hello")`, we're calling a function whose first parameter is of type `std::string`--and so we're implicitly constructing `std::string("hello")` to pass as the argument to `find`. In general, the argument to `m.find` is going to get implicitly converted to `decltype(m)::key_type`, which may be an expensive conversion.

If our `operator<` behaves properly, we can avoid this overhead by changing the comparator of `m` to some class with a *heterogeneous* `operator()` which also defines the member typedef `is_transparent`, like this:

```
struct MagicLess {
  using is_transparent = std::true_type;

  template<class T, class U>
  bool operator()(T&& t, U&& u) const {
    return std::forward<T>(t) < std::forward<U>(u);
  }
};

void test()
{
  std::map<std::string, std::string, MagicLess> m;

  // The STL provides std::less<> as a synonym for MagicLess.
  std::map<std::string, std::string, std::less<>> m2;

  // Now 'find' no longer constructs a std::string!
  auto it = m2.find("hello");
}
```

The "magic" here is all happening inside the library's implementation of `std::map`; the `find` member function specifically checks for the member `is_transparent` and changes its behavior accordingly. The member functions `count`, `lower_bound`, `upper_bound`, and `equal_range` all change their behavior as well. But oddly, the member function `erase` does not! This is probably because it would be too difficult for overload resolution to distinguish an intended `m.erase(v)` from an intended `m.erase(it)`. Anyway, if you want heterogeneous comparison during deletion as well, you can get it in two steps:

```
auto [begin, end] = m.equal_range("hello");
m.erase(begin, end);
```

The Container Zoo

Oddballs: std::multiset<T> and std::multimap<K, V>

In STL-speak, a "set" is an ordered, deduplicated collection of elements. So naturally, a "multiset" is an ordered, non-deduplicated collection of elements! Its memory layout is exactly the same as the layout of `std::set`; only its invariants are different. Notice in the following diagram that `std::multiset` allows two elements with value 42:

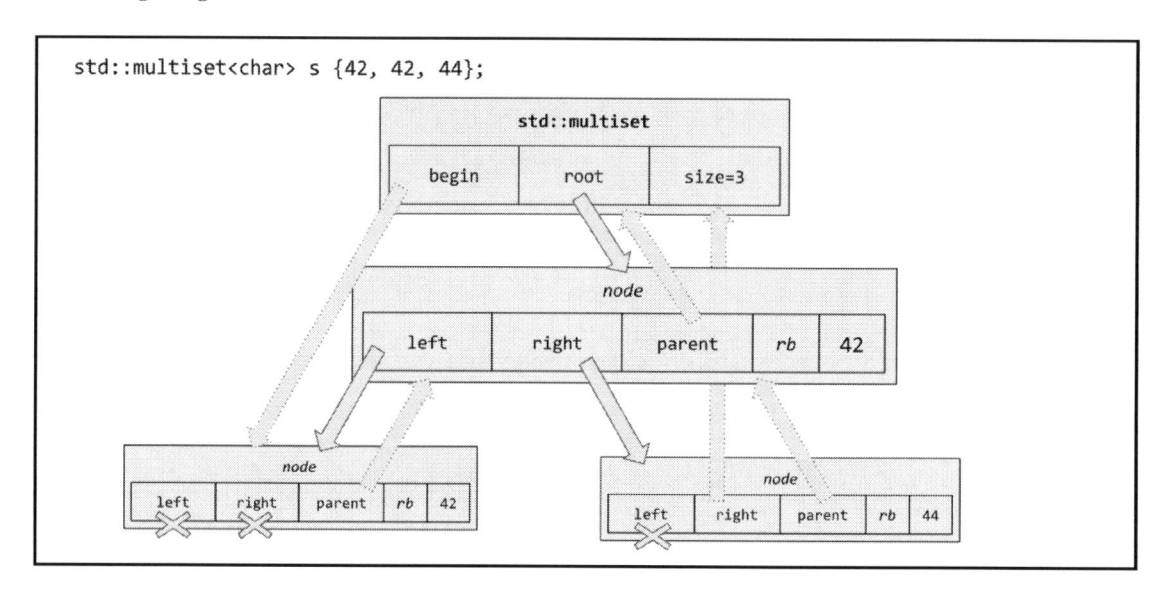

```
std::multiset<char> s {42, 42, 44};
```

`std::multiset<T, Cmp>` behaves just like `std::set<T, Cmp>`, except that it can store duplicate elements. The same goes for `std::multimap<K, V, Cmp>`:

```
std::multimap<std::string, std::string> mm;
mm.emplace("hello", "world");
mm.emplace("quick", "brown");
mm.emplace("hello", "dolly");
assert(mm.size() == 3);

// Key-value pairs are stored in sorted order.
// Pairs with identical keys are guaranteed to be
// stored in the order in which they were inserted.
auto it = mm.begin();
using Pair = decltype(mm)::value_type;
assert(*(it++) == Pair("hello", "world"));
assert(*(it++) == Pair("hello", "dolly"));
assert(*(it++) == Pair("quick", "brown"));
```

In a multiset or multimap, `mm.find(v)` returns an iterator to *some* element (or key-value pair) matching v--not necessarily the first one in iteration order. `mm.erase(v)` erases all the elements (or key-value pairs) with keys equal to v. And `mm[v]` doesn't exist. For example:

```
std::multimap<std::string, std::string> mm = {
  {"hello", "world"},
  {"quick", "brown"},
  {"hello", "dolly"},
};
assert(mm.count("hello") == 2);
mm.erase("hello");
assert(mm.count("hello") == 0);
```

Moving elements without moving them

Recall that, with `std::list`, we were able to splice lists together, move elements from one list to another, and so on, by using the "particular set of skills" of `std::list`. As of C++17, the tree-based containers have acquired similar skills!

The syntax for merging two sets or maps (or multisets or multimaps) is deceptively similar to the syntax for merging sorted `std::list`:

```
std::map<std::string, std::string> m = {
  {"hello", "world"},
  {"quick", "brown"},
};
std::map<std::string, std::string> otherm = {
  {"hello", "dolly"},
  {"sad", "clown"},
};

// This should look familiar!
m.merge(otherm);

assert((otherm == decltype(m){
  {"hello", "dolly"},
}));

assert((m == decltype(m){
  {"hello", "world"},
  {"quick", "brown"},
  {"sad", "clown"},
}));
```

The Container Zoo

However, notice what happens when there are duplicates! The duplicated elements are *not* transferred; they're left behind in the right-hand-side map! This is the exact opposite of what you'd expect if you're coming from a language such as Python, where `d.update(otherd)` inserts all the mappings from the right-hand dict into the left-hand dict, overwriting anything that was there already.

The C++ equivalent of `d.update(otherd)` is `m.insert(otherm.begin(), otherm.end()`. The only case in which it makes sense to use `m.merge(otherm)` is if you know that you don't want to overwrite duplicates, *and* you're okay with trashing the old value of `otherm` (for example, if it's a temporary that's going out of scope soon).

Another way to transfer elements between tree-based containers is to use the member functions `extract` and `insert` to transfer individual elements:

```cpp
std::map<std::string, std::string> m = {
  {"hello", "world"},
  {"quick", "brown"},
};
std::map<std::string, std::string> otherm = {
  {"hello", "dolly"},
  {"sad", "clown"},
};

using Pair = decltype(m)::value_type;

// Insertion may succeed...
auto nh1 = otherm.extract("sad");
assert(nh1.key() == "sad" && nh1.mapped() == "clown");
auto [it2, inserted2, nh2] = m.insert(std::move(nh1));
assert(*it2 == Pair("sad", "clown") && inserted2 == true &&
  nh2.empty());

// ...or be blocked by an existing element.
auto nh3 = otherm.extract("hello");
assert(nh3.key() == "hello" && nh3.mapped() == "dolly");
auto [it4, inserted4, nh4] = m.insert(std::move(nh3));
assert(*it4 == Pair("hello", "world") && inserted4 == false &&
  !nh4.empty());

// Overwriting an existing element is a pain.
m.insert_or_assign(nh4.key(), nh4.mapped());

// It is often easiest just to delete the element that's
// blocking our desired insertion.
m.erase(it4);
m.insert(std::move(nh4));
```

The type of the object returned by `extract` is something called a "node handle"--essentially a pointer into the guts of the data structure. You can use the accessor methods `nh.key()` and `nh.mapped()` to manipulate the pieces of the entry in a `std::map` (or `nh.value()` for the single piece of data in an element of a `std::set`). Thus you can extract, manipulate, and reinsert a key without ever copying or moving its actual data! In the following code sample, the "manipulation" consists of a call to `std::transform`:

```cpp
std::map<std::string, std::string> m = {
    {"hello", "world"},
    {"quick", "brown"},
};
assert(m.begin()->first == "hello");
assert(std::next(m.begin())->first == "quick");

// Upper-case the {"quick", "brown"} mapping, with
// absolutely no memory allocations anywhere.
auto nh = m.extract("quick");
std::transform(nh.key().begin(), nh.key().end(), nh.key().begin(),
    ::toupper);
m.insert(std::move(nh));

assert(m.begin()->first == "QUICK");
assert(std::next(m.begin())->first == "hello");
```

As you can see, the interface to this functionality isn't as tidy as `lst.splice(it, otherlst)`; the subtlety of the interface is one reason it took until C++17 to get this functionality into the standard library. There is one clever bit to notice, though: Suppose you `extract` a node from a set and then throw an exception before you've managed to `insert` it into the destination set. What happens to the orphaned node--does it leak? It turns out that the designers of the library thought of this possibility; if a node handle's destructor is called before the node handle has been inserted into its new home, the destructor will correctly clean up the memory associated with the node. Therefore, `extract` by itself (without `insert`) will behave just like `erase`!

The Container Zoo

The hashes: std::unordered_set<T> and std::unordered_map<K, V>

The `std::unordered_set` class template represents a chained hash table--that is, a fixed-size array of "buckets," each bucket containing a singly linked list of data elements. As new data elements are added to the container, each element is placed in the linked list associated with the "hash" of the element's value. This is almost exactly the same as Java's `HashSet`. In memory it looks like this:

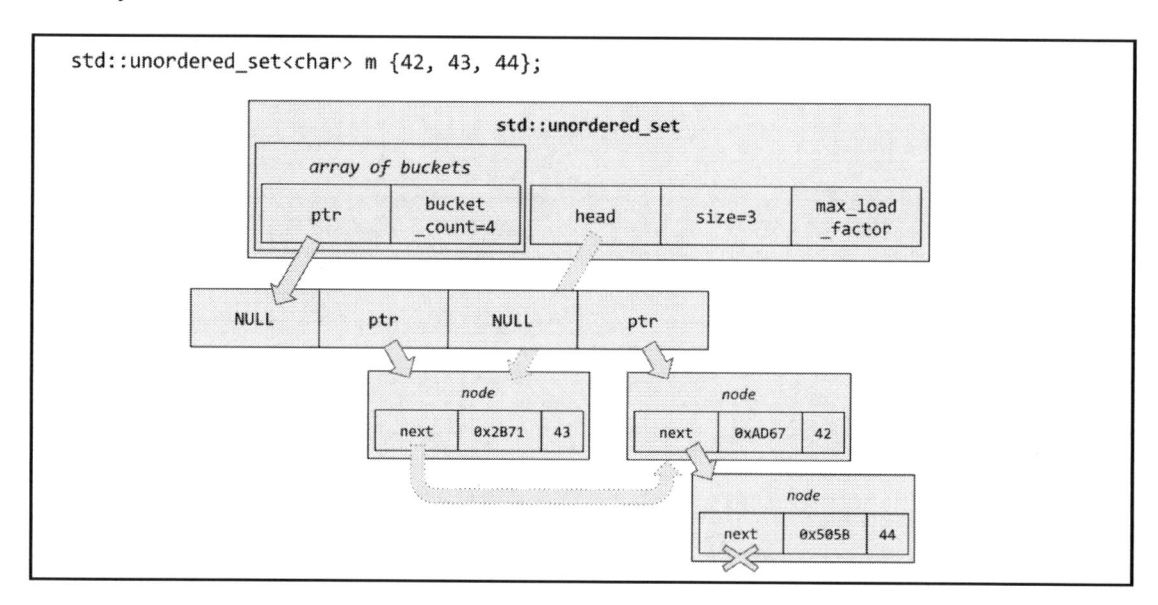

```
std::unordered_set<char> m {42, 43, 44};
```

```
                    std::unordered_set
            ┌─────────────────────────────────────────────┐
            │  array of buckets                           │
            │  ┌─────┬─────────┐                          │
            │  │ ptr │ bucket  │  head   size=3  max_load │
            │  │     │ _count=4│                  _factor │
            └──┴──┬──┴─────────┴────┬─────────────────────┘
                  │                 │
        ┌─────┬───▼─┬─────┬─────┐   │
        │NULL │ ptr │NULL │ ptr │   │
        └──┬──┴──┬──┴─────┴──┬──┘   │
           │     │           │      │
           ▼     ▼           ▼      ▼
              node              node
         ┌──────┬──────┬──┐  ┌──────┬──────┬──┐
         │ next │0x2B71│43│  │ next │0xAD67│42│
         └──────┴──────┴──┘  └──────┴──────┴──┘
                                      node
                                ┌──────┬──────┬──┐
                                │ next │0x505B│44│
                                └──────┴──────┴──┘
```

The literature on hash tables is extensive, and `std::unordered_set` does not represent even remotely the state of the art; but because it eliminates a certain amount of pointer-chasing, it tends to perform better than the tree-based `std::set`.

> **TIP:** To eliminate the rest of the pointers, you'd have to replace the linked lists with a technique called "open addressing," which is far out of scope for this book; but it's worth looking up if `std::unordered_set` proves too slow for your use-case.

[108]

`std::unordered_set` was designed to be a drop-in replacement for `std::set`, so it provides the same interface that we've already seen: `insert` and `erase`, plus iteration with `begin` and `end`. However, unlike `std::set`, the elements of a `std::unordered_set` are not stored in sorted order (it's *unordered*, you see?) and it provides only forward iterators, as opposed to the bidirectional iterators provided by `std::set`. (Check the preceding illustration--there are "next" pointers but no "previous" pointers, so iterating backwards in a `std::unordered_set` is impossible.)

`std::unordered_map<K, V>` is to `std::unordered_set<T>` as `std::map<K, V>` is to `std::set<T>`. That is, it looks exactly the same in memory, except that it stores key-value pairs instead of just keys:

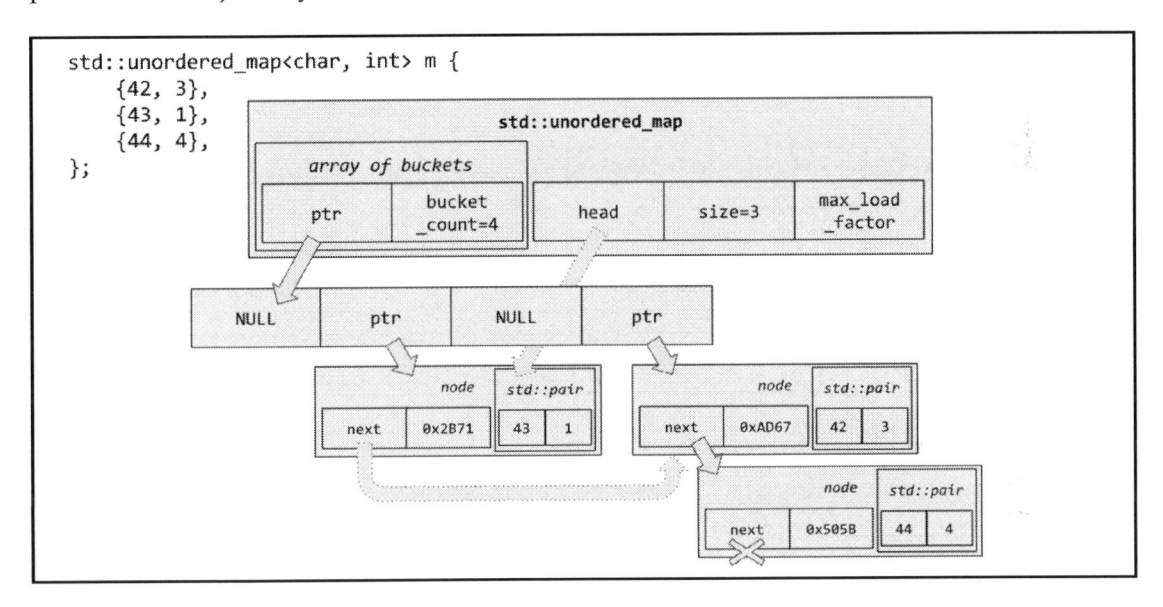

```
std::unordered_map<char, int> m {
    {42, 3},
    {43, 1},
    {44, 4},
};
```

                            std::unordered_map
          array of buckets
                    bucket   max_load
          ptr   _count=4   head   size=3   _factor

    NULL   ptr   NULL   ptr

              node   std::pair   node   std::pair
              next   0x2B71 43 1   next   0xAD67 42 3

                                                    node   std::pair
                                                    next   0x505B 44 4

Like `set` and `map`, which take an optional comparator parameter, `unordered_set` and `unordered_map` take some optional parameters as well. The two optional parameters are `Hash` (which defaults to `std::hash<K>`) and `KeyEqual` (which defaults to `std::equal_to<K>`, which is to say, `operator==`). Passing in a different hash function or a different key-comparison function causes the hash table to use those functions instead of the defaults. This might be useful if you're interfacing with some old-school C++ class type that doesn't implement value semantics or `operator==`:

```
class Widget {
public:
    virtual bool IsEqualTo(Widget const *b) const;
    virtual int GetHashValue() const;
```

```
};

struct myhash {
  size_t operator()(const Widget *w) const {
    return w->GetHashValue();
  }
};

struct myequal {
  bool operator()(const Widget *a, const Widget *b) const {
    return a->IsEqualTo(b);
  }
};

std::unordered_set<Widget *, myhash, myequal> s;
```

Load factor and bucket lists

Like Java's `HashSet`, `std::unordered_set` exposes all kinds of administrative details about its buckets. You probably will never need to interact with these administrative functions!

- `s.bucket_count()` returns the current number of buckets in the array.
- `s.bucket(v)` returns the index *i* of the bucket in which you'd find the element v, if it existed in this `unordered_set`.
- `s.bucket_size(i)` returns the number of elements in the *i*th bucket. Observe that invariably `s.count(v) <= s.bucket_size(s.bucket(v))`.
- `s.load_factor()` returns `s.size() / s.bucket_count()` as a `float` value.
- `s.rehash(n)` increases (or decreases) the size of the bucket array to exactly n.

You might have noticed that `load_factor` seems out of place so far; what's so important about `s.size() / s.bucket_count()` that it gets its own member function? Well, this is the mechanism by which `unordered_set` scales itself as its number of elements grows. Each `unordered_set` object s has a value `s.max_load_factor()` indicating exactly how large `s.load_factor()` is allowed to get. If an insertion would push `s.load_factor()` over the top, then s will reallocate its array of buckets and rehash its elements in order to keep `s.load_factor()` smaller than `s.max_load_factor()`.

`s.max_load_factor()` is `1.0` by default. You can set it to a different value `k` by using the one-parameter overload: `s.max_load_factor(k)`. However, that's basically never necessary or a good idea.

One administrative operation that *does* make sense is `s.reserve(k)`. Like `vec.reserve(k)` for vectors, this `reserve` member function means "I'm planning to do insertions that bring the size of this container up into the vicinity of `k`. Please pre-allocate enough space for those `k` elements right now." In the case of `vector`, that meant allocating an array of `k` elements. In the case of `unordered_set`, it means allocating a bucket array of `k / max_load_factor()` pointers, so that even if `k` elements are inserted (with the expected number of collisions), the load factor will still only be `max_load_factor()`.

Where does the memory come from?

Throughout this whole chapter, I've actually been lying to you! Each of the containers described in this chapter--except for `std::array`--takes one *more* optional template type parameter. This parameter is called the *allocator*, and it indicates where the memory comes from for operations such as "reallocating the underlying array" or "allocating a new node on the linked list." `std::array` doesn't need an allocator because it holds all of its memory inside itself; but every other container type needs to know where to get its allocations from.

The default value for this template parameter is the standard library type `std::allocator<T>`, which is certainly good enough for most users. We'll talk more about allocators in Chapter 8, *Allocators*.

Summary

In this chapter we've learned the following: A *container* manages the *ownership* of a collection of elements. STL containers are always class templates parameterized on the element type, and sometimes on other relevant parameters as well. Every container except `std::array<T, N>` can be parameterized by an *allocator* type to specify the manner in which it allocates and deallocates memory. Containers that use comparison can be parameterized by a *comparator* type. Consider using transparent comparator types such as `std::less<>` instead of homogeneous comparators.

When using `std::vector`, watch out for reallocation and address invalidation. When using most container types, watch out for iterator invalidation.

The standard library's philosophy is to support no operation that is naturally inefficient (such as `vector::push_front`); and to support any operation that is naturally efficient (such as `list::splice`). If you can think of an efficient implementation for a particular operation, odds are that the STL has already implemented it under some name; you just have to figure out how it's spelled.

When in doubt, use `std::vector`. Use other container types only when you need their particular set of skills. Specifically, avoid the pointer-based containers (`set`, `map`, `list`) unless you need their special skills (maintaining sorted order; extracting, merging, and splicing).

Online references such as `cppreference.com` are your best resource for figuring these things out.

5
Vocabulary Types

It has been increasingly recognized over the past decade that one of the important roles of a standard language or standard library is to provide *vocabulary types*. A "vocabulary" type is a type that purports to provide a single *lingua franca*, a common language, for dealing with its domain.

Notice that even before C++ existed, the C programming language had already made a decent shot at the vocabulary of some areas, providing standard types or type aliases for integer math (`int`), floating-point math (`double`), timepoints expressed in the Unix epoch (`time_t`), and byte counts (`size_t`).

In this chapter we'll learn:

- The history of vocabulary types in C++, from `std::string` to `std::any`
- The definitions of *algebraic data type*, *product type*, and *sum type*
- How to manipulate tuples and visit variants
- The role of `std::optional<T>` as "maybe a `T`" or "not yet a `T`"
- `std::any` as the algebraic-data-type equivalent of "infinity"
- How to implement type erasure, how it's used in `std::any` and `std::function`, and its intrinsic limitations
- Some pitfalls with `std::function`, and third-party libraries that fix them

Vocabulary Types

The story of std::string

Consider the domain of character strings; for example, the phrase `hello world`. In C, the *lingua franca* for dealing with strings was `char *`:

```
char *greet(const char *name) {
  char buffer[100];
  snprintf(buffer, 100, "hello %s", name);
  return strdup(buffer);
}

void test() {
  const char *who = "world";
  char *hw = greet(who);
  assert(strcmp(hw, "hello world") == 0);
  free(hw);
}
```

This was all right for a while, but dealing with raw `char *`s had some problems for the users of the language and the creators of third-party libraries and routines. For one thing, the C language was so old that `const` had not been invented at the outset, which meant that certain old routines would expect their strings as `char *` and certain newer ones expect `const char *`. For another thing, `char *` didn't carry a *length* with it; so some functions expected both a pointer and a length, and some functions expected only the pointer and simply couldn't deal with embedded bytes of value `'\0'`.

The most vital piece missing from the `char *` puzzle was *lifetime management* and *ownership* (as discussed at the start of `Chapter 4`, *The Container Zoo*). When a C function wants to receive a string from its caller, it takes `char *` and generally leaves it up to the caller to manage the ownership of the characters involved. But what if it wants to *return* a string? Then it has to return `char *` and hope that the caller remembers to free it (`strdup`, `asprintf`), or take in a buffer from the caller and hope it's big enough for the output (`sprintf`, `snprintf`, `strcat`). The difficulty of managing the ownership of strings in C (and in pre-standard C++) was so great that there was a proliferation of "string libraries" to deal with the problem: Qt's `QString`, glib's `GString`, and so on.

Into this chaos stepped C++ in 1998 with a miracle: a *standard* string class! The new `std::string` encapsulated the bytes of a string *and* its length, in a natural way; it could deal correctly with embedded null bytes; it supported formerly complicated operations such as `hello + world` by quietly allocating exactly as much memory as it needed; and because of RAII, it would never leak memory or incite confusion about who owned the underlying bytes. Best of all, it had an implicit conversion from `char *`:

```
std::string greet(const std::string& name) {
  return "hello " + name;
}

void test() {
  std::string who = "world";
  assert(greet(who) == "hello world");
}
```

Now C++ functions dealing with strings (such as `greet()` in the preceding code) could take `std::string` parameters and return `std::string` results. Even better, because the string type was *standardized*, within a few years you could be reasonably confident that when you picked up some third-party library to integrate it into your codebase, any of its functions that took strings (filenames, error messages, what-have-you) would be using `std::string`. Everybody could communicate more efficiently and effectively by sharing the *lingua franca* of `std::string`.

Tagging reference types with reference_wrapper

Another vocabulary type introduced in C++03 was `std::reference_wrapper<T>`. It has a simple implementation:

```
namespace std {
  template<typename T>
  class reference_wrapper {
    T *m_ptr;
  public:
    reference_wrapper(T& t) noexcept : m_ptr(&t) {}

    operator T& () const noexcept { return *m_ptr; }
    T& get() const noexcept { return *m_ptr; }
  };

  template<typename T>
```

Vocabulary Types

```
    reference_wrapper<T> ref(T& t);
} // namespace std
```

`std::reference_wrapper` has a slightly different purpose from vocabulary types such as `std::string` and `int`; it's meant specifically as a way to the "tag" values that we'd like to behave as references in contexts where passing native C++ references doesn't work the way we'd like:

```
int result = 0;
auto task = [](int& r) {
    r = 42;
};

// Trying to use a native reference wouldn't compile.
//std::thread t(task, result);

// Correctly pass result "by reference" to the new thread.
std::thread t(task, std::ref(result));
```

The constructor of `std::thread` is written with specific special cases to handle `reference_wrapper` parameters by "decaying" them into native references. The same special cases apply to the standard library functions `make_pair`, `make_tuple`, `bind`, `invoke`, and everything based on `invoke` (such as `std::apply`, `std::function::operator()`, and `std::async`).

C++11 and algebraic types

As C++11 took shape, there was growing recognition that another area ripe for vocabularization was that of the so-called *algebraic data types*. Algebraic types arise naturally in the functional-programming paradigm. The essential idea is to think about the domain of a type--that is, the set of all possible values of that type. To keep things simple, you might want to think about C++ `enum` types, because it's easy to talk about the number of different values that an object of `enum` type might assume at one time or another:

```
enum class Color {
    RED = 1,
    BLACK = 2,
};

enum class Size {
    SMALL = 1,
    MEDIUM = 2,
    LARGE = 3,
};
```

Given the types `Color` and `Size`, can you create a data type whose instances might assume any of 2 × 3 = 6 values? Yes; this type represents "one of each" of `Color` and `Size`, and is called a *product type*, because its set of possible values is the *Cartesian product* of its elements' sets of possible values.

How about a data type whose instances might assume any of 2 + 3 = 5 different values? Also yes; this type represents "either a `Color` or a `Size` but never both at once," and is called a *sum type*. (Confusingly, mathematicians do not use the term *Cartesian sum* for this concept.)

In a functional-programming language such as Haskell, these two exercises would be spelled like this:

```
data SixType = ColorandSizeOf Color Size;
data FiveType = ColorOf Color | SizeOf Size;
```

In C++, they're spelled like this:

```
using sixtype = std::pair<Color, Size>;
using fivetype = std::variant<Color, Size>;
```

The class template `std::pair<A, B>` represents an ordered pair of elements: one of type `A`, followed by one of type `B`. It's very similar to a plain old `struct` with two elements, except that you don't have to write the struct definition yourself:

```
template<class A, class B>
struct pair {
  A first;
  B second;
};
```

Notice that there are only cosmetic differences between `std::pair<A, A>` and `std::array<A, 2>`. We might say that `pair` is a *heterogeneous* version of `array` (except that `pair` is restricted to holding only two elements).

Working with std::tuple

C++11 introduced a full-fledged heterogeneous array; it's called `std::tuple<Ts...>`. A tuple of only two element types--for example, `tuple<int, double>`--is no different from `pair<int, double>`. But tuples can hold more than just a pair of elements; though the magic of C++11 variadic templates they can hold triples, quadruples, quintuples,... hence the generic name `tuple`. For example, `tuple<int, int, char, std::string>` is analogous to a `struct` whose members are an `int`, another `int`, a `char`, and finally a `std::string`.

Vocabulary Types

Because the first element of a tuple has a different type from the second element, we can't use the "normal" `operator[](size_t)` to access the elements by indices that might vary at runtime. Instead, we must tell the compiler *at compile time* which element of the tuple we're planning to access, so that the compiler can figure out what type to give the expression. The C++ way to provide information at compile time is to force it into the type system via template parameters, and so that's what we do. When we want to access the first element of a tuple t, we call `std::get<0>(t)`. To access the second element, we call `std::get<1>(t)`, and so on.

This becomes the pattern for dealing with `std::tuple`--where the homogeneous container types tend to have *member functions* for accessing and manipulating them, the heterogeneous algebraic types tend to have *free function templates* for accessing and manipulating them.

However, generally speaking, you won't do a lot of *manipulating* of tuples. Their primary use-case, outside of template metaprogramming, is as an economical way to temporarily bind a number of values together in a context that requires a single value. For example, you might remember `std::tie` from the example in section "The simplest container" in Chapter 4, *The Container Zoo*. It's a cheap way of binding together an arbitrary number of values into a single unit that can be compared lexicographically with `operator<`. The "sense" of the lexicographical comparison depends on the order in which you bind the values together:

```
using Author = std::pair<std::string, std::string>;
std::vector<Author> authors = {
  {"Fyodor", "Dostoevsky"},
  {"Sylvia", "Plath"},
  {"Vladimir", "Nabokov"},
  {"Douglas", "Hofstadter"},
};

// Sort by first name then last name.
std::sort(
  authors.begin(), authors.end(),
  [](auto&& a, auto&& b) {
    return std::tie(a.first, a.second) < std::tie(b.first, b.second);
  }
);
assert(authors[0] == Author("Douglas", "Hofstadter"));

// Sort by last name then first name.
std::sort(
  authors.begin(), authors.end(),
  [](auto&& a, auto&& b) {
    return std::tie(a.second, a.first) < std::tie(b.second, b.first);
```

```
        }
    );
    assert(authors[0] == Author("Fyodor", "Dostoevsky"));
```

The reason that `std::tie` is so cheap is that it actually creates a tuple of *references* to its arguments' memory locations, rather than copying its arguments' values. This leads to a second common use for `std::tie`: simulating the "multiple assignment" found in languages such as Python:

```
    std::string s;
    int i;

    // Assign both s and i at once.
    std::tie(s, i) = std::make_tuple("hello", 42);
```

> **TIP**: Notice that the phrase "at once" in the preceding comment doesn't have any bearing on concurrency (see Chapter 7, *Concurrency*) or the order in which the side effects are performed; I just mean that both values can be assigned in a single assignment statement, instead of taking two or more lines.

As the preceding example illustrates, `std::make_tuple(a, b, c...)` can be used to create a tuple of *values*; that is, `make_tuple` does construct copies of its arguments' values, rather than merely taking their addresses.

Lastly, in C++17 we are allowed to use constructor template parameter deduction to write simply `std::tuple(a, b, c...)`; but it's probably best to avoid this feature unless you know specifically that you want its behaviour. The only thing that template parameter deduction will do differently from `std::make_tuple` is that it will preserve `std::reference_wrapper` arguments rather than decaying them to native C++ references:

```
    auto [i, j, k] = std::tuple{1, 2, 3};

    // make_tuple decays reference_wrapper...
    auto t1 = std::make_tuple(i, std::ref(j), k);
    static_assert(std::is_same_v< decltype(t1),
        std::tuple<int, int&, int>
    >);

    // ...whereas the deduced constructor does not.
    auto t2 = std::tuple(i, std::ref(j), k);
    static_assert(std::is_same_v< decltype(t2),
        std::tuple<int, std::reference_wrapper<int>, int>
    >);
```

Vocabulary Types

Manipulating tuple values

Most of these functions and templates are useful only in the context of template metaprogramming; you're unlikely to use them on a daily basis:

- `std::get<I>(t)`: Retrieves a reference to the `I`th element of `t`.
- `std::tuple_size_v<decltype(t)>`: Tells the *size* of the given tuple. Because this is a compile-time constant property of the tuple's type, this is expressed as a variable template parameterized on that type. If you'd rather use more natural-looking syntax, you can write a helper function in either of the following ways:

  ```
  template<class T>
  constexpr size_t tuple_size(T&&)
  {
      return std::tuple_size_v<std::remove_reference_t<T>>;
  }

  template<class... Ts>
  constexpr size_t simpler_tuple_size(const std::tuple<Ts...>&)
  {
      return sizeof...(Ts);
  }
  ```

- `std::tuple_element_t<I, decltype(t)>`: Tells the *type* of the `I`th element of the given tuple type. Again, the standard library exposes this information in a more awkward way than the core language does. Generally, to find the type of the `I`th element of a tuple, you'd just write `decltype(std::get<I>(t))`.
- `std::tuple_cat(t1, t2, t3...)`: Concatenates all the given tuples together, end to end.
- `std::forward_as_tuple(a, b, c...)`: Creates a tuple of references, just like `std::tie`; but whereas `std::tie` demands lvalue references, `std::forward_as_tuple` will accept any kind of references as input, and perfectly forward them into the tuple so that they can later be extracted by `std::get<I>(t)...`:

  ```
  template<typename F>
  void run_zeroarg(const F& f);

  template<typename F, typename... Args>
  void run_multiarg(const F& f, Args&&... args)
  {
    auto fwd_args =
      std::forward_as_tuple(std::forward<Args>(args)...);
    auto lambda = [&f, fwd_args]() {
  ```

```
        std::apply(f, fwd_args);
    };
    run_zeroarg(f);
}
```

A note about named classes

As we saw in Chapter 4, *The Container Zoo*, when we compared `std::array<double, 3>` to `struct Vec3`, using an STL class template can shorten your development time and eliminate sources of error by reusing well-tested STL components; but it can also make your code less readable or give your types *too much* functionality. In our example from Chapter 4, *The Container Zoo*, `std::array<double, 3>` turned out to be a poor choice for `Vec3` because it exposed an unwanted `operator<`.

Using any of the algebraic types (`tuple`, `pair`, `optional`, or `variant`) directly in your interfaces and APIs is probably a mistake. You'll find that your code is easier to read, understand, and maintain if you write named classes for your own "domain-specific vocabulary" types, even if--*especially* if--they end up being thin wrappers around the algebraic types.

Expressing alternatives with std::variant

Whereas `std::tuple<A,B,C>` is a *product type*, `std::variant<A,B,C>` is a *sum type*. A variant is allowed to hold either an A, a B, or a C--but never more (or less) than one of those at a time. Another name for this concept is *discriminated union*, because a variant behaves a lot like a native C++ `union`; but unlike a native `union`, a variant is always able to tell you which of its elements, A, B, or C, is "active" at any given time. The official name for these elements is "alternatives," since only one can be active at once:

```
std::variant<int, double> v1;

v1 = 1; // activate the "int" member
assert(v1.index() == 0);
assert(std::get<0>(v1) == 1);

v1 = 3.14; // activate the "double" member
assert(v1.index() == 1);
assert(std::get<1>(v1) == 3.14);
assert(std::get<double>(v1) == 3.14);

assert(std::holds_alternative<int>(v1) == false);
```

Vocabulary Types

```
assert(std::holds_alternative<double>(v1) == true);

assert(std::get_if<int>(&v1) == nullptr);
assert(*std::get_if<double>(&v1) == 3.14);
```

As with `tuple`, you can get a specific element of the `variant` using `std::get<I>(v)`. If your variant object's alternatives are all distinct (which should be the most common case, unless you're doing deep metaprogramming), you can use `std::get<T>(v)` with types as well as with indices--for an example, look at the preceding code sample, where `std::get<0>(v1)` and `std::get<int>(v1)` work interchangeably because the zeroth alternative in the variant `v1` is of type `int`. Unlike `tuple`, however, `std::get` on a variant is allowed to fail! If you call `std::get<double>(v1)` while `v1` currently holds a value of type `int`, then you'll get an exception of type `std::bad_variant_access`. `std::get_if` is the "non-throwing" version of `std::get`. As shown in the preceding example, `get_if` returns a *pointer* to the specified alternative if it's the active one, and otherwise returns a null pointer. Therefore the following code snippets are all equivalent:

```
// Worst...
try {
   std::cout << std::get<int>(v1) << std::endl;
} catch (const std::bad_variant_access&) {}

// Still bad...
if (v1.index() == 0) {
   std::cout << std::get<int>(v1) << std::endl;
}

// Slightly better...
if (std::holds_alternative<int>(v1)) {
   std::cout << std::get<int>(v1) << std::endl;
}

// ...Best.
if (int *p = std::get_if<int>(&v1)) {
   std::cout << *p << std::endl;
}
```

Visiting variants

In the preceding example, we showed how when we had a variable `std::variant<int, double> v`, calling `std::get<double>(v)` would give us the current value *if* the variant currently held a `double`, but would throw an exception if the variant held an `int`. This might have struck you as odd--since `int` is convertible to `double`, why couldn't it just have given us the converted value?

We can get that behaviour if we want it, but not from `std::get`. We have to re-express our desire this way: "I have a variant. If it currently holds a `double`, call it d, then I want to get `double(d)`. If it holds an `int i`, then I want to get `double(i)`." That is, we have a list of behaviors in mind, and we want to invoke exactly one of those behaviors on whichever alternative is currently held by our variant v. The standard library expresses this algorithm by the perhaps obscure name `std::visit`:

```
struct Visitor {
  double operator()(double d) { return d; }
  double operator()(int i) { return double(i); }
  double operator()(const std::string&) { return -1; }
};

using Var = std::variant<int, double, std::string>;

void show(Var v)
{
  std::cout << std::visit(Visitor{}, v) << std::endl;
}

void test()
{
  show(3.14);
  show(1);
  show("hello world");
}
```

Vocabulary Types

Generally speaking, when we `visit` a variant, all of the behaviors that we have in mind are fundamentally similar. Because we're writing in C++, with its overloading of functions and operators, we can generally express our similar behaviors using exactly identical syntax. If we can express them with identical syntax, we can wrap them up into a template function or--the most common case--a C++14 generic lambda, like this:

```
std::visit([](const auto& alt) {
  if constexpr (std::is_same_v<decltype(alt), const std::string&>) {
    std::cout << double(-1) << std::endl;
  } else {
    std::cout << double(alt) << std::endl;
  }
}, v);
```

> **TIP**: Notice the use of C++17 `if constexpr` to take care of the one case that's fundamentally unlike the others. It's somewhat a matter of taste whether you prefer to use explicit switching on `decltype` like this, or to make a helper class such as the previous code sample's `Visitor` and rely on overload resolution to pick out the correct overload of `operator()` for each possible alternative.

There is also a variadic version of `std::visit` taking two, three, or even more `variant` objects, of the same or different types. This version of `std::visit` can be used to implement a kind of "multiple dispatch," as shown in the following code. However, you almost certainly will never need this version of `std::visit` unless you're doing really intense metaprogramming:

```
struct MultiVisitor {
  template<class T, class U, class V>
  void operator()(T, U, V) const { puts("wrong"); }

  void operator()(char, int, double) const { puts("right!"); }
};

void test()
{
  std::variant<int, double, char> v1 = 'x';
  std::variant<char, int, double> v2 = 1;
  std::variant<double, char, int> v3 = 3.14;
  std::visit(MultiVisitor{}, v1, v2, v3);  // prints "right!"
}
```

What about make_variant? and a note on value semantics

Since you can create a tuple object with `std::make_tuple`, or a pair with `make_pair`, you might reasonably ask, "Where is `make_variant`?" It turns out that there is none. The primary reason for its absence is that whereas `tuple` and `pair` are product types, `variant` is a sum type. To create a tuple, you always have to provide all *n* of its elements' values, and so the element types can always be inferred. With `variant`, you only have to provide one of its values--of type let's say `A`--but the compiler can't create a `variant<A,B,C>` object without knowing the identities of types `B` and `C` as well. So there'd be no point in providing a function `my::make_variant<A,B,C>(a)`, given that the actual class constructor can be spelled more concisely than that: `std::variant<A,B,C>(a)`.

We have already alluded to the secondary reason for the existence of `make_pair` and `make_tuple`: They automatically decay the special vocabulary type `std::reference_wrapper<T>` into `T&`, so that `std::make_pair(std::ref(a), std::cref(b))` creates an object of type `std::pair<A&, const B&>`. Objects of "pair-of-reference" or "tuple-of-reference" type behave very strangely: you can compare and copy them with the usual semantics, but when you assign to an object of this type, rather than "rebinding" the reference elements (so that they refer to the objects on the right-hand side), the assignment operator actually "assigns through," changing the values of the referred-to objects. As we saw in the code sample in section "Working with `std::tuple`", this deliberate oddity allows us to use `std::tie` as a sort of "multiple assignment" statement.

So another reason that we might expect or desire to see a `make_variant` function in the standard library would be for its reference-decaying ability. However, this is a moot point for one simple reason--the standard forbids making variants whose elements are reference types! We will see later in this chapter that `std::optional` and `std::any` are likewise forbidden from holding reference types. (However, `std::variant<std::reference_wrapper<T>, ...>` is perfectly legitimate.) This prohibition comes because the designers of the library have not come to a consensus as to what a variant of references should mean. Or, for that matter, what a *tuple* of references should mean! only reason we have tuples of references in the language today is because `std::tie` seemed like such a good idea in 2011. In 2017, nobody is particularly eager to compound the confusion by introducing variants, optionals, or "anys" of references.

Vocabulary Types

We have established that a `std::variant<A,B,C>` always holds exactly one value of type A, B, or C--no more and no less. Well, that's not technically correct. *Under very unusual circumstances*, it is possible to construct a variant with no value whatsoever. The only way to make this happen is to construct the variant with a value of type A, and then assign it a value of type B in such a way that the A is successfully destroyed but the constructor B throws an exception and the B is never actually emplaced. When this happens, the variant object enters a state known as "valueless by exception":

```
struct A {
  A() { throw "ha ha!"; }
};
struct B {
  operator int () { throw "ha ha!"; }
};
struct C {
  C() = default;
  C& operator=(C&&) = default;
  C(C&&) { throw "ha ha!"; }
};

void test()
{
  std::variant<int, A, C> v1 = 42;

  try {
    v1.emplace<A>();
  } catch (const char *haha) {}
  assert(v1.valueless_by_exception());

  try {
    v1.emplace<int>(B());
  } catch (const char *haha) {}
  assert(v1.valueless_by_exception());
}
```

This will never happen to you, unless you are writing code where your constructors or conversion operators throw exceptions. Furthermore, by using `operator=` instead of `emplace`, you can avoid valueless variants in every case except when you have a move constructor that throws:

```
v1 = 42;

// Constructing the right-hand side of this assignment
// will throw; yet the variant is unaffected.
try { v1 = A(); } catch (...) {}
assert(std::get<int>(v1) == 42);
```

```
    // In this case as well.
    try { v1 = B(); } catch (...) {}
    assert(std::get<int>(v1) == 42);

    // But a throwing move-constructor can still foul it up.
    try { v1 = C(); } catch (...) {}
    assert(v1.valueless_by_exception());
```

Recall from the discussion of `std::vector` in Chapter 4, *The Container Zoo*, that your types' move constructors should always be marked `noexcept`; so, if you follow that advice religiously, you'll be able to avoid dealing with `valueless_by_exception` at all.

Anyway, when a variant *is* in this state, its `index()` method returns `size_t(-1)` (a constant also known as `std::variant_npos`) and any attempt to `std::visit` it will throw an exception of type `std::bad_variant_access`.

Delaying initialization with std::optional

You might already be thinking that one potential use for `std::variant` would be to represent the notion of "Maybe I have an object, and maybe I don't." For example, we could represent the "maybe I don't" state using the standard tag type `std::monostate`:

```
    std::map<std::string, int> g_limits = {
      { "memory", 655360 }
    };

    std::variant<std::monostate, int>
    get_resource_limit(const std::string& key)
    {
      if (auto it = g_limits.find(key); it != g_limits.end()) {
        return it->second;
      }
      return std::monostate{};
    }

    void test()
    {
      auto limit = get_resource_limit("memory");
      if (std::holds_alternative<int>(limit)) {
        use( std::get<int>(limit) );
      } else {
        use( some_default );
      }
    }
```

[127]

Vocabulary Types

You'll be pleased to know that this is *not* the best way to accomplish that goal! The standard library provides the *vocabulary type* `std::optional<T>` specifically to deal with the notion of "maybe I have an object, maybe I don't."

```
std::optional<int>
get_resource_limit(const std::string& key)
{
  if (auto it = g_limits.find(key); it != g_limits.end()) {
    return it->second;
  }
  return std::nullopt;
}

void test()
{
  auto limit = get_resource_limit("memory");
  if (limit.has_value()) {
    use( *limit );
  } else {
    use( some_default );
  }
}
```

In the logic of algebraic data types, `std::optional<T>` is a sum type: it has exactly as many possible values as `T` does, plus one. This one additional value is called the "null," "empty," or "disengaged" state, and is represented in source code by the special constant `std::nullopt`.

> Do not confuse `std::nullopt` with the similarly named `std::nullptr`! They have nothing in common except that they're both vaguely null-ish.

Unlike `std::tuple` and `std::variant` with their mess of free (non-member) functions, the `std::optional<T>` class is full of convenient member functions. `o.has_value()` is true if the optional object `o` currently holds a value of type `T`. The "has-value" state is commonly known as the "engaged" state; an optional object containing a value is "engaged" and an optional object in the empty state is "disengaged."

The comparison operators ==, !=, <, <=, >, and >= are all overloaded for `optional<T>` if they are valid for `T`. To compare two optionals, or to compare an optional to a value of type `T`, all you need to remember is that an optional in the disengaged state compares "less than" any real value of `T`.

[128]

`bool(o)` is a synonym for `o.has_value()`, and `!o` is a synonym for `!o.has_value()`. Personally, I recommend that you always use `has_value`, since there's no difference in runtime cost; the only difference is in the readability of your code. If you do use the abbreviated conversion-to-`bool` form, be aware that for a `std::optional<bool>`, `o == false` and `!o` mean very different things!

`o.value()` returns a reference to the value contained by `o`. If `o` is currently disengaged, then `o.value()` throws an exception of type `std::bad_optional_access`.

`*o` (using the overloaded unary `operator*`) returns a reference to the value contained by `o`, without checking for engagement. If `o` is currently disengaged and you call `*o`, that's undefined behavior, just as if you called `*p` on a null pointer. You can remember this behavior by noticing that the C++ standard library likes to use punctuation for its most efficient, least sanity-checked operations. For example, `std::vector::operator[]` does less bounds-checking than `std::vector::at()`. Therefore, by the same logic, `std::optional::operator*` does less bounds-checking than `std::optional::value()`.

`o.value_or(x)` returns a copy of the value contained by `o`, or, if `o` is disengaged, it returns a copy of `x` converted to type `T`. We can use `value_or` to rewrite the preceding code sample into a one-liner of utter simplicity and readability:

```
std::optional<int> get_resource_limit(const std::string&);

void test() {
  auto limit = get_resource_limit("memory");
  use( limit.value_or(some_default) );
}
```

The preceding examples have shown how to use `std::optional<T>` as a way to handle "maybe a T" in flight (as a function return type, or as a parameter type). Another common and useful way to use `std::optional<T>` is as a way to handle "not yet a T" at rest, as a class data member. For example, suppose we have some type `L` which is not default-constructible, such as the closure type produced by a lambda expression:

```
auto make_lambda(int arg) {
  return [arg](int x) { return x + arg; };
}
using L = decltype(make_lambda(0));

static_assert(!std::is_default_constructible_v<L>);
static_assert(!std::is_move_assignable_v<L>);
```

Vocabulary Types

Then a class with a member of that type would also fail to be default-constructible:

```
class ProblematicAdder {
  L fn_;
};

static_assert(!std::is_default_constructible_v<ProblematicAdder>);
```

But, by giving our class a member of type `std::optional<L>`, we allow it to be used in contexts that require default-constructibility:

```
class Adder {
  std::optional<L> fn_;
public:
  void setup(int first_arg) {
    fn_.emplace(make_lambda(first_arg));
  }
  int call(int second_arg) {
    // this will throw unless setup() was called first
    return fn_.value()(second_arg);
  }
};

static_assert(std::is_default_constructible_v<Adder>);

void test() {
  Adder adder;
  adder.setup(4);
  int result = adder.call(5);
  assert(result == 9);
}
```

It would be very difficult to implement this behavior without `std::optional`. You could do it with placement-new syntax, or using a `union`, but essentially you'd have to reimplement at least half of `optional` yourself. Much better to use `std::optional`!

> And notice that if for some reason we wanted to get undefined behavior instead of the possibility of throwing from `call()`, we could just replace `fn_.value()` with `*fn_`.

`std::optional` is truly one of the biggest wins among the new features of C++17, and you'll benefit immensely by getting familiar with it.

Vocabulary Types

From `optional`, which could be described as a sort of limited one-type `variant`, we now approach the other extreme: the algebraic-data-type equivalent of *infinity*.

Revisiting variant

The `variant` data type is good at representing simple alternatives, but as of C++17, it is not particularly suitable for representing *recursive* data types such as JSON lists. That is, the following C++17 code will fail to compile:

```
using JSONValue = std::variant<
  std::nullptr_t,
  bool,
  double,
  std::string,
  std::vector<JSONValue>,
  std::map<std::string, JSONValue>
>;
```

There are several possible workarounds. The most robust and correct is to continue using the C++11 Boost library `boost::variant`, which specifically supports recursive variant types via the marker type `boost::recursive_variant_`:

```
using JSONValue = boost::variant<
  std::nullptr_t,
  bool,
  double,
  std::string,
  std::vector<boost::recursive_variant_>,
  std::map<std::string, boost::recursive_variant_>
>;
```

You could also get around the problem by introducing a new class type called `JSONValue`, which either **HAS-A** or **IS-A** `std::variant` of the recursive type.

> Notice that in the following example I chose HAS-A rather than IS-A; inheriting from non-polymorphic standard library types is almost always a really bad idea.

Since forward references to class types are acceptable to C++, this will compile:

```
struct JSONValue {
  std::variant<
    std::nullptr_t,
```

[131]

Vocabulary Types

```
        bool,
        double,
        std::string,
        std::vector<JSONValue>,
        std::map<std::string, JSONValue>
    > value_;
};
```

The final possibility is to switch to an algebraic type from the standard library that is even more powerful than `variant`.

Infinite alternatives with std::any

To paraphrase Henry Ford, an object of type `std::variant<A, B, C>` can hold a value of any type--as long as it's A, B, or C. But suppose we wanted to hold a value of *truly* any type? Perhaps our program will load plugins at runtime that might contain new types impossible to predict. We can't specify those types in a `variant`. Or perhaps we are in the "recursive data type" situation detailed in the preceding section.

For these situations, the C++17 standard library provides an algebraic-data-type version of "infinity": the type `std::any`. This is a sort of a container (see Chapter 4, *The Container Zoo*) for a single object of any type at all. The container may be empty, or it may contain an object. You can perform the following fundamental operations on an `any` object:

- Ask if it currently holds an object
- Put a new object into it (destroying the old object, whatever it was)
- Ask the type of the held object
- Retrieve the held object, by correctly naming its type

In code the first three of these operations look like this:

```cpp
std::any a;  // construct an empty container

assert(!a.has_value());

a = std::string("hello");
assert(a.has_value());
assert(a.type() == typeid(std::string));

a = 42;
assert(a.has_value());
assert(a.type() == typeid(int));
```

The fourth operation is a little more fiddly. It is spelled `std::any_cast`, and, like `std::get` for variants, it comes in two flavors: a `std::get`-like flavor that throws `std::bad_any_cast` on failure, and a `std::get_if`-like flavor that returns a null pointer on failure:

```
if (std::string *p = std::any_cast<std::string>(&a)) {
  use(*p);
} else {
  // go fish!
}

try {
  std::string& s = std::any_cast<std::string&>(a);
  use(s);
} catch (const std::bad_any_cast&) {
  // go fish!
}
```

Observe that in either case, you must name the type that you want to retrieve from the `any` object. If you get the type wrong, then you'll get an exception or a null pointer. There is no way to say "Give me the held object, no matter what type it is," since then what would be the type of that expression?

Recall that when we faced a similar problem with `std::variant` in the preceding section, we solved it by using `std::visit` to visit some generic code onto the held alternative. Unfortunately, there is no equivalent `std::visit` for `any`. The reason is simple and insurmountable: separate compilation. Suppose in one source file, a.cc, I have:

```
template<class T> struct Widget {};

std::any get_widget() {
  return std::make_any<Widget<int>>();
}
```

And in another source file, b.cc, (perhaps compiled into a different plugin, .dll, or shared object file) I have:

```
template<class T> struct Widget {};

template<class T> int size(Widget<T>& w) {
  return sizeof w;
}

void test()
{
  std::any a = get_widget();
```

Vocabulary Types

```
    int sz = hypothetical_any_visit([](auto&& w){
      return size(w);
    }, a);
    assert(sz == sizeof(Widget<int>));
}
```

How should the compiler know, when compiling `b.cc`, that it needs to output a template instantiation for `size(Widget<int>&)` as opposed to, let's say, `size(Widget<double>&)`? When someone changes `a.cc` to return `make_any(Widget<char>&)`, how should the compiler know that it needs to recompile `b.cc` with a fresh instantiation of `size(Widget<char>&)` and that the instantiation of `size(Widget<int>&)` is no longer needed--unless of course we're anticipating being linked against a `c.cc` that *does* require that instantiation! Basically, there's no way for the compiler to figure out what kind of code-generation might possibly be needed by visitation, on a container that can by definition contain *any* type and trigger *any* code-generation.

Therefore, in order to extract any function of the contained value of an `any`, you must know up front what the type of that contained value might be. (And if you guess wrong--go fish!)

std::any versus polymorphic class types

`std::any` occupies a position in between the compile-time polymorphism of `std::variant<A, B, C>` and the runtime polymorphism of polymorphic inheritance hierarchies and `dynamic_cast`. You might wonder whether `std::any` interacts with the machinery of `dynamic_cast` at all. The answer is "no, it does not"--nor is there any standard way to get that behavior. `std::any` is one hundred percent statically type-safe: there is no way to break into it and get a "pointer to the data" (for example, a `void *`) without knowing the exact static type of that data:

```
    struct Animal {
      virtual ~Animal() = default;
    };

    struct Cat : Animal {};

    void test()
    {
      std::any a = Cat{};

      // The held object is a "Cat"...
      assert(a.type() == typeid(Cat));
      assert(std::any_cast<Cat>(&a) != nullptr);
```

```
        // Asking for a base "Animal" will not work.
        assert(a.type() != typeid(Animal));
        assert(std::any_cast<Animal>(&a) == nullptr);

        // Asking for void* certainly will not work!
        assert(std::any_cast<void>(&a) == nullptr);
    }
```

Type erasure in a nutshell

Let's look briefly at how `std::any` might be implemented by the standard library. The core idea is called "type erasure," and the way we achieve it is to identify the salient or relevant operations that we want to support for *all* types T, and then "erase" every other idiosyncratic operation that might be supported by any specific type T.

For `std::any`, the salient operations are as follows:

- Constructing a copy of the contained object
- Constructing a copy of the contained object "by move"
- Getting `typeid` of the contained object

Construction and destruction are also required, but those two operations are concerned with the lifetime management of the contained object itself, not "what you can do with it," so at least in this case we don't need to consider them.

So we invent a polymorphic class type (call it `AnyBase`) which supports only those three operations as overrideable `virtual` methods, and then we create a brand-new derived class (call it `AnyImpl<T>`) each time the programmer actually stores an object of a specific type T into any:

```
class any;

struct AnyBase {
  virtual const std::type_info& type() = 0;
  virtual void copy_to(any&) = 0;
  virtual void move_to(any&) = 0;
  virtual ~AnyBase() = default;
};

template<typename T>
struct AnyImpl : AnyBase {
  T t_;
  const std::type_info& type() {
```

Vocabulary Types

```
      return typeid(T);
    }
    void copy_to(any& rhs) override {
      rhs.emplace<T>(t_);
    }
    void move_to(any& rhs) override {
      rhs.emplace<T>(std::move(t_));
    }
    // the destructor doesn't need anything
    // special in this case
};
```

With these helper classes, the code to implement `std::any` becomes fairly trivial, especially when we use a smart pointer (see Chapter 6, *Smart Pointers*) to manage the lifetime of our `AnyImpl<T>` object:

```
class any {
  std::unique_ptr<AnyBase> p_ = nullptr;
  public:
  template<typename T, typename... Args>
  std::decay_t<T>& emplace(Args&&... args) {
    p_ = std::make_unique<AnyImpl<T>>(std::forward<Args>(args)...);
  }

  bool has_value() const noexcept {
    return (p_ != nullptr);
  }

  void reset() noexcept {
    p_ = nullptr;
  }

  const std::type_info& type() const {
    return p_ ? p_->type() : typeid(void);
  }

  any(const any& rhs) {
    *this = rhs;
  }

  any& operator=(const any& rhs) {
    if (rhs.has_value()) {
      rhs.p_->copy_to(*this);
    }
    return *this;
  }
};
```

The preceding code sample omits the implementation of move-assignment. It can be done in the same way as copy-assignment, or it can be done by simply swapping the pointers. The standard library actually prefers to swap pointers when possible, because that is guaranteed to be noexcept; the only reason that you might see std::any *not* swapping pointers is if it uses a "small object optimization" to avoid heap allocation altogether for very small, nothrow-move-constructible types T. As of this writing, libstdc++ (the library used by GCC) will use small object optimization and avoid heap allocation for types up to 8 bytes in size; libc++ (the library used by Clang) will use small object optimization for types up to 24 bytes in size.

Unlike the standard containers discussed in Chapter 4, *The Container Zoo*, std::any does *not* take an allocator parameter and does *not* allow you to customize or configure the source of its heap memory. If you use C++ on a real-time or memory-constrained system where heap allocation is not allowed, then you should not use std::any. Consider an alternative such as Tiemo Jung's tj::inplace_any<Size, Alignment>. If all else fails, you have now seen how to roll your own!

std::any and copyability

Notice that our definition of AnyImpl<T>::copy_to required T to be copy-constructible. This is true of the standard std::any as well; there is simply no way to store a move-only type into a std::any object. The way to work around this is with a sort of a "shim" wrapper, whose purpose is to make its move-only object conform to the syntactic requirement of copy-constructibility while eschewing any actual copying:

```
using Ptr = std::unique_ptr<int>;

template<class T>
struct Shim {
  T get() { return std::move(*t_); }

  template<class... Args>
  Shim(Args&&... args) : t_(std::in_place,
    std::forward<Args>(args)...) {}

  Shim(Shim&&) = default;
  Shim& operator=(Shim&&) = default;
  Shim(const Shim&) { throw "oops"; }
  Shim& operator=(const Shim&) { throw "oops"; }
private:
  std::optional<T> t_;
};
```

Vocabulary Types

```
void test()
{
  Ptr p = std::make_unique<int>(42);

  // Ptr cannot be stored in std::any because it is move-only.
  // std::any a = std::move(p);

  // But Shim<Ptr> can be!
  std::any a = Shim<Ptr>(std::move(p));
  assert(a.type() == typeid(Shim<Ptr>));

  // Moving a Shim<Ptr> is okay...
  std::any b = std::move(a);

  try {
    // ...but copying a Shim<Ptr> will throw.
    std::any c = b;
  } catch (...) {}

  // Get the move-only Ptr back out of the Shim<Ptr>.
  Ptr r = std::any_cast<Shim<Ptr>&>(b).get();
  assert(*r == 42);
}
```

Notice the use of `std::optional<T>` in the preceding code sample; this guards our fake copy constructor against the possibility that T might not be default-constructible.

Again with the type erasure: std::function

We observed that for `std::any`, the salient operations were as follows:

- Constructing a copy of the contained object
- Constructing a copy of the contained object "by move"
- Getting the `typeid` of the contained object

Suppose we were to add one to this set of salient operations? Let's say our set is:

- Constructing a copy of the contained object
- Constructing a copy of the contained object "by move"
- Getting the `typeid` of the contained object
- Calling the contained object with a particular fixed sequence of argument types A..., and converting the result to some particular fixed type R

The type-erasure of this set of operations corresponds to the standard library type `std::function<R(A...)>`!

```cpp
int my_abs(int x) { return x < 0 ? -x : x; }
long unusual(long x, int y = 3) { return x + y; }

void test()
{
  std::function<int(int)> f; // construct an empty container
  assert(!f);

  f = my_abs; // store a function in the container
  assert(f(-42) == 42);

  f = [](long x) { return unusual(x); }; // or a lambda!
  assert(f(-42) == -39);
}
```

Copying `std::function` always makes a copy of the contained object, if the contained object has state. Of course if the contained object is a function pointer, you won't observe any difference; but you can see the copying happen if you try it with an object of user-defined class type, or with a stateful lambda:

```cpp
f = [i=0](int) mutable { return ++i; };
assert(f(-42) == 1);
assert(f(-42) == 2);

auto g = f;
assert(f(-42) == 3);
assert(f(-42) == 4);
assert(g(-42) == 3);
assert(g(-42) == 4);
```

Just as with `std::any`, `std::function<R(A...)>` allows you to retrieve the `typeid` of the contained object, or to retrieve a pointer to the object itself as long as you statically know (or can guess) its type:

- `f.target_type()` is the equivalent of `a.type()`
- `f.target<T>()` is the equivalent of `std::any_cast<T*>(&a)`

```cpp
if (f.target_type() == typeid(int(*)(int))) {
  int (*p)(int) = *f.target<int (*)(int)>();
  use(p);
} else {
  // go fish!
}
```

[139]

Vocabulary Types

That said, I have never seen a use-case for these methods in real life. Generally, if you have to ask what the contained type of a `std::function` is, you've already done something wrong.

The most important use-case for `std::function` is as a vocabulary type for passing "behaviors" across module boundaries, where using a template would be impossible--for example, when you need to pass a callback to a function in an external library, or when you're writing a library that needs to receive a callback from its caller:

```
// templated_for_each is a template and must be visible at the
// point where it is called.
template<class F>
void templated_for_each(std::vector<int>& v, F f) {
  for (int& i : v) {
    f(i);
  }
}

// type_erased_for_each has a stable ABI and a fixed address.
// It can be called with only its declaration in scope.
extern void type_erased_for_each(std::vector<int>&,
  std::function<void(int)>);
```

We started this chapter talking about `std::string`, the standard vocabulary type for passing strings between functions; now, as the end of the chapter draws near, we're talking about `std::function`, the standard vocabulary type for passing *functions* between functions!

std::function, copyability, and allocation

Just like `std::any`, `std::function` requires that whatever object you store in it must be copy-constructible. This can present a problem if you are using a lot of lambdas that capture `std::future<T>`, `std::unique_ptr<T>`, or other move-only types: such lambda types will be move-only themselves. One way to fix that was demonstrated in the *std::any and copyability* section in this chapter: we could introduce a shim that is syntactically copyable but throws an exception if you try to copy it.

When working with `std::function` and lambda captures, it might often be preferable to capture your move-only lambda captures by `shared_ptr`. We'll cover `shared_ptr` in the next chapter:

```
auto capture = [](auto& p) {
  using T = std::decay_t<decltype(p)>;
  return std::make_shared<T>(std::move(p));
};

std::promise<int> p;

std::function<void()> f = [sp = capture(p)]() {
  sp->set_value(42);
};
```

Like `std::any`, `std::function` does *not* take an allocator parameter and does *not* allow you to customize or configure the source of its heap memory. If you use C++ on a real-time or memory-constrained system where heap allocation is not allowed, then you should not use `std::function`. Consider an alternative such as Carl Cook's `sg14::inplace_function<R(A...), Size, Alignment>`.

Summary

Vocabulary types like `std::string` and `std::function` allow us to share a *lingua franca* for dealing with common programming concepts. In C++17, we have a rich set of vocabulary types for dealing with the *algebraic data types*: `std::pair` and `std::tuple` (product types), `std::optional` and `std::variant` (sum types), and `std::any` (the ultimate in sum types--it can store almost anything). However, don't get carried away and start using `std::tuple` and `std::variant` return types from every function! Named class types are still the most effective way to keep your code readable.

Use `std::optional` to signal the possible lack of a value, or to signal the "not-yet-ness" of a data member.

Use `std::get_if<T>(&v)` to query the type of a `variant`; use `std::any_cast<T>(&a)` to query the type of an `any`. Remember that the type you provide must be an exact match; if it's not, you'll get `nullptr`.

Vocabulary Types

Be aware that `make_tuple` and `make_pair` do more than construct `tuple` and `pair` objects; they also decay `reference_wrapper` objects into native references. Use `std::tie` and `std::forward_as_tuple` to create tuples of references. `std::tie` is particularly useful for multiple assignment and for writing comparison operators. `std::forward_as_tuple` is useful for metaprogramming.

Be aware that `std::variant` always has the possibility of being in a "valueless by exception" state; but know that you don't have to worry about that case unless you write classes with throwing move-constructors. Separately: don't write classes with throwing move-constructors!

Be aware that the *type-erased* types `std::any` and `std::function` implicitly use the heap. Third-party libraries provide non-standard `inplace_` versions of these types. Be aware that `std::any` and `std::function` require copyability of their contained types. Use "capture by `shared_ptr`" to deal with this case if it arises.

6
Smart Pointers

C++ holds its grip on large swaths of the software industry by virtue of its performance--well-written C++ code runs faster than anything else out there, *almost* by definition, because C++ gives the programmer almost complete control over the code that is ultimately generated by the compiler.

One of the classic features of low-level, performant code is the use of *raw pointers* (`Foo*`). However, raw pointers come with many pitfalls, such as memory leaks and dangling pointers. The C++11 library's "smart pointer" types can help you avoid these pitfalls at little to no expense.

In this chapter we'll learn the following:

- The definition of "smart pointer" and how you might write your own
- The usefulness of `std::unique_ptr<T>` in preventing resource leaks of all types (not just memory leaks)
- How `std::shared_ptr<T>` is implemented, and its implications for memory usage
- The meaning and uses of the Curiously Recurring Template Pattern

The origins of smart pointers

Raw pointers have many uses in C:

- As a cheap, non-copying view of an object owned by the caller
- As a way for the callee to modify an object owned by the caller

Smart Pointers

- As one-half of a pointer/length pair, used for arrays
- As an optional argument (either a valid pointer *or* null)
- As a way to manage memory on the heap

In C++, we have native references (`const Foo&` and `Foo&`) to handle the first two bullets; plus, move semantics makes it cheap for a callee to take and pass back a complex object by value in most cases, thus completely avoiding aliasing. In C++17 we can use `std::string_view` to address some of the first and third bullet. And we've just seen in Chapter 5, *Vocabulary Types*, that passing an `optional<T>`--or perhaps getting fancy with an `optional<reference_wrapper<T>>`--is sufficient to handle the fourth bullet.

This chapter will be concerned with the fifth bullet.

Heap allocation comes with a host of problems in C, and all those problems (and more!) applied to C++ prior to 2011. As of C++11, though, almost all of those problems have disappeared. Let's enumerate them:

- **Memory leaks**: You might allocate a piece of memory or an object on the heap, and accidentally forget to write the code that frees it.
- **Memory leaks**: You might have written that code, but due to an early return or an exception being thrown, the code never runs and the memory remains unfreed!
- **Use-after-free**: You take a copy of a pointer to an object on the heap, and then free that object through the original pointer. The holder of the copied pointer doesn't realize that their pointer is no longer valid.
- **Heap corruption via pointer arithmetic**: You allocate an array on the heap at address *A*. Having a raw pointer to an array tempts you to do pointer arithmetic, and in the end you accidentally free a pointer to address *A+k*. When *k*=0 (as Murphy's Law ensures it will be, in testing) there is no problem; when *k*=1 you corrupt your heap and cause a crash.

The first two problems are compounded by the fact that heap allocation is semantically allowed to fail--`malloc` can return null, `operator new` can throw `std::bad_alloc`--which means that if you're writing pre-C++11 code that allocates memory, you are probably writing a lot of cleanup code to deal with allocation failure. (In C++, you're "writing" that code whether you know it or not, because the control flow paths due to exception handling are there even if you're not consciously thinking about them.) The upshot of all this is that managing heap-allocated memory in C++ is *hard*.

Unless you use smart pointers!

Smart pointers never forget

The idea of a "smart pointer" type (not to be confused with a "fancy pointer" type, which we'll cover in `Chapter 8`, *Allocators*) is that it's a class--typically a class template--which behaves syntactically just like a pointer, but whose special member functions (construction, destruction, and copying/moving) have additional bookkeeping to ensure certain invariants. For example, we might ensure the following:

- The pointer's destructor also frees its pointee--helping to solve memory leaks
- Maybe the pointer cannot be copied--helping to solve use-after-free
- Or maybe the pointer *can* be copied, but it knows how many copies exist and won't free the pointee until the last pointer to it has been destroyed
- Or maybe the pointer can be copied, and you can free the pointee, but if you do, all other pointers to it magically become null
- Or maybe the pointer has no built-in `operator+`--helping to solve corruption due to pointer arithmetic
- Or maybe you're allowed to adjust the pointer's value arithmetically, but the arithmetic "what object is pointed-to" is managed separately from the identity of "what object is to be freed"

The standard smart pointer types are `std::unique_ptr<T>`, `std::shared_ptr<T>`, and (not really a pointer type, but we'll lump it in with them) `std::weak_ptr<T>`. In this chapter we'll cover all three of those types, plus one non-standard smart pointer that you might find useful--and which might become a standard smart pointer type in a future C++ standard!

Automatically managing memory with std::unique_ptr<T>

The fundamental properties of a smart pointer type are simple: it should support `operator*`, and it should overload the special member functions to preserve its class invariants, whatever those are.

Smart Pointers

`std::unique_ptr<T>` supports the same interface as `T*`, but with the class invariant that, once you construct a `unique_ptr` pointing to a given heap-allocated object, that object *will* be freed when the destructor `unique_ptr` is called. Let's write some code supporting that `T*` interface:

```
template<typename T>
class unique_ptr {
  T *m_ptr = nullptr;
public:
  constexpr unique_ptr() noexcept = default;
  constexpr unique_ptr(T *p) noexcept : m_ptr(p) {}

  T *get() const noexcept { return m_ptr; }
  operator bool() const noexcept { return bool(get()); }
  T& operator*() const noexcept { return *get(); }
  T* operator->() const noexcept { return get(); }
```

If we stopped here--with just a way to construct a pointer object from a `T*` and a way to get the pointer out again--we'd have the `observer_ptr<T>` discussed at the end of this chapter. But we'll keep going. We'll add methods `release` and `reset`:

```
  void reset(T *p = nullptr) noexcept {
    T *old_p = std::exchange(m_ptr, p);
    delete old_p;
  }

  T *release() noexcept {
    return std::exchange(m_ptr, nullptr);
  }
```

`p.release()` is just like `p.get()`, but in addition to returning a copy of the original raw pointer, it nulls out the contents of `p` (without freeing the original pointer, of course, because presumably our caller wants to take ownership of it).

`p.reset(q)` *does* free the current contents of `p`, and then puts the raw pointer `q` in its place.

Notice that we have implemented both of these member functions in terms of the standard algorithm `std::exchange`, which we didn't cover in Chapter 3, *The Iterator-Pair Algorithms*. It's sort of a value-returning version of `std::swap`: pass in a new value, get out the former value.

Finally, with these two primitive operations, we can implement the special member functions of `std::unique_ptr<T>` so as to preserve our invariant--which, again, is this: once a raw pointer has been acquired by a `unique_ptr` object, it will remain valid as long as the `unique_ptr` object has the same value, and when that's no longer true--when the `unique_ptr` is adjusted to point elsewhere, or destroyed--the raw pointer will be freed correctly. Here are the special member functions:

```
    unique_ptr(unique_ptr&& rhs) noexcept {
      this->reset(rhs.release());
    }

    unique_ptr& operator=(unique_ptr&& rhs) noexcept {
      reset(rhs.release());
      return *this;
    }

    ~unique_ptr() {
      reset();
    }
};
```

In memory, our `std::unique_ptr<T>` will look like this:

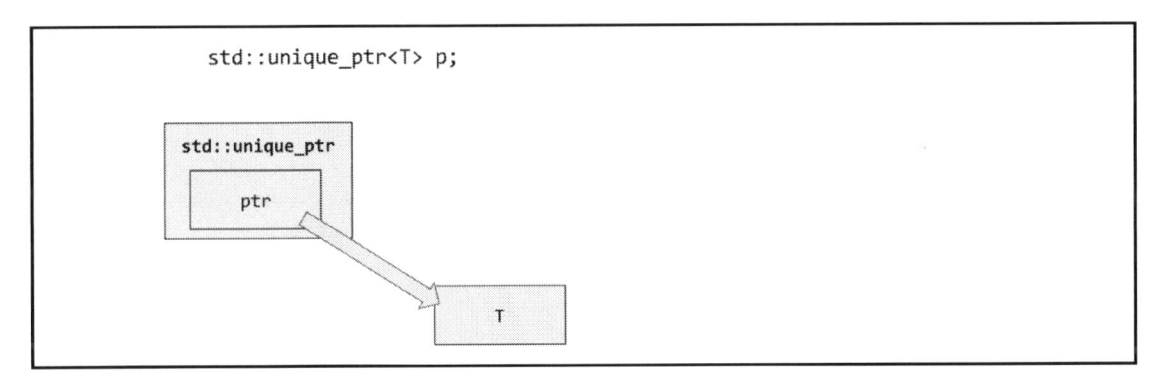

There is one more little helper function we need, so as never to touch raw pointers with our hands:

```
template<typename T, typename... Args>
unique_ptr<T> make_unique(Args&&... args)
{
   return unique_ptr<T>(new T(std::forward<Args>(args)...));
}
```

[147]

With `unique_ptr` in our toolbox, we can replace old-style code such as this:

```
struct Widget {
  virtual ~Widget();
};
struct WidgetImpl : Widget {
  WidgetImpl(int size);
};
struct WidgetHolder {
  void take_ownership_of(Widget *) noexcept;
};
void use(WidgetHolder&);

void test() {
  Widget *w = new WidgetImpl(30);
  WidgetHolder *wh;
  try {
    wh = new WidgetHolder();
  } catch (...) {
    delete w;
    throw;
  }
  wh->take_ownership_of(w);
  try {
    use(*wh);
  } catch (...) {
    delete wh;
    throw;
  }
  delete wh;
}
```

It can be replaced with modern C++17 code like this:

```
void test() {
  auto w = std::make_unique<WidgetImpl>(30);
  auto wh = std::make_unique<WidgetHolder>();
  wh->take_ownership_of(w.release());
  use(*wh);
}
```

Notice that `unique_ptr<T>` is yet another application of **RAII**--in this case, quite literally. Although the "interesting" action (the freeing of the underlying raw pointer) still happens during destruction (of the `unique_ptr`), the only way you'll get the full benefit of `unique_ptr` is if you make sure that whenever you *allocate* a *resource,* you also *initialize* a `unique_ptr` to manage it. The `std::make_unique<T>()` function shown in the previous section (and introduced to the standard library in C++14) is the key to safe memory management in modern C++.

While it is *possible* to use `unique_ptr` without using `make_unique`, you should not do it:

```
std::unique_ptr<Widget> bad(new WidgetImpl(30));
bad.reset(new WidgetImpl(40));

std::unique_ptr<Widget> good = std::make_unique<WidgetImpl>(30);
good = std::make_unique<WidgetImpl>(40);
```

Why C++ doesn't have the finally keyword

Consider again this snippet of code from the preceding section's "pre-modern" code sample:

```
try {
  use(*wh);
} catch (...) {
  delete wh;
  throw;
}
delete wh;
```

In other languages such as Java and Python, these semantics might be expressed more compactly using the `finally` keyword:

```
try {
  use(*wh);
} finally {
  delete wh;
}
```

C++ doesn't have the `finally` keyword, and shows no signs that it will ever enter the language. This is simply due to a philosophical difference between C++ and those other languages: the C++ philosophy is that if you're concerned with *enforcing some invariant*--such as "this pointer shall always be freed at the end of this block, no matter how we get there"--then you shouldn't ever be writing *explicit code,* because then there's always a chance for you to write it wrong, and then you'll have bugs.

Smart Pointers

If you have some *invariant* that you want to enforce, then the right place to enforce it is *in the type system*, using constructors, destructors, and other special member functions--the tools of RAII. Then, you can ensure that *any possible* use of your new type preserves its invariants--such as "the underlying pointer shall be freed whenever it's no longer held by an object of this type"--and when you go to write your business logic, you won't have to write anything explicitly; the code will look simple and yet always--provably--have correct behavior.

So if you find yourself writing code that looks like the preceding example, or if you find yourself wishing you could just write `finally`, stop and think: "Should I be using `unique_ptr` for this?" or "Should I write an RAII class type for this?"

Customizing the deletion callback

Speaking of custom RAII types, you might be wondering whether it's possible to use `std::unique_ptr` with a customized deletion callback: for example, instead of passing the underlying pointer to `delete`, you might want to pass it to `free()`. Yes you can!

`std::unique_ptr<T,D>` has a second template type parameter: a *deletion callback type*. The parameter `D` defaults to `std::default_delete<T>`, which just calls `operator delete`, but you can pass in any type you want--typically a user-defined class type with an overloaded `operator()`:

```cpp
struct fcloser {
  void operator()(FILE *fp) const {
    fclose(fp);
  }

  static auto open(const char *name, const char *mode) {
    return std::unique_ptr<FILE, fcloser>(fopen(name, mode));
  }
};

void use(FILE *);

void test() {
  auto f = fcloser::open("test.txt", "r");
  use(f.get());
  // f will be closed even if use() throws
}
```

Smart Pointers

Incidentally, notice that the destructor of `std::unique_ptr` is carefully written so that it guarantees never to call your callback with a null pointer. This is absolutely critical in the preceding example, because `fclose(NULL)` is a special case that means "close all open file handles in the current process"--which is never what you wanted to do!

Observe also that `std::make_unique<T>()` only ever takes one template type parameter; there is no `std::make_unique<T,D>()`. But the rule to avoid touching raw pointers with your hands is still a good one; that's why our preceding example wraps the `fopen` and `unique_ptr` construction into a small reusable helper function `fcloser::open`, rather than inlining the call to `fopen` into the body of `test`.

The space for your custom deleter will be allocated in the body of the `std::unique_ptr<T,D>` object itself, which means `sizeof(unique_ptr<T,D>)` may be bigger than `sizeof(unique_ptr<T>)` if D has any member data:

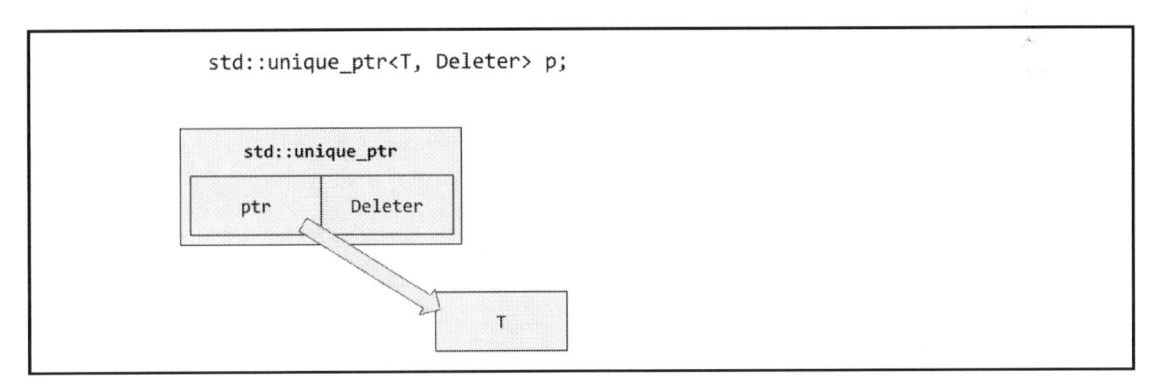

```
std::unique_ptr<T, Deleter> p;

    std::unique_ptr
    ┌──────┬─────────┐
    │ ptr  │ Deleter │
    └──┬───┴─────────┘
       │
       ▼
      ┌───┐
      │ T │
      └───┘
```

Managing arrays with std::unique_ptr<T[]>

Another case where `delete p` is not the appropriate way to free a raw pointer is if p is a pointer to the first element of an array; in that case, `delete [] p` should be used instead. Fortunately, as of C++14, `std::unique_ptr<T[]>` exists and does the right thing in this case (by virtue of the fact that `std::default_delete<T[]>` also exists and does the right thing, which is to call `operator delete[]`).

An overload of `std::make_unique` for array types does exist, although be careful--it assigns a different meaning to its argument! `std::make_unique<T[]>(n)` essentially calls `new T[n]()`, where the parentheses on the end signify that it's going to value-initialize all the elements; that is, it will zero out primitive types. In the rare case that you don't want this behavior, you'll have to call `new` yourself and wrap the return value in a `std::unique_ptr<T[]>`, preferably using a helper function as we did in the example in the preceding section (where we used `fcloser::open`).

Reference counting with std::shared_ptr<T>

Having completely solved the problem of memory leaks, we now tackle the problem of use-after-free bugs. The essential problem to be solved here is *unclear ownership*--or rather *shared ownership*--of a given resource or chunk of memory. This chunk of memory might have several people looking at it at different times, maybe from different data structures or from different threads, and we want to make sure that all these stakeholders are involved in the decision about when to free it. The ownership of the underlying chunk of memory should be *shared*.

For this, the standard has provided `std::shared_ptr<T>`. Its interface appears very similar to `std::unique_ptr<T>`; all of the differences are hidden under the hood, in the implementations of the special member functions.

`std::shared_ptr<T>` provides an approach to memory management that is often known as *reference counting*. Each object managed by a `shared_ptr` keeps count of how many references to it are in the system--that is, how many stakeholders care about it right now--and as soon as that number drops to zero, the object knows it's time to clean itself up. Of course, it's not really "the object" that cleans itself up; the entity that knows how to count references and clean things up is a small wrapper, or "control block," which is created on the heap whenever you transfer ownership of an object to `shared_ptr`. The control block is handled invisibly by the library, but if we were to view its layout in memory, it might look something like this:

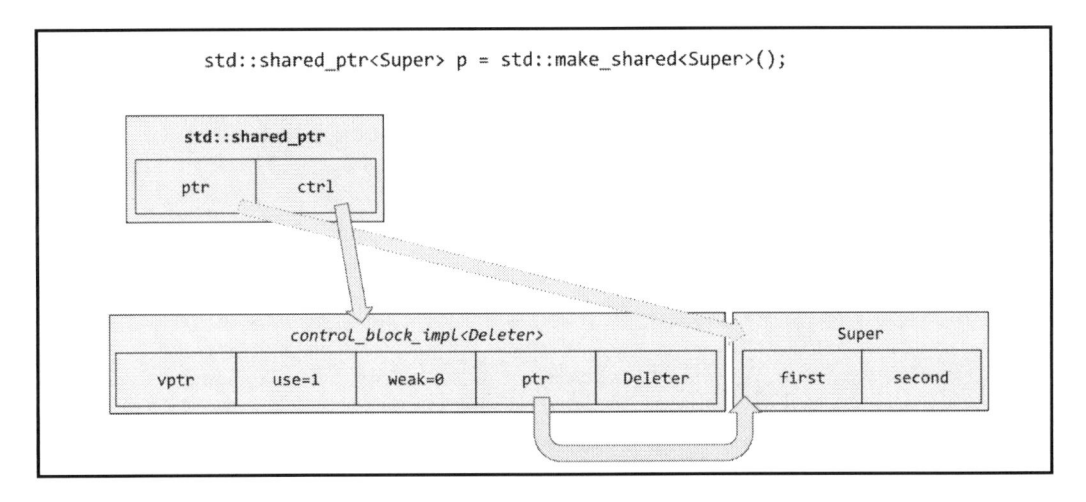

Figure: std::shared_ptr<Super> p = std::make_shared<Super>(); showing shared_ptr (ptr, ctrl) pointing to control_block_impl<Deleter> (vptr, use=1, weak=0, ptr, Deleter) adjacent to Super (first, second).

Just as `unique_ptr` has `make_unique`, the standard library provides `shared_ptr` with `make_shared` so that you never have to touch raw pointers with your hands. The other advantage of using `std::make_shared<T>(args)` to allocate shared objects is that transferring ownership into a `shared_ptr` requires allocating additional memory for the control block. When you call `make_shared`, the library is permitted to allocate a single chunk of memory that's big enough for both the control block *and* your T object, in one allocation. (This is illustrated by the physical placement of the rectangles for `control_block_impl` and `Super` in the preceding diagram.)

Copying a `shared_ptr` increments the "use-count" of its associated control block; destroying a `shared_ptr` decrements its use-count. Assigning over the value of a `shared_ptr` will decrement the use-count of its old value (if any), and increment the use-count of its new value. Here are some examples of playing with `shared_ptr`:

```
std::shared_ptr<X> pa, pb, pc;

pa = std::make_shared<X>();
// use-count always starts at 1

pb = pa;
// make a copy of the pointer; use-count is now 2

pc = std::move(pa);
assert(pa == nullptr);
// moving the pointer keeps the use-count at 2

pb = nullptr;
// decrement the use-count back to 1
assert(pc.use_count() == 1);
```

[153]

Smart Pointers

The following diagram illustrates an interesting and occasionally useful aspect of `shared_ptr`: the ability for two instances of `shared_ptr` to refer to the same control block and yet point to different pieces of the memory being managed by that control block:

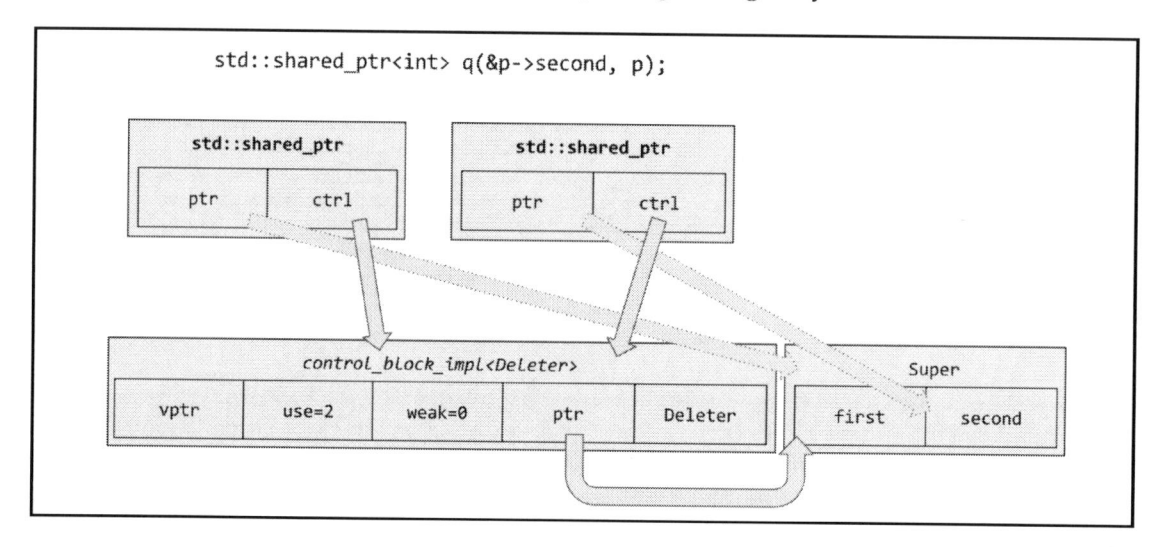

```
                    std::shared_ptr<int> q(&p->second, p);

        ┌─────────────────────────┐   ┌─────────────────────────┐
        │    std::shared_ptr      │   │    std::shared_ptr      │
        │  ┌──────┬──────┐        │   │  ┌──────┬──────┐        │
        │  │ ptr  │ ctrl │        │   │  │ ptr  │ ctrl │        │
        │  └──────┴──────┘        │   │  └──────┴──────┘        │
        └─────────────────────────┘   └─────────────────────────┘

   ┌──────────────────────────────────────────┐   ┌──────────────────┐
   │       control_block_impl<Deleter>        │   │      Super       │
   │ ┌─────┬─────┬──────┬─────┬─────────┐     │   │ ┌───────┬──────┐ │
   │ │vptr │use=2│weak=0│ ptr │ Deleter │     │   │ │ first │second│ │
   │ └─────┴─────┴──────┴─────┴─────────┘     │   │ └───────┴──────┘ │
   └──────────────────────────────────────────┘   └──────────────────┘
```

The constructor being used in the preceding diagram, which is also used in the `get_second()` function, is often called the "aliasing constructor" of `shared_ptr`. It takes an existing non-null `shared_ptr` object of any type, whose control block will be shared by the newly constructed object. In the following code sample, the message "destroying `Super`" will not be printed until *after* the message "accessing `Super::second`":

```
struct Super {
  int first, second;
  Super(int a, int b) : first(a), second(b) {}
  ~Super() { puts("destroying Super"); }
};

auto get_second() {
  auto p = std::make_shared<Super>(4, 2);
  return std::shared_ptr<int>(p, &p->second);
}

void test() {
  std::shared_ptr<int> q = get_second();
  puts("accessing Super::second");
  assert(*q == 2);
}
```

As you can see, once ownership has been transferred into the `shared_ptr` system, the responsibility for remembering how to free a managed resource rests entirely on the shoulders of the control block. It isn't necessary for your code to deal in `shared_ptr<T>` just because the underlying managed object happens to be of type `T`.

Don't double-manage!

While `shared_ptr<T>` has the potential to eliminate nasty double-free bugs from your pointer code, it is sadly all too common for inexperienced programmers to write the same bugs using `shared_ptr` simply by over-using the constructors that take raw pointer arguments. Here's an example:

```
std::shared_ptr<X> pa, pb, pc;

pa = std::make_shared<X>();
  // use-count always starts at 1

pb = pa;
  // make a copy of the pointer; use-count is now 2

pc = std::shared_ptr<X>(pb.get()); // WRONG!
  // give the same pointer to shared_ptr again,
  // which tells shared_ptr to manage it -- twice!
assert(pb.use_count() == 2);
assert(pc.use_count() == 1);

pc = nullptr;
  // pc's use-count drops to zero and shared_ptr
  // calls "delete" on the X object

*pb; // accessing the freed object yields undefined behavior
```

Remember that your goal should be never to touch raw pointers with your hands! The place where this code goes wrong is the very first time it calls `pb.get()` to fetch the raw pointer out of `shared_ptr`.

It would have been correct to call the aliasing constructor here, `pc = std::shared_ptr<X>(pb, pb.get())`, but that would have had the same effect as a simple assignment `pc = pb`. So another general rule we can state is: if you have to use the word `shared_ptr` explicitly in your code, you're doing something out of the ordinary--and perhaps dangerous. *Without* naming `shared_ptr` in your code, you can already allocate and manage heap objects (using `std::make_shared`) and manipulate a managed object's use-count by creating and destroying copies of the pointer (using `auto` to declare variables as you need them). The one place this rule definitely breaks down is when you sometimes need to declare a class data member of type `shared_ptr<T>`; you generally can't do that without writing the name of the type!

Holding nullable handles with weak_ptr

You may have noticed in the previous diagrams, an unexplained data member of the control block marked "weak count". It's time to explain what that is.

Sometimes--it's rare, but sometimes--we have a situation where we're using `shared_ptr` to manage the ownership of shared objects, and we'd like to keep a pointer to an object without actually expressing ownership of that object. Of course we could use a raw pointer, reference, or `observer_ptr<T>` to express the idea of "non-owning reference," but the danger then would be that the actual owners of the referenced object could decide to free it, and then when we went to dereference our non-owning pointer, we'd visit a freed object and get undefined behavior. `DangerousWatcher` in the following code sample illustrates this dangerous behavior:

```
struct DangerousWatcher {
  int *m_ptr = nullptr;

  void watch(const std::shared_ptr<int>& p) {
    m_ptr = p.get();
  }
  int current_value() const {
    // By now, *m_ptr might have been deallocated!
    return *m_ptr;
  }
};
```

We could alternatively use a `shared_ptr` to express the idea of "reference," but of course that would give us an owning reference, making us less of a `Watcher` and more of a `Participant`:

```
struct NotReallyAWatcher {
  std::shared_ptr<int> m_ptr;

  void watch(const std::shared_ptr<int>& p) {
    m_ptr = p;
  }
  int current_value() const {
    // Now *m_ptr cannot ever be deallocated; our
    // mere existence is keeping *m_ptr alive!
    return *m_ptr;
  }
};
```

What we really want is a non-owning reference that is nevertheless aware of the `shared_ptr` system for managing memory, and is able to query the control block and find out whether the referenced object still exists. But by the time we found out that the object existed and went to access it, it might have been deallocated by some other thread! So the primitive operation we need is "atomically get an owning reference (a `shared_ptr`) to the referenced object if it exists, or otherwise indicate failure." That is, we don't want a *non-owning reference*; what we want is a *ticket that we can exchange at some future date for an owning reference*.

The standard library provides this "ticket for a `shared_ptr`" under the name `std::weak_ptr<T>`. (It's called "weak" in opposition to the "strong" owning references of `shared_ptr`.) Here's an example of how to use `weak_ptr` to solve our `Watcher` problem:

```
struct CorrectWatcher {
  std::weak_ptr<int> m_ptr;

  void watch(const std::shared_ptr<int>& p) {
    m_ptr = std::weak_ptr<int>(p);
  }
  int current_value() const {
    // Now we can safely ask whether *m_ptr has been
    // deallocated or not.
    if (auto p = m_ptr.lock()) {
        return *p;
    } else {
      throw "It has no value; it's been deallocated!";
    }
  }
};
```

Smart Pointers

The only two operations you need to know with `weak_ptr` are that you can construct a `weak_ptr<T>` from a `shared_ptr<T>` (by calling the constructor, as shown in the `watch()` function), and you can attempt to construct a `shared_ptr<T>` from a `weak_ptr<T>` by calling `wptr.lock()`. If the `weak_ptr` has expired, you'll get back a null `shared_ptr`.

There's also the member function `wptr.expired()`, which can tell you if the `weak_ptr` in question has already expired; but notice that it's essentially useless, since even if it returns `false` right now, it might return `true` a few microseconds later.

The following diagram continues the narrative started in the previous diagram by creating `weak_ptr` from `q` and then nulling out the `shared_ptr` it came from:

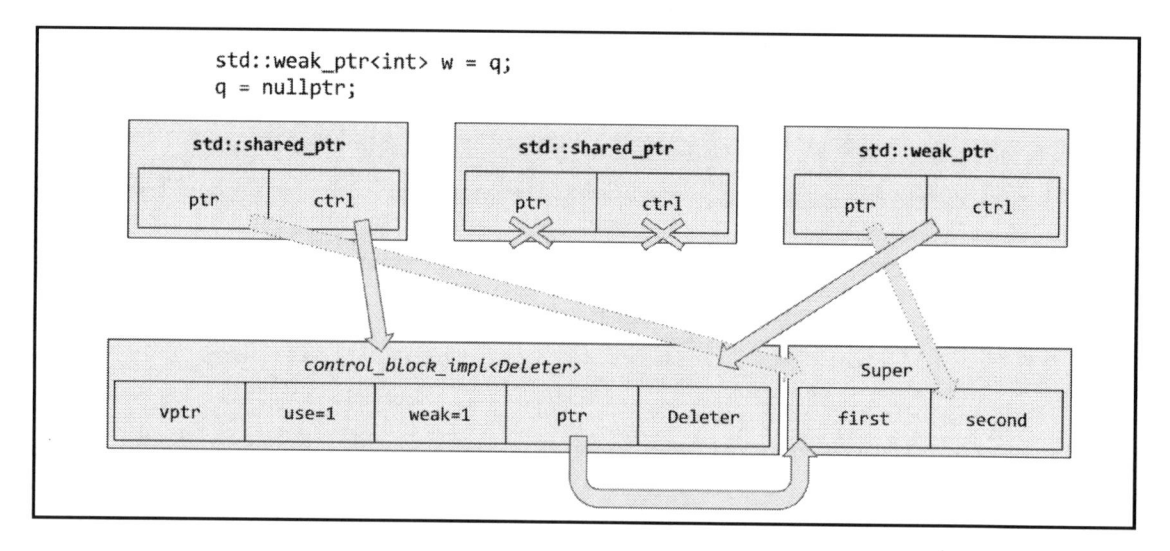

Copying a `weak_ptr` increments the weak-count associated with the referenced object's control block, and destroying a `weak_ptr` decrements the weak-count. When the use-count hits zero, the system knows it's safe to deallocate the controlled object; but the control block itself will not be deallocated until the weak-count hits zero, at which point we know that there are no more `weak_ptr` objects pointing at this control block:

```
p = nullptr;   // decrement the use-count to zero
```

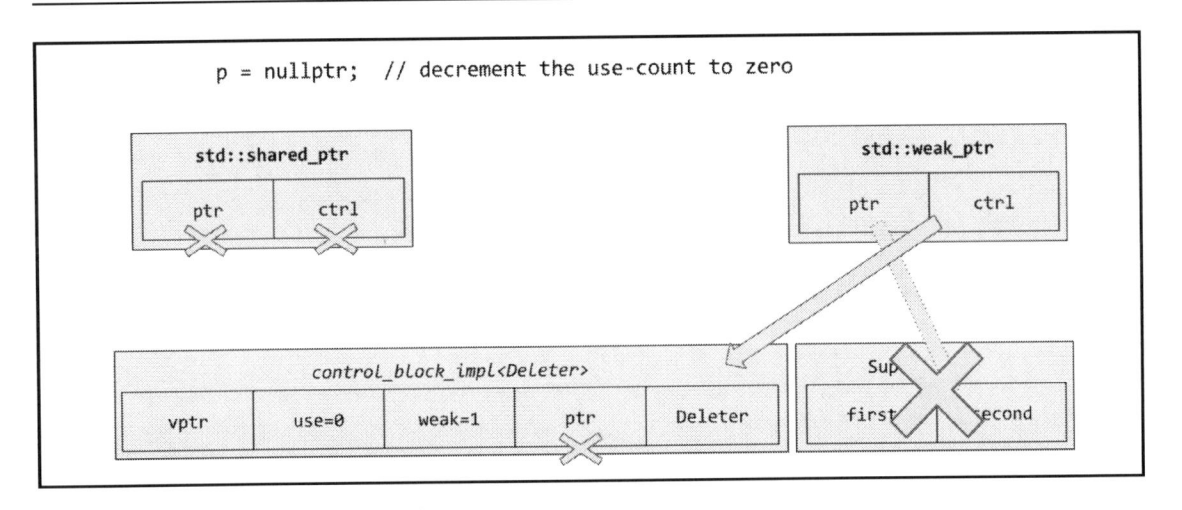

[Diagram: std::shared_ptr (ptr, ctrl) both crossed out; std::weak_ptr (ptr, ctrl) pointing to control_block_impl<Deleter> with vptr, use=0, weak=1, ptr (crossed out), Deleter; Sub-object with first, second crossed out]

You might have noticed that `shared_ptr` is using the same trick on its `Deleter` that we saw in the context of `std::any` and `std::function` in Chapter 5, *Vocabulary Types*--it is using *type erasure*. And, like `std::any` and `std::function`, `std::shared_ptr` provides a "go fish" function--`std::get_deleter<Deleter>(p)`--to retrieve the original deleter object. This tidbit will be entirely useless to you in your work; I mention it only to call attention to the importance of type erasure in modern C++. Even `shared_ptr`, whose ostensible purpose has nothing to do with erasing types, relies on type erasure in one little corner of its functionality.

Talking about oneself with std::enable_shared_from_this

There's just one more piece of the `shared_ptr` ecosystem that we should discuss. We've mentioned the danger of "double-managing" a pointer by creating multiple control blocks. So we might want a way to ask, given a pointer to a heap-allocated object, just who exactly is managing it right now.

The most common use-case for this feature is in object-oriented programming, where a method `A::foo()` wants to invoke some external function `bar()`, and `bar()` needs a pointer back to the `A` object. If we weren't worrying about lifetime management, this would be easy; `A::foo()` would simply invoke `bar(this)`. But let's say our `A` is being managed by `shared_ptr`, and let's say that `bar()` is likely to stash a copy of the `this` pointer somewhere internally--maybe we're registering a callback for later, or maybe we're spawning a new thread that will run concurrently while `A::foo()` finishes up and returns to its caller. So we need some way to keep `A` alive while `bar()` is still running.

Smart Pointers

Clearly `bar()` should take a parameter of type `std::shared_ptr<A>`; this will keep our A alive. But within `A::foo()`, where do we get that `shared_ptr` from? We could give A a member variable of type `std::shared_ptr<A>`, but then A would be keeping *itself* alive--it would never die! That's certainly not what we want!

A preliminary solution is that A should keep a member variable of type `std::weak_ptr<A>` pointing to itself, and when it invokes `bar`, it should do so with `bar(this->m_wptr.lock())`. This has quite a bit of syntactic overhead, though, and besides it's unclear how the pointer `m_wptr` ought to get initialized. So, C++ took this idea and built it right into the standard library!

```
template<class T>
class enable_shared_from_this {
  weak_ptr<T> m_weak;
public:
  enable_shared_from_this(const enable_shared_from_this&) {}
  enable_shared_from_this& operator=(const enable_shared_from_this&) {}
  shared_ptr<T> shared_from_this() const {
    return shared_ptr<T>(m_weak);
  }
};
```

The `std::enable_shared_from_this<A>` class holds our member variable of type `std::weak_ptr<A>`, and exposes the operation "get a `shared_ptr` to myself" under the name `x.shared_from_this()`. There are a couple of interesting details to notice in the preceding code: First, if you try to call `x.shared_from_this()` on an object that isn't currently being managed by the `shared_ptr` system, you'll get an exception of type `std::bad_weak_ptr`. Second, notice the empty copy constructor and copy assignment operator. Empty braces in this case is *not* the same thing as `=default`! If we had used `=default` to make the copy operations defaulted, they would have performed memberwise copying. Every time you made a copy of a managed object, the new object would receive a copy of the original's `m_weak`; which isn't what we want here at all. The "identity" of the `enable_shared_from_this` portion of a C++ object is tied to its *location in memory*, and therefore it does not (and should not) follow the rules of copying and value semantics for which we typically strive.

Smart Pointers

The last question to answer is: how does the member `m_weak` (which remember is a *private* member; we're using the name `m_weak` purely for exposition) get initialized in the first place? The answer is that the constructor of `shared_ptr` includes some lines of code to detect whether T publicly inherits from `enable_shared_from_this<T>`, and, if so, to set its `m_weak` member through some hidden back door. Notice that the inheritance must be *public* and *unambiguous*, since the constructor of `shared_ptr` is just another user-defined function as far as the rules of C++ are concerned; it can't crack open your class to find its private base classes, or to disambiguate between multiple copies of `enable_shared_from_this`.

> **TIP**
> These restrictions imply that you should only ever inherit from `enable_shared_from_this` publicly; that once a class derives from `enable_shared_from_this` you should only ever inherit from *it* publicly; and to keep things simple you probably ought to inherit from `enable_shared_from_this` only at the very leaves of your inheritance hierarchy. Of course, if you do not make deep inheritance hierarchies in the first place, following these rules will be fairly easy!

Let's put everything we know about `enable_shared_from_this` together into a single example:

```
struct Widget : std::enable_shared_from_this<Widget> {
  template<class F>
  void call_on_me(const F& f) {
    f(this->shared_from_this());
  }
};

void test() {
  auto sa = std::make_shared<Widget>();

  assert(sa.use_count() == 1);
  sa->call_on_me([](auto sb) {
    assert(sb.use_count() == 2);
  });

  Widget w;
  try {
    w.call_on_me([](auto) {});
  } catch (const std::bad_weak_ptr&) {
    puts("Caught!");
  }
}
```

[161]

The Curiously Recurring Template Pattern

You may already have noticed, but especially after seeing the preceding code sample it should be apparent, that whenever you inherit from `enable_shared_from_this` the name of *your class* always appears in the template parameter list of its own base class! This pattern of "X inherits from A<X>" is known as the **Curiously Recurring Template Pattern**, or **CRTP** for short. It's common whenever some aspect of the base class depends on its derived class. For example, in our case the name of the derived class is incorporated into the return type of the `shared_from_this` method.

Another common case where the CRTP is warranted is when some *behavior* of the derived class is incorporated into the behavior provided by the base class. For example, using the CRTP we can write a base class template that provides a value-returning `operator+` for any derived class that implements `operator+=` and copy-construction. Notice the required `static_cast` from `addable<Derived>` to `Derived`, so that we call the copy constructor of `Derived` instead of the copy constructor of the base class `addable<Derived>`:

```
template<class Derived>
class addable {
public:
  auto operator+(const Derived& rhs) const {
    Derived lhs = static_cast<const Derived&>(*this);
    lhs += rhs;
    return lhs;
  }
};
```

In fact, this is almost exactly the service provided by `boost::addable` in the Boost Operators library; except that `boost::addable` uses the so-called "Barton-Nackman trick" to make its `operator+` a friend free function instead of a member function:

```
template<class Derived>
class addable {
public:
  friend auto operator+(Derived lhs, const Derived& rhs) {
    lhs += rhs;
    return lhs;
  }
};
```

Even if you never use `enable_shared_from_this` in your codebase, you should be aware of the Curiously Recurring Template Pattern and be able to pull it out of your toolbox whenever you need to "inject" some derived-class behavior into a method of your base class.

A final warning

The mini-ecosystem of `shared_ptr`, `weak_ptr`, and `enable_shared_from_this` is one of the coolest parts of modern C++; it can give your code the safety of a garbage-collected language while preserving the speed and deterministic destruction that have always characterized C++. However, be careful not to abuse `shared_ptr`! Most of your C++ code shouldn't be using `shared_ptr` at all, because you shouldn't be *sharing* the ownership of heap-allocated objects. Your first preference should always be to avoid heap-allocation altogether (by using value semantics); your second preference should be to make sure each heap-allocated object has a unique owner (by using `std::unique_ptr<T>`); and only if both of those are really impossible should you consider use of shared ownership and `std::shared_ptr<T>`.

Denoting un-special-ness with observer_ptr<T>

We've now seen two or three different smart pointer types (depending on whether you count `weak_ptr` as a pointer type in its own right, or more like a ticket for a `shared_ptr`). Each of these types carries with it some useful source-level information about lifetime management. For example, just from the function signatures of these two C++ functions, what can we say about their semantics?

```
void remusnoc(std::unique_ptr<Widget> p);

std::unique_ptr<Widget> recudorp();
```

We see that `remusnoc` takes a `unique_ptr` by value, which means that ownership of the controlled object is transferred to `remusnoc`. When we call this function, we must have *unique ownership* of a `Widget`, and after we call this function, we will no longer be able to access that `Widget`. We don't know whether `remusnoc` is going to destroy the `Widget`, keep it around, or attach it to some other object or thread; but it's explicitly *no longer our concern*. The `remusnoc` function is a *consumer* of widgets.

More subtly, we can also say that when we call `remusnoc`, we must have unique ownership of a `Widget` that was allocated with `new`, and which it is safe to `delete`!

Smart Pointers

And vice versa: when I call `recudorp`, I know that whatever `Widget` we receive will be *uniquely owned* by me. It isn't a reference to someone else's `Widget`; it isn't a pointer to some static data. It's explicitly a heap-allocated `Widget` owned by me and me alone. Even if the first thing I do with the return value is to call `.release()` on it and stuff the raw pointer into some "pre-modern" struct, I can be sure that it is *safe* to do so, because I am definitely the *unique owner* of the return value.

What can we say about the semantics of this C++ function?

```
void suougibma(Widget *p);
```

It's ambiguous. Maybe this function will take ownership of the passed pointer; maybe it won't. We can tell (we hope) from the documentation of `suougibma`, or from certain stylistic conventions in our codebase (such as "a raw pointer shall never denote ownership," which is a reasonable convention), but we can't tell from the signature alone. Another way to express this distinction is to say that `unique_ptr<T>` is a *vocabulary type* for expressing ownership transfer, whereas `T*` is not a vocabulary type for anything at all; it's the C++ equivalent of a nonsense word or a Rorschach blot, in that no two people will necessarily agree on what it means.

So, if you find yourself passing around a lot of non-owning pointers in your codebase, you might want a *vocabulary type* to represent the idea of a non-owning pointer. (Your first step should be to pass references instead of pointers whenever possible, but let's say that you've already exhausted that avenue.) Such a vocabulary type does exist, although it is not (yet) in the C++ standard library: due to Walter Brown, it's called "the world's dumbest smart pointer," and is merely a class-shaped wrapper around a raw non-owning pointer:

```
template<typename T>
class observer_ptr {
  T *m_ptr = nullptr;
public:
  constexpr observer_ptr() noexcept = default;
  constexpr observer_ptr(T *p) noexcept : m_ptr(p) {}
  T *get() const noexcept { return m_ptr; }
  operator bool() const noexcept { return bool(get()); }
  T& operator*() const noexcept { return *get(); }
  T* operator->() const noexcept { return get(); }
};

void revresbo(observer_ptr<Widget> p);
```

With `observer_ptr` in our toolbox, it becomes crystal clear that `revresbo` merely *observes* its argument; it definitely doesn't take ownership of it. In fact, we can assume that it doesn't even keep a copy of the passed-in pointer, because the validity of that pointer would depend on the lifetime of the controlled object, and `revresbo` is explicitly claiming not to have any stake in the lifetime of that object. If it wanted a stake in the lifetime of the controlled object, it would ask for that stake explicitly, by requesting `unique_ptr` or `shared_ptr` from its caller. By requesting `observer_ptr`, `revresbo` is "opting out" of the whole ownership debate.

As I said, `observer_ptr` is not part of the C++17 standard. One of the main objections keeping it out is its terrible name (being as it has nothing to do with the "observer pattern"). There are also many knowledgeable people who would say that `T*` *should* be the vocabulary type for "non-owning pointer," and that all old code using `T*` for ownership transfer should be rewritten or at least re-annotated with constructs such as `owner<T*>`. This is the approach currently recommended by the editors of the C++ Core Guidelines, including C++ inventor Bjarne Stroustrup. One thing is certain, though: *never use raw pointers for ownership transfer!*

Summary

In this chapter, we have learned a few things about smart pointers.

`std::unique_ptr<T>` is a vocabulary type for ownership, and for ownership transfer; prefer it over raw `T*`. Consider the use of `observer_ptr` in situations where ownership is explicitly *not* being transferred, or where raw `T*` might be ambiguous to the reader.

`std::shared_ptr<T>` is a good (and standard) tool for dealing with shared ownership, where many different entities are all stakeholders in the lifetime of a single controlled object. `std::weak_ptr<T>` is a "ticket for `shared_ptr`"; it provides `.lock()` instead of `operator*`. If your class needs the ability to get `shared_ptr` to itself, inherit from `std::enable_shared_from_this<T>`. Remember to inherit publicly, and generally speaking, only at the leaves of your inheritance graph. And don't overuse these features in situations that do not absolutely require shared ownership!

Smart Pointers

Never touch raw pointers with your hands: use `make_unique` and `make_shared` to create heap-allocated objects and manage them in a single swoop. And remember the Curiously Recurring Template Pattern whenever you need to "inject" derived-class behaviors back into a function provided by your base class.

In the next chapter, we'll talk about a different kind of "sharing": the kind that arises in multi-threaded programming.

7
Concurrency

In the previous chapter, we discussed how `std::shared_ptr<T>` implements reference-counting memory management, so that an object's lifetime can be cooperatively controlled by stakeholders who might be otherwise unaware of each other--for example, the stakeholders might live in different threads. In C++ before C++11, this would have posed a stumbling block right away: if one stakeholder decrements the reference count while, simultaneously, a stakeholder in another thread is in the process of decrementing the reference count, then don't we have a *data race* and therefore undefined behavior?

In C++ before C++11, the answer was generally "yes." (In fact, C++ before C++11 didn't have a standard concept of "threads," so another reasonable answer might have been that the question itself was irrelevant.) In C++ as of 2011, though, we have a standard memory model that accounts for concepts such as "threading" and "thread-safety," and so the question is meaningful and the answer is categorically "No!" Accesses to the reference count of `std::shared_ptr` are guaranteed not to race with each other; and in this chapter we'll show you how you can implement similarly thread-safe constructions using the tools the standard library provides.

In this chapter we'll cover the following topics:

- The difference between `volatile T` and `std::atomic<T>`
- `std::mutex`, `std::lock_guard<M>`, and `std::unique_lock<M>`
- `std::recursive_mutex` and `std::shared_mutex`
- `std::condition_variable` and `std::condition_variable_any`
- `std::promise<T>` and `std::future<T>`
- `std::thread` and `std::async`
- The dangers of `std::async`, and how to build a thread pool to replace it

Concurrency

The problem with volatile

If you've been living under a rock for the past ten years--or if you're coming from old-style C--you might ask, "What's wrong with the `volatile` keyword? When I want to make sure some access really hits memory, I make sure it's done `volatile`."

The official semantics of `volatile` are that volatile accesses are evaluated strictly according to the rules of the abstract machine, which means, more or less, that the compiler is not allowed to reorder them or combine multiple accesses into one. For example, the compiler cannot assume that the value of x remains the same between these two loads; it must generate machine code that performs two loads, one on either side of the store to y:

```
volatile int& x = memory_mapped_register_x();
volatile bool& y = memory_mapped_register_y();
int stack;

stack = x;  // load
y = true;   // store
stack += x; // load
```

If x were not volatile, then the compiler would be perfectly within its rights to reorder the code like this:

```
stack = 2*x; // load
y = true;    // store
```

The compiler could do this (if x weren't volatile) because the write to a `bool` variable y cannot possibly affect the value of the `int` variable x. However, since x is volatile, this reordering optimization is not allowed.

The most common reason you'd use the `volatile` keyword is suggested by the names I chose for that example: the use-case is when you are working directly with hardware, such as memory-mapped registers, where something that looks like a load or store at the source-code level actually maps onto a more complex hardware operation. In the preceding example, perhaps x is a view onto some hardware buffer, and the store to memory location y is the signal for the hardware to load the next four bytes of data into the x register. It might help to view the situation as an operator overloading, but in hardware. And if "operator overloading, but in hardware" sounds crazy to you, then you probably have zero reason to use `volatile` in your programs!

So that's what `volatile` does. But why can't we use `volatile` to make our programs thread-safe? In essence, the problem with `volatile` is that it's too old. The keyword has been in C++ ever since we split off from C, and it was in C since the original standard in 1989. Back then, there was very little concern about multithreading, and compilers were simpler, which meant that some potentially problematic optimizations had not yet been dreamt of. By the late 1990s and early 2000s, when C++'s lack of a thread-aware memory model started to become a real concern, it was too late to make `volatile` do everything that was required for thread-safe memory access, because every vendor had already implemented `volatile` and documented exactly what it did. Changing the rules at that point would have broken a lot of people's code--and the code that would have broken would have been low-level hardware interface code, the kind of code you really don't want bugs in.

Here are a couple of examples of the kind of guarantee we need in order to get thread-safe memory accesses:

```
// Global variables:
int64_t x = 0;
bool y = false;

void thread_A() {
    x = 0x42'00000042;
    y = true;
}

void thread_B() {
  if (x) {
     assert(x == 0x42'00000042);
  }
}

void thread_C() {
  if (y) {
     assert(x == 0x42'00000042);
  }
}
```

Concurrency

Suppose `thread_A`, `thread_B`, and `thread_C` are all running concurrently in different threads. How could this code go wrong? Well, `thread_B` is checking that x always holds exactly either zero or `0x42'00000042`. On a 32-bit computer, however, it may not be possible to make that guarantee; the compiler might have to implement the assignment in `thread_A` as a pair of assignments "set the upper half of x to 42; set the lower half of x to 42." If the test in `thread_B` happens to run at the right (wrong) time, it could end up seeing x as `0x42'00000000`. Making x volatile will not help with this one; in fact, nothing will, because our 32-bit hardware simply doesn't support this operation! It would be nice for the compiler to detect that we're trying to get an atomic 64-bit assignment, and give us a compile-time error if it knows our goal is impossible. In other words, `volatile` accesses are not guaranteed to be *atomic*. In practice, they often are atomic--and so are non-volatile accesses, but they aren't *guaranteed* to be, and sometimes you have to go down to the machine code level to figure out whether you're getting the code you expected. We'd like a way to guarantee that an access will be atomic (or if that's impossible, we'd like a compiler error).

Now consider `thread_C`. It's checking that *if* the value of y is visibly true, *then* the value of x must already be set to its final value. In other words, it's checking that the write to x "happened before" the write to y. This is definitely true from the point of view of `thread_A`, at least if x and y are both volatile, because we have seen that the compiler is not allowed to reorder volatile accesses. However, the same is not necessarily true from the point of view of `thread_C`! If `thread_C` is running on a different physical CPU, with its own data cache, then it may become aware of the updated values of x and y at different times, depending on when it refreshes their respective cache lines. We would like a way to say that when the compiler loads from y, it must also ensure that its entire cache is up-to-date--that it will never read a "stale" value for x. However, on some processor architectures, that requires special instructions, or additional memory-barrier logic. The compiler doesn't generate those instructions for "old-style" volatile accesses, because threading wasn't a concern when `volatile` was invented; and the compiler can't be *made* to generate those instructions for volatile accesses, because that would unnecessarily slow down or maybe even break, all the existing low-level code that uses old-style `volatile` for its old-style meaning. So we're left with the problem that even though volatile accesses happen in sequential order from the point of view of their own thread, they may well appear in a different order from the point of view of another thread. In other words, `volatile` accesses are not guaranteed to be *sequentially consistent*. We'd like a way to guarantee that an access will be sequentially consistent with respect to other accesses.

The solution to both of our problems was added to C++ in 2011. That solution is `std::atomic`.

Using std::atomic<T> for thread-safe accesses

In C++11 and later, the `<atomic>` header contains the definition of class template `std::atomic<T>`. There are two different ways you can think about `std::atomic`: you can think of it as a class template just like `std::vector`, with overloaded operators that just happen to implement thread-safe operations; or you can think of it as a magical built-in family of types whose names just happen to contain angle brackets. The latter way of thinking about it is actually pretty useful, because it suggests--correctly--that `std::atomic` is partly built into the compiler, and so the compiler will usually generate optimal code for atomic operations. The latter also suggests a way in which `atomic` is different from `vector`: with `std::vector<T>`, the `T` can be pretty much anything you like. With `std::atomic<T>`, the `T` is *can* be anything you like, but in practice it is a bad idea to use any `T` that doesn't belong to a small set of *atomic-friendly* types. More on this topic in a moment.

The *atomic-friendly* types are the integral types (at least, those no bigger than a machine register) and the pointer types. Generally speaking, on common platforms, you'll find that operations on `std::atomic` objects of these types will do exactly what you want:

```
// Global variables:
std::atomic<int64_t> x = 0;
std::atomic<bool> y = false;

void thread_A() {
  x = 0x42'00000042; // atomic!
  y = true; // atomic!
}

void thread_B() {
  if (x) {
    // The assignment to x happens atomically.
    assert(x == 0x42'00000042);
  }
}

void thread_C() {
  if (y) {
    // The assignment to x "happens before" the
    // assignment to y, even from another thread's
    // point of view.
    assert(x == 0x42'00000042);
  }
}
```

`std::atomic<T>` overloads its assignment operator to perform atomic, thread-safe assignment; and likewise its `++`, `--`, `+=`, and `-=` operators; and for integral types, also the `&=`, `|=`, and `^=` operators.

It's important to bear in mind the difference between *objects* of type `std::atomic<T>` (which conceptually live "out there" in memory) and short-lived *values* of type `T` (which conceptually live "right here," close at hand; for example, in CPU registers). So, for example, there is no copy-assignment operator for `std::atomic<int>`:

```
std::atomic<int> a, b;
a = b; // DOES NOT COMPILE!
```

There's no copy-assignment operator (nor move-assignment operator) because it wouldn't have a clear meaning: Does the programmer mean that the computer should load the value of b into a register and then store the value of that register into a? That sounds like two different atomic operations, not one operation! Or the programmer might mean that the computer should copy the value from b to a in a single atomic operation; but that involves touching two different memory locations in a single atomic operation, which is not within the capabilities of most computer hardware. So instead, C++ requires that you write out explicitly what you mean: a single atomic load from object b into a register (represented in C++ by a non-atomic stack variable), and then a single atomic store into object a:

```
int shortlived = b; // atomic load
a = shortlived; // atomic store
```

`std::atomic<T>` provides the member functions `.load()` and `.store(v)` for the benefit of programmers who like to see what they're doing at every step. Using them is optional:

```
int shortlived = b.load(); // atomic load
a.store(shortlived); // atomic store
```

In fact, by using these member functions, you *could* write the assignment in a single line of code as `b.store(a.load());` but I advise strongly against doing that. Writing both function calls on one line of code does *not* mean that they'll happen "closer together" in time, and *certainly* doesn't mean they'll happen "atomically" (as we've just seen, that's impossible on most hardware), but writing both function calls on one line of code might very well *deceive you into thinking* that the calls happen "together."

Dealing with threaded code is hard enough when you're doing only one thing at a time. If you start getting clever and doing several things at once, in a single line of code, the potential for bugs skyrockets. Stick to a single atomic operation per source line; you'll find that it clarifies your thinking process and incidentally makes your code easier to read.

Doing complicated operations atomically

You may have noticed that the operators `*=`, `/=`, `%=`, `<<=`, and `>>=` were omitted from the list of overloaded operators in the preceding section. These operators were deleted by `std::atomic<int>` and all the rest of the integral atomic types because they were perceived as being difficult to provide efficiently on any real hardware. However, even among the operations that were included in `std::atomic<int>`, most of them require a slightly expensive implementation trick.

Let's suppose that our hardware doesn't have an "atomic multiply" instruction, but we'd still like to implement `operator*=`). How would we do it? The trick is to use a primitive atomic operation known as "compare and swap," or in C++ "compare-exchange."

```
std::atomic<int> a = 6;

a *= 9; // This isn't allowed.

// But this is:

int expected, desired;
do {
  expected = a.load();
  desired = expected * 9;
} while (!a.compare_exchange_weak(expected, desired));

// At the end of this loop, a's value will
// have been "atomically" multiplied by 9.
```

The meaning of `a.compare_exchange_weak(expected, desired)` is that the processor should look at `a`; and *if* its value is currently `expected`, then set its value to `desired`; otherwise don't. The function call returns `true` if `a` was set to `desired` and `false` otherwise.

But there's one more thing it does, too. Notice that every time through the preceding loop, we're loading the value of `a` into `expected`; but the compare-exchange function is also loading the value of `a` in order to compare it with `expected`. The second time we go through the loop, we'd prefer not to load `a` a second time; we'd prefer simply to set `expected` to the value that the compare-exchange function saw. Fortunately, `a.compare_exchange_weak(expected, desired)` anticipates this desire of ours, and preemptively--if it would return `false`--updates `expected` to the value it saw. That is, whenever we use `compare_exchange_weak`, we must provide a modifiable value for `expected` because the function takes it by reference.

Therefore, we should really write our example like this:

```
int expected = a.load();
while (!a.compare_exchange_weak(expected, expected * 9)) {
  // continue looping
}
```

The `desired` variable isn't really necessary except if it helps to clarify the code.

The dirty little secret of `std::atomic` is that most of the compound assignment operations are implemented as compare-exchange loops just like this. On RISC processors, this is practically always the case. On x86 processors, this is the case only if you want to use the return value of the operator, as in `x = (a += b)`.

When the atomic variable `a` isn't being modified very frequently by other threads, there's no harm in doing a compare-exchange loop. But when `a` is being frequently modified--when it is highly *contended*--then we might see the loop being taken several times before it succeeds. In an absolutely pathological case, we might even see starvation of the looping thread; it might just keep looping forever, until the contention died down. However, notice that every time our compare-exchange returns `false` and we loop around again, it is because the value of `a` in memory has changed; which means that some other thread must have made a little bit of progress. Compare-exchange loops by themselves will never cause the program to enter a state where *nobody* is making progress (a state known technically as "livelock").

The previous paragraph probably sounds scarier than it ought to. There's generally no need to worry about this pathological behavior, since it manifests itself only under really high contention and even then doesn't really cause any terrible problem. The real takeaway you should take from this section is how you can use a compare-exchange loop to implement complicated, non-built-in "atomic" operations on `atomic<T>` objects. Just remember the order of the parameters to `a.compare_exchange_weak(expected, desired)` by remembering what it does to `a`: "if `a` has the expected value, give it the desired value."

Big atomics

The compiler will recognize and generate optimal code for `std::atomic<T>` when T is an integral type (including `bool`), or when T is a pointer type such as `void *`. But what if T is a bigger type, such as `int[100]`? In that case, the compiler will generally call out to a routine in the C++ runtime library which will perform the assignment under a *mutex*. (We'll look at mutexes in a moment.) Since the assignment is being performed out in a library which doesn't know how to copy arbitrary user-defined types, the C++17 standard restricts `std::atomic<T>` to work only with types that are *trivially copyable*, which is to say they can be copied safely using `memcpy`. So, if you wanted `std::atomic<std::string>`, tough luck--you'll have to write that one yourself.

The other catch when using big (trivially copyable) types with `std::atomic` is that the relevant C++ runtime routines often live in a different place from the rest of the C++ standard library. On some platforms, you'd be required to add `-latomic` to your linker command line. But this is only a problem if you actually do use big types with `std::atomic`, and as you really shouldn't, there's generally no reason to worry.

Now let's look at how you'd write that atomic string class!

Taking turns with std::mutex

Suppose we want to write a class type that behaves basically like `std::atomic<std::string>` would, if it existed. That is, we'd like to make it support atomic, thread-safe loads and stores, so that if two threads are accessing the `std::string` concurrently, neither one will ever observe it in a "halfway assigned" state, the way we observed a "halfway assigned" `int64_t` in the code sample in the previous section "The problem with volatile."

The best way to write this class is to use a standard library type called `std::mutex`. The name "mutex" is so common in technical circles that these days it basically just stands for itself, but originally its name is derived from "*mut*ual *ex*clusion." This is because a mutex acts as a way to ensure that only one thread is allowed into a particular section of code (or set of sections of code) at once--that is, to ensure that the possibilities "thread A is executing this code" and "thread B is executing this code" are *mutually exclusive* possibilities.

At the start of such a critical section, to indicate that we don't want to be disturbed by any other thread, we *take a lock* on the associated mutex. When we leave the critical section, we *release the lock*. The library takes care of making sure that no two threads can hold locks on the same mutex at the same time. Specifically, this means that if thread B comes in while thread A is already holding the lock, thread B must *wait* until thread A leaves the critical section and releases the lock. As long as thread A holds the lock, thread B's progress is *blocked*; therefore this phenomenon is referred to as either *waiting* or *blocking*, interchangeably.

"Taking a lock on a mutex" is often shortened to "locking the mutex," and "releasing the lock" shortened to "unlocking the mutex."

Sometimes (albeit rarely) it can be useful to test whether a mutex is currently locked. For this purpose `std::mutex` exposes not only the member functions `.lock()` and `.unlock()` but also the member function `.try_lock()`, which returns `true` if it was able to acquire a lock on the mutex (in which case the mutex will be locked) and `false` if the mutex was already locked by some thread.

In some languages, like Java, each object carries with it its own mutex; this is how Java implements its `synchronized` blocks, for example. In C++, a mutex is its own object type; when you want to use a mutex to control a section of code, you need to think about the lifetime semantics of the mutex object itself. Where can you put the mutex so that there will be just a single mutex object that is visible to everyone who wants to use it? Sometimes, if there is just one critical section that needs protection, you can put the mutex in a function-scoped static variable:

```
void log(const char *message)
{
  static std::mutex m;
  m.lock(); // avoid interleaving messages on stdout
  puts(message);
  m.unlock();
}
```

The `static` keyword here is very important! If we had omitted it, then `m` would have been a plain old stack variable, and each thread that entered `log` would have received its own distinct copy of `m`. That wouldn't have helped us with our goal, because the library merely ensures that no two threads have a lock on the *same* mutex object at once. If each thread is locking and unlocking its own distinct mutex object, then the library has nothing to do; none of the mutexes are being *contended*.

If we want to make sure that two different functions are mutually exclusive with each other, such that only one thread is allowed in either `log1` or `log2` at any given time, we must put the mutex object somewhere that can be seen by both critical sections:

```
static std::mutex m;

void log1(const char *message) {
  m.lock();
  printf("LOG1: %s\n", message);
  m.unlock();
}

void log2(const char *message) {
  m.lock();
  printf("LOG2: %s\n", message);
  m.unlock();
}
```

Generally, if you find yourself needing to do this, you should try to eliminate the global variable by creating a class type and making the mutex object a member variable of that class, like this:

```
struct Logger {
  std::mutex m_mtx;

  void log1(const char *message) {
    m_mtx.lock();
    printf("LOG1: %s\n", message);
    m_mtx.unlock();
  }

  void log2(const char *message) {
    m_mtx.lock();
    printf("LOG2: %s\n", message);
    m_mtx.unlock();
  }
};
```

Now messages printed by one `Logger` may interleave with messages printed by another `Logger`, but concurrent accesses to the same `Logger` object will take locks on the same `m_mtx`, which means they will block each other and nicely take turns entering the critical functions `log1` and `log2`, one at a time.

"Taking locks" the right way

Recall from `Chapter 6`, *Smart Pointers*, that one of the major problems of programs written in C and "old-style" C++ is the presence of pointer bugs--memory leaks, double-frees, and heap corruption--and that the way we eliminate those bugs from "new-style" C++ programs is via the use of RAII types such as `std::unique_ptr<T>`. Multi-threaded programming with raw mutexes have failure modes that are analogous to the failure modes of heap programming with raw pointers:

- **Lock leaks**: You might take a lock on a particular mutex, and accidentally forget to write the code that frees it.
- **Lock leaks**: You might have written that code, but due to an early return or an exception being thrown, the code never runs and the mutex remains locked!
- **Use-outside-of-lock**: Because a raw mutex is just another variable, it is physically disassociated from the variables it "guards." You might accidentally access one of those variables without taking the lock first.
- **Deadlock**: Suppose thread A takes a lock on mutex 1 and thread B takes a lock on mutex 2. Then, thread A attempts to acquire a lock on mutex 2 (and blocks); and while thread A is still blocked, thread B attempts to acquire a lock on mutex 1 (and blocks). Now both threads are blocked, and will never make progress again.

This is not an exhaustive list of concurrency pitfalls; for example, we've already briefly mentioned "livelock" in connection with `std::atomic<T>`. For a thorough treatment of concurrency bugs and how to avoid them, consult a book on multithreaded or concurrent programming.

The C++ standard library has some tools that help us eliminate these bugs from our multithreaded programs. Unlike the situation with memory management, the standard library's solutions in this case are not 100 percent guaranteed to fix your issues-- multithreading is much harder than single-threaded programming, and in fact a good rule of thumb is *not to do it* if you can help it. But if you must do concurrent programming, the standard library can help somewhat.

Just as in `Chapter 6`, *Smart Pointers*, we can eliminate bugs related to "lock leaks" by the conscientious use of RAII. You might have noticed that I have been consistently using the phrase "take a lock on the mutex" instead of "lock the mutex"; now we'll see why. In the phrase "lock the mutex," "lock" is a *verb*; this phrasing corresponds exactly to the C++ code `mtx.lock()`. But in the phrase "take a lock *on* the mutex," "lock" is a *noun*. Let's invent a type that reifies the idea of "lock"; that is, that turns it into a noun (an RAII class) instead of a verb (a method on a non-RAII class):

```cpp
template<typename M>
class unique_lock {
  M *m_mtx = nullptr;
  bool m_locked = false;
public:
  constexpr unique_lock() noexcept = default;
  constexpr unique_lock(M *p) noexcept : m_mtx(p) {}

  M *mutex() const noexcept { return m_mtx; }
  bool owns_lock() const noexcept { return m_locked; }

  void lock() { m_mtx->lock(); m_locked = true; }
  void unlock() { m_mtx->unlock(); m_locked = false; }

  unique_lock(unique_lock&& rhs) noexcept {
    m_mtx = std::exchange(rhs.m_mtx, nullptr);
    m_locked = std::exchange(rhs.m_locked, false);
  }

  unique_lock& operator=(unique_lock&& rhs) {
    if (m_locked) {
        unlock();
    }
    m_mtx = std::exchange(rhs.m_mtx, nullptr);
    m_locked = std::exchange(rhs.m_locked, false);
    return *this;
  }

  ~unique_lock() {
    if (m_locked) {
        unlock();
    }
  }
};
```

As suggested by the name, `std::unique_lock<M>` is a "unique ownership" RAII class, similar in spirit to `std::unique_ptr<T>`. If you stick to using the noun `unique_ptr` instead of the verbs `new` and `delete`, you'll never forget to free a pointer; and if you stick to using the noun `unique_lock` instead of the verbs `lock` and `unlock`, you'll never forget to release a mutex lock.

Concurrency

`std::unique_lock<M>` does expose the member functions `.lock()` and `.unlock()`, but generally you will not need to use those. They can be useful if you need to acquire or release a lock in the middle of a block of code, far away from the natural point of destruction of the `unique_lock` object. We will also see in the next section a function that takes as a parameter a locked `unique_lock`, which the function unlocks and re-locks as part of its functionality.

Notice that because `unique_lock` is movable, it must have a "null" or "empty" state, just like `unique_ptr`. In most cases, you won't need to move your locks around; you'll just unconditionally take the lock at the start of some scope, and unconditionally release it at the end of the scope. For this use-case, there's `std::lock_guard<M>`. `lock_guard` is much like `unique_lock`, but it is not movable, nor does it have the `.lock()` and `.unlock()` member functions. Therefore, it doesn't need to carry around an `m_locked` member, and its destructor can unconditionally unlock the mutex the object has been guarding, without any extra tests.

In both cases (`unique_lock` and `lock_guard`), the class template is parameterized on the kind of mutex being locked. (We'll look at a couple more kinds of mutexes in a minute, but almost invariably, you'll want to use `std::mutex`.) C++17 has a new language feature called *class template argument deduction* that, in most cases, allows you to elide the template parameter: to write simply `std::unique_lock` instead of `std::unique_lock<std::mutex>`, for example. This is one of the very few cases where I would personally recommend relying on class template argument deduction, because writing out the parameter type `std::mutex` really adds so little information for your reader.

Let's see some examples of `std::lock_guard`, with and without class template argument deduction:

```
struct Lockbox {
  std::mutex m_mtx;
  int m_value = 0;

  void locked_increment() {
    std::lock_guard<std::mutex> lk(m_mtx);
    m_value += 1;
  }

  void locked_decrement() {
    std::lock_guard lk(m_mtx);  // C++17 only
    m_value -= 1;
  }
};
```

Before we can see similarly practical examples of `std::unique_lock`, we'll have to explain a good reason to use `std::unique_lock` in the first place.

Always associate a mutex with its controlled data

Consider the following sketch of a thread-safe `StreamingAverage` class. There is a bug here; can you find it?

```cpp
class StreamingAverage {
  double m_sum = 0;
  int m_count = 0;
  double m_last_average = 0;
  std::mutex m_mtx;
public:
  // Called from the single producer thread
  void add_value(double x) {
    std::lock_guard lk(m_mtx);
    m_sum += x;
    m_count += 1; // A
  }

  // Called from the single consumer thread
  double get_current_average() {
    std::lock_guard lk(m_mtx);
    m_last_average = m_sum / m_count; // B
    return m_last_average;
  }

  // Called from the single consumer thread
  double get_last_average() const {
    return m_last_average; // C
  }

  // Called from the single consumer thread
  double get_current_count() const {
    return m_count; // D
  }
};
```

[181]

The bug is the line A, which writes to `this->m_count` in the producer thread, races with line D, which reads from `this->m_count` in the consumer thread. Line A correctly takes a lock on `this->m_mtx` before writing, but line D fails to take a similar lock, which means that it will happily barge in and attempt to read `m_count` even while line A is writing to it.

Lines B and C look superficially similar, which is probably how the bug originally crept in. Line C doesn't need to take a lock; why should line D have to? Well, line C is called only from the consumer thread, which is the same thread that writes to `m_last_average` on line B. Since lines B and C are executed only by the single consumer thread, they can't both be executed simultaneously--at least as long as the rest of the program conforms to the comments! (Let's assume the code comments are correct. This is often sadly untrue in practice, but for the sake of this example let's assume it.)

We have a recipe for confusion here: Locking `m_mtx` is required when touching `m_sum` or `m_count`, but it is not required when touching `m_last_average`. If this class becomes even more complicated, it might even have several mutexes involved (although at that point, it would clearly be violating the Single Responsibility Principle and would probably benefit from refactoring into smaller components). Therefore, a very good practice when dealing with mutexes is to place the mutex in the tightest possible relationship to the variables it "guards." One way to do this is simply via careful naming:

```
class StreamingAverage {
    double m_sum = 0;
    int m_count = 0;
    double m_last_average = 0;
    std::mutex m_sum_count_mtx;

    // ...
};
```

A better way is via a nested struct definition:

```
class StreamingAverage {
    struct {
        double sum = 0;
        int count = 0;
        std::mutex mtx;
    } m_guarded_sc;
    double m_last_average = 0;

    // ...
};
```

The hope above is that when the programmer is forced to write
`this->m_guarded_sc.sum`, it reminds him to make sure he's already gotten a lock on
`this->m_guarded_sc.mtx`. We could use the GNU extension of "anonymous struct
members" to avoid retyping `m_guarded_sc` all over our code; but this would defeat the
purpose of this approach, which is to make sure that every place the data is accessed *must*
use the word "guarded," reminding the programmer to take that lock on
`this->m_guarded_sc.mtx`.

An even more bulletproof, but somewhat inflexible, approach is to place the mutex in a
class that allows access to its private members only when the mutex is locked, by returning
an RAII handle. The handle-returning class would look more or less like this:

```
template<class Data>
class Guarded {
  std::mutex m_mtx;
  Data m_data;

  class Handle {
    std::unique_lock<std::mutex> m_lk;
    Data *m_ptr;
  public:
    Handle(std::unique_lock<std::mutex> lk, Data *p) :
      m_lk(std::move(lk)), m_ptr(p) {}
    auto operator->() const { return m_ptr; }
  };
public:
  Handle lock() {
    std::unique_lock lk(m_mtx);
    return Handle{std::move(lk), &m_data};
  }
};
```

And our `StreamingAverage` class could use it like this:

```
class StreamingAverage {
  struct Guts {
    double m_sum = 0;
    int m_count = 0;
  };
  Guarded<Guts> m_sc;
  double m_last_average = 0;

  // ...

  double get_current_average() {
    auto h = m_sc.lock();
    m_last_average = h->m_sum / h->m_count;
```

Concurrency

```
            return m_last_average;
      }
};
```

Notice that in the preceding code snippet, it is *impossible* for any member function of `StreamingAverage` to access `m_sum` without owning a lock on `m_mtx`; access to the guarded `m_sum` is possible only via the RAII `Handle` type.

> **TIP**: This pattern is included in Facebook's Folly library under the name `folly::Synchronized<T>`, and many more variations on it are available in Ansel Sermersheim and Barbara Geller's "libGuarded" template library.

Notice the use of `std::unique_lock<std::mutex>` in the `Handle` class! We're using `unique_lock` here, not `lock_guard`, because we want the ability to pass this lock around, return it from functions, and so on--so it needs to be movable. This is the main reason you'd reach into your toolbox for `unique_lock`.

Do be aware that this pattern does not solve all lock-related bugs--it solves only the simplest "forget to lock the mutex" cases--and it might encourage programming patterns that lead to more concurrency bugs of other types. For example, consider the following rewrite of `StreamingAverage::get_current_average`:

```
double get_sum() {
   return m_sc.lock()->m_sum;
}

int get_count() {
   return m_sc.lock()->m_count;
}

double get_current_average() {
   return get_sum() / get_count();
}
```

Because of the two calls to `m_sc.lock()`, there is a gap between the read of `m_sum` and the read of `m_count`. If the producer thread calls `add_value` during this gap, we will compute an incorrect average (too low by a factor of $1 / m\_count$). And if we try to "fix" this bug by taking a lock around the entire computation, we'll find ourselves in deadlock:

```
double get_sum() {
   return m_sc.lock()->m_sum;  // LOCK 2
}

int get_count() {
```

[184]

```
      return m_sc.lock()->m_count;
    }

    double get_current_average() {
      auto h = m_sc.lock();  // LOCK 1
      return get_sum() / get_count();
    }
```

The line marked LOCK 1 causes the mutex to become locked; then, on the line marked LOCK 2, we try to lock the mutex again. The general rule with mutexes is, if you're trying to lock a mutex and it's already locked, then you must *block* and wait for it to become unlocked. So our thread blocks and waits for the mutex to unlock--which will never happen, since the lock is being held by our own thread!

This problem (deadlock with oneself) should generally be dealt with by careful programming--that is, you should try not to take locks you already hold! But if taking locks this way is unavoidably part of your design, then the standard library has your back, so let's talk about recursive_mutex.

Special-purpose mutex types

Recall that std::lock_guard<M> and std::unique_lock<M> are parameterized on the mutex type. So far we've seen only std::mutex. However, the standard library does contain a few other mutex types which can be useful in special circumstances.

std::recursive_mutex is like std::mutex, but remembers *which* thread has locked it. If that particular thread tries to lock it a second time, the recursive mutex will merely increment an internal reference count of "how many times I've been locked." If some other thread tries to lock the recursive mutex, that thread will block until the original thread has unlocked the mutex the appropriate number of times.

std::timed_mutex is like std::mutex, but is aware of the passage of time. It has as member functions not only the usual .try_lock(), but also .try_lock_for() and .try_lock_until(), which interact with the standard <chrono> library. Here's an example of try_lock_for:

```
    std::timed_mutex m;
    std::atomic<bool> ready = false;

    std::thread thread_b([&]() {
      std::lock_guard lk(m);
      puts("Thread B got the lock.");
      ready = true;
```

Concurrency

```cpp
    std::this_thread::sleep_for(100ms);
  });

  while (!ready) {
    puts("Thread A is waiting for thread B to launch.");
    std::this_thread::sleep_for(10ms);
  }

  while (!m.try_lock_for(10ms)) {
    puts("Thread A spent 10ms trying to get the lock and failed.");
  }

  puts("Thread A finally got the lock!");
  m.unlock();
```

And here's an example of `try_lock_until`:

```cpp
  std::timed_mutex m1, m2;
  std::atomic<bool> ready = false;

  std::thread thread_b([&]() {
    std::unique_lock lk1(m1);
    std::unique_lock lk2(m2);
    puts("Thread B got the locks.");
    ready = true;
    std::this_thread::sleep_for(50ms);
    lk1.unlock();
    std::this_thread::sleep_for(50ms);
  });

  while (!ready) {
    std::this_thread::sleep_for(10ms);
  }

  auto start_time = std::chrono::system_clock::now();
  auto deadline = start_time + 100ms;

  bool got_m1 = m1.try_lock_until(deadline);
  auto elapsed_m1 = std::chrono::system_clock::now() - start_time;

  bool got_m2 = m2.try_lock_until(deadline);
  auto elapsed_m2 = std::chrono::system_clock::now() - start_time;

  if (got_m1) {
    printf("Thread A got the first lock after %dms.\n",
      count_ms(elapsed_m1));
    m1.unlock();
  }
```

```
    if (got_m2) {
      printf("Thread A got the second lock after %dms.\n",
        count_ms(elapsed_m2));
      m2.unlock();
    }
```

Incidentally, the `count_ms` function being used here is just a little lambda that factors out some of the usual `<chrono>` boilerplate:

```
    auto count_ms = [](auto&& d) -> int {
      using namespace std::chrono;
      return duration_cast<milliseconds>(d).count();
    };
```

In both of the preceding examples, pay attention to our use of `std::atomic<bool>` to synchronize threads A and B. We simply initialize the atomic variable to `false`, and then loop until it becomes `true`. The body of the polling loop is a call to `std::this_thread::sleep_for`, which is a sufficient hint to the compiler that the value of the atomic variable might change. Be careful never to write a polling loop that does not contain a sleep, because in that case the compiler is within its rights to collapse all the consecutive loads of `ready` down into a single load and a (necessarily infinite) loop.

`std::recursive_timed_mutex` is like you took `recursive_mutex` and `timed_mutex` and smushed them together; it provides the "counting" semantics of `recursive_mutex`, *plus* the `try_lock_for` and `try_lock_until` methods of `timed_mutex`.

`std::shared_mutex` is perhaps poorly named. It implements behavior that in most concurrency textbooks would be called a *read-write lock* (also known as a *rwlock* or *readers-writer lock*). The defining characteristic of a read-write lock, or `shared_mutex`, is that it can be "locked" in two different ways. You can take a normal exclusive ("write") lock by calling `sm.lock()`, or you can take a non-exclusive ("read") lock by calling `sm.lock_shared()`. Many different threads are allowed to take read locks at the same time; but if *anybody* is reading, then *nobody* can be writing; and if *anybody* is writing, then *nobody* can be doing anything else (neither reading nor writing). These happen to be fundamentally the same rules that define "race conditions" in the C++ memory model: two threads reading from the same object simultaneously is fine, as long as no thread is writing to it at the same time. What `std::shared_mutex` adds to the mix is safety: it ensures that if anyone *does* try to write (at least if they play nice and take a write lock on the `std::shared_mutex` first), they'll block until all the readers have exited and it's safe to write.

Concurrency

`std::unique_lock<std::shared_mutex>` is the noun corresponding to an exclusive ("write") lock on a `std::shared_mutex`. As you might expect, the standard library also provides `std::shared_lock<std::shared_mutex>` to reify the idea of a non-exclusive ("read") lock on a `std::shared_mutex`.

Upgrading a read-write lock

Suppose you have a read lock on a `shared_mutex` (that is to say, you have a `std::shared_lock<std::shared_mutex> lk` such that `lk.owns_lock()`), and you want to get a write lock. Can you "upgrade" your lock?

No, you can't. Consider what would happen if threads A and B both hold read locks, and simultaneously attempt to upgrade to write locks without first releasing their read locks. Neither one would be able to acquire a write lock, and so they'd deadlock with each other.

There *are* third-party libraries that attempt to solve this problem, such as `boost::thread::upgrade_lock`, which works with `boost::thread::shared_mutex`; but they are outside the scope of this book. The standard solution is that if you hold a read lock and want a write lock, you must release your read lock and then go stand in line for a write lock with everyone else:

```
template<class M>
std::unique_lock<M> upgrade(std::shared_lock<M> lk)
{
  lk.unlock();
  // Some other writer might sneak in here.
  return std::unique_lock<M>(*lk.mutex());
}
```

Downgrading a read-write lock

Suppose you have an exclusive write lock on a `shared_mutex` and you want to get a read lock. Can you "downgrade" your lock?

[188]

In principle the answer is yes, it should be possible to downgrade a write lock to a read lock; but in standard C++17 the answer is no, you can't do it directly. As in the upgrade case, you can use `boost::thread::shared_mutex`. The standard solution is that if you hold a write lock and want a read lock, you must release your write lock and then go stand in line for a read lock with everyone else:

```
template<class M>
std::shared_lock<M> downgrade(std::unique_lock<M> lk)
{
  lk.unlock();
  // Some other writer might sneak in here.
  return std::shared_lock<M>(*lk.mutex());
}
```

As you can see from these examples, C++17's `std::shared_mutex` is a bit half-baked at the moment. If your architectural design calls for a read-write lock, I strongly recommend using something like `boost::thread::shared_mutex`, which comes "batteries included."

You may have noticed that since new readers can come in while a read lock is held, but new writers cannot, it is conceivable and even likely for a prospective writer thread to be "starved" by a steady stream of prospective readers, unless the implementation goes out of its way to provide a strong "no starvation" guarantee. `boost::thread::shared_mutex` provides such a guarantee (at least, it avoids starvation if the underlying operating system's scheduler does). The standard wording for `std::shared_mutex` provides no such guarantee, although any implementation that allowed starvation in practice would be considered a pretty poor one. In practice you'll find that your standard library vendor's implementation of `shared_mutex` is pretty close to the Boost one, except for the missing upgrade/downgrade functionality.

Waiting for a condition

In the section titled "Special-purpose mutex types," we launched a task in a separate thread and then needed to wait until a certain bit of initialization was done before continuing. We used a polling loop around a `std::atomic<bool>` in that case. But there are better ways to wait!

The problem with our 50-millisecond polling loop is that it *never* spends the right amount of time asleep. Sometimes our thread will wake up, but the condition it's waiting for hasn't been satisfied, so it'll go back to sleep--that means we didn't sleep long enough the first time. Sometimes our thread will wake up and see that the condition it's waiting for *has* been satisfied, sometime in the past 50 milliseconds, but we don't know how long ago--that means we've *overslept* by about 25 milliseconds on average. Whatever happens, the chance that we slept *just precisely the right amount of time* is slim to none.

So, if we don't want to waste time, the right thing to do is to avoid polling loops. The standard library provides a way to wait just the *right* amount of time; it's called `std::condition_variable`.

Given a variable `cv` of type `std::condition_variable`, our thread can "wait on" `cv` by calling `cv.wait(lk);` that puts our thread to sleep. Calling `cv.notify_one()` or `cv.notify_all()` wakes up one, or all of, the threads currently waiting on `cv`. However, this is not the only way that those threads might wake up! It's possible that an interrupt from outside (such as a POSIX signal) might jar your thread awake without anybody's having called `notify_one`. This phenomenon is called a *spurious wakeup*. The usual way to guard against spurious wakeups is to check your condition when you wake up. For example, if you're waiting for some input to arrive in a buffer `b`, then when you wake up, you ought to check `b.empty()` and, if it's empty, go back to waiting.

By definition, some other thread is going to be putting that data into `b`; so when you read `b.empty()`, you'd better do it under some kind of mutex. Which means the first thing you'll do when you wake up is take a lock on that mutex, and the last thing you'll do when you go back to sleep is release your lock on that mutex. (In fact, you need to release your lock on that mutex atomically with the going-to-sleep operation, so that nobody can slip in, modify `b`, and call `cv.notify_one()` before you've managed to get to sleep.) This chain of logic leads us to the reason that `cv.wait(lk)` takes that parameter `lk`--it's a `std::unique_lock<std::mutex>` that will be released upon going to sleep and regained upon awaking!

Here's an example of waiting for some condition to be satisfied. First the simple but wasteful polling loop on a `std::atomic` variable:

```
std::atomic<bool> ready = false;

std::thread thread_b([&]() {
  prep_work();
  ready = true;
  main_work();
});

// Wait for thread B to be ready.
while (!ready) {
  std::this_thread::sleep_for(10ms);
}
// Now thread B has completed its prep work.
```

And now the preferable and more efficient `condition_variable` implementation:

```
bool ready = false; // not atomic!
std::mutex ready_mutex;
std::condition_variable cv;

std::thread thread_b([&]() {
  prep_work();
  {
    std::lock_guard lk(ready_mutex);
    ready = true;
  }
  cv.notify_one();
  main_work();
});

// Wait for thread B to be ready.
{
  std::unique_lock lk(ready_mutex);
  while (!ready) {
    cv.wait(lk);
  }
}
// Now thread B has completed its prep work.
```

If we're waiting to read from a structure protected by a read-write lock (that is, a `std::shared_mutex`), then we don't want to pass in a `std::unique_lock<std::mutex>`; we want to pass in a `std::shared_lock<std::shared_mutex>`. We can do this, if (and sadly only if) we plan ahead and define our condition variable to be of type `std::condition_variable_any` instead of `std::condition_variable`. In practice, there is unlikely to be any performance difference between `std::condition_variable_any` and `std::condition_variable`, which means you should choose between them based on your program's needs, or, if either one would serve, then based on the clarity of the resulting code. Generally this means saving four characters and using `std::condition_variable`. However, notice that because of the layer of insulating abstraction provided by `std::shared_lock`, the actual code for waiting on cv under a read-write lock is almost identical to the code for waiting on cv under a plain old mutex. Here is the read-write lock version:

```
bool ready = false;
std::shared_mutex ready_rwlock;
std::condition_variable_any cv;
std::thread thread_b([&]() {
  prep_work();
  {
    std::lock_guard lk(ready_rwlock);
    ready = true;
  }
  cv.notify_one();
  main_work();
});

// Wait for thread B to be ready.
{
  std::shared_lock lk(ready_rwlock);
  while (!ready) {
    cv.wait(lk);
  }
}
// Now thread B has completed its prep work.
```

This is perfectly correct code, and as efficient as it can be. However, manually fiddling with mutex locks and condition variables is almost as dangerous to one's health as fiddling with raw mutexes or raw pointers. We can do better! The better solution is the subject of our next section.

Promises about futures

If you haven't encountered concurrent programming topics before, the last few sections probably got progressively more and more challenging. Mutexes are pretty simple to understand because they model a familiar idea from daily life: getting exclusive access to some resource by putting a lock on it. Read-write locks (`shared_mutex`) aren't much harder to understand. However, we then took a significant jump upward in esotericism with condition variables--which are hard to grasp partly because they seem to model not a noun (like "padlock") but a sort of prepositional verb phrase: "sleep until, but also, wake." Their opaque name doesn't help much either.

Now we continue our journey into concurrent programming with a topic that may be unfamiliar even if you've taken an undergraduate course in concurrent programming, but is well worth the learning: *promises* and *futures*.

In C++11, the types `std::promise<T>` and `std::future<T>` always appear in pairs. Someone coming from the Go language might think of a promise-future pair as a sort of *channel*, in that if one thread shoves a value (of type `T`) into the "promise" side of the pair, that value will eventually emerge at the "future" side (which is typically in a different thread by then). However, promise-future pairs are also like unstable wormholes: as soon as you've shoved a single value through the wormhole, it collapses.

We might say that a promise-future pair is like a directed, portable, one-shot wormhole. It's "directed" because you're allowed to shove data into only the "promise" side and retrieve data only via the "future" side. It's "portable" because if you own one end of the wormhole, you can move that end around and even move it between threads; you won't break the tunnel between the two ends. And it's "one-shot" because once you've shoved one piece of data into the "promise" end, you can't shove any more.

Another metaphor for the pair is suggested by their names: A `std::future<T>` is not actually a value of type `T`, but it is in some sense a *future* value--it will, at some point in the future, give you access to a `T`, but "not yet." (In this way, it is also something like a thread-safe `optional<T>`.) Meanwhile, a `std::promise<T>` object is like an unfulfilled promise, or an I-O-U. The holder of the promise object *promises* to put a value of type `T` into it at some point; if he doesn't ever put in a value, then he's "broken his promise."

Concurrency

Generally speaking, you use a promise-future pair by first creating a `std::promise<T>`, where `T` is the type of data you're planning to send through it; then creating the wormhole's "future" end by calling `p.get_future()`. When you're ready to fulfill the promise, you call `p.set_value(v)`. Meanwhile, in some other thread, when you're ready to retrieve the value, you call `f.get()`. If a thread calls `f.get()` before the promise has been fulfilled, that thread will block until the promise is fulfilled and the value is ready to retrieve. On the other hand, when the promise-holding thread calls `p.set_value(v)`, if nobody's waiting, that's fine; `set_value` will just record the value v in memory so that it's ready and waiting whenever anyone *does* ask for it via `f.get()`.

Let's see `promise` and `future` in action!

```
std::promise<int> p1, p2;
std::future<int> f1 = p1.get_future();
std::future<int> f2 = p2.get_future();

  // If the promise is satisfied first,
  // then f.get() will not block.
p1.set_value(42);
assert(f1.get() == 42);

  // If f.get() is called first, then it
  // will block until set_value() is called
  // from some other thread.
std::thread t([&](){
  std::this_thread::sleep_for(100ms);
  p2.set_value(43);
});
auto start_time = std::chrono::system_clock::now();
assert(f2.get() == 43);
auto elapsed = std::chrono::system_clock::now() - start_time;
printf("f2.get() took %dms.\n", count_ms(elapsed));
t.join();
```

(For the definition of `count_ms`, see the previous section, *Special-purpose mutex types*.)

One nice detail about the standard library's `std::promise` is that it has a specialization for void. The idea of `std::future<void>` might seem a little silly at first--what good is a wormhole if the only data type you can shove through it is a type with no values? But in fact `future<void>` is extremely useful, whenever we don't care so much about the *value* that was received as about the fact that some signal was received at all. For example, we can use `std::future<void>` to implement yet a third version of our "wait for thread B to launch" code:

```
std::promise<void> ready_p;
std::future<void> ready_f = ready_p.get_future();

std::thread thread_b([&]() {
  prep_work();
  ready_p.set_value();
  main_work();
});

  // Wait for thread B to be ready.
ready_f.wait();
  // Now thread B has completed its prep work.
```

Compare this version to the code samples from the section titled "Waiting for a condition." This version is much cleaner! There's practically no cruft, no boilerplate at all. The "signal B's readiness" and "wait for B's readiness" operations both take only a single line of code. So this is definitely the preferred way to signal between a single pair of threads, as far as syntactic cleanliness is concerned. For yet a fourth way to signal from one thread to a group of threads, see this chapter's subsection titled "Identifying individual threads and the current thread."

Concurrency

There *is* a price to pay for `std::future`, though. The price is dynamic memory allocation. You see, `promise` and `future` both need access to a shared storage location, so that when you store `42` in the promise side, you'll be able to pull it out from the future side. (That shared storage location also holds the mutex and condition variable required for synchronizing between the threads. The mutex and condition variable haven't disappeared from our code; they've just moved down a layer of abstraction so that we don't have to worry about them.) So, `promise` and `future` both act as a sort of "handle" to this shared state; but they're both movable types, so neither of them can actually hold the shared state as a member. They need to allocate the shared state on the heap, and hold pointers to it; and since the shared state isn't supposed to be freed until *both* handles are destroyed, we're talking about shared ownership via something like `shared_ptr` (see Chapter 6, *Smart Pointers*). Schematically, `promise` and `future` look like this:

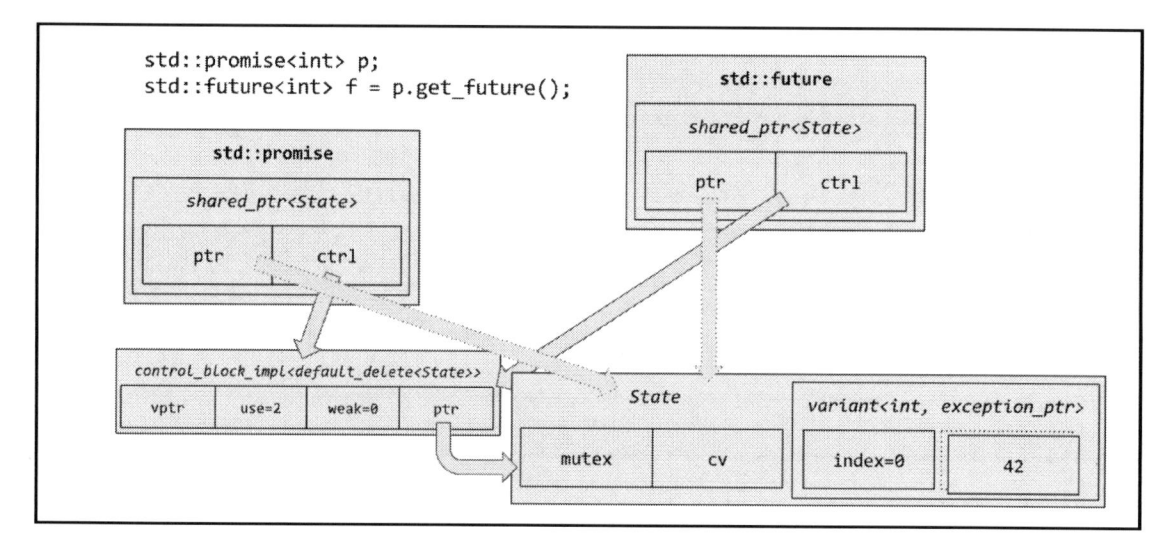

The shared state in this diagram will be allocated with `operator new`, unless you use a special "allocator-aware" version of the constructor `std::promise`. To use `std::promise` and `std::future` with an allocator of your choice, you'd write the following:

```
MyAllocator myalloc{};
std::promise<int> p(std::allocator_arg, myalloc);
std::future<int> f = p.get_future();
```

`std::allocator_arg` is defined in the `<memory>` header. See Chapter 8, *Allocators*, for the details of `MyAllocator`.

Packaging up tasks for later

Another thing to notice about the preceding diagram is that the shared state doesn't just contain an `optional<T>`; it actually contains a `variant<T, exception_ptr>` (for `variant` and `optional`, see Chapter 5, *Vocabulary Types*). This implies that not only can you shove data of type `T` through the wormhole; you can also shove *exceptions* through. This is particularly convenient and symmetrical because it allows `std::future<T>` to represent all the possible outcomes of calling a function with the signature `T()`. Maybe it returns a `T`; maybe it throws an exception; and of course maybe it never returns at all. Similarly, a call to `f.get()` may return a `T`; or throw an exception; or (if the promise-holding thread loops forever) might never return at all. In order to shove an exception through the wormhole, you'd use the method `p.set_exception(ex)`, where `ex` is an object of type `std::exception_ptr` such as might be returned from `std::current_exception()` inside a catch handler.

Let's take a function of signature `T()` and package it up in a future of type `std::future<T>`:

```
template<class T>
class simple_packaged_task {
  std::function<T()> m_func;
  std::promise<T> m_promise;
public:
  template<class F>
  simple_packaged_task(const F& f) : m_func(f) {}

  auto get_future() { return m_promise.get_future(); }

  void operator()() {
    try {
      T result = m_func();
      m_promise.set_value(result);
    } catch (...) {
      m_promise.set_exception(std::current_exception());
    }
  }
};
```

Concurrency

This class superficially resembles the standard library type `std::packaged_task<R(A...)>`; the difference is that the standard library type takes arguments, and uses an extra layer of indirection to make sure that it can hold even move-only functor types. Back in Chapter 5, *Vocabulary Types*, we showed you some workarounds for the fact that `std::function` can't hold move-only function types; fortunately those workarounds are not needed when dealing with `std::packaged_task`. On the other hand, you'll probably never have to deal with `std::packaged_task` in your life. It's interesting mainly as an example of how to compose promises, futures, and functions together into user-friendly class types with externally very simple interfaces. Consider for a moment: The `simple_packaged_task` class above uses type-erasure in `std::function`, and then has the `std::promise` member, which is implemented in terms of `std::shared_ptr`, which does reference counting; and the shared state pointed to by that reference-counted pointer holds a mutex and a condition variable. That's quite a lot of ideas and techniques packed into a very small volume! And yet the interface to `simple_packaged_task` is indeed simple: construct it with a function or lambda of some kind, then call `pt.get_future()` to get a future that you can `f.get()`; and meanwhile call `pt()` (probably from some other thread) to actually execute the stored function and shove the result through the wormhole into `f.get()`.

If the stored function throws an exception, then `packaged_task` will catch that exception (in the promise-holding thread) and shove it into the wormhole. Then, whenever the other thread calls `f.get()` (or maybe it already called it and it's blocked inside `f.get()` right now), `f.get()` will throw that exception out into the future-holding thread. In other words, by using promises and futures, we can actually "teleport" exceptions across threads. The exact mechanism of this teleportation, `std::exception_ptr`, is unfortunately outside the scope of this book. If you do library programming in a codebase that uses a lot of exceptions, it is definitely worth becoming familiar with `std::exception_ptr`.

The future of futures

As with `std::shared_mutex`, the standard library's own version of `std::future` is only half-baked. A much more complete and useful version of `future` is coming, perhaps in C++20, and there are very many third-party libraries that incorporate the best features of the upcoming version. The best of these libraries include `boost::future` and Facebook's `folly::Future`.

The major problem with `std::future` is that it requires "touching down" in a thread after each step of a potentially multi-step computation. Consider this pathological usage of `std::future`:

```cpp
template<class T>
auto pf() {
  std::promise<T> p;
  std::future<T> f = p.get_future();
  return std::make_pair(std::move(p), std::move(f));
}

void test() {
  auto [p1, f1] = pf<Connection>();
  auto [p2, f2] = pf<Data>();
  auto [p3, f3] = pf<Data>();

  auto t1 = std::thread([p1 = std::move(p1)]() mutable {
    Connection conn = slowly_open_connection();
    p1.set_value(conn);
    // DANGER: what if slowly_open_connection throws?
  });
  auto t2 = std::thread([p2 = std::move(p2)]() mutable {
    Data data = slowly_get_data_from_disk();
    p2.set_value(data);
  });
  auto t3 = std::thread(
    [p3 = std::move(p3), f1 = std::move(f1)]() mutable {
    Data data = slowly_get_data_from_connection(f1.get());
    p3.set_value(data);
  });
  bool success = (f2.get() == f3.get());

  assert(success);
}
```

Notice the line marked DANGER: each of the three thread bodies has the same bug, which is that they fail to catch and `.set_exception()` when an exception is thrown. The solution is a `try...catch` block, just like we used in our `simple_packaged_task` in the preceding section; but since that would get tedious to write out every time, the standard library provides a neat wrapper function called `std::async()`, which takes care of creating a promise-future pair and spawning a new thread. Using `std::async()`, we have this much cleaner-looking code:

```cpp
void test() {
  auto f1 = std::async(slowly_open_connection);
  auto f2 = std::async(slowly_get_data_from_disk);
```

[199]

Concurrency

```
auto f3 = std::async([f1 = std::move(f1)]() mutable {
    return slowly_get_data_from_connection(f1.get());
    // No more danger.
});
bool success = (f2.get() == f3.get());

assert(success);
}
```

However, this code is cleaner only in its aesthetics; it's equally horrifically bad for the performance and robustness of your codebase. This is *bad* code!

Every time you see a .get() in that code, you should think, "What a waste of a context switch!" And every time you see a thread being spawned (whether explicitly or via async), you should think, "What a possibility for the operating system to run out of kernel threads and for my program to start throwing unexpected exceptions from the constructor of std::thread!" Instead of either of the preceding codes, we'd prefer to write something like this, in a style that might look familiar to JavaScript programmers:

```
void test() {
    auto f1 = my::async(slowly_open_connection);
    auto f2 = my::async(slowly_get_data_from_disk);
    auto f3 = f1.then([](Connection conn) {
        return slowly_get_data_from_connection(conn);
    });
    bool success = f2.get() == f3.get();

    assert(success);
}
```

Here, there are no calls to .get() except at the very end, when we have nothing to do but wait for the final answer; and there is one fewer thread spawned. Instead, before f1 finishes its task, we attach a "continuation" to it, so that when f1 does finish, the promise-holding thread can immediately segue right into working on the continuation task (if original task of f1 threw an exception, we won't enter this continuation at all. The library should provide a symmetrical method, f1.on_error(continuation), to deal with the exceptional codepath).

Something like this is already available in Boost; and Facebook's Folly library contains a particularly robust and fully featured implementation even better than Boost's. While we wait for C++20 to improve the situation, my advice is to use Folly if you can afford the cognitive overhead of integrating it into your build system. The single advantage of std::future is that it's standard; you'll be able to use it on just about any platform without needing to worry about downloads, include paths, or licensing terms.

Speaking of threads...

Throughout this entire chapter, we've been using the word "thread" without ever defining exactly what we mean by it; and you've probably noticed that many of our multithreaded code examples have used the class type `std::thread` and the namespace `std::this_thread` without much explanation. We've been focusing on *how* to synchronize behavior between different threads of execution, but so far we have glossed over exactly *who* is doing the executing!

To put it another way: When execution reaches the expression `mtx.lock()`, where `mtx` is a locked mutex, the semantics of `std::mutex` say that the current thread of execution should block and wait. While that thread is blocked, what is happening? Our C++ program is still "in charge" of what's going on, but clearly *this particular C++ code* is no longer executing; so who *is* executing? The answer is: another thread. We specify the existence of other threads, and the code we want them to execute, by using the standard library class `std::thread`, defined in the `<thread>` header.

To spawn a new thread of execution, simply construct an object of type `std::thread`, and pass a single argument to the constructor: a lambda or function that tells you what code you want to run in the new thread. (Technically, you are allowed to pass multiple arguments; all arguments after the first will be passed along to the first argument as *its* function parameters, after undergoing `reference_wrapper` decay as described in Chapter 5, *Vocabulary Types*. As of C++11, lambdas have made the extra arguments to the `thread` constructor unnecessary and even error-prone; I recommend avoiding them.)

The new thread will immediately start running; if you want it to "start up paused," you'll have to build that functionality yourself using one of the synchronization tricks shown in the section titled "Waiting for a condition," or the alternative trick shown in "Identifying individual threads and the current thread."

The new thread will run through the code it's given, and when it gets to the end of the lambda or function you provided to it, it will "become joinable." This idea is very similar to what happens with `std::future` when it "becomes ready": the thread has completed its computation and is ready to deliver the result of that computation to you. Just as with `std::future<void>`, the result of that computation is "valueless"; but the very fact that the computation *has finished* is valuable nonetheless--no pun intended!

Concurrency

Unlike `std::future<void>`, though, it is not permitted to destroy a `std::thread` object without fetching that valueless result. By default, if you destroy any new thread without dealing with its result, the destructor will call `std::terminate`, which is to say, it will bluntly kill your program. The way to avoid this fate is to indicate to the thread that you see and acknowledge its completion--"Good job, thread, well done!"--by calling the member function `t.join()`. Alternatively, if you do not expect the thread to finish (for example if it is a background thread running an infinite loop) or don't care about its result (for example if it represents some short-lived "fire and forget" task), you can dismiss it to the background--"Go away, thread, I don't want to hear from you again!"--via `t.detach()`.

Here are some complete examples of how to use `std::thread`:

```
using namespace std::literals;  // for "ms"

std::thread a([](){
  puts("Thread A says hello ~0ms");
  std::this_thread::sleep_for(10ms);
  puts("Thread A says goodbye ~10ms");
});

std::thread b([](){
  puts("Thread B says hello ~0ms");
  std::this_thread::sleep_for(20ms);
  puts("Thread B says goodbye ~20ms");
});

puts("The main thread says hello ~0ms");
a.join();     // waits for thread A
b.detach();   // doesn't wait for thread B
puts("The main thread says goodbye ~10ms");
```

Identifying individual threads and the current thread

Objects of type `std::thread`, like every other type described in this chapter, do not support `operator==`. You can't directly ask "Are these two thread objects the same?" This also means that you can't use `std::thread` objects as the keys in an associative container such as `std::map` or `std::unordered_map`. However, you *can* ask about equality indirectly, via a feature called *thread-ids*.

The member function `t.get_id()` returns a unique identifier of type `std::thread::id`, which, although it is technically a class type, behaves an awful lot like an integer type. You can compare thread-ids using operators `<` and `==`; and you can use thread-ids as keys in associative containers. Another valuable feature of thread-id objects is that they can be *copied*, unlike `std::thread` objects themselves, which are move-only. Remember, each `std::thread` object represents an actual thread of execution; if you could copy `thread` objects, you would be "copying" threads of execution, which doesn't make a whole lot of sense--and would certainly lead to some interesting bugs!

The third valuable feature of `std::thread::id` is that it is possible to get the thread-id of the *current* thread, or even of the main thread. From within a thread, there is no way to say "Please give me the `std::thread` object that manages this thread." (This would be a trick analogous to `std::enable_shared_from_this<T>` from Chapter 6, *Smart Pointers*; but as we've seen, such a trick requires support from the part of the library that creates managed resources--which in this case would be the constructor of `std::thread`.) And the main thread, the thread in which `main` begins execution, doesn't have a corresponding `std::thread` object at all. But it still has a thread-id!

Finally, thread-ids are convertible in some implementation-defined manner to a string representation, which is guaranteed to be unique--that is, `to_string(id1) == to_string(id2)` if and only if `id1 == id2`. Unfortunately this string representation is exposed only via the stream operator (see Chapter 9, *Iostreams*); if you want to use the syntax `to_string(id1)` you need to write a simple wrapper function:

```
std::string to_string(std::thread::id id)
{
  std::ostringstream o;
  o << id;
  return o.str();
}
```

You can get the thread-id of the current thread (including of the main thread, if that happens to be your current thread) by calling the free function `std::this_thread::get_id()`. Look carefully at the syntax! `std::thread` is the name of a class, but `std::this_thread` is the name of a *namespace*. In this namespace live some free functions (unassociated with any C++ class instance) that manipulate the current thread. `get_id()` is one of those functions. Its name was chosen to be reminiscent of `std::thread::get_id()`, but in fact it is a completely different function: `thread::get_id()` is a member function and `this_thread::get_id()` is a free function.

Using two thread-ids, you can find out, for example, which of an existing list of threads represents your current thread:

```
std::mutex ready;
std::unique_lock lk(ready);
std::vector<std::thread> threads;

auto task = [&](){
    // Block here until the main thread is ready.
  (void)std::lock_guard(ready);
    // Now go. Find my thread-id in the vector.
  auto my_id = std::this_thread::get_id();
  auto iter = std::find_if(
    threads.begin(), threads.end(),
    [=](const std::thread& t) {
      return t.get_id() == my_id;
    }
  );
  printf("Thread %s %s in the list.\n",
    to_string(my_id).c_str(),
    iter != threads.end() ? "is" : "is not");
};

std::vector<std::thread> others;
for (int i = 0; i < 10; ++i) {
  std::thread t(task);
  if (i % 2) {
    threads.push_back(std::move(t));
  } else {
    others.push_back(std::move(t));
  }
}

    // Let all the threads run.
ready.unlock();

    // Join all the threads.
for (std::thread& t : threads) t.join();
for (std::thread& t : others) t.join();
```

What you cannot do, ever, is go the other direction; you cannot reconstruct the `std::thread` object corresponding to a given `std::thread::id`. Because if you could, you'd have two different objects in your program representing that thread of execution: the original `std::thread` wherever it is, and the one you just reconstructed from its thread-id. And you can never have two `std::thread` objects controlling the same thread.

The two other free functions in the `std::this_thread` namespace are `std::this_thread::sleep_for(duration)`, which you've seen me use extensively in this chapter, and `std::this_thread::yield()`, which is basically the same thing as `sleep_for(0ms)`: it tells the runtime that it would be a good idea to context-switch to a different thread right now, but doesn't connote any *particular* time delay on the current thread.

Thread exhaustion and std::async

In this chapter's section *The future of futures*, we introduced `std::async`, which is a simple wrapper around a thread constructor with the result captured into a `std::future`. Its implementation looks more or less like this:

```cpp
template<class F>
auto async(F&& func) {
  using ResultType = std::invoke_result_t<std::decay_t<F>>;
  using PromiseType = std::promise<ResultType>;
  using FutureType = std::future<ResultType>;

  PromiseType promise;
  FutureType future = promise.get_future();
  auto t = std::thread([
    func = std::forward<F>(func),
    promise = std::move(promise)
  ]() mutable {
    try {
      ResultType result = func();
      promise.set_value(result);
    } catch (...) {
      promise.set_exception(std::current_exception());
    }
  });
  // This special behavior is not implementable
  // outside of the library, but async does do it.
  // future.on_destruction([t = std::move(t)]() {
  //   t.join();
  // });
  return future;
}
```

Concurrency

Notice the commented-out lines indicating a special behavior "on destruction" of the `std::future` returned from `std::async`. This is a strange and awkward behavior of the standard library's `std::async` implementation, and a good reason to avoid or reimplement `std::async` in your own code: The futures returned from `std::async` have destructors that call `.join()` on their underlying threads! This means that their destructors can block, and that the task certainly will not be "executing in the background" as you might naturally expect. If you call `std::async` and don't assign the returned future to a variable, the return value will be destroyed right then and there, which means ironically that a line containing nothing but a call to `std::async` will actually execute the specified function *synchronously*:

```
template<class F>
void fire_and_forget_wrong(const F& f) {
  // WRONG! Runs f in another thread, but blocks anyway.
  std::async(f);
}

template<class F>
void fire_and_forget_better(const F& f) {
  // BETTER! Launches f in another thread without blocking.
  std::thread(f).detach();
}
```

The original reason for this limitation seems to have been a concern that if `std::async` launched background threads in the usual way, it would lead to people overusing `std::async` and possibly introducing dangling-reference bugs, as in this example:

```
int test() {
  int i = 0;
  auto future = std::async([&]() {
    i += 1;
  });
  // suppose we do not call f.wait() here
  return i;
}
```

If we didn't wait for the result of this future, the function `test()` might return to its caller before the new thread got a chance to run; then, when the new thread did finally run and attempt to increment `i`, it would be accessing a stack variable that no longer existed. So, rather than run the risk of people writing such buggy code, the Standards Committee decided that `std::async` should return futures with special, "magic" destructors that join their threads automatically.

Anyway, overuse of `std::async` is problematic for other reasons as well. The biggest reason is that on all popular operating systems, `std::thread` represents a *kernel thread*--a thread whose scheduling is under the control of the OS kernel. Because the OS has only finite resources to track these threads, the number of threads available to any one process is fairly limited: often only a few tens of thousands. If you're using `std::async` as your thread manager, spawning a new `std::thread` every time you have another task that might benefit from concurrency, you'll quickly find yourself running out of kernel threads. When this happens, the constructor of `std::thread` will start throwing exceptions of type `std::system_error`, often with the text `Resource temporarily unavailable`.

Building your own thread pool

If you use `std::async` to spawn a thread every time you have a new task, you risk exhausting the kernel's number of available threads for your process. A better way to run tasks concurrently is to use a *thread pool*--a small number of "worker threads" whose sole job is to run tasks as they are provided by the programmer. If there are more tasks than workers, the excess tasks are placed in a *work queue*. Whenever a worker finishes a task, it checks the work queue for new tasks.

This is a well-known idea, but has not yet been taken up into the standard library as of C++17. However, you can combine the ideas shown in this chapter to create your own production-quality thread pool. I'll walk through a simple one here; it's not "production quality" in terms of performance, but it *is* properly thread-safe and correct in all its functionality. Some performance tweaks will be discussed at the end of the walkthrough.

Concurrency

We'll start with the member data. Notice that we are using the rule that all the data controlled by a mutex should be located together under a single visual namespace; in this case, a nested struct definition. We're also going to use `std::packaged_task<void()>` as our move-only function type; if your codebase already has a move-only function type, you'll probably want to use that instead. If you don't already have a move-only function type, consider adopting Folly's `folly::Function` or Denis Blank's `fu2::unique_function`:

```
class ThreadPool {
  using UniqueFunction = std::packaged_task<void()>;
  struct {
    std::mutex mtx;
    std::queue<UniqueFunction> work_queue;
    bool aborting = false;
  } m_state;
  std::vector<std::thread> m_workers;
  std::condition_variable m_cv;
```

The `work_queue` variable will hold tasks as they come in to us. The member variable `m_state.aborting` will be set to `true` when it's time for all the workers to stop working and "come home to rest." `m_workers` holds the worker threads themselves; and `m_state.mtx` and `m_cv` are just for synchronization. (The workers will spend much of their time asleep when there's no work to do. When a new task comes in and we need to wake up some worker, we'll notify `m_cv`.)

The constructor of `ThreadPool` spawns worker threads and populates the `m_workers` vector. Each worker thread will be running the member function `this->worker_loop()`, which we'll see in a minute:

```
public:
  ThreadPool(int size) {
    for (int i=0; i < size; ++i) {
      m_workers.emplace_back([this]() { worker_loop(); });
    }
  }
```

As promised, the destructor sets `m_state.aborting` to `true` and then waits for all of the worker threads to notice the change and terminate. Notice that when we touch `m_state.aborting`, it's only under a lock on `m_state.mtx`; we are following good hygiene in order to avoid bugs!

```
  ~ThreadPool() {
    if (std::lock_guard lk(m_state.mtx); true) {
      m_state.aborting = true;
    }
```

```
      m_cv.notify_all();
      for (std::thread& t : m_workers) {
        t.join();
      }
    }
```

Now let's see how we enqueue tasks into the work queue. (We have not yet seen how workers grab tasks out; we'll see that happening in the `worker_loop` member function.) It's very straightforward; we just have to make sure that we access `m_state` only under the mutex lock, and that once we have enqueued the task, we call `m_cv.notify_one()` so that some worker will wake up to handle the task:

```
    void enqueue_task(UniqueFunction task) {
      if (std::lock_guard lk(m_state.mtx); true) {
        m_state.work_queue.push(std::move(task));
      }
      m_cv.notify_one();
    }
```

At last, here is the worker loop. This is the member function that each worker runs:

```
  private:
    void worker_loop() {
      while (true) {
        std::unique_lock lk(m_state.mtx);
        while (m_state.work_queue.empty() && !m_state.aborting) {
          m_cv.wait(lk);
        }
        if (m_state.aborting) break;
        // Pop the next task, while still under the lock.
        assert(!m_state.work_queue.empty());
        UniqueFunction task = std::move(m_state.work_queue.front());
        m_state.work_queue.pop();

        lk.unlock();
        // Actually run the task. This might take a while.
        task();
        // When we're done with this task, go get another.
      }
    }
```

Notice the inevitable loop around `m_cv.wait(lk)`, and notice that we hygienically access `m_state` only under the mutex lock. Also notice that when we actually call out to perform `task`, we release the mutex lock first; this ensures that we are not holding the lock for a very long time while the user's task executes. If we *were* to hold the lock for a long time, then no other worker would be able to get in and grab its next task--we'd effectively reduce the concurrency of our pool. Also, if we were to hold the lock during `task`, and if `task` itself tried to enqueue a new task on this pool (which requires taking the lock itself), then `task` would deadlock and our whole program would freeze up. This is a special case of the more general rule never to call a user-provided callback while holding a mutex lock: that's generally a recipe for deadlock.

Finally, let's round out our `ThreadPool` class by implementing a safe version of `async`. Our version will allow calling `tp.async(f)` for any f that is callable without arguments, and just like `std::async`, we'll return a `std::future` via which our caller can retrieve the result of f once it's ready. Unlike the futures returned from `std::async`, our futures will be safe to drop on the floor: If the caller decides that he doesn't want to wait for the result after all, the task will remain enqueued and will eventually be executed, and the result will simply be ignored:

```
public:
  template<class F>
  auto async(F&& func) {
    using ResultType = std::invoke_result_t<std::decay_t<F>>;

    std::packaged_task<ResultType()> pt(std::forward<F>(func));
    std::future<ResultType> future = pt.get_future();

    UniqueFunction task(
        [pt = std::move(pt)]() mutable { pt(); }
    );

    enqueue_task(std::move(task));

    // Give the user a future for retrieving the result.
    return future;
  }
}; // class ThreadPool
```

We can use our `ThreadPool` class to write code like this function, which creates 60,000 tasks:

```
void test() {
  std::atomic<int> sum(0);
  ThreadPool tp(4);
  std::vector<std::future<int>> futures;
  for (int i=0; i < 60000; ++i) {
    auto f = tp.async([i, &sum](){
      sum += i;
      return i;
    });
    futures.push_back(std::move(f));
  }
  assert(futures[42].get() == 42);
  assert(903 <= sum && sum <= 1799970000);
}
```

We could try to do the same with `std::async`, but we'd likely run into thread exhaustion when we tried to create 60,000 kernel threads. The preceding example uses only four kernel threads, as indicated by the parameter to the `ThreadPool` constructor.

When you run this code, you'll see at least the numbers 0 through 42 printed to standard output, in some order. We know that 42 must be printed because the function definitely waits for `futures[42]` to be ready before it exits, and all the previous numbers must be printed because their tasks were placed in the work queue ahead of task number 42. The numbers 43 through 59,999 might or might not be printed, depending on the scheduler; because as soon as task 42 is completed, we exit `test` and thus destroy the thread pool. The thread pool's destructor, as we've seen, notifies all of its workers to stop working and come home after they complete their current tasks. So it is likely that we'll see a few more numbers printed, but then all the workers will come home and the remaining tasks will be dropped on the floor.

Of course if you wanted the destructor of `ThreadPool` to block until all enqueued tasks were completed, you could do that, by changing the code of the destructor. However, typically when you're destroying a thread pool, it's because your program (such as a web server) is exiting, and that's because you've received a signal such as the user pressing *Ctrl + C*. In that situation, you *probably* want to exit as soon as you can, as opposed to trying to clear the queue. Personally, I'd prefer to add a member function `tp.wait_for_all_enqueued_tasks()`, so that the user of the thread pool could decide whether they want to block or just drop everything on the floor.

Improving our thread pool's performance

The biggest performance bottleneck in our `ThreadPool` is that every worker thread is vying for the same mutex, `this->m_state.mtx`. The reason they're all contending that mutex is because that is the mutex that guards `this->m_state.work_queue`, and every worker needs to touch that queue in order to find out its next job. So one way to reduce contention and speed up our program is to find a way of distributing work to our workers that doesn't involve a single central work queue.

The simplest solution is to give each worker its own "to-do list"; that is, to replace our single `std::queue<Task>` with a whole `std::vector<std::queue<Task>>`, with one entry for each worker thread. Of course then we'd also need a `std::vector<std::mutex>` so that we had one mutex for each work queue. The `enqueue_task` function distributes tasks to the work queues in a round-robin fashion (using atomic increments of a `std::atomic<int>` counter to deal with simultaneous enqueues).

You could alternatively use a `thread_local` counter per enqueuing thread, if you are fortunate enough to work on a platform that supports C++11's `thread_local` keyword. On x86-64 POSIX platforms, access to a `thread_local` variable is approximately as fast as access to a plain old global variable; all the complication of setting up thread-local variables happens under the hood and only when you spawn a new thread. However, because that complication *does* exist and needs runtime support, many platforms do not yet support the `thread_local` storage class specifier. (On those that do, `thread_local int x` is basically the same thing as `static int x`, except that when your code accesses x by name, the actual memory address of x will vary depending on `std::this_thread::get_id()`. In principle, there is a whole array of x somewhere behind the scenes, indexed by thread-id and populated by the C++ runtime as threads are created and destroyed.)

The next significant performance improvement to our `ThreadPool` would be "work-stealing": now that each worker has its own to-do list, it might happen by chance or malice that one worker becomes overworked while all the other workers lie idle. In this case, we want the idle workers to scan the queues of the busy workers and "steal" tasks if possible. This re-introduces lock contention among the workers, but only when an inequitable assignment of tasks has already produced inefficiency--inefficiency which we are hoping to *correct* via work-stealing.

Implementing separate work queues and work-stealing is left as an exercise for the reader; but I hope that after seeing how simple the basic `ThreadPool` turned out, you won't be too daunted by the idea of modifying it to include those extra features.

Of course, there also exists professionally written thread-pool classes. Boost.Asio contains one, for example, and Asio is on track to be brought into the standard perhaps in C++20. Using Boost.Asio, our `ThreadPool` class would look like this:

```
class ThreadPool {
  boost::thread_group m_workers;
  boost::asio::io_service m_io;
  boost::asio::io_service::work m_work;
public:
  ThreadPool(int size) : m_work(m_io) {
    for (int i=0; i < size; ++i) {
      m_workers.create_thread([&](){ m_io.run(); });
    }
  }

  template<class F>
  void enqueue_task(F&& func) {
    m_io.post(std::forward<F>(func));
  }

  ~ThreadPool() {
    m_io.stop();
    m_workers.join_all();
  }
};
```

An explanation of Boost.Asio is, of course, far outside the scope of this book.

Any time you use a thread pool, be careful that the tasks you enqueue never block indefinitely on conditions controlled by other tasks in the same thread pool. A classic example would be a task A that waits on a condition variable, expecting that some later task B will notify the condition variable. If you make a `ThreadPool` of size 4 and enqueue four copies of task A followed by four copies of task B, you'll find that task B never runs--the four worker threads in your pool are all occupied by the four copies of task A, which are all asleep waiting for a signal that will never come! "Handling" this scenario is tantamount to writing your own user-space threading library; if you don't want to get into that business, then the only sane answer is to be careful that the scenario cannot arise in the first place.

Summary

Multithreading is a difficult and subtle subject, with many pitfalls that are obvious only in hindsight. In this chapter we have learned:

`volatile`, while useful for dealing directly with hardware, is insufficient for thread-safety. `std::atomic<T>` for scalar `T` (up to the size of a machine register) is the right way to access shared data without races and without locks. The most important primitive atomic operation is compare-and-swap, which in C++ is spelled `compare_exchange_weak`.

To force threads to take turns accessing shared non-atomic data, we use `std::mutex`. Always lock mutexes via an RAII class such as `std::unique_lock<M>`. Remember that although C++17 class template argument deduction allows us to omit the `<M>` from these templates' names, that is just a syntactic convenience; they remain template classes.

Always clearly indicate which data is controlled by each mutex in your program. One good way to do this is with a nested struct definition.

`std::condition_variable` allows us to "sleep until" some condition is satisfied. If the condition can be satisfied only once, such as a thread becoming "ready," then you probably want to use a promise-future pair instead of a condition variable. If the condition can be satisfied over and over again, consider whether your problem can be rephrased in terms of the *work queue* pattern.

`std::thread` reifies the idea of a thread of execution. The "current thread" is not directly manipulable as a `std::thread` object, but a limited set of operations are available as free functions in the `std::this_thread` namespace. The most important of these operations are `sleep_for` and `get_id`. Each `std::thread` must always be joined or detached before it can be destroyed. Detaching is useful only for background threads that you will never need to shut down cleanly.

The standard function `std::async` takes a function or lambda for execution on some other thread, and returns a `std::future` that becomes ready when the function is done executing. While `std::async` itself is fatally flawed (destructors that `join`; kernel thread exhaustion) and thus should not be used in production code, the general idea of dealing with concurrency via futures is a good one. Prefer to use an implementation of promises and futures that supports the `.then` method. Folly's implementation is the best.

Multithreading is a difficult and subtle subject, with many pitfalls that are obvious only in hindsight.

8
Allocators

We've seen in the preceding chapters that C++ has a love-hate relationship with dynamic memory allocation.

On one hand, dynamic memory allocation from the heap is a "code smell"; chasing pointers can hurt a program's performance, the heap can be exhausted unexpectedly (leading to exceptions of type `std::bad_alloc`), and manual memory management is so subtly difficult that C++11 introduced several different "smart pointer" types to manage the complexity (see Chapter 6, *Smart Pointers*). Successive versions of C++ after 2011 have also added a great number of non-allocating algebraic data types, such as `tuple`, `optional`, and `variant` (see Chapter 5, *Vocabulary Types*) that can express ownership or containment without ever touching the heap.

On the other hand, the new smart pointer types do effectively manage the complexity of memory management; in modern C++ you can safely allocate and deallocate memory without ever using raw `new` or `delete` and without fear of memory leaks. And heap allocation is used "under the hood" of many of the new C++ features (`any`, `function`, `promise`) just as it continues to be used by many of the old ones (`stable_partition`, `vector`).

So there's a conflict here: How can we use these great new features (and the old ones) that depend on heap allocation, if we are simultaneously being told that good C++ code avoids heap allocation?

Allocators

In most cases, you should err on the side of *using the features that C++ provides*. If you want a resizeable vector of elements, you *should* be using the default `std::vector`, unless you have measured an actual performance problem with using it in your case. But there also exists a class of programmers--working in very constrained environments such as flight software--who have to avoid touching the heap for a very simple reason: "the heap" does not exist on their platforms! In these embedded environments, the entire footprint of the program must be laid out at compile time. Some such programs simply avoid any algorithm that resembles heap allocation--you can never encounter unexpected resource exhaustion if you never dynamically allocate resources of any kind! Other such programs do use algorithms resembling heap allocation, but require that the "heap" be represented explicitly in their program (say, by a very large array of `char` and functions for "reserving" and "returning" consecutive chunks of that array).

It would be extremely unfortunate if programs of this last kind were unable to use the features that C++ provides, such as `std::vector` and `std::any`. So, ever since the original standard in 1998, the standard library has provided a feature known as *allocator-awareness*. When a type or an algorithm is *allocator-aware*, it provides a way for the programmer to specify exactly how the type or algorithm ought to reserve and return dynamic memory. This "how" is reified into an object known as an *allocator*.

In this chapter we'll learn:

- The definitions of "allocator" and "memory resource"
- How to create your own memory resource that allocates out of a static buffer
- How to make your own containers "allocator-aware"
- The standard memory-resource types from namespace `std::pmr`, and their surprising pitfalls
- That many of the strange features of the C++11 allocator model are intended purely to support `scoped_allocator_adaptor`
- What makes a type a "fancy pointer" type, and where such types might be useful

An allocator is a handle to a memory resource

In reading this chapter, you'll have to keep in mind the difference between two fundamental concepts, which I am going to call *memory resource* and *allocator*. A *memory resource* (a name inspired by the standard's own terminology--you might find it more natural to call it "a heap") is a long-lived object that can dole out chunks of memory on request (usually by carving them out of a big block of memory that is owned by the memory resource itself). Memory resources have classically object-oriented semantics (see Chapter 1, *Classical Polymorphism and Generic Programming*): you create a memory resource once and never move or copy it, and equality for memory resources is generally defined by *object identity*. On the other hand, an *allocator* is a short-lived handle *pointing* to a memory resource. Allocators have pointer semantics: you can copy them, move them around, and generally mess with them as much as you want, and equality for allocators is generally defined by whether they point to the same memory resource. Instead of saying an allocator "points to" a particular memory resource, we might also say that the allocator is "backed by" that memory resource; the terms are interchangeable.

When I talk about "memory resources" and "allocators" in this chapter, I will be talking about the preceding concepts. The standard library also has a couple of types named memory_resource and allocator; whenever I'm talking about those types I'll be careful to use typewriter text. It shouldn't be too confusing. The situation is similar to Chapter 2, *Iterators and Ranges*, where we talked about "iterators" and also about std::iterator. Of course that was easier because I only mentioned std::iterator in order to tell you never to use it; it has no place in well-written C++ code. In this chapter we'll learn that std::pmr::memory_resource *does* have a place in certain C++ programs!

Even though I described an allocator as a handle "pointing to" a memory resource, you should notice that sometimes the memory resource in question is a global singleton--one example of such a singleton is the global heap, whose accessors are the global operator new and operator delete. Just as a lambda which "captures" a global variable doesn't actually capture anything, an allocator backed by the global heap doesn't actually need any state. In fact, std::allocator<T> is just such a stateless allocator type--but we're getting ahead of ourselves here!

Refresher - Interfaces versus concepts

Recall from Chapter 1, *Classical Polymorphism and Generic Programming*, that C++ offers two mostly incompatible ways of dealing with polymorphism. Static, compile-time polymorphism is called *generic programming*; it relies on expressing the polymorphic interface as a *concept* with many possible *models*, and the code that interacts with the interface is expressed in terms of *templates*. Dynamic, runtime polymorphism is called *classical polymorphism*; it relies on expressing the polymorphic interface as a *base class* with many possible *derived classes*, and the code that interacts with the interface is expressed in terms of calls to *virtual methods*.

In this chapter we'll have our first (and last) really close encounter with generic programming. It is impossible to make sense of C++ allocators unless you can hold in your mind two ideas at once: on one hand the *concept* Allocator, which defines an interface, and on the other hand some particular *model*, such as std::allocator, that implements behavior conforming to the Allocator concept.

To complicate matters further, the Allocator concept is really a templated family of concepts! It would be more accurate to talk about the family of concepts Allocator<T>; for example, Allocator<int> would be the concept defining "an allocator that allocates int objects," and Allocator<char> would be the concept defining "an allocator that allocates char objects," and so on. And, for example, the concrete class std::allocator<int> is a model of the concept Allocator<int>, but it is *not* a model of Allocator<char>.

Every allocator of T (every Allocator<T>) is required to provide a member function named allocate, such that a.allocate(n) returns a pointer to enough memory for an array of n objects of type T. (That pointer will come from the memory resource that backs the allocator instance.) It is not specified whether the allocate member function ought to be static or non-static, nor whether it ought to take exactly one parameter (n) or perhaps some additional parameters with default values. So both of the following class types would be acceptable models of Allocator<int> in that respect:

```
struct int_allocator_2014 {
  int *allocate(size_t n, const void *hint = nullptr);
};

struct int_allocator_2017 {
  int *allocate(size_t n);
};
```

Allocators

The class designated `int_allocator_2017` is obviously a *simpler* way to model `Allocator<int>`, but `int_allocator_2014` is just as correct a model, because in both cases the expression `a.allocate(n)` will be accepted by the compiler; and that's all we ask for, when we're talking about *generic programming*.

In contrast, when we do classical polymorphism, we specify a fixed signature for each method of the base class, and derived classes are not allowed to deviate from that signature:

```
struct classical_base {
   virtual int *allocate(size_t n) = 0;
};

struct classical_derived : public classical_base {
   int *allocate(size_t n) override;
};
```

The derived class `classical_derived` is not allowed to add any extra parameters onto the signature of the `allocate` method; it's not allowed to change the return type; it's not allowed to make the method `static`. The interface is more "locked down" with classical polymorphism than it is with generic programming.

Because a "locked-down" classical interface is naturally easier to describe than a wide-open conceptual one, we'll start our tour of the allocator library with C++17's brand-new, classically polymorphic `memory_resource`.

Defining a heap with memory_resource

Recall that on resource-constrained platforms, we might not be permitted to use "the heap" (for example via `new` and `delete`), because the platform's runtime might not support dynamic memory allocation. But we can make our own little heap--not "the heap," just "a heap"--and simulate the effect of dynamic memory allocation by writing a couple of functions `allocate` and `deallocate` that reserve chunks of a big statically allocated array of `char`, something like this:

```
static char big_buffer[10000];
static size_t index = 0;

void *allocate(size_t bytes) {
   if (bytes > sizeof big_buffer - index) {
      throw std::bad_alloc();
   }
   index += bytes;
   return &big_buffer[index - bytes];
```

Allocators

```
    }

    void deallocate(void *p, size_t bytes) {
      // drop it on the floor
    }
```

To keep the code as simple as possible, I made `deallocate` a no-op. This little heap allows the caller to allocate up to 10,000 bytes of memory, and then starts throwing `bad_alloc` from then on.

With a little more investment in the code, we can allow the caller to allocate and deallocate an infinite number of times, as long as the total outstanding amount of allocated memory doesn't exceed 10,000 bytes and as long as the caller always follows a "last-allocated-first-deallocated" protocol:

```
    void deallocate(void *p, size_t bytes) {
      if ((char*)p + bytes == &big_buffer[index]) {
        // aha! we can roll back our index!
        index -= bytes;
      } else {
        // drop it on the floor
      }
    }
```

The salient point here is that our heap has some *state* (in this case, `big_buffer` and `index`), and a couple of functions that manipulate this state. We've seen two different possible implementations of `deallocate` already--and there are other possibilities, with additional shared state, that wouldn't be so "leaky"--yet the interface, the signatures of `allocate` and `deallocate` themselves, has remained constant. This suggests that we could wrap up our state and accessor functions into a C++ object; and the wide variety of implementation possibilities plus the constancy of our function signatures suggests that we could use some classical polymorphism.

The C++17 allocator model does exactly that. The standard library provides the definition of a classically polymorphic base class, `std::pmr::memory_resource`, and then we implement our own little heap as a derived class. (In practice we might use one of the derived classes provided by the standard library, but let's finish up our little example before talking about those.) The base class `std::pmr::memory_resource` is defined in the standard header `<memory_resource>`:

```
    class memory_resource {
      virtual void *do_allocate(size_t bytes, size_t align) = 0;
      virtual void do_deallocate(void *p, size_t bytes, size_t align) = 0;
      virtual bool do_is_equal(const memory_resource& rhs) const = 0;
    public:
```

```cpp
    void *allocate(size_t bytes, size_t align) {
      return do_allocate(bytes, align);
    }
    void deallocate(void *p, size_t bytes, size_t align) {
      return do_deallocate(p, bytes, align);
    }
    bool is_equal(const memory_resource& rhs) const {
      return do_is_equal(rhs);
    }
};
```

Notice the curious layer of indirection between the `public` interface of the class and the `virtual` implementation. Usually when we're doing classical polymorphism, we have just one set of methods that are both `public` and `virtual`; but in this case, we have a `public` non-virtual interface that calls down into the private virtual methods. This splitting of the interface from the implementation has a few obscure benefits--for example, it prevents any child class from invoking `this->SomeBaseClass::allocate()` using the "directly invoke a virtual method non-virtually" syntax--but honestly, its main benefit to us is that when we define a derived class, we don't have to use the `public` keyword at all. Because we are specifying only the *implementation*, not the interface, all the code we write can be `private`. Here's our trivial little leaky heap:

```cpp
class example_resource : public std::pmr::memory_resource {
  alignas(std::max_align_t) char big_buffer[10000];
  size_t index = 0;
  void *do_allocate(size_t bytes, size_t align) override {
    if (align > alignof(std::max_align_t) ||
        (-index % align) > sizeof big_buffer - index ||
        bytes > sizeof big_buffer - index - (-index % align))
    {
        throw std::bad_alloc();
    }
    index += (-index % align) + bytes;
    return &big_buffer[index - bytes];
  }
  void do_deallocate(void *, size_t, size_t) override {
    // drop it on the floor
  }
  bool do_is_equal(const memory_resource& rhs) const override {
    return this == &rhs;
  }
};
```

Allocators

Notice that the standard library's `std::pmr::memory_resource::allocate` takes not only a size in bytes, but also an alignment. We need to make sure that whatever pointer we return from `do_allocate` is suitably aligned; for example, if our caller is planning to store `int` in the memory we give him, he might ask for four-byte alignment.

The last thing to notice about our derived class `example_resource` is that it represents the actual resources controlled by our "heap"; that is, it actually contains, owns, and manages the `big_buffer` out of which it's allocating memory. For any given `big_buffer`, there will be exactly one `example_resource` object in our program that manipulates that buffer. Just as we said earlier: objects of type `example_resource` are "memory resources," and thus they are *not* intended to be copied or moved around; they are classically object-oriented, not value-semantic.

The standard library provides several species of memory resource, all derived from `std::pmr::memory_resource`. Let's look at a few of them.

Using the standard memory resources

Memory resources in the standard library come in two flavors. Some of them are actual class types, of which you can create instances; and some of them are "anonymous" class types accessed only via singleton functions. Generally you can predict which is which by thinking about whether two objects of the type could ever possibly be "different," or whether the type is basically a singleton anyway.

The simplest memory resource in the `<memory_resource>` header is the "anonymous" singleton accessed via `std::pmr::null_memory_resource()`. The definition of this function is something like this:

```
class UNKNOWN : public std::pmr::memory_resource {
  void *do_allocate(size_t, size_t) override {
    throw std::bad_alloc();
  }
  void do_deallocate(void *, size_t, size_t) override {}
  bool do_is_equal(const memory_resource& rhs) const override {
    return this == &rhs;
  }
};

std::pmr::memory_resource *null_memory_resource() noexcept {
  static UNKNOWN singleton;
  return &singleton;
}
```

Notice that the function returns a pointer to the singleton instance. Generally, `std::pmr::memory_resource` objects will be manipulated via pointers, because the `memory_resource` objects themselves cannot move around.

`null_memory_resource` seems fairly useless; all it does is throw an exception when you try to allocate from it. However, it can be useful when you start using the more complicated memory resources which we'll see in a moment.

The next most complicated memory resource is the singleton accessed via `std::pmr::new_delete_resource()`; it uses `::operator new` and `::operator delete` to allocate and deallocate memory.

Now we move on to talking about the named class types. These are resources where it makes sense to have multiple resources of identical type in a single program. For example, there's `class std::pmr::monotonic_buffer_resource`. This memory resource is fundamentally the same as our `example_resource` from earlier, except for two differences: Instead of holding its big buffer as member data (`std::array`-style), it just holds a pointer to a big buffer allocated from somewhere else (`std::vector`-style). And when its first big buffer runs out, rather than immediately starting to throw `bad_alloc`, it will attempt to allocate a *second* big buffer, and allocate chunks out of that buffer until *it's* all gone; at which point it will allocate a third big buffer... and so on, until eventually it cannot even allocate any more big buffers. As with our `example_resource`, none of the deallocated memory is ever freed until the resource object itself is destroyed. There is one useful escape valve: If you call the method `a.release()`, the `monotonic_buffer_resource` will release all of the buffers it's currently holding, sort of like calling `clear()` on a vector.

When you construct a resource of type `std::pmr::monotonic_buffer_resource`, you need to tell it two things: Where is its first big buffer located? and, when that buffer is exhausted, who it should ask for another buffer? The first of these questions is answered by providing a pair of arguments `void*, size_t` that describes the first big buffer (optionally `nullptr`); and the second question is answered by providing a `std::pmr::memory_resource*` that points to this resource's "upstream" resource. One sensible thing to pass in for the "upstream" resource would be `std::pmr::new_delete_resource()`, so as to allocate new buffers using `::operator new`. Or, another sensible thing to pass in would be `std::pmr::null_memory_resource()`, so as to put a hard cap on the memory usage of this particular resource. Here's an example of the latter:

```
alignas(16) char big_buffer[10000];

std::pmr::monotonic_buffer_resource a(
  big_buffer, sizeof big_buffer,
```

```
        std::pmr::null_memory_resource()
);

void *p1 = a.allocate(100);
assert(p1 == big_buffer + 0);

void *p2 = a.allocate(100, 16);  // alignment
assert(p1 == big_buffer + 112);

// Now clear everything allocated so far and start over.
a.release();
void *p3 = a.allocate(100);
assert(p3 == big_buffer + 0);

// When the buffer is exhausted, a will go upstream
// to look for more buffers... and not find any.
try {
  a.allocate(9901);
} catch (const std::bad_alloc&) {
  puts("The null_memory_resource did its job!");
}
```

If you forget what upstream resource a particular `monotonic_buffer_resource` is using, you can always find out by calling `a.upstream_resource()`; that method returns a pointer to the upstream resource that was provided to the constructor.

Allocating from a pool resource

The final kind of memory resource provided by the C++17 standard library is what's called a "pool resource." A pool resource doesn't just manage one big buffer, such as `example_resource`; or even a monotonically increasing chain of buffers, such as `monotonic_buffer_resource`. Instead it manages a whole lot of "blocks" of various sizes. All the blocks of a given size are stored together in a "pool," so that we can talk about "the pool of blocks of size 4," "the pool of blocks of size 16," and so on. When a request comes in for an allocation of size *k*, the pool resource will look in the pool of blocks of size *k*, pull one out and return it. If the pool for size *k* is empty, then the pool resource will attempt to allocate some more blocks from its upstream resource. Also, if a request comes in for an allocation so large that we don't even have a pool for blocks of that size, then the pool resource is allowed to pass the request directly on to its upstream resource.

Pool resources come in two flavors: *synchronized* and *unsynchronized*, which is to say, thread-safe and thread-unsafe. If you're going to be accessing a pool from two different threads concurrently, then you should use `std::pmr::synchronized_pool_resource`, and if you're definitely never going to do that, and you want raw speed, then you should use `std::pmr::unsynchronized_pool_resource`. (By the way, `std::pmr::monotonic_buffer_resource` is always thread-unsafe; and `new_delete_resource()` is effectively thread-safe, since all it does is call `new` and `delete`.)

When you construct a resource of type `std::pmr::synchronized_pool_resource`, you need to tell it three things: Which block sizes it should keep in its pools; how many blocks it should glom together into a "chunk" when it goes to get more blocks from the upstream resource; and who is its upstream resource. Unfortunately, the standard interface leaves much to be desired here--so much so that frankly I recommend that if these parameters truly matter to you, you should be implementing your own derived `memory_resource` and not touching the standard library's version at all. The syntax for expressing these options is also fairly wonky:

```
std::pmr::pool_options options;
options.max_blocks_per_chunk = 100;
options.largest_required_pool_block = 256;

std::pmr::synchronized_pool_resource a(
  options,
  std::pmr::new_delete_resource()
);
```

Notice that there is no way to specify exactly which block sizes you want; that's left up to the vendor's implementation of `synchronized_pool_resource`. If you're lucky, it will choose decent block sizes that match your use-case; but personally I wouldn't rely on that assumption. Notice also that there's no way to use different upstream resources for the different block sizes, nor a different upstream resource for the "fallback" resource that's used when the caller requests an unusually sized allocation.

In short, I would steer clear of the built-in `pool_resource` derived classes for the foreseeable future. But the fundamental idea of deriving your own classes from `memory_resource` is solid. If you're concerned about memory allocation and managing your own little heaps, I'd recommend adopting `memory_resource` into your codebase.

Allocators

Now, so far we've only been talking about various allocation strategies, as "personified" by the different `memory_resource` derived classes. We still need to see how to hook `memory_resource` into the algorithms and containers of the Standard Template Library. And to do that, we'll have to transition from the classically polymorphic world of `memory_resource` back into the value-semantic world of the C++03 STL.

The 500 hats of the standard allocator

The standard allocator model must have seemed amazing in 2011. We're about to see how, with just one C++ type, we can accomplish all of the following feats:

- Specify a memory resource to be used for allocating memory.
- Annotate each allocated pointer with some metadata that will be carried along for its whole lifetime, all the way to deallocation time.
- Associate a container object with a particular memory resource, and make sure that association is "sticky"--this container object will always use the given heap for its allocations.
- Associate a container *value* with a particular memory resource, meaning that the container can be efficiently moved around using value semantics without forgetting how to deallocate its contents.
- Choose between the two mutually exclusive behaviors above.
- Specify a strategy for allocating memory at all levels of a multi-level container, such as a vector of vectors.
- Redefine what it means to "construct" the contents of a container, so that for example, `vector<int>::resize` could be defined to default-initialize new elements instead of zero-initializing them.

This is just an *insane* number of hats for any one class type to wear--a massive violation of the Single Responsibility Principle. Nevertheless, this is what the standard allocator model does; so let's try to explain all these features.

Remember that a "standard allocator" is just any class type that satisfies the concept `Allocator<T>` for some type `T`. The standard library provides three standard allocator types: `std::allocator<T>`, `std::pmr::polymorphic_allocator<T>`, and `std::scoped_allocator_adaptor<A...>`.

Let's start by looking at `std::allocator<T>`:

```
template<class T>
struct allocator {
  using value_type = T;

  T *allocate(size_t n) {
    return static_cast<T *>(::operator new(n * sizeof (T)));
  }
  void deallocate(T *p, size_t) {
    ::operator delete(static_cast<void *>(p));
  }

  // NOTE 1
  template<class U>
  explicit allocator(const allocator<U>&) noexcept {}

  // NOTE 2
  allocator() = default;
  allocator(const allocator&) = default;
};
```

`std::allocator<T>` has the member functions `allocate` and `deallocate` that are required by the `Allocator<T>` concept. Remember that we are in the world of concept-based generic programming now! The classically polymorphic `memory_resource` *also* had member functions named `allocate` and `deallocate`, but they always returned `void*`, not `T*`. (Also, `memory_resource::allocate()` took two arguments--bytes and align-- whereas `allocator<T>::allocate()` takes only one argument. The first reason for this is that `allocator<T>` predated the mainstream understanding that alignment was a big deal; remember that the `sizeof` operator was inherited from C in the 1980s but the `alignof` operator only showed up in C++11. The second reason is that in the context of `std::allocator<T>`, we know that the type of the objects being allocated is `T`, and thus the requested alignment must necessarily be `alignof(T)`. `std::allocator<T>` doesn't use that information, because it predates `alignof`; but in principle it could, and that's why the `Allocator<T>` concept requires only the signature `a.allocate(n)` instead of `a.allocate(n, align)`.)

The constructor marked NOTE 1 is important; every allocator needs a templated constructor modeled after this one. The constructors following the line marked NOTE 2 are unimportant; the only reason we wrote them explicitly in the code is because if we had not written them, they would have been implicitly deleted due to the presence of a user-defined constructor (namely, the NOTE 1 constructor).

Allocators

The idea of any standard allocator is that we can plug it in as the very last template type parameter of any standard container (Chapter 4, *The Container Zoo*) and the container will then use that allocator instead of its usual mechanisms anytime it needs to allocate memory for any reason. Let's see an example:

```
template<class T>
struct helloworld {
  using value_type = T;

  T *allocate(size_t n) {
    printf("hello world %zu\n", n);
    return static_cast<T *>(::operator new(n * sizeof (T)));
  }
  void deallocate(T *p, size_t) {
    ::operator delete(static_cast<void *>(p));
  }
};

void test() {
  std::vector<int, helloworld<int>> v;
  v.push_back(42); // prints "hello world 1"
  v.push_back(42); // prints "hello world 2"
  v.push_back(42); // prints "hello world 4"
}
```

Here our class `helloworld<int>` models `Allocator<int>`; but we've omitted the templated constructor. This is fine if we're dealing only with `vector`, because `vector` will allocate only arrays of its element type. However, watch what happens if we change the test case to use `list` instead:

```
void test() {
  std::list<int, helloworld<int>> v;
  v.push_back(42);
}
```

Under libc++, this code spews several dozen lines of error messages, which boil down to the essential complaint "no known conversion from `helloworld<int>` to `helloworld<std::__1::__list_node<int, void *>>`." Recall from the diagram in Chapter 4, *The Container Zoo*, that `std::list<T>` stores its elements in nodes that are larger than the size of `T` itself. So `std::list<T>` isn't going to be trying to allocate any `T` objects; it wants to allocate objects of type `__list_node`. To allocate memory for `__list_node` objects, it needs an allocator that models the concept `Allocator<__list_node>`, not `Allocator<int>`.

Internally, the constructor of `std::list<int>` takes our `helloworld<int>` and attempts to "rebind" it to allocate `__list_node` objects instead of `int` objects. This is accomplished via a *traits class*--a C++ idiom that we first encountered in Chapter 2, *Iterators and Ranges*:

```
using AllocOfInt = helloworld<int>;

using AllocOfChar =
   std::allocator_traits<AllocOfInt>::rebind_alloc<char>;

// Now alloc_of_char is helloworld<char>
```

The standard class template `std::allocator_traits<A>` wraps up a lot of information about the allocator type `A` into one place, so it's easy to get at. For example, `std::allocator_traits<A>::value_type` is an alias for the type `T` whose memory is allocated by `A`; and `std::allocator_traits<A>::pointer` is an alias for the corresponding pointer type (generally `T*`).

The nested alias template `std::allocator_traits<A>::rebind_alloc<U>` is a way of "converting" an allocator from one type `T` to another type `U`. This type trait uses metaprogramming to crack open the type `A` and see: first, whether `A` has a nested template alias `A::rebind<U>::other` (this is rare), and second, whether type `A` can be expressed in the form `Foo<Bar,Baz...>` (where `Baz...` is some list of types which might be an empty list). If `A` can be expressed that way, then `std::allocator_traits<A>::rebind_alloc<U>` will be a synonym for `Foo<U,Baz...>`. Philosophically, this is completely arbitrary; but in practice it works for every allocator type you'll ever see. In particular, it works for `helloworld<int>`--which explains why we didn't have to muck around with providing a nested alias `rebind<U>::other` in our `helloworld` class. By providing a sensible default behavior, the `std::allocator_traits` template has saved us some boilerplate. This is the reason `std::allocator_traits` exists.

You might wonder why `std::allocator_traits<Foo<Bar,Baz...>>::value_type` doesn't default to `Bar`. Frankly, I don't know either. It seems like a no-brainer; but the standard library doesn't do it. Therefore, every allocator type you write (remember now we're talking about classes modeling `Allocator<T>`, and *not* about classes derived from `memory_resource`) must provide a nested typedef `value_type` that is an alias for `T`.

Allocators

However, once you've defined the nested typedef for `value_type`, you can rely on `std::allocator_traits` to infer the correct definitions for its nested typedef `pointer` (that is, `T*`), and `const_pointer` (that is, `const T*`), and `void_pointer` (that is, `void*`), and so on. If you were following the previous discussion of `rebind_alloc`, you might guess that "converting" a pointer type like `T*` to `void*` is just as difficult or easy as "converting" an allocator type `Foo<T>` to `Foo<void>`; and you'd be correct! The values of these pointer-related type aliases are all computed via a *second* standard traits class, `std::pointer_traits<P>`:

```
using PtrToInt = int*;

using PtrToChar =
  std::pointer_traits<PtrToInt>::rebind<char>;

// Now PtrToChar is char*

using PtrToConstVoid =
  std::pointer_traits<PtrToInt>::rebind<const void>;

// Now PtrToConstVoid is const void*
```

This traits class becomes very important when we talk about the next responsibility of `Allocator<T>`, which was "annotate each allocated pointer with some metadata that will be carried along for its whole lifetime."

Carrying metadata with fancy pointers

Consider the following high-level design for a memory resource, which should remind you very much of `std::pmr::monotonic_buffer_resource`:

- Keep a list of chunks of memory we've gotten from the system. For each chunk, also store an `index` of how many bytes we've allocated from the beginning of the chunk; and store a count `freed` of how many bytes we've deallocated from this specific chunk.
- When someone calls `allocate(n)`, increment any one of our chunks' `index` by the appropriate number of bytes if possible, or get a new chunk from the upstream resource if absolutely necessary.
- When someone calls `deallocate(p, n)`, figure out which of our chunks `p` came from and increment its `freed += n`. If `freed == index`, then the entire chunk is empty, so set `freed = index = 0`.

It's pretty straightforward to turn the foregoing description into code. The only problematic item is: in `deallocate(p, n)`, how do we figure out which of our chunks p came from?

This would be easy if we simply recorded the identity of the chunk in the "pointer" itself:

```
template<class T>
class ChunkyPtr {
    T *m_ptr = nullptr;
    Chunk *m_chunk = nullptr;
public:
    explicit ChunkyPtr(T *p, Chunk *ch) :
        m_ptr(p), m_chunk(ch) {}

    T& operator *() const {
        return *m_ptr;
    }
    explicit operator T *() const {
        return m_ptr;
    }
    // ... and so on ...

    // ... plus this extra accessor:
    auto chunk() const {
        return m_chunk;
    }
};
```

Then in our `deallocate(p, n)` function, all we'd have to do is to look at `p.chunk()`. But to make this work, we'd need to change the signature of the `allocate(n)` and `deallocate(p, n)` functions so that `deallocate` took a `ChunkyPtr<T>` instead of `T*`, and `allocate` returned `ChunkyPtr<T>` instead of `T*`.

Fortunately, the C++ standard library gives us a way to do this! All we need to do is define our own type that models `Allocator<T>` and give it a member typedef `pointer` that evaluates to `ChunkyPtr<T>`:

```
template<class T>
struct ChunkyAllocator {
    using value_type = T;
    using pointer = ChunkyPtr<T>;

    ChunkyAllocator(ChunkyMemoryResource *mr) :
        m_resource(mr) {}

    template<class U>
    ChunkyAllocator(const ChunkyAllocator<U>& rhs) :
        m_resource(rhs.m_resource) {}
```

Allocators

```
    pointer allocate(size_t n) {
      return m_resource->allocate(
        n * sizeof(T), alignof(T));
    }
    void deallocate(pointer p, size_t n) {
      m_resource->deallocate(
        p, n * sizeof(T), alignof(T));
    }
  private:
    ChunkyMemoryResource *m_resource;

    template<class U>
    friend struct ChunkyAllocator;
};
```

The traits classes `std::allocator_traits` and `std::pointer_traits` will take care of inferring the other typedefs--such as `void_pointer`, which through the magic of `pointer_traits::rebind` will end up as an alias for `ChunkyPtr<void>`.

I've left out the implementations of the `allocate` and `deallocate` functions here because they would depend on the interface of `ChunkyMemoryResource`. We might implement `ChunkyMemoryResource` something like this:

```
class Chunk {
  char buffer[10000];
  int index = 0;
  int freed = 0;
public:
  bool can_allocate(size_t bytes) {
    return (sizeof buffer - index) >= bytes;
  }
  auto allocate(size_t bytes) {
    index += bytes;
    void *p = &buffer[index - bytes];
    return ChunkyPtr<void>(p, this);
  }
  void deallocate(void *, size_t bytes) {
    freed += bytes;
    if (freed == index) {
        index = freed = 0;
    }
  }
};

class ChunkyMemoryResource {
  std::list<Chunk> m_chunks;
public:
```

```
    ChunkyPtr<void> allocate(size_t bytes, size_t align) {
      assert(align <= alignof(std::max_align_t));
      bytes += -bytes % alignof(std::max_align_t);
      assert(bytes <= 10000);

      for (auto&& ch : m_chunks) {
        if (ch.can_allocate(bytes)) {
          return ch.allocate(bytes);
        }
      }
      return m_chunks.emplace_back().allocate(bytes);
    }
    void deallocate(ChunkyPtr<void> p, size_t bytes, size_t) {
      bytes += -bytes % alignof(std::max_align_t);
      p.chunk()->deallocate(static_cast<void*>(p), bytes);
    }
  };
```

Now we can use our `ChunkyMemoryResource` to allocate memory for standard allocator-aware containers like this:

```
    ChunkyMemoryResource mr;
    std::vector<int, ChunkyAllocator<int>> v{&mr};
    v.push_back(42);
    // All the memory for v's underlying array
    // is coming from blocks owned by "mr".
```

Now, I've chosen this example to make it look very simple and straightforward; and I've left out a lot of the details of the `ChunkyPtr<T>` type itself. If you try copying this code yourself, you'll find that you need to provide `ChunkyPtr` with a lot of overloaded operators such as `==`, `!=`, `<`, `++`, `--`, and `-`; and you'll also need to provide a specialization for `ChunkyPtr<void>` that omits the overloaded `operator*`. Most of the details are the same as what we covered in Chapter 2, *Iterators and Ranges*, when we implemented our own iterator type. In fact, every "fancy pointer" type is required to be usable as a *random-access iterator*--which means that you must provide the five nested typedefs listed at the end of Chapter 2, *Iterators and Ranges*: `iterator_category`, `difference_type`, `value_type`, `pointer`, and `reference`.

Finally, if you want to use certain containers such as `std::list` and `std::map`, you'll need to implement a static member function with the surprising name `pointer_to(r)`:

```
    static ChunkyPtr<T> pointer_to(T &r) noexcept {
      return ChunkyPtr<T>(&r, nullptr);
    }
```

Allocators

This is because--as you may recall from Chapter 4, *The Container Zoo*--a few containers such as `std::list` store their data in nodes whose `prev` and `next` pointers need to be able to point *either* to an allocated node *or* to a node which is contained within the member data of the `std::list` object itself. There are two obvious ways to accomplish this: Either every `next` pointer must be stored in a sort of tagged union of a fancy pointer and a raw pointer (perhaps a `std::variant` as described in Chapter 5, *Vocabulary Types*), or else we must find a way of encoding a raw pointer *as* a fancy pointer. The standard library chose the latter approach. So, whenever you write a fancy pointer type, not only must it do all the things required of it by the allocator, and not only must it satisfy the requirements of a random-access iterator, but it must *also* have a way of representing any arbitrary pointer in the program's address space--at least if you want to use your allocator with node-based containers such as `std::list`.

Even after jumping through all these hoops, you'll find that (as of press time) neither libc++ nor libstdc++ can handle fancy pointers in any container more complicated than `std::vector`. They support just enough to work with a single fancy pointer type--`boost::interprocess::offset_ptr<T>`, which carries no metadata. And the standard continues to evolve; `std::pmr::memory_resource` was newly introduced in C++17, and as of this writing it is still not implemented by libc++ nor libstdc++.

You may also have noticed the lack of any standard base class for memory resources that use fancy pointers. Fortunately, this is easy to write yourself:

```
namespace my {

  template<class VoidPtr>
  class fancy_memory_resource {
  public:
    VoidPtr allocate(size_t bytes,
        size_t align = alignof(std::max_align_t)) {
      return do_allocate(bytes, align);
    }
    void deallocate(VoidPtr p, size_t bytes,
        size_t align = alignof(std::max_align_t)) {
      return do_deallocate(p, bytes, align);
    }
    bool is_equal(const fancy_memory_resource& rhs) const noexcept {
      return do_is_equal(rhs);
    }
    virtual ~fancy_memory_resource() = default;
  private:
    virtual VoidPtr do_allocate(size_t bytes, size_t align) = 0;
    virtual void do_deallocate(VoidPtr p, size_t bytes,
        size_t align) = 0;
    virtual bool do_is_equal(const fancy_memory_resource& rhs)
```

```
            const noexcept = 0;
    };

    using memory_resource = fancy_memory_resource<void*>;

} // namespace my
```

The standard library provides no allocators that use fancy pointers; every library-provided allocator type uses raw pointers.

Sticking a container to a single memory resource

The next hat worn by the standard allocator model--the next feature controlled by `std::allocator_traits`--is the ability to associate specific container objects with specific heaps. We used three bullet points to describe this feature earlier:

- Associate a container object with a particular memory resource, and make sure that association is "sticky"--this container object will always use the given heap for its allocations.
- Associate a container *value* with a particular memory resource, meaning that the container can be efficiently moved around using value semantics without forgetting how to deallocate its contents.
- Choose between the two mutually exclusive behaviors just mentioned.

Let's look at an example, using `std::pmr::monotonic_buffer_resource` for our resource but using a hand-written class type for our allocator type. (Just to reassure you that you haven't missed anything: Indeed, we *still* haven't covered any standard-library-provided allocator types--except for `std::allocator<T>`, the trivial stateless allocator that is a handle to the global heap managed by `new` and `delete`.)

```
    template<class T>
    struct WidgetAlloc {
      std::pmr::memory_resource *mr;

      using value_type = T;

      WidgetAlloc(std::pmr::memory_resource *mr) : mr(mr) {}

      template<class U>
      WidgetAlloc(const WidgetAlloc<U>& rhs) : mr(rhs.mr) {}
```

```
    T *allocate(size_t n) {
      return (T *)mr->allocate(n * sizeof(T), alignof(T));
    }
    void deallocate(void *p, size_t n) {
      mr->deallocate(p, n * sizeof(T), alignof(T));
    }
};

class Widget {
  char buffer[10000];
  std::pmr::monotonic_buffer_resource mr {buffer, sizeof buffer};
  std::vector<int, WidgetAlloc<int>> v {&mr};
  std::list<int, WidgetAlloc<int>> lst {&mr};
public:
  static void swap_elems(Widget& a, Widget& b) {
    std::swap(a.v, b.v);
  }
};
```

Here our `Widget` is a classically object-oriented class type; we expect it to live at a specific memory address for its entire lifetime. Then, to reduce heap fragmentation or to improve cache locality, we've placed a large buffer inside each `Widget` object and made the `Widget` use that buffer as the backing store for its data members `v` and `lst`.

Now look at the `Widget::swap_elems(a, b)` function. It swaps the `v` data members of `Widget` a and `Widget` b. You might recall from Chapter 4, *The Container Zoo*, that a `std::vector` is little more than a pointer to a dynamically allocated array, and so *usually* the library can swap two instances of `std::vector` by simply swapping their underlying pointers, without moving any of the underlying data--making vector swap an O(1) operation instead of an O(*n*) operation.

Furthermore, vector is smart enough to know that if it swaps pointers, it also needs to swap allocators--so that the information about how to deallocate travels along with the pointer that will eventually be in need of deallocation.

But in this case, if the library just swapped the pointers and allocators, it would be disastrous! We'd have a vector `a.v` whose underlying array was now "owned" by `b.mr`, and vice versa. If we destroyed `Widget` b, then the next time we accessed the elements of `a.v` we'd be accessing freed memory. And furthermore, even if we never accessed `a.v` again, our program would likely crash when the destructor of `a.v` attempted to call the `deallocate` method of the long-dead `b.mr`!

Fortunately, the standard library saves us from this fate. One of the responsibilities of an allocator-aware container is to appropriately *propagate* its allocator on copy-assignment, move-assignment, and swap. For historical reasons this is handled by a whole mess of typedefs in the `allocator_traits` class template, but in order to *use* allocator propagation correctly, you only have to know a couple of things:

- Whether the allocator propagates itself, or whether it sticks firmly to a specific container, is a property of the *allocator type*. If you want one allocator to "stick" while another propagates, you *must* make them different types.
- When an allocator is "sticky," it sticks to a particular (classical, object-oriented) container object. Operations that with a non-sticky allocator type would be O(1) pointer-swaps may become O(*n*), because "adopting" elements from some other allocator's memory space into our own requires allocating room for them in our own memory space.
- Stickiness has a clear use-case (as we have just shown with `Widget`), and the effects of non-stickiness can be disastrous (again, see `Widget`). Therefore, `std::allocator_traits` assumes by default that an allocator type is sticky, unless it can tell that the allocator type is *empty* and thus is quite definitely *stateless*. The default for *empty* allocator types is effectively non-stickiness.
- As a programmer, you basically always want the default: stateless allocators might as well propagate, and stateful allocators *probably* don't have much use outside of `Widget`-like scenarios where stickiness is required.

Using the standard allocator types

Let's talk about the allocator types provided by the standard library.

`std::allocator<T>` is the default allocator type; it is the default value of the template type parameter to every standard container. So for example when you write `std::vector<T>` in your code, that's secretly the exact same type as `std::vector<T, std::allocator<T>>`. As we've mentioned before in this chapter, `std::allocator<T>` is a stateless empty type; it is a "handle" to the global heap managed by `new` and `delete`. Because `std::allocator` is a stateless type, `allocator_traits` assumes (correctly) that it should be non-sticky. This means that operations such as `std::vector<T>::swap` and `std::vector<T>::operator=` are guaranteed to be very efficient pointer-swaps--because any object of type `std::vector<T, std::allocator<T>>` always knows how to deallocate memory that was originally allocated by any other `std::vector<T, std::allocator<T>>`.

Allocators

`std::pmr::polymorphic_allocator<T>` is a new addition in C++17. It is a stateful, non-empty type; its one data member is a pointer to a `std::pmr::memory_resource`. (In fact, it is almost identical to `WidgetAlloc` in our sample code from earlier in this chapter!) Two different instances of `std::pmr::polymorphic_allocator<T>` are not necessarily interchangeable, because their pointers might point to completely different `memory_resources`; this means that an object of type `std::vector<T, std::pmr::polymorphic_allocator<T>>` does *not* necessarily know how to deallocate memory that was originally allocated by some other `std::vector<T, std::pmr::polymorphic_allocator<T>>`. That, in turn, means that `std::pmr::polymorphic_allocator<T>` is a "sticky" allocator type; and *that* means that operations such as `std::vector<T, std::pmr::polymorphic_allocator<T>>::operator=` can end up doing lots of copying.

By the way, it's quite tedious to write out the name of the type `std::vector<T, std::pmr::polymorphic_allocator<T>>` over and over. Fortunately, the standard library implementors came to the same realization, and so the standard library provides type aliases in the `std::pmr` namespace:

```
namespace std::pmr {

  template<class T>
  using vector = std::vector<T,
    polymorphic_allocator<T>>;

  template<class K, class V, class Cmp = std::less<K>>
  using map = std::map<K, V, Cmp,
    polymorphic_allocator<typename std::map<K, V>::value_type>>;

  // ...

} // namespace std::pmr
```

Setting the default memory resource

The biggest difference between the standard `polymorphic_allocator` and our example `WidgetAlloc` is that `polymorphic_allocator` is default-constructible. Default-constructibility is arguably an attractive feature of an allocator; it means that we can write the second of these two lines instead of the first:

```
std::pmr::vector<int> v2({1, 2, 3}, std::pmr::new_delete_resource());
    // Specifying a specific memory resource
```

```
std::pmr::vector<int> v1 = {1, 2, 3};
    // Using the default memory resource
```

On the other hand, when you look at that second line, you might wonder, "Where is the underlying array actually being allocated?" After all, the main point of specifying an allocator is that we want to know where our bytes are coming from! That's why the *normal* way to construct a standard `polymorphic_allocator` is to pass in a pointer to a `memory_resource`--in fact, this idiom is expected to be *so* common that the conversion from `std::pmr::memory_resource*` to `std::pmr::polymorphic_allocator` is an implicit conversion. But `polymorphic_allocator` does have a default, zero-argument constructor as well. When you default-construct a `polymorphic_allocator`, you get a handle to the "default memory resource," which by default is `new_delete_resource()`. However, you can change this! The default memory resource pointer is stored in a global atomic (thread-safe) variable which can be manipulated with the library functions `std::pmr::get_default_resource()` (which returns the pointer) and `std::pmr::set_default_resource()` (which assigns a new value to the pointer and returns the previous value).

If you want to avoid heap allocation via `new` and `delete` altogether, it might make sense to call `std::pmr::set_default_resource(std::pmr::null_memory_resource())` at the start of your program. Of course you can't stop any other part of your program from going rogue and calling `set_default_resource` itself; and because the same global variable is shared by every thread in your program, you might run into some very strange behavior if you *try* to modify the default resource during the program's execution. There is no way to say "set the default resource only for my current thread," for example. Furthermore, calling `get_default_resource()` (such as from the default constructor of `polymorphic_allocator`) performs an atomic access, which will tend to be marginally slower than if the atomic access could have been avoided. Therefore, your best course of action is to avoid the default constructor of `polymorphic_allocator`; always be explicit as to which memory resource you're trying to use. For absolute foolproofness, you might consider simply using the above `WidgetAlloc` instead of `polymorphic_allocator`; having *no* default constructor, `WidgetAlloc` flatly cannot be misused.

Making a container allocator-aware

Having covered memory resources (heaps) and allocators (handles to heaps), let's turn now to the third leg of the tripod: container classes. Inside each allocator-aware container, at least four things have to happen:

- The container instance must store an allocator instance as member data. (Therefore the container must take the type of the allocator as a template parameter; otherwise it can't know how much space to reserve for that member variable.)
- The container must provide constructors taking an allocator argument.
- The container must actually use its allocator to allocate and deallocate memory; every use of `new` or `delete` must be banished.
- The container's move constructor, move assignment operator, and `swap` function must all propagate the allocator according to its `allocator_traits`.

Here is a very simple allocator-aware container--a container of just one single object, allocated on the heap. This is something like an allocator-aware version of `std::unique_ptr<T>` from Chapter 6, *Smart Pointers*:

```cpp
template<class T, class A = std::allocator<T>>
class uniqueish {
  using Traits = std::allocator_traits<A>;
  using FancyPtr = typename Traits::pointer;

  A m_allocator;
  FancyPtr m_ptr = nullptr;

public:
  using allocator_type = A;

  uniqueish(A a = {}) : m_allocator(a) {
    this->emplace();
  }

  ~uniqueish() {
    clear();
  }

  T& value() { return *m_ptr; }
  const T& value() const { return *m_ptr; }

  template<class... Args>
  void emplace(Args&&... args) {
```

```
    clear();
    m_ptr = Traits::allocate(m_allocator, 1);
    try {
      T *raw_ptr = static_cast<T *>(m_ptr);
      Traits::construct(m_allocator, raw_ptr,
          std::forward<Args>(args)...
      );
    } catch (...) {
      Traits::deallocate(m_allocator, m_ptr, 1);
      throw;
    }
  }

  void clear() noexcept {
    if (m_ptr) {
      T *raw_ptr = static_cast<T *>(m_ptr);
      Traits::destroy(m_allocator, raw_ptr);
      Traits::deallocate(m_allocator, m_ptr, 1);
      m_ptr = nullptr;
    }
  }
};
```

Notice that where `unique_ptr` uses `T*`, our present code uses `allocator_traits<A>::pointer`; and where `make_unique` uses `new` and `delete`, our present code uses the one-two punch of `allocator_traits<A>::allocate/construct` and `allocator_traits<A>::destroy/deallocate`. We've already discussed the purpose of `allocate` and `deallocate`--they deal with getting memory from the appropriate memory resource. But those chunks of memory are just raw bytes; to turn a chunk of memory into a usable object we have to construct an instance of T at that address. We could use "placement `new`" syntax for this purpose; but we'll see in the next section why it's important to use `construct` and `destroy` instead.

Finally, before we proceed, notice that the destructor of `uniqueish` checks to see whether an allocation exists before trying to deallocate it. This is important because it gives us a value of `uniqueish` representing the "empty object"--a value that can be constructed without allocating any memory, and that is a suitably "moved-from" representation for our type.

Allocators

Now let's implement the move operations for our type. We'd like to ensure that after you move out of a uniqueish<T> object, the moved-from object is "empty." Furthermore, if the left-hand object and the right-hand object share the same allocator, or if the allocator type is "not sticky," then we'd like to avoid calling the move constructor of T at all--we'd like to transfer ownership of the allocated pointer from the right-hand-side object to the left-hand object:

```
uniqueish(uniqueish&& rhs) : m_allocator(rhs.m_allocator)
{
  m_ptr = std::exchange(rhs.m_ptr, nullptr);
}

uniqueish& operator=(uniqueish&& rhs)
{
  constexpr bool pocma =
    Traits::propagate_on_container_move_assignment::value;
  if constexpr (pocma) {
    // We can adopt the new allocator, since
    // our allocator type is not "sticky".
    this->clear(); // using the old allocator
    this->m_allocator = rhs.m_allocator;
    this->m_ptr = std::exchange(rhs.m_ptr, nullptr);
  } else if (m_allocator() == rhs.m_allocator()) {
    // Our allocator is "stuck" to this container;
    // but since it's equivalent to rhs's allocator,
    // we can still adopt rhs's memory.
    this->clear();
    this->m_ptr = std::exchange(rhs.m_ptr, nullptr);
  } else {
    // We must not propagate this new allocator
    // and thus cannot adopt its memory.
    if (rhs.m_ptr) {
      this->emplace(std::move(rhs.value()));
      rhs.clear();
    } else {
      this->clear();
    }
  }
  return *this;
}
```

The move *constructor* is just about as simple as it ever was. The only minor difference is that we have to remember to construct our m_allocator as a copy of the right-hand object's allocator.

> We could use `std::move` to move the allocator instead of copying it, but I didn't think it was worth it for this example. Remember that an allocator is just a thin "handle" pointing to the actual memory resource, and that a lot of allocator types, such as `std::allocator<T>`, are actually empty. Copying an allocator type should always be relatively cheap. Still, using `std::move` here wouldn't have hurt.

The move *assignment operator*, on the other hand, is very complicated! The first thing we need to do is check whether our allocator type is "sticky" or not. Non-stickiness is denoted by having a true value for `propagate_on_container_move_assignment::value`, which we abbreviate to "pocma." (Actually, the standard says that `propagate_on_container_move_assignment` ought to be *exactly* the type `std::true_type`; and GNU's libstdc++ will hold you firmly to that requirement. So watch out when defining your own allocator types.) If the allocator type is non-sticky, then our most efficient course of action for move-assignment is to destroy our current value (if any)--making sure to use our old `m_allocator`--and then adopt the right-hand object's pointer along with its allocator. Because we adopt the allocator along with the pointer, we can be sure that we'll know how to deallocate the pointer down the road.

On the other hand, if our allocator type *is* "sticky," then we cannot adopt the allocator of the right-hand object. If our current ("stuck") allocator instance happens to be equal to the right-hand object's allocator instance, then we can adopt the right-hand object's pointer anyway; we already know how to deallocate pointers allocated by this particular allocator instance.

Finally, if we cannot adopt the right-hand object's allocator instance, and our current allocator instance isn't equal to the right-hand object's, then we cannot adopt the right-hand object's pointer--because at some point down the road we're going to have to free that pointer, and the only way to free that pointer is to use the right-hand object's allocator instance, and we're not allowed to adopt the right-hand object's allocator instance because our own instance is "stuck." In this case, we actually have to allocate a completely new pointer using our own allocator instance, and then copy over the data from `rhs.value()` to our own value by invoking the move constructor of `T`. This final case is the only one where we actually call the move constructor of `T`!

Copy assignment follows similar logic for the propagation of the right-hand allocator instance, except that it looks at the trait `propagate_on_container_copy_assignment`, or "pocca."

Allocators

Swap is particularly interesting because its final case (when the allocator type is "sticky" and the allocator instances are unequal) requires extra allocations:

```
void swap(uniqueish& rhs) noexcept {
  constexpr bool pocs =
    Traits::propagate_on_container_swap::value;
  using std::swap;
  if constexpr (pocs) {
    // We can swap allocators, since
    // our allocator type is not "sticky".
    swap(this->m_allocator, rhs.m_allocator);
    swap(this->m_ptr, rhs.m_ptr);
  } else if (m_allocator == rhs.m_allocator) {
    // Our allocator is "stuck" to this container;
    // but since it's equivalent to rhs's allocator,
    // we can still adopt rhs's memory and vice versa.
    swap(this->m_ptr, rhs.m_ptr);
  } else {
    // Neither side can adopt the other's memory, and
    // so one side or the other must allocate.
    auto temp = std::move(*this);
    *this = std::move(rhs);  // might throw
    rhs = std::move(temp);   // might throw
  }
}
```

On each of the two lines marked "might throw," we're calling the move assignment operator, which in this case might call `emplace`, which will ask the allocator for memory. If the underlying memory resource has been exhausted, then `Traits::allocate(m_allocator, 1)` might well throw an exception--and then we'd be in trouble, for two reasons. First, we've already started moving state around and deallocating old memory, and we might find it impossible to "unwind" back to a reasonable state. Second, and more importantly, `swap` is one of those functions that is so primitive and so fundamental that the standard library makes no provision for its failing--for example, the `std::swap` algorithm (Chapter 3, *The Iterator-Pair Algorithms*) is declared as `noexcept`, which means it *must* succeed; it is not allowed to throw an exception.

Thus, if allocation fails during our `noexcept` swap function, we'll see a `bad_alloc` exception percolate up through the call stack until it reaches our `noexcept` swap function declaration; at which point the C++ runtime will stop unwinding and call `std::terminate`, which (unless the programmer has altered its behavior via `std::set_terminate`) will cause our program to crash and burn.

The C++17 Standard goes several steps further than this in its specification of what *ought* to happen during the swapping of standard container types. First, instead of saying that allocation failure during `swap` will result in a call to `std::terminate`, the Standard simply says that allocation failure during `swap` will result in *undefined behavior*. Second, the Standard does not limit that undefined behavior to allocation failure! According to the C++17 Standard, merely *calling* `swap` on any standard library container instances whose allocators do not compare equally will result in undefined behavior, whether an allocation failure would have been encountered or not!

In fact, libc++ exploits this optimization opportunity to generate code for all standard container `swap` functions that looks roughly like this:

```
void swap(uniqueish& rhs) noexcept {
  constexpr bool pocs =
    Traits::propagate_on_container_swap::value;
  using std::swap;
  if constexpr (pocs) {
    swap(this->m_allocator, rhs.m_allocator);
  }
  // Don't even check that we know how to free
  // the adopted pointer; just assume that we can.
  swap(this->m_ptr, rhs.m_ptr);
}
```

Notice that if you use this code (as libc++ does) to `swap` two containers with unequal allocators, you'll wind up with a mismatch between pointers and their allocators, and then your program will probably crash--or worse--the next time you try to deallocate one of those pointers using the mismatched allocator. It is supremely important that you remember this pitfall when dealing with the C++17 "convenience" types such as `std::pmr::vector`!

```
char buffer[100];
auto mr = std::pmr::monotonic_buffer_resource(buffer, 100);

std::pmr::vector<int> a {1,2,3};
std::pmr::vector<int> b({4,5,6}, &mr);

std::swap(a, b);
  // UNDEFINED BEHAVIOR

a.reserve(a.capacity() + 1);
  // this line will undoubtedly crash, as
  // it tries to delete[] a stack pointer
```

Allocators

If your code design allows containers backed by different memory resources to be swapped with each other, then you must avoid `std::swap` and instead use this safe idiom:

```
auto temp = std::move(a);  // OK
a = std::move(b);  // OK
b = std::move(temp);  // OK
```

When I say "avoid `std::swap`," I mean "avoid any of the permutative algorithms in the STL," including such algorithms as `std::reverse` and `std::sort`. This would be quite an undertaking and I do not advise attempting it!

If your code design allows containers backed by different memory resources to be swapped with each other, then really, you *might* want to reconsider your design. If you can fix it so that you only ever swap containers that share the same memory resource, or if you can avoid stateful and/or sticky allocators entirely, then you will never need to think about this particular pitfall.

Propagating downwards with scoped_allocator_adaptor

In the preceding section, we introduced `std::allocator_traits<A>::construct(a, ptr, args...)` and described it as a preferable alternative to the placement-new syntax `::new ((void*)ptr) T(args...)`. Now we'll see why the author of a particular allocator might want to give it different semantics.

One perhaps obvious way to change the semantics of `construct` for our own allocator type would be to make it trivially default-initialize primitive types instead of zero-initializing them. That code would look like this:

```
template<class T>
struct my_allocator : std::allocator<T>
{
  my_allocator() = default;

  template<class U>
  my_allocator(const my_allocator<U>&) {}

  template<class... Args>
  void construct(T *p, Args&&... args) {
    if (sizeof...(Args) == 0) {
      ::new ((void*)p) T;
    } else {
```

```
            ::new ((void*)p) T(std::forward<Args>(args)...);
        }
    }
};
```

Now you can use `std::vector<int, my_allocator<int>>` as a "vector-like" type satisfying all the usual invariants of `std::vector<int>`, except that when you implicitly create new elements via `v.resize(n)` or `v.emplace_back()`, the new elements are created uninitialized, just like stack variables, instead of being zero-initialized.

In a sense, what we've designed here is an "adaptor" that fits over the top of `std::allocator<T>` and modifies its behavior in an interesting way. It would be even better if we could modify or "adapt" any arbitrary allocator in the same way; to do that, we'd just change our `template<class T>` to `template<class A>` and inherit from `A` where the old code inherited from `std::allocator<T>`. Of course our new adaptor's template parameter list no longer starts with `T`, so we'd have to implement `rebind` ourselves; this path quickly gets into deep metaprogramming, so I won't digress to show it.

However, there's another useful way we could fiddle with the `construct` method for our own allocator type. Consider the following code sample, which creates a vector of vectors of `int`:

```
std::vector<std::vector<int>> vv;
vv.emplace_back();
vv.emplace_back();
vv[0].push_back(1);
vv[1].push_back(2);
vv[1].push_back(3);
```

Suppose we wanted to "stick" this container to a memory resource of our own devising, such as our favorite `WidgetAlloc`. We'd have to write something repetitive like this:

```
char buffer[10000];
std::pmr::monotonic_buffer_resource mr {buffer, sizeof buffer};

using InnerAlloc = WidgetAlloc<int>;
using InnerVector = std::vector<int, InnerAlloc>;
using OuterAlloc = WidgetAlloc<InnerVector>;

std::vector<InnerVector, OuterAlloc> vv(&mr);
vv.emplace_back(&mr);
vv.emplace_back(&mr);
vv[0].push_back(1);
vv[1].push_back(2);
vv[1].push_back(3);
```

Notice the repetition of the allocator object's initializer `&mr` at both levels. The need to repeat `&mr` makes it difficult to use our vector `vv` in generic contexts; for example, we can't easily pass it to a function template to populate it with data, because every time the callee would want to `emplace_back` a new vector-of-`int`, it would need to know the address `&mr` that is only known to the caller. What we'd like to do is wrap up and reify the notion that "every time you construct an element of the vector-of-vectors, you need to tack `&mr` onto the end of the argument list." And the standard library has us covered!

Since C++11, the standard library has provided (in the header named `<scoped_allocator>`) a class template called `scoped_allocator_adaptor<A>`. Just like our default-initializing "adaptor," `scoped_allocator_adaptor<A>` inherits from `A`, thus picking up all of `A`'s behaviors; and then it overrides the `construct` method to do something different. Namely, it attempts to figure out whether the `T` object it's currently constructing "uses an allocator," and if so, it will pass itself down as an extra argument to the constructor of `T`.

To decide whether type `T` "uses an allocator," `scoped_allocator_adaptor<A>::construct` defers to the type trait `std::uses_allocator_v<T, A>`, which (unless you've specialized it, which you probably shouldn't) will be true if and only if `A` is implicitly convertible to `T::allocator_type`. If `T` doesn't have an `allocator_type`, then the library will assume that `T` doesn't care about allocators, except in the special cases of `pair` and `tuple` (which all have special overloads of their constructors intended specifically to propagate allocators downward to their members) and in the special case of `promise` (which can allocate its shared state with an allocator even though it provides no way of referring to that allocator object afterward; we say that `promise`'s allocator support is "type-erased" even more thoroughly than the examples of type erasure we saw in `Chapter 5`, *Vocabulary Types*).

For historical reasons, the constructors of allocator-aware types can follow either of two different patterns, and `scoped_allocator_adaptor` is smart enough to know them both. Older and simpler types (that is, everything except `tuple` and `promise`) tend to have constructors of the form `T(args..., A)` where the allocator `A` comes at the end. For `tuple` and `promise`, the standard library has introduced a new pattern: `T(std::allocator_arg, A, args...)` where the allocator `A` comes at the beginning but is preceded by the special tag value `std::allocator_arg`, whose sole purpose is to indicate that the next argument in the argument list represents an allocator, similarly to how the sole purpose of the tag `std::nullopt` is to indicate that an `optional` has no value (see `Chapter 5`, *Vocabulary Types*). Just as the standard forbids creating the type `std::optional<std::nullopt_t>`, you will also find yourself in a world of trouble if you attempt to create `std::tuple<std::allocator_arg_t>`.

Using `scoped_allocator_adaptor`, we can rewrite our cumbersome example from earlier in a slightly less cumbersome way:

```
char buffer[10000];
std::pmr::monotonic_buffer_resource mr {buffer, sizeof buffer};

using InnerAlloc = WidgetAlloc<int>;
using InnerVector = std::vector<int, InnerAlloc>;
using OuterAlloc =
   std::scoped_allocator_adaptor<WidgetAlloc<InnerVector>>;

std::vector<InnerVector, OuterAlloc> vv(&mr);
vv.emplace_back();
vv.emplace_back();
vv[0].push_back(1);
vv[1].push_back(2);
vv[1].push_back(3);
```

Notice that the allocator type has gotten *more* cumbersome, but the important thing is that the `&mr` argument to `emplace_back` has disappeared; we can now use `vv` in contexts that expect to be able to push back elements in a natural way, without having to remember to add `&mr` all over the place. In our case, because we're using our `WidgetAlloc`, which is not default-constructible, the symptom of a forgotten `&mr` is a spew of compile-time errors. But you may recall from preceding sections in this chapter that `std::pmr::polymorphic_allocator<T>` will happily allow you to default-construct it, with potentially disastrous results; so if you are planning to use `polymorphic_allocator`, it might also be wise to look into `scoped_allocator_adaptor` just in order to limit the number of places in which you might forget to specify your allocation strategy.

Propagating different allocators

In my introduction of `scoped_allocator_adaptor<A>`, I left out one more complication. The template parameter list isn't limited to just one allocator type argument! You can actually create a scoped-allocator type with multiple allocator type arguments, like this:

```
using InnerAlloc = WidgetAlloc<int>;
using InnerVector = std::vector<int, InnerAlloc>;

using MiddleAlloc = std::scoped_allocator_adaptor<
    WidgetAlloc<InnerVector>,
    WidgetAlloc<int>
>;
using MiddleVector = std::vector<InnerVector, MiddleAlloc>;
```

Allocators

```
using OuterAlloc = std::scoped_allocator_adaptor<
  WidgetAlloc<MiddleVector>,
  WidgetAlloc<InnerVector>,
  WidgetAlloc<int>
>;
using OuterVector = std::vector<MiddleVector, OuterAlloc>;
```

Having set up these typedefs, we proceed to set up three distinct memory resources and construct an instance of `scoped_allocator_adaptor` capable of remembering all three of the memory resources (because it contains three distinct instances of `WidgetAlloc`, one per "level"):

```
char bi[1000];
std::pmr::monotonic_buffer_resource mri {bi, sizeof bi};
char bm[1000];
std::pmr::monotonic_buffer_resource mrm {bm, sizeof bm};
char bo[1000];
std::pmr::monotonic_buffer_resource mro {bo, sizeof bo};

OuterAlloc saa(&mro, &mrm, &mri);
```

Finally, we can construct an instance of `OuterVector`, passing in our `scoped_allocator_adaptor` argument; and that's all! The overridden `construct` method hidden deep within our carefully crafted allocator type takes care of passing the argument `&bm` or `&bi` to any constructor that needs one of them:

```
OuterVector vvv(saa);

vvv.emplace_back();
  // This allocation comes from buffer "bo".

vvv[0].emplace_back();
  // This allocation comes from buffer "bm".

vvv[0][0].emplace_back(42);
  // This allocation comes from buffer "bi".
```

As you can see, a deeply nested `scoped_allocator_adaptor` is not for the faint of heart; and they're really only usable at all if you make a lot of "helper" typedefs along the way, as we did in this example.

One last note about `std::scoped_allocator_adaptor<A...>`: if the nesting of containers goes deeper than the number of allocator types in the template parameter list, then `scoped_allocator_adaptor` will act as if the last allocator type in its parameter list repeats forever. For example:

```
using InnerAlloc = WidgetAlloc<int>;
using InnerVector = std::vector<int, InnerAlloc>;

using MiddleAlloc = std::scoped_allocator_adaptor<
    WidgetAlloc<InnerVector>
>;
using MiddleVector = std::vector<InnerVector, MiddleAlloc>;

using TooShortAlloc = std::scoped_allocator_adaptor<
    WidgetAlloc<MiddleVector>,
    WidgetAlloc<InnerVector>
>;
using OuterVector = std::vector<MiddleVector, TooShortAlloc>;

TooShortAlloc tsa(&mro, WidgetAlloc<InnerVector>(&mri));
OuterVector tsv(tsa);

tsv.emplace_back();
    // This allocation comes from buffer "bo".

tsv[0].emplace_back();
    // This allocation comes from buffer "bi".

tsv[0][0].emplace_back(42);
    // This allocation AGAIN comes from buffer "bi"!
```

We actually relied on this behavior in our very first `scoped_allocator_adaptor` example, the one involving vv, even though I didn't mention it at the time. Now that you know about it, you might want to go back and study that example to see where the "repeat forever" behavior is being used, and how you'd change that code if you wanted to use a different memory resource for the inner array of `int` than for the outer array of `InnerVector`.

Summary

Allocators are a fundamentally arcane topic in C++, mainly for historical reasons. Several different interfaces, with different obscure use-cases, are piled one on top of the other; all of them involve intense metaprogramming; and vendor support for many of these features, even relatively old C++11 features such as fancy pointers, is still lacking.

Allocators

C++17 offers the standard library type `std::pmr::memory_resource` to clarify the existing distinction between *memory resources* (a.k.a. *heaps*) and `allocators` (a.k.a. *handles to heaps*). Memory resources provide `allocate` and `deallocate` methods; allocators provide those methods as well as `construct` and `destroy`.

If you implement your own allocator type `A`, it must be a template; its first template parameter should be the type `T` that it expects to `allocate`. Your allocator type `A` must also have a templated constructor to support "rebinding" from `A<U>` to `A<T>`. Just like any other kind of pointer, an allocator type must support the `==` and `!=` operators.

A heap's `deallocate` method is allowed to require additional metadata attached to the incoming pointer. C++ handles this via *fancy pointers*. C++17's `std::pmr::memory_resource` does not support fancy pointers, but it's easy to implement your own.

Fancy pointer types must satisfy all the requirements of random access iterators, and must be nullable, and must be convertible to plain raw pointers. If you want to use your fancy pointer type with node-based containers such as `std::list`, you must give it a static `pointer_to` member function.

C++17 distinguishes between "sticky" and "non-sticky" allocator types. Stateless allocator types such as `std::allocator<T>` are non-sticky; stateful allocator types such as `std::pmr::polymorphic_allocator<T>` are sticky by default. Making your own allocator type of a non-default stickiness requires setting all three of the member typedefs familiarly known as "POCCA," "POCMA," and "POCS." Sticky allocator types such as `std::pmr::polymorphic_allocator<T>` are useful primarily--perhaps only--in classical object-oriented situations, where a container object is pinned to a particular memory address. Value-oriented programming (with lots of moves and swaps) calls for stateless allocator types, or else for everyone in the program to use the same heap and a single sticky but *effectively stateless* allocator type.

`scoped_allocator_adaptor<A...>` can help simplify the usage of deeply nested containers that use custom allocators or memory resources. Just about any deeply nested container using a non-default allocator type requires a lot of helper typedefs to remain even remotely readable.

Swapping two containers with unequal sticky allocators: in theory this invokes undefined behavior, and in practice it corrupts memory and segfaults. Don't do it!

9
Iostreams

So far, we've seen classical polymorphism in just a couple of places in the standard library. We just saw the classically polymorphic `std::pmr::memory_resource` in Chapter 8, *Allocators*; and polymorphism is used "behind the scenes" in the type-erased types `std::any` and `std::function`, as detailed in Chapter 5, *Vocabulary Types*. However, by and large, the standard library gets by without classical polymorphism.

Two places in the standard library, however, make *massive* use of classical polymorphism. One is the standard exception hierarchy--for convenience, all exceptions thrown by the standard library are subclasses of `std::exception`. (We don't cover the exception hierarchy in this book.) The other is the contents of the standard `<iostream>` header, which we will cover in this chapter. However, we have a lot of background to cover before we get there!

In this chapter, we will cover the following topics:

- The division of output into buffering and formatting; and of input into buffering, lexing, and parsing
- The POSIX API for unformatted file I/O
- The "C" API in `<stdio.h>`, which adds both buffering and formatting
- The pros and cons of the classical `<iostream>` API
- The dangers of *locale-dependent* formatting, and new C++17 features that can help avoid them
- Many ways to convert numeric data to and from strings

The trouble with I/O in C++

A common measure of a programming language's ease of use is what's called **TTHW**--"**time to hello world**." Many popular programming languages have a very low TTHW: in many scripting languages, such as Python and Perl, the "hello world" program is literally the single line: `print "hello world"`.

C++ and its ancestor C are systems programming languages, which is to say that their primary concerns are with "power": control over the machine, speed, and (in C++'s case) the ability to leverage the type system with generic algorithms. This is a mixture of concerns not suited to small "hello world" programs.

The canonical "hello world" program in C is as follows:

```
#include <stdio.h>

int main()
{
  puts("hello world");
}
```

In C++, it is as follows:

```
#include <iostream>

int main()
{
  std::cout << "hello world" << std::endl;
}
```

The canonical C++ source code is not much longer than the canonical C source code, but it has many more "parameters" or "knobs" that can be adjusted--knobs that the novice user must learn about even if all he learns is not to adjust them. For example, where, in C, we called a function named `puts` (informally, a "verb"), in C++, we apply an *operator* to an object named `std::cout` (so, informally, we have both a "verb" and an "indirect object"). In the C++ example, we also had to learn a special name for the end-of-line (newline) character--`std::endl`--a detail that C's `puts` function hid from us.

Sometimes, this complexity "turns off" newcomers to C++, especially if they're learning C++ in school and maybe aren't sure they want to be learning it in the first place. However, this is an unfortunate misunderstanding! You see, the preceding "C" source code (using `puts`) is also perfectly valid C++, and there is nothing wrong with using the facilities of the `<stdio.h>` header. In fact, in this chapter, we'll explain the facilities of `<stdio.h>` before we even tackle the facilities of `<iostream>`. However, we'll see that C++14 and C++17 have introduced some little-known new features--in headers such as `<string>` and `<utility>`-- that help with some common I/O tasks.

A note on header naming: I've been using the `<stdio.h>` name for the header that contains "C-style" I/O facilities. Ever since C++03, there has been a similar standard header named `<cstdio>`. The only difference between `<stdio.h>` and `<cstdio>` is that in `<stdio.h>`, all of the facilities are guaranteed to be in the global namespace (for example, `::printf`) and may or may not be in the `std` namespace (for example, `std::printf`); whereas, in `<cstdio>`, they are guaranteed to be in `std` (for example, `std::printf`), but not necessarily in the global namespace (for example, `::printf`). In practice, there is no difference at all, because all major vendors put the facilities in both namespaces, no matter which header you include. My recommendation is merely to pick a style and stick with it. If your code base uses a lot of POSIX headers, such as `<unistd.h>`, which only ever have names with `.h`; it may be aesthetically preferable to stick with the `.h` names of the standard "C-style" headers as well.

Buffering versus formatting

It will be easier for you to understand both "C-style" I/O and "iostream-style" I/O if you remember that there are at least two fundamentally different things going on when you "output" some data (and likewise, in reverse, when you input some data). Just to have some sort of name for them, let's refer to them as *formatting* and *buffering*:

- *Formatting* is the task of taking a bunch of strongly typed data values from the program--ints, strings, floating-point numbers, user-defined class types--and translating or serializing them into "text." For example, when the number 42 is printed out as `"42"` (or `"+42"` or `"0x002A"`), that's *formatting*. Generally, a formatting library will have its own "mini-language" to describe how you want each value to be formatted.

- *Buffering* is the task of taking a bunch of raw bytes from the program and sending them to some output device (on output), or collecting data from some input device and making it available to the program as a bunch of raw bytes (on input). The part of the library concerned with buffering may do things such as "collect 4096 bytes of data at a time, then flush"; or it might be concerned with *where* the data is going: to a file in the filesystem, a network socket, or an array of bytes in memory?

Now, I deliberately said that the output of the *formatting* stage is "text" and the input to the *buffering* stage is "a bunch of bytes." On sensible operating systems, "text" and "bytes" are the same thing. However, if you're on one of those strange operating systems where newlines are encoded as two bytes, or where the expected encoding for text files is not UTF-8, then there must be some additional processing going on in one or both of these stages, or even further downstream (such as in the operating system syscall that writes the data to the file). We won't talk much more about that kind of thing, because my hope is that you're not using that kind of operating system (or locale) for actual production use. In production, you should *always* be using UTF-8 for character encoding, and UTC for your time zone, and `C.UTF-8` for your locale. So, for our purposes, we can pretend that "formatting" and "buffering" are the only pieces of the pipeline we need to worry about.

When we're doing input, we do the "buffering" first, to read some unformatted bytes from the input device; and then we do "formatting" to turn the bytes into strongly typed data values. The "formatting" stage for input may be subdivided further into *lexing* (to determine the length of an individual data item in the stream) and *parsing* (to determine the actual value of the item from those bytes). We'll talk more about lexing in `Chapter 10`, *Regular Expressions*.

Using the POSIX API

The most important thing to keep in mind whenever we're talking about file I/O is that everything I/O-related in C and C++ is built on top of the POSIX standard. POSIX is a very low-level specification, almost at the level of Linux system calls, that has quite a bit of overlap with the C and C++ standards for I/O; and, if you don't understand the gist of the POSIX layer, you'll have a very hard time understanding the concepts that come later.

Bear in mind that technically, *none* of what follows is standard C++! It is, rather, *valid* C++ that conforms to a *non-C++ standard*: the POSIX standard. In practice, this means that it'll work on any operating system except Windows, and may even work on modern Windows systems via the **Windows Subsystem for Linux** (**WSL**). Regardless, all the standard APIs (both `<stdio.h>` and `<iostream>`) are built on top of this model.

The non-standard headers that define most of what follows are <unistd.h> and <fcntl.h>.

In POSIX, the term *file* refers to an actual file on disk (or at least in some sort of *file system*; forgive me if I occasionally use the word "disk" to refer to the file system). Multiple programs can read or write the same file concurrently, via operating system resources known as *file descriptors*. In a C or C++ program, you'll never see a file descriptor object itself; all you'll see is a handle (or pointer) to a file descriptor. These handles (or pointers) present themselves not as pointer types, but as small integers--literally, values of type int. (The committee behind POSIX is not nearly as obsessed with type-safety as your average C++ programmer!)

To create a new file descriptor and get an integer handle to it, you use the open function; for example, int fd = open("myfile.txt", O_RDONLY). The second argument is a bitmask, which may contain any of the following bit-flags, or'ed together:

- **Required**: One and only one "access mode." The possible "access modes" are O_RDONLY (read only), O_WRONLY (write only), and O_RDWR (both read and write).
- **Optionally**: Some "open-time flags," describing actions you want the system to take at the time the file is opened. For example, O_CREAT means "if the named file doesn't exist, please create it for me" (as opposed to returning failure); and you can even add O_EXCL, which means "...and if the named file *does* exist already, then *do* return failure." The other important open-time flag is O_TRUNC, which means "truncate--clear out, empty, reset--the file after opening it."
- **Optionally**: Some "operating modes," describing the manner in which I/O is to be done via this file descriptor. The important one here is O_APPEND.

O_APPEND indicates "append mode." When a file is in "append mode," you can seek around in it (as you'll see next) as usual, but every time you write to the file, your write is implicitly preceded by a seek to the end of the file (which means that after the write, your cursor will be located at the end of the file, even if you had just been reading from a different position). Opening a file descriptor in append mode is useful if you're using it for logging, especially if you're using it for logging from different threads. Some standard utility programs, such as logrotate, work best when the program doing the logging has correctly opened their log file in "append mode." In short, append mode is so broadly useful that we'll see it coming back again and again in every one of the higher-level APIs.

Iostreams

Now to explain "cursor" and "seek." Each POSIX file descriptor has some associated data--basically its "member variables." One of those pieces of associated data is the descriptor's current operating mode; another is the descriptor's current *file position indicator*, henceforth referred to as a "cursor." Like the cursor in a text editor, this cursor points to the place in the underlying file where the next read or write will take place. Using `read` or `write` on a descriptor advances its cursor. And, as described in the previous paragraph, using `write` on a file descriptor in "append mode" will reset the cursor to the very end of the file. Notice that there is only a single cursor per file descriptor! If you open a file descriptor with O_RDWR, you don't get a read cursor and a write cursor; you get just a single cursor that is advanced by reading *and* by writing.

- `read(fd, buffer, count)`: This reads raw bytes from the underlying file and stores them in the given buffer--up to `count` bytes, or until it encounters some sort of temporary or permanent error (for example, if we'd need to wait for more data over a network connection, or if someone unmounts the underlying filesystem in the middle of the read). It returns the number of bytes read; and remember, it advances the cursor.
- `write(fd, buffer, count)`: This writes raw bytes from the given buffer into the underlying file--up to `count` bytes, or until it encounters some sort of temporary or permanent error. It returns the number of bytes written; and remember, it advances the cursor. (And *before* it writes any data, if the file descriptor is in append mode, it will seek to the end of the file.)
- `lseek(fd, offset, SEEK_SET)`: This seeks (that is, moves the cursor) to the given offset from the start of the file, and returns that offset (or -1 if the operation fails, for example, by running off the end of the file).
- `lseek(fd, offset, SEEK_CUR)`: This seeks to the given offset relative to the *current* cursor. Relative movements like this generally aren't important, but the special case of `lseek(fd, 0, SEEK_CUR)` is very important because that's how you find out the current position of your cursor!
- `lseek(fd, offset, SEEK_END)`: This seeks to the given offset relative to the end of the file. Again, this version is most useful when `offset` is zero.

Incidentally, there is no way to "copy-construct" a POSIX file descriptor so that you can get a second cursor to the same file. If you want two cursors, you'll need to `open` the file twice. Confusingly, there *is* a POSIX function named `dup`, which takes an integer file descriptor handle and returns a different integer that can be used as a second handle to the *same* descriptor; this is a kind of primitive reference-counting.

When you're done with a file descriptor, you call `close(fd)` to release your handle; if this was the last handle to the descriptor (that is, if nobody has called `dup` on it in the meantime), then the file descriptor itself will be reclaimed by the operating system--which is to say, the underlying file will be "closed."

Putting it all together, we can write a simple program like this using the POSIX API to open, read, write, seek, and close file descriptors:

```cpp
#include <cassert>
#include <string>
#include <unistd.h>
#include <fcntl.h>

int main()
{
  int fdw = open("myfile.txt", O_WRONLY | O_CREAT | O_TRUNC);
  int fdr = open("myfile.txt", O_RDONLY);
  if (fdw == -1 || fdr == -1)
    return EXIT_FAILURE;

  write(fdw, "hello world", 11);
  lseek(fdw, 6, SEEK_SET);
  write(fdw, "neighbor", 8);

  std::string buffer(14, '\0');
  int b = read(fdr, buffer.data(), 14);
  assert(b == 14);
  assert(buffer == "hello neighbor");
  close(fdr);
  close(fdw);
}
```

Notice that the POSIX API doesn't bother with anything related to *formatting*. It is merely concerned with making sure that we can get raw bytes into and out of files on disk; that is, with about half of the *buffering* stage--the "where the data is going" half. POSIX doesn't bother with the "buffered output"; when you call `write`, your data will be written out. That is, it may still be sitting in a buffer at the OS level, or at the disk-controller level, or in the hardware, but as far as your program is concerned, the data is *on its way*. Any further delay in the output is out of your control and not your fault. This, in turn, means that if you need to write a lot of data efficiently using the POSIX API, your program must take charge of writing data to a buffer and then sending that whole buffer to `write` at once. A single 4096-byte `write` will be much faster than a 4,096 one-byte `write`!

Or, instead of writing your own buffer-management code, you could step up one level of abstraction and use the C API.

Using the standard C API

This description is necessarily almost as brief and incomplete as our discussion of POSIX earlier. For a complete description of the facilities in `<stdio.h>`, you'll have to consult another source, such as `cppreference.com` or your local `man` pages.

In the "C-style" API, POSIX *file descriptors* are given a new name: the thing corresponding to a file descriptor is called `FILE`, and the thing corresponding to an integer file descriptor handle is (naturally) called `FILE*`. Just as in the POSIX API, though, you'll never construct an instance of `FILE` yourself.

To create a new `FILE` object and get a pointer to it, you use the `fopen` function; for example, `FILE *fp = fopen("myfile.txt", "r")`. The second argument is a string (that is, a pointer to a null-terminated array of characters--generally, you'll just use a string literal, as I did here), which must be one of the following:

- `"r"`: This is equivalent to POSIX `O_RDONLY`. Open for reading. Fail (that is, return `nullptr`) if the file doesn't exist.
- `"w"`: This is equivalent to POSIX `O_WRONLY | O_CREAT | O_TRUNC`. Open for writing. Create the file if it doesn't exist. Regardless, make the file empty before proceeding.
- `"r+"`: This is equivalent to POSIX `O_RDWR | O_CREAT`. Open for both reading *and* writing. Create the file empty if it doesn't exist.
- `"w+"`: This is equivalent to POSIX `O_RDWR | O_CREAT | O_TRUNC`. Open for both reading and writing. Create the file if it doesn't exist. Regardless, make the file empty before proceeding.
- `"a"`: This is equivalent to POSIX `O_WRONLY | O_CREAT | O_APPEND`. Open for writing. Create the file empty if it doesn't exist. Enter append mode.
- `"a+"`: This is equivalent to POSIX `O_RDWR | O_CREAT | O_APPEND`. Open for both reading *and* writing. Create the file empty if it doesn't exist. Enter append mode.

Notice that there is some pattern to the preceding strings--strings with `'+'` always map to `O_RDWR`, strings with `'w'` always map to `O_TRUNC`, and strings with `'a'` always map to `O_APPEND`; however, there is no perfectly regular pattern that describes the mapping from `fopen` mode strings into POSIX `open` flags.

Some platforms support appending additional characters to the mode string; for example, a common extension on POSIX platforms is that an added `'x'` means `O_EXCL`; on GNU platforms, an added `'e'` means `O_CLOEXEC`; and on Windows, a similar behavior can be gotten by adding a capital `'N'`.

The one character that can be appended to the mode string on any platform (that is, it's guaranteed by the C++ standard to be available everywhere) is `'b'`, for "binary." This matters only on Windows, where, if you do *not* specify this character, the library will automatically translate every `'\n'` byte you output into the Windows line terminator sequence, `'\r'`, `'\n'`. If you specifically do want this translation when running on Windows, a useful convention is to add `'t'` to your mode string. All vendors' libraries will recognize and ignore this character; it merely serves as an indication to the human reader that indeed you meant to open the file in "text" mode, and didn't accidentally omit an intended `'b'`.

When you're done using a file, you must call `fclose(fp)`, which corresponds to calling `close(fd)` on the underlying file descriptor handle.

To deal with the bookkeeping on C-style `FILE` pointers, you may want to use the RAII smart pointers from Chapter 5, *Vocabulary Types*. You can write a "unique FILE pointer" like this:

```
struct fcloser {
  void operator()(FILE *fp) const {
    fclose(fp);
  }

  static auto open(const char *name, const char *mode) {
    return std::unique_ptr<FILE, fcloser>(fopen(name, mode));
  }
};

void test() {
  auto f = fcloser::open("test.txt", "w");
  fprintf(f.get(), "hello world\n");
    // f will be closed automatically
}
```

Moreover, remember that you can always move `unique_ptr` into `shared_ptr` if you want the reference-counted, "last person out of the room turns out the lights" semantics:

```
auto f = fcloser::open("test.txt", "w");
std::shared_ptr<FILE> g1 = std::move(f);
  // now f is empty and g1's use-count is 1
if (true) {
```

```
        std::shared_ptr<FILE> g2 = g1;
           // g1's use-count is now 2
        fprintf(g2.get(), "hello ");
           // g1's use-count drops back to 1
    }
    fprintf(g1.get(), "world\n");
       // g1's use-count drops to 0; the file is closed
```

Buffering in the standard C API

The standard C API offers a family of functions that look just like the POSIX functions, but with the letter f on the front.

The `fread(buffer, 1, count, fp)` method reads raw bytes from the underlying file and stores them in the given buffer--up to count bytes, or until it encounters some sort of permanent error (for example, if someone unmounts the underlying filesystem in the middle of the read). It returns the number of bytes read and advances the cursor.

The literal 1 in that call is not a mistake! Technically, the function signature is `fread(buffer, k, count, fp)`. It reads up to k * count bytes, or until it encounters a permanent error and returns the number of bytes read divided by k. However, in your own code, k should always be the literal 1; using anything else is a mistake, for at least two reasons. First, since the return value is always divided by k, and if k is anything but 1, you will lose information. For example, if k is 8, a return value of 3 indicates that "somewhere between 24 and 31" bytes were read and stored into the buffer, but buffer[3] may now contain a partially written value--that is to say, garbage--and you have no way of detecting that. Second, since the library internally multiplies k * count, passing any k other than 1 runs the risk of overflow and an incorrectly computed buffer length. No popular implementation checks that multiplication for overflow; this is for performance reasons if nothing else. It doesn't make sense to spend CPU time on an expensive division operation if every programmer already knows never to pass any other value for k but 1!

The `fwrite(buffer, 1, count, fp)` method writes raw bytes from the given buffer into the underlying file--up to count bytes, or until it encounters some sort of permanent error. It returns the number of bytes written, and advances the cursor. (And *before* it writes any data, if the file descriptor is in append mode, it will seek to the end of the file.)

The `fseek(fp, offset, SEEK_SET)` method seeks (that is, moves the cursor) to the given offset from the start of the file; `fseek(fp, offset, SEEK_CUR)` seeks to the given offset relative to the *current* cursor; and `fseek(fp, offset, SEEK_END)` seeks to the given offset relative to the end of the file. Unlike the POSIX `lseek`, the standard C version `fseek` does *not* return the value of the current cursor; it merely returns 0 on success or -1 on failure.

The `ftell(fp)` method returns the value of the current cursor; that is, it's equivalent to the underlying POSIX call `lseek(fd, 0, SEEK_CUR)`.

Speaking of underlying POSIX calls: if you are on a POSIX platform and need to do something non-portable with the POSIX file descriptor underlying a standard C `FILE *`, you can always retrieve the file descriptor by calling `fileno(fp)`. So, for example, we could express `ftell` as follows:

```
long ftell(FILE *fp)
{
   int fd = fileno(fp);
   return lseek(fd, 0, SEEK_CUR);
}
```

Working with `fread` and `fwrite` is quite possible, but it is not the most common way of using the C API. Many programs prefer to deal with input and output not in terms of large chunks of data but rather character by character, or byte by byte. The original "Unix philosophy" is oriented toward small simple command-line utilities that read and transform a "stream" of bytes; these small stream-oriented programs are known as "filters," and they really shine when you link them together with the Unix shell's pipes. For example, here is a tiny program that opens a file and counts the number of bytes, space-separated "words," and lines in that file using the `<stdio.h>` API:

```
struct LWC {
   int lines, words, chars;
};

LWC word_count(FILE *fp)
{
  LWC r {};
  bool in_space = true;
  while (true) {
    int ch = getc(fp);
    if (ch == EOF) break;
    r.lines += (ch == '\n');
    r.words += (in_space && !isspace(ch));
    r.chars += 1;
    in_space = isspace(ch);
```

```
      }
      return r;
}

int main(int argc, const char **argv)
{
  FILE *fp = (argc < 2) ? stdin : fopen(argv[1], "r");
  auto [lines, words, chars] = word_count(fp);
  printf("%8d %7d %7d\n", lines, words, chars);
}
```

(Do you recognize it? This is the command-line utility `wc`.)

This program introduces two new ideas (besides the standard guarantee that all the `FILE` objects are implicitly closed at program exit so that it is safe for us to omit the `fclose` bookkeeping and save a few lines in this example). The first is the idea of *standard streams*. There are three standard streams in C and C++: `stdin`, `stdout`, and `stderr`. In our word-counting program, we follow the rule that if the command-line user has not explicitly told us any filename to read from, we'll read from `stdin`, the *standard input stream*, which is usually a synonym for the console (or terminal or keyboard--point is, it's the human being sitting there typing). Various mechanisms within the operating system and the command-line shell can be used to *redirect* the standard input stream from other inputs; these mechanisms (such as typing `wc <myfile.txt` at the shell prompt) are far outside the scope of this book. The main things to remember about the three standard streams are that they are automatically available to you by name without having to `fopen` them; and that it is always an error to `fclose` any of them.

The second new idea introduced in our word-counting program is the `getc` function. The `getc(fp)` function reads a single byte from the given `FILE *` and returns the byte it read. If there was an error, or (more likely) if it hit end-of-file, it returns a special value named `EOF`. The numerical value of `EOF` is usually `-1;`, but the guaranteed thing about it is that it is completely different from any possible *valid* byte. For this reason, `getc(fp)` does not return its return value as `char`; it returns it as `int`, which is big enough to store any possible `char` and, in addition, big enough to store the value `EOF` distinct from any of those `char` values (if `char` is a signed type on your platform--as it is on many platforms--then `getc` will convert `char` it read into `unsigned char` before returning it; this ensures that if the `0xFF` byte appears in the input file, it will be returned as `255`, which is a different integer value than `-1` that represents `EOF`).

Now, for the crucial difference between `fread`/`fwrite` and `read`/`write`.
Recall that the POSIX API doesn't do any additional buffering of input or output bytes; when you call `read`, you're going all the way to the operating system to retrieve the next chunk of input bytes. If `getc(fp)` were implemented as `fread(&ch, 1, 1, fp)`, and `fread(buf, 1, count, fp)` were implemented as `read(fileno(fp), buf, count)`, then our word-counting program would be horrendously inefficient--reading a file of a million bytes would result in a million system calls! So, when the C library wraps a file descriptor handle in a `FILE` object, it also adds one more feature: *buffering*.

`FILE` streams may be "unbuffered" (meaning that every `fread` really does correspond to `read`, and every `fwrite` to `write`); "fully buffered," also known as "block buffered" (meaning that writes will be accumulated into a private buffer that is sent to the underlying file descriptor only when it becomes full, and likewise, reads will be served from a private buffer that is refilled from the underlying file descriptor only when it becomes empty); or "line-buffered" (meaning that there is a private buffer just like the previous case, but writing `'\n'` causes a flush even if the buffer is not yet full). When the program starts up and opens its standard streams, `stdin` and `stdout` will be line-buffered, and `stderr` will be unbuffered. Any files you open yourself via `fopen` will generally be fully buffered, although the operating system may have something to say about that as well; for example, if the "file" you're opening is actually a terminal device, it may end up being line-buffered by default.

In the very rare case that you need to control the buffering mode of a `FILE` stream, you can do it via the standard `setvbuf` function. You can also use `setvbuf` to provide your own buffer, as shown in the following example:

```
FILE *fp = fopen("myfile.txt", "w");
    int fd = fileno(fp);
    char buffer[150];
    setvbuf(fp, buffer, _IOFBF, 150);
       // setvbuf returns 0 on success, or EOF on failure.

    std::string AAAA(160, 'A');
    int bytes_written = fwrite(AAAA.data(), 1, 160, fp);
       // This fills the buffer with 150 bytes, flushes it,
       // and writes 10 more bytes into the buffer.

    assert(bytes_written == 160);
    assert(lseek(fd, 0, SEEK_CUR) == 150);
    assert(ftell(fp) == 160);
```

Notice the discrepancy between `ftell(fp)` and `lseek(fd, 0, SEEK_CUR)` in the last line of the example. Ten bytes remain buffered in the buffer of FILE; so FILE reports that your cursor is currently at offset 160, but, in actuality, the underlying POSIX file descriptor's cursor is still at offset 150, and will remain there until the FILE's buffer fills up and is flushed a second time--at which point the underlying POSIX file descriptor's cursor will jump to offset 300. This feels awkward, but it's actually exactly what we want! We *want* the efficiency that comes with writing the underlying file descriptor in large chunks. (Note that 150 bytes is not "large" in reality. A typical default file buffer size, if you don't use `setvbuf` at all, would be more like 4096 bytes.)

On some platforms, calling `ftell` will cause the buffer to be flushed as a side effect, since that makes the library's bookkeeping easier; the library doesn't like to be caught telling lies. (Calling `fseek` is also a likely way to cause a flush.) However, on other platforms, `ftell` and even `fseek` don't always flush the buffer. To make sure that your FILE stream's buffer has definitely been flushed to the underlying file, use `fflush`. Let's continue the previous example as follows:

```
// Flush the FILE's buffer by force.
fflush(fp);
// Now, fd and fp agree about the state of the file.
assert(lseek(fd, 0, SEEK_CUR) == 160);
```

Putting it all together, we can rewrite our simple program from the *Using the POSIX API* section like this, using the `<stdio.h>` API to open, read, write, seek, flush, and close file streams:

```
#include <cassert>
#include <cstdio>
#include <string>

int main()
{
  FILE *fpw = fopen("myfile.txt", "w");
  FILE *fpr = fopen("myfile.txt", "r");
  if (fpw == nullptr || fpr == nullptr)
    return EXIT_FAILURE;

  fwrite("hello world", 1, 11, fpw);
  fseek(fpw, 6, SEEK_SET);
  fwrite("neighbor", 1, 8, fpw);
  fflush(fpw);

  std::string buffer(14, '\0');
  int b = fread(buffer.data(), 1, 14, fpr);
  assert(b == 14 && buffer == "hello neighbor");
```

```
        fclose(fpr);
        fclose(fpw);
}
```

This concludes our exploration of the *buffering* capabilities of the standard `<stdio.h>` API; now, we move on to consider how `<stdio.h>` deals with *formatting*.

Formatting with printf and snprintf

In the formatting stage, we start with the high-level data values that we want to print out; for example, we might want to print the number of piano tuners in Chicago, which our program has computed as 225. Printing out the *three-byte string* `"225"` is easy; we've solved that in the preceding sections. The task of *formatting* is to get us from the number 225 (an `int`, let's say) to that three-byte string `"225"`.

When printing numbers, we have many possible concerns: should the number be printed in base 10, base 16, base 8, base 2, or some other base? If the number is negative, presumably, we should prefix it with –; if it is positive, should we prefix it with +? Should we use thousands-separators, and if so, should we use commas, periods, or spaces? What about decimal points? Once we're talking about floating-point numbers, how many digits after the decimal point should we print? Or should we use scientific notation, and if so, to how many significant digits?

Then, there are concerns that extend even to non-numeric input. Should the printed value be aligned within a fixed-width column, and if so, should it be left-aligned, right-aligned, or even aligned in some other clever way? (And what character should we use to fill the unoccupied columns?) What if the value doesn't fit in the given column width--should it be truncated left or right or just overflow the column's bounds?

Similarly, when reading formatted input (that is, *parsing*), we have to answer many of the same questions about numerics: do we expect thousands-separators? Scientific notation? Leading + signs? What numeric base do we expect? And even for non-numerics: do we expect leading whitespace? If we're reading in a value of type "string," what indicates the end of the value other than EOF?

The standard C API provides a whole family of formatting functions with names ending in `printf`, and a matching family of parsing functions with names ending in `scanf`. A commonality of every function in this family is that it takes a variadic argument list (using C-style varargs, not C++ variadic templates) and, prior to the variadic arguments, a single "format string" that answers many of the above questions (but not all of them) for each argument to be formatted, and also provides a "shape" for the overall message, into which the library will insert the formatted arguments:

```
int tuners = 225;
const char *where = "Chicago";
printf("There are %d piano tuners in %s.\n", tuners, where);
```

There is also `fprintf(fp, "format", args...)` to print to any arbitrary stream (not necessarily `stdout`); `snprintf(buf, n, "format", args...)` to write to a buffer, about which we'll discuss more in a moment; and a matching family of `vprintf`, `vfprintf`, and `vsnprintf` functions that are useful in building your own printf-like functions. As you've probably learned to expect in this chapter, a complete treatment of C-style format strings is out of the scope of this book. However, the C-style "format string language" is widely used even in languages that don't directly descend from C; for example, in Python 2, you can say:

```
tuners = 225
where = "Chicago"
print "There are %d piano tuners in %s." % (tuners, where)
```

However, there are major differences between what's happening in C and what's happening in Python!

The biggest difference is that Python is dynamically typed, so if you write `"%s tuners" % (tuners)`, it will still be able to do the right thing. With C-style variadic argument lists, the original type of `tuners` is lost; if you use the `"%s"` format specifier (which expects a `const char *` argument) with an argument of type `int`, you'll get a friendly compiler warning at best and undefined behavior at worst. That is to say, when you use `<stdio.h>` formatting functions, the format string does double duty: it encodes not only *how to format* each data value, but also *the type of* each data value--and if you get one of those types wrong, such as by using `"%s"` when you meant `"%d"`, then your program will have a bug. Fortunately, all major compilers can detect and diagnose such mismatches these days, as long as your format string is passed directly to `printf` or to a function annotated with the (non-standard) `format` attribute, as demonstrated in the code sample we'll see shortly. Unfortunately, these diagnostics can be unreliable when you're dealing with typedefs for platform-dependent types; for example, some 64-bit compilers will not diagnose an attempt to format a `size_t` value with the `"%llu"` format specifier, even though the properly portable specifier would be `"%zu"`.

Another difference is that in C, `printf` is effectively writing directly to the standard output stream, `stdout`; the formatting of the data is interleaved with the buffering of the output bytes. In Python, the `"There are %d piano tuners in %s." % (tuners, where)` construct is actually an *expression* of type `str` (string); all of the formatting happens right there, producing a single string value with the proper bytes, before we decide that the string is to be printed to `stdout` at all.

To produce a formatted string using the `<stdio.h>` API, we will use `snprintf`:

```
char buf[13];
int needed = snprintf(
  buf, sizeof buf,
    "There are %d piano tuners in %s", tuners, where
);
assert(needed == 37);
assert(std::string_view(buf) == "There are 22");
```

Notice that `snprintf` always null-terminates its buffer, even if it means not writing the entire message into it; and it returns `strlen` of the message that it *wanted* to write. A common idiom to format an arbitrarily long message is to call `snprintf` first with `nullptr`, to learn the message's final size; and then call it a second time with a buffer of that size:

```
template<class... Args>
std::string format(const char *fmt, const Args&... args)
{
  int needed = snprintf(nullptr, 0, fmt, args...);
  std::string s(needed + 1, '\0');
  snprintf(s.data(), s.size(), fmt, args...);
  s.pop_back(); // remove the written '\0'
  return s;
}

void test()
{
  std::string s = format("There are %d piano tuners in %s", tuners, where);
  assert(s == "There are 225 piano tuners in Chicago");
}
```

The preceding implementation of `format` uses a variadic function template, which will tend to produce a lot of similar copies of the code. A more efficient implementation (in terms of compile time and code bloat) would be to use a single (non-template) function with a C-style variadic argument list, and use `vsnprintf` for formatting. Sadly, further discussion of `va_list` and `vsnprintf` is far outside the scope of this book.

```
std::string better_format(const char *fmt, ...)
{
  va_list ap;
  va_start(ap, fmt);
  int needed = vsnprintf(nullptr, 0, fmt, ap);
  va_end(ap);
  std::string s(needed + 1, '\0');
  va_start(ap, fmt);
  vsnprintf(s.data(), s.size(), fmt, ap);
  va_end(ap);
  s.pop_back(); // remove the written '\0'
  return s;
}
```

We'll defer the discussion of the `scanf` format strings until the *recipes* portion of this chapter. For a complete treatment of `scanf`, consult cppreference.com or a book on the C standard library.

Having seen how both buffering and formatting (at least, output formatting) work in the `<stdio.h>` regime, we now move on to the standard C++ `<iostream>` API.

The classical iostreams hierarchy

The `<stdio.h>` API suffers from at least three problems. First, the formatting functionality is far from type-safe. Second, the buffering functionality is awkwardly split up into "buffering into a file stream" (`FILE *` and `fprintf`) and "buffering into a character buffer" (`snprintf`). (Okay, technically, the GNU C library provides `fopencookie` to construct `FILE *` that buffers into anything you want; but this is fairly obscure and extremely non-standard.) Third, there is no easy way to extend the formatting functionality for user-defined classes; I cannot even `printf` a `std::string`, let alone `my::Widget`!

When C++ was being developed in the mid-1980s, the designers felt a need for a type-safe, composable, and extensible I/O library. Thus was born the feature known as "iostreams," or simply as "C++ streams" (not to be confused with the <stdio.h> streams we just finished talking about). The fundamental architecture of iostreams has not changed since the mid-1980s, which makes it very different from anything else in the standard library with the possible exception (no pun intended) of the std::exception hierarchy.

The C++ iostreams library consists of two major pieces: *streams*, which are concerned with formatting, and streambufs, which are concerned with buffering. The majority of C++ programmers will never interact with streambufs; only with streams. However, let's very quickly explain what a streambuf is.

A streambuf is very similar to FILE in the C API. It tells the program where the input (in the form of raw bytes) should come from, and where the output should go to. It also maintains a buffer of bytes to reduce the number of round-trips to those destinations (such as the POSIX read and write functions). In order to allow different kinds of streambufs with the same interface--well, remember my promise that we'd see classical polymorphism in this chapter? We've finally gotten to it!

std::streambuf (which is actually an alias for std::basic_streambuf<char, char_traits<char>>, but let's not make this any more complicated) is the base class of an inheritance hierarchy whose derived classes are std::filebuf and std::stringbuf. The virtual methods provided by the streambuf interface are too many to list, but they include sb.setbuf(buf, n) (corresponding to setvbuf(fp, buf, _IO_FBF, n)), sb.overflow() (corresponding to fflush(fp)), and sb.seekpos(offset, whence) (corresponding to fseek(fp, offset, whence)). When I say corresponding, I mean corresponding for std::filebuf, of course. These methods have implementation-defined (and in practice, non-portable) behavior when called on std::stringbuf.

Any streambuf derived class must also support some primitive operations to interact with its buffer (to put in and take out bytes). These primitive operations are not for use by normal programmers, though; they're for use by the *stream* object that wraps this streambuf and provides a more programmer-friendly interface.

A C++ *stream* encapsulates a streambuf and restricts the set of operations you can do on it. For example, notice that streambuf doesn't have any conception of "access mode": you can put bytes into it ("write") as easily as you can take bytes out ("read"). However, when we take that streambuf and wrap it in a std::ostream, the ostream object exposes only a write method; there is no read method on ostream.

Iostreams

The following diagram expresses the class hierarchy of streams and streambufs in C++17, as defined in the standard `<iostream>`, `<fstream>`, and/or `<sstream>` headers. The `streambuf`, `istream`, `ostream`, and `iostream` base classes are "abstract-ish": while they have no pure virtual methods, they contain only the `streambuf*` member variable inherited from `ios`. To protect you from accidentally constructing instances of these "abstract-ish" types, the standard library defines their constructors as `protected`. Contrariwise, the classes with names containing `stringstream` and `fstream` actually contain instances of `stringbuf` and `filebuf` respectively, to which their constructors initialize the inherited `streambuf*` member to point. Later in this chapter, in the *Solving the sticky-manipulator problem* section, we'll see how to construct an `ostream` object whose `streambuf*` member points to a streambuf instance not owned by `*this`:

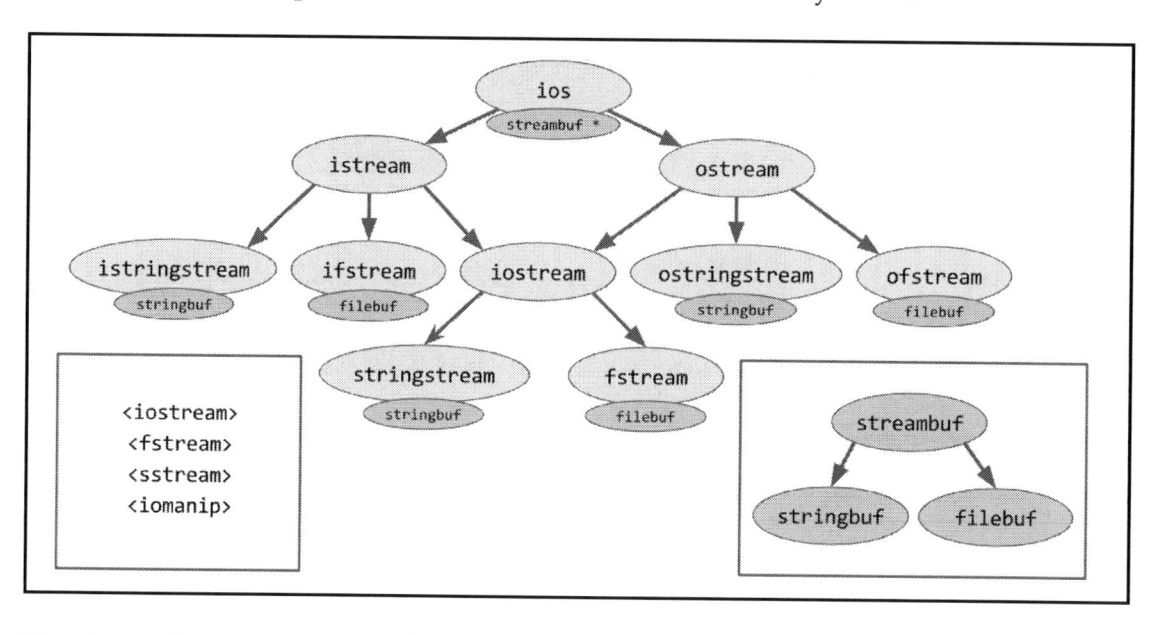

The stream classes expose a motley collection of methods that correspond, more or less exactly, to the functions we've seen twice before. In particular, the `fstream` class wraps `filebuf` and, together, they behave a lot like `FILE` from the C API: `filebuf` has a "cursor" that you can manipulate with the `seekp` method of `fstream`. (The name `seekp` is inherited from the `ostream` class. On `ifstream`, the method is named `seekg`: "g" for "get" and "p" for "put." On a full `fstream`, you can use either `seekg` or `seekp`; they are synonyms in that case. As always, remember that there is just a single cursor, even though the iostreams API has two different *names* for the cursor in this case!)

The constructor of `fstream` takes a bitmask or'ed together from the `std::ios_base::in`, `out`, `app` (for "append mode"), `trunc`, `ate`, and `binary` flag values; however, just as we saw with `fopen`, there is only a very small dash of rhyme and reason as to how those flags are translated into POSIX `open` flags:

- `in`: This is equivalent to `fopen("r")`, or POSIX `O_RDONLY`.
- `out`: This is equivalent to `fopen("w")`, or POSIX `O_WRONLY | O_CREAT | O_TRUNC`. (Notice that `out` alone means `O_TRUNC` even if `trunc` was not passed!)
- `in|out`: This is equivalent to `fopen("r+")`, or POSIX `O_RDWR | O_CREAT`.
- `in|out|trunc`: This is equivalent to `fopen("w+")`, or POSIX `O_RDWR | O_CREAT | O_TRUNC`. (Notice that the iostreams syntax makes more sense than the `fopen` syntax, in this case.)
- `out|app`: This is equivalent to `fopen("a")`, or POSIX `O_WRONLY | O_CREAT | O_APPEND`.
- `in|out|app`: This is equivalent to `fopen("a+")`, or POSIX `O_RDWR | O_CREAT | O_APPEND`.

Adding `binary` to the bitmask is just like adding "b" to `fopen`. Adding `ate` tells the stream to begin with a seek to the end of the file, even if the file is not being opened in `O_APPEND` mode.

Passing an unsupported set of flags, such as `app|trunc`, will still construct the stream object, but place it into the "fail" state, which we'll discuss soon. In general, you should design your own classes' constructors so that failure is indicated by an exception. That rule is broken here partly because this class hierarchy was designed almost forty years ago, and partly because we need a "failure" mechanism anyway, to deal with the relatively likely possibility that the named file cannot be opened (for example, if it doesn't exist).

Putting it all together, we can rewrite our simple program from "Using the POSIX API" like this, using the `<fstream>` API to open, read, write, seek, flush, and close file streams:

```
#include <cassert>
#include <fstream>
#include <string>

int main()
{
  std::fstream fsw("myfile.txt", std::ios_base::out);
  std::fstream fsr("myfile.txt", std::ios_base::in);
  if (fsw.fail() || fsr.fail())
    return EXIT_FAILURE;
```

```
        fsw.write("hello world", 11);
        fsw.seekp(6, std::ios_base::beg);
        fsw.write("neighbor", 8);
        fsw.flush();

        std::string buffer(14, '\0');
        fsr.read(buffer.data(), 14);
        assert(fsr.gcount() == 14 && buffer == "hello neighbor");
    }
```

One odd thing about the preceding example is that `fsr.read(buffer.data(), 14)` does not return any indication of how many bytes were read! Instead, it stores the count of bytes read in a member variable, and you must retrieve the count yourself via the accessor `fsr.gcount()` function. And the `write` method doesn't even allow you to find out how many bytes were written. This may seem like a problem; but, in general, if a stream encounters an error on reading or writing, the error is often essentially "unrecoverable" anyway, due to the uncertain number of bytes *actually* read from or written to the underlying file descriptor and due to the several layers of buffers between the application program and hardware. When a read or write error is encountered, we pretty much have to give up on understanding the state of that stream at all--*except* in the special case of "end of file" on input. If we intended to read 100 bytes and instead hit "end of file," it is meaningful to ask, "How many bytes did we succeed at reading?" However, if we intended to *write* 100 bytes and instead received a network error, or a disk error, it's not so meaningful to ask, "How many bytes did we succeed at writing?" We simply cannot tell whether our "written" bytes managed to reach their destination or not.

If we asked for 100 bytes and only read 99 (or fewer) before hitting end-of-file, then not only will `fs.gcount()` report a number less than 100, but also the *eof indicator* will be set on the stream object's state. You can ask any stream about its current state with the accessor functions `fs.good()` (is it hunky-dory?), `fs.bad()` (did the underlying stream encounter an unrecoverable error?), `fs.eof()` (did the last input operation hit end-of-file?), and `fs.fail()` (did the last operation "fail" for any reason?). Notice that `fs.good()` is not the inverse of `fs.bad()`; it is possible for a stream to be in a state, such as *eof*, that is, `!good() && !bad()`.

We have now seen the simplest, most primitive way to do buffered input and output using `fstream` streams. However, if you're using C++ streams like this, you may as well just be using `FILE *`, or even the POSIX API. The "new and (arguably) improved" thing about C++ streams is the way they handle *formatting*.

Streaming and manipulators

Recall that with `printf`, the original types of the arguments are lost, and so the format string must do double duty, encoding not only *how to format* each data value, but also *the type of* each data value. When we use iostreams, this disadvantage goes away. Formatting with iostreams looks like this:

```
int tuners = 225;
const char *where = "Chicago";
std::cout << "There are " << tuners << " piano tuners in " << where << "\n";
```

Here, `std::cout` is a global variable of type `ostream`, corresponding to `stdout` or POSIX file descriptor 1. There's also `std::cerr`, corresponding to unbuffered `stderr` or POSIX file descriptor 2; `std::clog`, again corresponding to file descriptor 2 but fully buffered this time; and `std::cin`, a global variable of type `istream`, corresponding to `stdin` or POSIX file descriptor 0.

The standard `ostream` class, which, again, is really `basic_ostream<char, char_traits<char>>`, but let's ignore that) has many, many non-member overloads of `operator<<`. For example, here's the simplest possible overloaded `operator<<`:

```
namespace std {
  ostream& operator<< (ostream& os, const string& s)
  {
    os.write(s.data(), s.size());
    return os;
  }
} // namespace std
```

As this function returns a reference to the same `os` it received, we can chain the `<<` operators together, as shown in the previous example. This allows us to format complicated messages.

Unfortunately, our simple `operator<<(ostream&, const string&)` is not nearly sufficient to satisfy the variety of formatting concerns described in the *Formatting with printf and snprintf* section. Suppose we wanted to print that left-aligned string in a column of width 7; how would we do that? The `operator<<` syntax doesn't allow us to pass any additional "formatting option" parameters, which means that we simply *cannot* do complicated formatting unless the formatting options are carried along in either the left-hand side of `<<` (the ostream object itself) or the right-hand side (the object to be formatted). The standard library uses a mix of both approaches. Generally, functionality that first appeared in the 1980s and 1990s carried its formatting options in the ostream object itself; and anything added later--not being able to add new member variables to `ostream` without breaking binary compatibility--has had to make do by fiddling with the right-hand side of the `<<` operator. Let's look at alignment within a column, as an example of the 1980s approach. This is a slightly more full-featured version of our `operator<<` for `std::string`:

```
void pad(std::ostream& os, size_t from, size_t to)
{
  char ch = os.fill();
  for (auto i = from; i < to; ++i) {
    os.write(&ch, 1);
  }
}

std::ostream& operator<< (std::ostream& os, const std::string& s)
{
  auto column_width = os.width();
  auto padding = os.flags() & std::ios_base::adjustfield;

  if (padding == std::ios_base::right) {
    pad(os, s.size(), column_width);
  }
  os.write(s.data(), s.size());
  if (padding == std::ios_base::left) {
    pad(os, s.size(), column_width);
  }
  os.width(0); // reset "column width" to 0
  return os;
}
```

Here, `os.width()`, `os.flags()`, and `os.fill()` are all built-in members of the `std::ostream` class. There's also `os.precision()` for floating-point numbers, and `os.flags()` can indicate the base-10, base-16, or base-8 output for some numeric types as well. You can set the "column width" state on a stream by calling `os.width(n)`; however, it would be quite painful (and silly!) if we had to set up by writing `std::cout.width(10)`, `std::cout.setfill('.')`, and so on, before each output operation. So, the iostreams library provides some standard *stream manipulators* that can be used to get the effect of these member functions but in a more "fluent" manner. These manipulators are generally defined in a standard header, `<iomanip>`, not in `<iostream>` proper. For example, here's a manipulator that sets the column width of a stream:

```
struct WidthSetter { int n; };

auto& operator<< (std::ostream& os, WidthSetter w)
{
    os.width(w.n);
    return os;
}

auto setw(int n) { return WidthSetter{n}; }
```

And here are two more standard manipulators, one of which should look very familiar to you by now. The `std::endl` manipulator streams a newline to the output stream and then flushes it:

```
using Manip = std::ostream& (*)(std::ostream&);

auto& operator<< (std::ostream& os, Manip f) {
    return f(os);
}

std::ostream& flush(std::ostream& os) {
    return os.flush();
}

std::ostream& endl(std::ostream& os) {
    return os << '\n' << flush;
}
```

Iostreams

Once we have `std::setw`; its friends, `std::left`, `std::right`, `std::hex`, `std::dec`, `std::oct`, `std::setfill`, and `std::precision`; and all the rest--I say once we have all these manipulators--, we can write iostreams code that looks almost natural, if extremely verbose. Compare these `<stdio.h>` and `<iostream>` snippets:

```
printf("%-10s.%6x\n", where, tuners);
  // "Chicago   .    e1"

std::cout << std::setw(8) << std::left << where << "."
          << std::setw(4) << std::right << std::hex
          << tuners << "\n";
  // "Chicago   .    e1"
```

Bear in mind that every time we use one of these manipulators, we are imperatively affecting the state of the stream object itself; this effect may persist for longer than just the current output statement. For example, our preceding snippet may continue like this:

```
printf("%d\n", 42); // "42"

std::cout << 42 << "\n"; // "2a" -- oops!
```

The `std::hex` manipulator from the previous example set the mode of this stream to "hexadecimal output for numbers," and nothing ever set it back to the "default" decimal mode. So now we've unintentionally made everything later in the program also print in hex! This is a major disadvantage of the iostreams library (and of stateful, imperative programming in general).

Streaming and wrappers

The parameters provided by `std::ios_base` (`left`, `right`, `hex`, `width`, `precision`, and so on) are a closed set--a set defined in the mid-1980s and basically untouched since then. Since each manipulator modifies one of these parameters in the state of the stream, the set of manipulators is essentially closed as well. The modern way to affect the formatting of a particular data value is to wrap it in a *wrapper*. For example, suppose that we have written a generic algorithm for quoting values in a data file:

```
template<class InputIt, class OutputIt>
OutputIt do_quote(InputIt begin, InputIt end,
    OutputIt dest)
{
    *dest++ = '"';
    while (begin != end) {
        auto ch = *begin++;
        if (ch == '"') {
```

```
            *dest++ = '\\';
        }
        *dest++ = ch;
    }
    *dest++ = '"';
    return dest;
}
```

(This algorithm is not part of the standard library.) Having this algorithm in hand, we could easily construct a wrapper class, where the wrapper class' `operator<<` would invoke the following algorithm:

```
struct quoted {
    std::string_view m_view;
    quoted(const char *s) : m_view(s) {}
    quoted(const std::string& s) : m_view(s) {}
};

std::ostream& operator<< (std::ostream& os, const quoted& q)
{
    do_quote(
        q.m_view.begin(),
        q.m_view.end(),
        std::ostreambuf_iterator<char>(os)
    );
    return os;
}
```

(The `std::ostreambuf_iterator<char>` type is part of the standard library; it comes from the `<iterator>` header. We'll see its friend, `istream_iterator`, later in this chapter.) Then, having the wrapper class, we'd be able to write very reasonable-looking code to print quoted values to an output stream:

```
std::cout << quoted("I said \"hello\".");
```

The wrapper we just invented bears a deliberate resemblance to the `std::quoted` wrapper function found in the standard library's `<iomanip>` header. The major difference is that `std::quoted` doesn't use an iterator-based algorithm to produce its output; it constructs the entire output in a local `std::string` variable and then uses `os << str` to print it out in one fell swoop. This means that `std::quoted` is *not allocator-aware* (see Chapter 8, *Allocators*) and thus is not suitable for environments where heap allocation is forbidden. While the fine details may have been botched in this case,
the fundamental idea of using a wrapper function or class to adjust the formatting of a data value is a good one. You can see it taken to extremes in libraries like Boost.Format, where syntax like the following is legal:

```
std::cout << boost::format("There are %d piano tuners in %s.") % tuners
    % where
        << std::endl;
```

Prefer to use wrappers that describe self-contained formatting operations instead of manipulators, which "stickily" mutate the state of the stream. In the preceding code, we saw how an ill-placed `std::hex` can put a curse on everyone "downstream." Now, we'll look at two ways to solve that problem--and two new problems that crop up in its place!

Solving the sticky-manipulator problem

Our "sticky `std::hex`" problem can be solved by saving and restoring the state of the ostream around each complicated output operation, or by creating a brand-new ostream each time we want to output something. An example of the former is as follows:

```
void test() {
  std::ios old_state(nullptr);
  old_state.copyfmt(std::cout);
    std::cout << std::hex << 225; // "e1"
  std::cout.copyfmt(old_state);

  std::cout << 42; // "42"
}
```

An example of the latter is as follows:

```
void test() {
  std::ostream os(std::cout.rdbuf());
    os << std::hex << 225; // "e1"

  std::cout << 42; // "42"
}
```

Notice how convenient it is that the iostreams library separates the idea of a "streambuf" from the idea of a "stream"; in the preceding example, we easily strip all the formatting-related fields away from a stream by extracting just its streambuf: `std::cout.rdbuf()`) and then layer a brand new stream (with its own formatting-related fields) on top of that same streambuf.

However, iostreams formatting has another major disadvantage. Each piece of our intended message is output "eagerly" as soon as its respective `operator<<` is reached--or, if you prefer, each piece of our intended message is computed "lazily" only when its respective `operator<<` is reached--so that we have the following piece of code:

```
void test() {
  try {
    std::cout << "There are "
              << computation_that_may_throw()
              << "piano tuners here.\n";
  } catch (...) {
    std::cout << "An exception was thrown";
  }
}
```

We'll see the output `There are An exception was thrown` for the preceding piece of code.

Also, iostreams formatting is *intensely* disagreeable to internationalization ("i18n"), because the "shape" of the overall message is never present in the source code. Instead of a single string literal `"There are %d piano tuners here.\n"` representing a complete thought, which could be translated by a human and stored in an external file of translated messages; we have two sentence fragments: `"There are "` and `"piano tuners here.\n"`, neither of which can be translated in isolation.

For all these reasons, I strongly discourage you from attempting to use iostreams as the *foundation* of your codebase. Using `<stdio.h>` or a third-party library such as `fmt` for formatting is preferable. Boost.Format is also a possibility, although it tends to have very long compile times and poor runtime performance compared to either of the other two options. If you find yourself typing `<<`, `std::hex`, or `os.rdbuf()` more than once or twice a week, you're doing something wrong.

Yet the iostreams library still has some usable and even useful features! Let's look at one of them.

Formatting with ostringstream

So far, we've been talking mostly about `fstream`, which roughly corresponds to the `fprintf` and `vfprintf` formatting functions in the C API. There is also `stringstream`, which corresponds to `snprintf` and `vsnprintf`.

An `ostringstream` is just like `ostream`, exposing all the usual `operator<<` functionality; however, it is backed by `stringbuf` that writes not to a file descriptor but to a resizable character buffer--in practice, `std::string`! You can use the `oss.str()` method to get a copy of this string for your own use. This leads to the following idiom for, for example, "stringifying" an object of any type `T`:

```
template<class T>
std::string to_string(T&& t)
{
  std::ostringstream oss;
  oss << std::forward<T>(t);
  return oss.str();
}
```

In C++17, you may even consider a multi-argument version of `to_string`:

```
template<class... Ts>
std::string to_string(Ts&&... ts)
{
  std::ostringstream oss;
  (oss << ... << std::forward<Ts>(ts));
  return oss.str();
}
```

With this version, a call such as `to_string(a, " ", b)` or `to_string(std::hex, 42)` will have the appropriate semantics.

A note on locales

There is still a pernicious pitfall to beware any time you use either `printf` or `ostream` for string formatting (or string parsing). That pitfall is *locales*. A full treatment of locales is out of the scope of this book; however, in short, the *locale* is "the subset of a user's environment that depends on language and cultural conventions." Locale information is exposed programmatically via the operating system, allowing a single program to adjust its behavior depending on the current user's preferred locale, for example, to control whether "á" is considered an alphabetic character, whether the week begins with Sunday or Monday, whether dates print as "23-01-2017" or "01-23-2017", and whether floating-point numbers print as "1234.56" or "1.234,56". Now, a programmer from the 21st century may look at all of those examples and say, "This is crazy! You mean, not one of these things is specified by a *standard*? It seems like this situation would inevitably lead to subtle and painful bugs!" And you'd be correct!

```
std::setlocale(LC_ALL, "C.UTF-8");
std::locale::global(std::locale("C.UTF-8"));

auto json = to_string('[', 3.14, ']');
assert(json == "[3.14]");  // Success!

std::setlocale(LC_ALL, "en_DK.UTF-8");
std::locale::global(std::locale("en_DK.UTF-8"));

json = to_string('[', 3.14, ']');
assert(json == "[3,14]");  // Silent, abject failure!
```

By changing the *global locale* to `"en_DK.UTF-8"`, we've made it so that none of our JSON printing works anymore. Woe betide the hapless user who attempts to run a web server or a database in any locale other than `"C.UTF-8"`!

Besides the correctness costs of locale-specific programming, we must also contend with the performance costs. Notice that "current locale" is a *global variable*, which means that every access to it must be guarded by either an atomic access or--worse--a global mutex lock. And, every call to `snprintf` or `operator<<(ostream&, double)` must access the current locale. This is a horrendous performance cost, and, in certain scenarios, can actually be the performance bottleneck in multi-threaded code.

Iostreams

As an application programmer, for applications above a certain level of complexity, you should get in the habit of writing `std::locale::global(std::locale("C"))` as the first line of `main()`. (If you write only `setlocale(LC_ALL, "C")`, as you would in a C program, you'll make `<stdio.h>` work correctly but not affect the locale used by `<iostream>`. In other words, setting the C++ library's "global locale" also modifies the C library's "global locale," but not vice versa.)

> **TIP**: If you don't even trust your users to be using UTF-8, perhaps prefer the locale name `"C.UTF-8"` instead of just `"C"`; however, be aware that the name `"C.UTF-8"` has been around only since about 2015, and may not be available on older systems. In fact, the availability of *any* locale other than `"C"` depends on the user. Locales are similar to time zones in this way: there is only one locale and one timezone that is *guaranteed* to be available on any platform in the world, and not coincidentally, it's the one you should always be using.

As a programmer of third-party libraries, you have two possible paths. The easier path is to assume that your library will only ever be used in applications that have set their global locale to `"C"`, and so you don't need to worry about locales; go ahead and use `snprintf` and `operator<<` to your heart's content. (However, notice that this does not solve the performance problem associated with locale-aware programming. That global mutex lock will still be there, taking up valuable cycles.) The harder path--harder because it requires conscientious adherence to a subtle guideline--is to avoid all use of locale-aware formatting functions. This path has only really become feasible as of C++17, with some of the very newest library facilities, to which we will turn now.

Converting numbers to strings

Consider the following declarations:

```
std::ostringstream oss;
std::string str;
char buffer[100];
int intvalue = 42;
float floatvalue = 3.14;
std::to_chars_result r;
```

To convert the `intvalue` integer to a string of digits, C++17 offers us the following options:

```
snprintf(buffer, sizeof buffer, "%d", intvalue);
  // available in <stdio.h>
  // locale-independent (%d is unaffected by locales)
```

```
    // non-allocating
    // bases 8, 10, 16 only

oss << intvalue;
str = oss.str();
    // available in <sstream>
    // locale-problematic (thousands separator may be inserted)
    // allocating; allocator-aware
    // bases 8, 10, 16 only

str = std::to_string(intvalue);
    // available since C++11 in <string>
    // locale-independent (equivalent to %d)
    // allocating; NOT allocator-aware
    // base 10 only

r = std::to_chars(buffer, std::end(buffer), intvalue, 10);
*r.ptr = '\0';
    // available since C++17 in <charconv>
    // locale-independent by design
    // non-allocating
    // bases 2 through 36
```

All four alternatives have their advantages. The main advantage of `std::to_string` is that it is conveniently composable into larger messages in a high-level code:

```
std::string response =
    "Content-Length: " + std::to_string(body.size()) + "\r\n" +
    "\r\n" +
    body;
```

The main advantages of `std::to_chars` are that it is locale-independent and that it can easily be composed in low-level code:

```
char *write_string(char *p, char *end, const char *from)
{
  while (p != end && *from != '\0') *p++ = *from++;
  return p;
}

char *write_response_headers(char *p, char *end, std::string body)
{
  p = write_string(p, end, "Content-Length: ");
  p = std::to_chars(p, end, body.size(), 10).ptr;
  p = write_string(p, end, "\r\n\r\n");
  return p;
}
```

Iostreams

The main disadvantage of `std::to_chars` is that it is a very new feature of C++17; as of this writing, the `<charconv>` header is not present in any major implementation of the standard library.

To convert the floating-point `floatvalue` number to a string of digits, C++17 offers us the following options:

```
snprintf(buffer, sizeof buffer, "%.6e", floatvalue);
snprintf(buffer, sizeof buffer, "%.6f", floatvalue);
snprintf(buffer, sizeof buffer, "%.6g", floatvalue);
  // available in <stdio.h>
  // locale-problematic (decimal point)
  // non-allocating

oss << floatvalue;
str = oss.str();
  // available in <sstream>
  // locale-problematic (decimal point)
  // allocating; allocator-aware

str = std::to_string(floatvalue);
  // available since C++11 in <string>
  // locale-problematic (equivalent to %f)
  // allocating; NOT allocator-aware
  // no way to adjust the formatting

r = std::to_chars(buffer, std::end(buffer), floatvalue,
            std::chars_format::scientific, 6);
r = std::to_chars(buffer, std::end(buffer), floatvalue,
            std::chars_format::fixed, 6);
r = std::to_chars(buffer, std::end(buffer), floatvalue,
            std::chars_format::general, 6);
*r.ptr = '\0';
  // available since C++17 in <charconv>
  // locale-independent by design
  // non-allocating
```

Notice that when printing the floating-point, every method except `std::to_string` offers the possibility of adjusting the formatting; and every method except `std::to_chars` is locale-aware and thus problematic in a portable code. All of these methods are available for the `double` and `long double` data types, as well as for `float`. In any case, the same respective advantages and disadvantages apply for integer formatting.

[286]

Converting strings to numbers

The reverse problem of formatting numbers for output is *parsing* numbers from the user's input. Parsing is intrinsically much more subtle and difficult than formatting, because we must account for the possibility of error. Every number can plausibly be turned into a string of digits, but not every string (or even every string of digits!) can plausibly be turned into a number. So, any function that purports to parse numbers must have some way of dealing with strings that do not represent valid numbers.

Consider the following declarations:

```
std::istringstream iss;
std::string str = "42";
char buffer[] = "42";
int intvalue;
float floatvalue;
int rc;
char *endptr;
size_t endidx;
std::from_chars_result r;
```

To convert the string in `buffer` or `str` to an `intvalue` integer, C++17 offers us the following options:

```
intvalue = strtol(buffer, &endptr, 10);
  // saturates on overflow
  // sets global "errno" on most errors
  // sets endptr==buffer when input cannot be parsed
  // available in <stdlib.h>
  // locale-problematic, in theory
  // non-allocating
  // bases 0 and 2 through 36
  // always skips leading whitespace
  // skips leading 0x for base 16
  // recognizes upper and lower case

rc = sscanf(buffer, "%d", &intvalue);
  // fails to detect overflow
  // returns 0 (instead of 1) when input cannot be parsed
  // available in <stdio.h>
  // locale-problematic (equivalent to strtol)
  // non-allocating
  // bases 0, 8, 10, 16 only
  // always skips leading whitespace
  // skips leading 0x for base 16
  // recognizes upper and lower case
```

```
intvalue = std::stoi(str, &endidx, 10);
  // throws on overflow or error
  // available since C++11 in <string>
  // locale-problematic (equivalent to strtol)
  // NOT allocator-aware
  // bases 0 and 2 through 36
  // always skips leading whitespace
  // skips leading 0x for base 16
  // recognizes upper and lower case

iss.str("42");
iss >> intvalue;
  // saturates on overflow
  // sets iss.fail() on any error
  // available in <sstream>
  // locale-problematic
  // allocating; allocator-aware
  // bases 8, 10, 16 only
  // skips leading 0x for base 16
  // skips whitespace by default

r = std::from_chars(buffer, buffer + 2, intvalue, 10);
  // sets r.ec != 0 on any error
  // available since C++17 in <charconv>
  // locale-independent by design
  // non-allocating
  // bases 2 through 36
  // always skips leading whitespace
  // recognizes lower case only
```

There are more parsing methods here than there were formatting methods in the previous section; this is because the C standard library alone offers us three different methods: `atoi`, the oldest method, and the only one whose behavior on invalid input is *literally undefined*, so avoid it in production code; `strtol`, the standard replacement for `atoi`, it communicates overflow errors via the global variable `errno`, which may be inappropriate for threaded or high-performance code); and `sscanf`, a function in the same family as `snprintf`.

`std::stoi` is a very good replacement for `atoi` in one-off parsing of user input, and a very bad option for high-performance work. It does a very good job of detecting errors--`std::stoi("2147483648")` throws `std::out_of_range` and `std::stoi("abc")` throws `std::invalid_argument`. (And, although `std::stoi("42abc")` returns 42 without complaint, the `std::stoi("42abc", &endidx)` invocation will set endidx to 2 instead of 5, indicating that something may be amiss.) The major disadvantage of `std::stoi` is that it works only on the exact type `std::string`--there is no overload of `std::stoi` for `string_view`, no overload for `std::pmr::string`, and *certainly* no overload for `const char *`!

`std::from_chars` is the most modern and performant option to parse integers. Its main advantage is that unlike any of the other contenders, `from_chars` does not require its input buffer to be null-terminated--it takes a pair of `begin`, `end` pointers to indicate the range of characters to be parsed, and will never read past `end`. It still has some unfortunate limitations--for example, it cannot be taught not to skip whitespace, nor can it be taught to parse uppercase hexadecimal input. The idiom to test `r.ec` for error is shown near the beginning of Chapter 12, *Filesystem*.

The `strtol`, `sscanf`, and `stoi` functions indicate that they recognize "base 0." This is a special-case syntax in the library, where passing a base of 0 (or, in the case of `sscanf`, a format specifier of `"%i"`) tells the library to parse the input as if it were a C integer literal: `0123` will parse as the octal representation of decimal 83, `0x123` will parse as the hexadecimal representation of 291, and `019` will parse as the octal representation of the integer 1, with the character `9` left unparsed because it is not a valid octal. "Base 0" is never an appropriate behavior for a computer program, and `from_chars` wisely chucks it to the trash can, where it belongs.

To convert a string to a floating-point `floatvalue`, C++17 offers the following options:

```
        floatvalue = strtof(buffer, &endptr);
          // saturates on overflow
          // sets global "errno" on most errors
          // sets endptr==buffer when input cannot be parsed
          // available in <stdlib.h>
          // locale-problematic
          // non-allocating
          // base 10 or 16, auto-detected
          // always skips leading whitespace

        rc = sscanf(buffer, "%f", &floatvalue);
          // fails to detect overflow
          // returns 0 (instead of 1) when input cannot be parsed
          // available in <stdio.h>
```

```cpp
                // locale-problematic (equivalent to strtof)
                // non-allocating
                // base 10 or 16, auto-detected
                // always skips leading whitespace

        floatvalue = std::stof(str, &endidx);
                // throws on overflow or error
                // available since C++11 in <string>
                // locale-problematic (equivalent to strtol)
                // NOT allocator-aware
                // base 10 or 16, auto-detected
                // always skips leading whitespace

        iss.str("3.14");
        iss >> floatvalue;
                // saturates on overflow
                // sets iss.fail() on any error
                // available in <sstream>
                // locale-problematic
                // allocating; allocator-aware
                // base 10 or 16, auto-detected
                // skips whitespace by default
                // non-portable behavior on trailing text

        r = std::from_chars(buffer, buffer + 2, floatvalue,
                            std::chars_format::general);
                // sets r.ec != 0 on any error
                // available since C++17 in <charconv>
                // locale-independent by design
                // non-allocating
                // base 10 or 16, auto-detected
                // always skips leading whitespace
```

All of these parsers--even `std::from_chars`--accept input strings, `"Infinity"` and `"Nan"` (case-insensitively), and also accept "hex float" inputs so that, for example, `"0x1.c"` parses as the decimal number 1.75. All but `std::from_chars` are locale-aware, and thus problematic in portable code. Where the locale problems with integer parsing are largely theoretical, the widespread real-world use of locales where . is not the decimal separator means that it is very easy to run into cases where `std::stof` and `std::stod` don't work as expected:

```cpp
        std::setlocale(LC_ALL, "C.UTF-8");
        assert(std::stod("3.14") == 3.14); // Success!
        std::setlocale(LC_ALL, "en_DK.UTF-8");
        assert(std::stod("3.14") == 3.00); // Silent, abject failure!
```

Notice in passing the "non-portable behavior on trailing text" mentioned in connection with `istringstream`. Different library vendors do different things with stream input, and it's not always clear which should be considered "correct":

```
double d = 17;
std::istringstream iss("42abc");
iss >> d;
if (iss.good() && d == 42) {
  puts("Your library vendor is libstdc++");
} else if (iss.fail() && d == 0) {
  puts("Your library vendor is libc++");
}
```

Because of these portability issues--symptoms of the subtle complexity of stream input in general--, I recommend you avoid using `istringstream` for input parsing, even though `ostringstream` may sometimes be the most appropriate choice for output formatting.

Another good rule of thumb is to separate the *validation* (or *lexing*) of input from the *parsing* of input. If you can validate beforehand that a certain string contains all digits, or matches the regular-expression syntax of a valid floating-point number, then you merely have to pick a parsing method that can detect overflow and/or trailing text; for example, `std::stof` or `std::from_chars`. For more on lexing input with regular expressions, see Chapter 10, *Regular Expressions*.

Reading a line or word at a time

Reading from standard input one line at a time is a very common task in simple scripts, and most scripting languages make it a one-liner. For example, in Python:

```
for line in sys.stdin:
# preserves trailing newlines
process(line)
```

And in Perl:

```
while (<>) {
  # preserves trailing newlines
  process($_);
}
```

In C++, the task is almost as easy. Notice that C++'s `std::getline` function, unlike the other languages' idioms, removes the trailing newline (if any) from each line it reads:

```
std::string line;
while (std::getline(std::cin, line)) {
  // automatically chomps trailing newlines
    process(line);
}
```

In each of these cases, the entire input never lives in memory at once; we are indeed "streaming" the lines through our program in an efficient manner. (And the `std::getline` function is allocator-aware; if we absolutely need to avoid heap allocation, we can exchange `std::string line` for `std::pmr::string`.) The `process` function may take each line and use a regular expression (see Chapter 10, *Regular Expressions*) to validate and split the line into fields for further parsing.

To read a word, instead of a line, at a time, we can use the following code snippet as our guide (as long as we trust the current locale's definition of `isspace` to separate words correctly, of course):

```
template<class T>
struct streamer {
  std::istream& m_in;
  explicit streamer(std::istream& in) : m_in(in) {}
  auto begin() const
    { return std::istream_iterator<T>(m_in); }
  auto end() const
    { return std::istream_iterator<T>{}; }
};

int main()
{
  for (auto word : streamer<std::string>(std::cin)) {
    process(word);
  }
}
```

`std::istream_iterator<T>` is a standard library type, defined in the `<iterator>` header, which wraps a pointer to `istream`. The iterator's `operator++` reads a value of type T from the istream, as if by `operator>>`, and that value is returned by the iterator's `operator*`. Putting it all together, this allows us to read a whole sequence of whitespace-delimited words from `std::cin` by relying on the fact that `std::istream::operator>>(std::string&)` reads a single whitespace-delimited word.

We can reuse our `streamer` class template to read a whole sequence of integers from `std::cin` and do something with each of them:

```
// Double every int the user gives us
for (auto value : streamer<int>(std::cin)) {
  printf("%d\n", 2*value);
}
```

While the I/O facilities of C++ are certainly very complicated, as befits a system's programming language with its roots in the 1980s, we see from these last few examples that it is nonetheless possible to hide this complexity under a layer of abstraction and end up with code that looks almost as simple as Python.

Summary

Data output can be divided roughly into *formatting* and *buffering*. Data input can be divided just as roughly into *buffering* and *parsing*; although, the parsing step gets easier if you can put a *lexing* step in front. (We'll talk more about lexing in the very next chapter!)

The classical iostreams API is built on top of `<stdio.h>`, which in turn is built on top of the POSIX file-descriptor API. You can't understand the higher levels without a good understanding of the levels beneath it. In particular, the mess of `fopen` mode strings and `fstream` constructor flags can be understood only by reference to lookup tables mapping them onto the actual underlying POSIX `open` flags.

The POSIX API is concerned only with moving chunks of data to and from file descriptors; it does not "buffer" data in the naive sense. The `<stdio.h>` API adds a layer of buffering on top of POSIX; the C `FILE` may be fully buffered, line-buffered, or unbuffered. Furthermore, `<stdio.h>` provides performant (but locale-aware) formatting routines, of which the most important are `fprintf`, `snprintf`, and `sscanf`.

The `<iostream>` API separates the "streambuf", (which identifies the source or sink of raw bytes, and its buffering mode) from the "stream" (which holds the state related to formatting). The different kinds of streams (input or output? file or string?) form a classical polymorphic hierarchy with complicated and, at times, unintuitive inheritance relationships. Avoiding `<iostream>` in production code is preferable as it is slow and opaque compared to the `<stdio.h>` or POSIX interfaces. Either way, beware of locale-dependent formatting routines.

For one-off quick tasks, prefer parsing numbers via `std::stoi`, which detects and throws on error, and formatting with `std::to_string` or `snprintf`. For high-performance situations, parsing with `std::from_chars` and formatting with `std::to_chars` is preferable if you can find a library implementation that supports these brand new functions from the `<charconv>` header.

10
Regular Expressions

In the previous chapter, we learned all about formatted input and output in C++. We saw that there are good solutions for formatted output--as long as you make sure you're in the C locale--but that despite the many approaches to input parsing, even the simple task of parsing an `int` out of a string can be quite difficult. (Recall that of the two most foolproof methods, `std::stoi(x)` requires converting x to a heap-allocated `std::string`, and the verbose `std::from_chars(x.begin(), x.end(), &value, 10)` is lagging the rest of C++17 in vendor adoption.) The fiddliest part of parsing numbers is figuring out what to do with the part of the input that *isn't* numeric!

Parsing gets easier if you can split it into two subtasks: First, figure out exactly how many bytes of the input correspond to one "input item" (this is called *lexing*); and second, parse the value of that item, with some error recovery in the case that the item's value is out of range or otherwise nonsensical. If we apply this approach to integer input, *lexing* corresponds to finding the longest initial sequence of digits in the input, and *parsing* corresponds to computing the numeric value of that sequence in base 10.

Regular expressions (or *regexes*) is a tool provided by many programming languages that solve the lexing problem, not just for sequences of digits but for arbitrarily complicated input formats. Regular expressions have been part of the C++ standard library since 2011, in the `<regex>` header. In this chapter we'll show you how to use regexes to simplify some common parsing tasks.

Regular Expressions

Bear in mind that regexes are likely to be overkill for *most* parsing tasks that you'll face in your daily work. They can be slow and bloated, and unavoidably require heap allocation (that is, the regex data types are not *allocator-aware* as described in `Chapter 8`, *Allocators*). Where regexes really shines is for complicated tasks where hand-written parsing code would be just as slow anyway; and for extremely simple tasks where the readability and robustness of regular expressions outweigh their performance costs. In short, regex support has taken C++ one step closer to the everyday usability of scripting languages such as Python and Perl.

In this chapter we'll learn:

- "Modified ECMAScript", the dialect used by C++ regexes
- How to match, search, and even replace substrings using regexes
- Further dangers of dangling iterators
- Regex features to avoid

What are regular expressions?

A *regular expression* is a way of writing down the rules for recognizing a string of bytes or characters as belonging (or not belonging) to a certain "language." In this context, a "language" can be anything from "the set of all digit-sequences" to "the set of all sequences of valid C++ tokens." Essentially, a "language" is just a rule for dividing the world of all strings into two sets--the set of strings matching the rules of the language, and the set of strings that *don't* match.

Some kinds of languages follow simple enough rules that they can be recognized by a *finite state machine*, a computer program with no memory at all--just a program counter and a pointer that scans over the input in a single pass. The language of "digit-sequences" is certainly in the category of languages that can be recognized by a finite state machine. We call these languages *regular languages*.

There also exist non-regular languages. One very common non-regular language is "valid arithmetic expressions," or, to boil it down to its essence, "properly matched parentheses." Any program that can distinguish the properly matched string (((()))) from the improperly matched strings (((())) and (((())))) must essentially be able to "count"-- to distinguish the case of *four* parentheses from the cases of *three* or *five*. Counting in this way cannot be done without a modifiable variable or a push-down stack; so parenthesis-matching is *not* a regular language.

It turns out that, given any regular language, there is a nice straightforward way to write a representation of the finite state machine that recognizes it, which of course is also a representation of the rules of the language itself. We call this representation a *regular expression*, or *regex*. The standard notation for regexes was developed in the 1950s, and was really set in stone by the late 1970s in Unix programs such as `grep` and `sed`--programs which are still very much worth learning today, but which are of course outside the scope of this book.

The C++ standard library offers several different "flavors" of regex syntax, but the default flavor (and the one you should always use) was borrowed wholesale from the standard for ECMAScript--the language better known as JavaScript--with only minor modifications in the vicinity of square-bracket constructs. I've included a primer on ECMAScript regex syntax near the end of this chapter; but if you've ever used `grep`, you'll be able to follow the rest of this chapter easily without consulting that section.

A note on backslash-escaping

In this chapter, we'll be referring frequently to strings and regular expressions that contain literal backslashes. As you know, to write a string containing a literal backslash in C++, you have to *escape* the backslash with another backslash: thus `"\n"` represents a newline character but `"\\n"` represents the two-character string of "backslash" followed by "n". This kind of thing is usually easy to keep track of, but in this chapter we're going to have to take special pains. Regexes are implemented purely as a library feature; so when you write `std::regex("\n")` the regex library will see a "regex" containing only a single whitespace character, and if you write `std::regex("\\n")` the library will see a two-character string starting with a backslash, which *the library will interpret* as a two-character escape sequence meaning "newline." If you want to communicate the idea of a *literal* backslash-n to the regex library, you'll have to get the regex library to see the three-character string \\\n, which means writing the five-character string `"\\\\n"` in your C++ source code.

You might have noticed in the preceding paragraph the solution I'm going to be using in this chapter. When I talk about a C++ *string literal* or string value, I will put it in double quotes, like this: `"cat"`, `"a\\.b"`. When I talk about a *regular expression* as you would type it in an email or a text editor, or hand it to the library for evaluation, I will express it without quotes: cat, a\.b. Just remember that when you see an unquoted string, that's a literal sequence of characters, and if you want to put it into a C++ string literal, you'll need to double up all the backslashes, thus: a\.b goes into your source code as `std::regex("a\\.b")`.

[297]

Regular Expressions

I hear some of you asking: What about *raw string literals*? Raw string literals are a C++11 feature that allows you to write the character sequence `a\.b` by "escaping" the entire string with an `R` and some parentheses, like this--`R"(a\.b)"`--instead of escaping each backslash in the string. If your string contains parentheses itself, then you can get fancier by writing any arbitrary string before the first parenthesis and after the last, like this: `R"fancy(a\.b)fancy"`. A raw string literal like this one is allowed to contain any characters--backslashes, quotation marks, even newlines--as long as it doesn't contain the consecutive sequence `)fancy"` (and if you think there's a chance it might contain that sequence, then you just pick a new arbitrary string, such as `)supercalifragilisticexpialidocious"`).

The syntax of C++ raw string literals, with its leading `R`, is reminiscent of the raw string literal syntax in Python (with its leading `r`). In Python, `r"a\.b"` similarly represents the literal string `a\.b`; and it is both common and idiomatic to represent regular expressions in code by strings such as `r"abc"` even if they don't contain any special characters. But notice the all-important difference between `r"a\.b"` and `R"(a\.b)"`--the C++ version has an extra set of parentheses! And parentheses are *significant special characters* in the regex grammar. The C++ string literals `"(cat)"` and `R"(cat)"` are as different as night and day-- the former represents the five-character regex `(cat)`, and the latter represents the three-character regex `cat`. If you trip up and write `R"(cat)"` when you meant `"(cat)"` (or equivalently, `R"((cat))"`), your program will have a very subtle bug. Even more sadistically, `R"a*(b*)a*"` is a valid regex with a surprising meaning! Therefore, I recommend that you use raw string literals for regexes with great caution; generally it is safer and clearer to double *all* your backslashes than to worry about doubling only the *outermost* of your parentheses.

Where raw string literals *are* useful is for what other languages call "heredocs":

```
void print_help() {
  puts(R"(The regex special characters are:
\ - escaping
| - separating alternatives
. - match any character
[] - character class or set
() - capturing parentheses, or lookahead
?*+ - "zero or one", "zero or more", "one or more"
{} - "exactly N" or "M to N" repetitions
^$ - beginning and end of a "line"
\b - word boundary
\d \s \w - digit, space, and word
(?=foo) (?!foo) - lookahead; negative lookahead
)");
```

That is, raw string literals are the only kind of string literal in C++ that can encode newline characters without any kind of escaping. This is useful for printing long messages to the user, or maybe for things such as HTTP headers; but raw strings' behavior with parentheses makes them mildly dangerous for use with regular expressions--I will not be using them in this book.

Reifying regular expressions into std::regex objects

To use regular expressions in C++, you can't use a string such as `"c[a-z]*t"` directly. Instead, you have to use that string to construct a *regular expression object* of type `std::regex`, and then pass the `regex` object as one of the arguments to a *matching function* such as `std::regex_match`, `std::regex_search`, or `std::regex_replace`. Each object of type `std::regex` encodes a complete finite state machine for the given expression, and constructing this finite state machine requires a lot of computation and memory allocation; so if we are going to match a lot of input text against the same regex, it is convenient that the library gives us a way to pay for that expensive construction just once. On the other hand, this means that the `std::regex` objects are relatively slow to construct and expensive to copy; constructing a regex inside a tight inner loop is a good way to kill your program's performance:

```cpp
std::regex rx("(left|right) ([0-9]+)");
// Construct the regex object "rx" outside the loop.
std::string line;
while (std::getline(std::cin, line)) {
  // Inside the loop, use the same "rx" over and over.
  if (std::regex_match(line, rx)) {
    process_command(line);
  } else {
    puts("Unrecognized command.");
  }
}
```

Keep in mind that this `regex` object has value semantics; when we "match" an input string against a regex, we aren't mutating the `regex` object itself. A regex has no memory of what it's been matched against. Therefore, when we want to pull information out of a regex-matching operation--such as "did the command say to move left or right? what was the number we saw?"--we'll have to introduce a new entity that we can mutate.

A `regex` object offers the following methods:

`std::regex(str, flags)` constructs a new `std::regex` object by translating (or "compiling") the given `str` into a finite state machine. Options affecting the compilation process itself can be specified via the bitmask argument `flags`:

- `std::regex::icase`: Treat all alphabetic characters as case-insensitive
- `std::regex::nosubs`: Treat all parenthesized groups as non-capturing
- `std::regex::multiline`: Make the non-consuming assertion ^ (and $) match immediately after (and before) a "\n" character in the input, rather than only at the beginning (and end) of the input

There are several other options that you could bitwise-OR into flags; but the others either change the "flavor" of regex syntax away from ECMAScript towards less well-documented and less well-tested flavors (`basic`, `extended`, `awk`, `grep`, `egrep`), introduce locale dependencies (`collate`), or simply don't do anything at all (`optimize`). Therefore, you should avoid all of them in production code.

Notice that even though the process of turning a string into a `regex` object is often called "compiling the regex," it is still a dynamic process that happens at runtime when the `regex` constructor is called, not during the compilation of your C++ program. If you make a syntax error in your regular expression, it will be caught not at compile time, but at runtime--the `regex` constructor will throw an exception of type `std::regex_error`, which is a subclass of `std::runtime_error`. Properly robust code should also be prepared for the `regex` constructor to throw `std::bad_alloc`; recall that `std::regex` is not allocator-aware.

`rx.mark_count()` returns the number of parenthesized capturing groups in the regex. The name of this method comes from the phrase "marked subexpression," an older synonym for "capturing group."

`rx.flags()` returns the bit-mask that was passed to the constructor originally.

Matching and searching

To ask whether a given input string `haystack` conforms to a given regex `rneedle`, you can use `std::regex_match(haystack, rneedle)`. The regex always comes last, which is reminiscent of JavaScript's syntax `haystack.match(rneedle)` and Perl's `haystack =~ rneedle` even as it's opposed to Python's `re.match(rneedle, haystack)`. The `regex_match` function returns `true` if the regex matches the entire input string, and `false` otherwise:

```cpp
std::regex rx("(left|right) ([0-9]+)");
std::string line;
while (std::getline(std::cin, line)) {
  if (std::regex_match(line, rx)) {
    process_command(line);
  } else {
    printf("Unrecognized command '%s'.\n",
      line.c_str());
  }
}
```

The `regex_search` function returns `true` if the regex matches any portion of the input string. Essentially, it just puts `.*` on both sides of the regex you provided and then runs the `regex_match` algorithm; but implementations can generally perform a `regex_search` faster than they could recompile a whole new regex.

To match within just part of a character buffer (such as you might do when pulling data in bulk over a network connection or from a file), you can pass an iterator pair to `regex_match` or `regex_search`, very similarly to what we saw in Chapter 3, *The Iterator-Pair Algorithms*. In the following example, bytes outside the range `[p, end)` are never considered, and the "string" p doesn't need to be null-terminated:

```cpp
void parse(const char *p, const char *end)
{
  static std::regex rx("(left|right) ([0-9]+)");
  if (std::regex_match(p, end, rx)) {
    process_command(p, end);
  } else {
    printf("Unrecognized command '%.*s'.\n",
      int(end - p), p);
  }
}
```

This interface is similar to what we saw with `std::from_chars` in Chapter 9, *Iostreams*.

Pulling submatches out of a match

To use regexes for the *lexing* stage of input, you'll need a way to pull out the input substrings that matched each capturing group. The way you do this in C++ is by creating a *match object* of type `std::smatch`. No, that's not a typo! The name of the match-object type really is `smatch`, which stands for `std::string` match; there is also `cmatch` for `const char *` match. The difference between `smatch` or `cmatch` is the *type of iterator* they store internally: `smatch` stores `string::const_iterator`, while `cmatch` stores `const char *`.

Having constructed an empty `std::smatch` object, you'll pass it by reference as the middle parameter to `regex_match` or `regex_search`. Those functions will "fill in" the `smatch` object with information about the substrings that matched, *if* the regex match actually succeeded. If the match failed, then the `smatch` object will become (or remain) empty.

Here's an example of using `std::smatch` to pull out the substrings matching the direction and the integer distance from our "robot command":

```
std::pair<std::string, std::string>
parse_command(const std::string& line)
{
  static std::regex rx("(left|right) ([0-9]+)");
  std::smatch m;
  if (std::regex_match(line, m, rx)) {
    return { m[1], m[2] };
  } else {
    throw "Unrecognized command!";
  }
}

void test() {
  auto [dir, dist] = parse_command("right 4");
  assert(dir == "right" && dist == "4");
}
```

Notice that we use a `static` regex object to avoid constructing ("compiling") a new regex object every time the function is entered. Here's the same code using `const char *` and `std::cmatch` just for comparison:

```
std::pair<std::string, std::string>
parse_command(const char *p, const char *end)
{
  static std::regex rx("(left|right) ([0-9]+)");
  std::cmatch m;
  if (std::regex_match(p, end, m, rx)) {
    return { m[1], m[2] };
```

```
      } else {
        throw "Unrecognized command!";
      }
    }

    void test() {
      char buf[] = "left 20";
      auto [dir, dist] = parse_command(buf, buf + 7);
      assert(dir == "left" && dist == "20");
    }
```

In both cases, something interesting happens on the line with the `return`. Having successfully matched the input string against our regex, we can query the match object `m` to find out which pieces of the input string correspond to the individual capturing groups in our regex. The first capturing group (`(left|right)` in our example) corresponds to `m[1]`, the second group (`([0-9]+)` in our example) corresponds to `m[2]`, and so on. If you try to refer to a group that doesn't exist in the regex, such as `m[3]` in our example, you'll get an empty string; accessing a match object will never throw an exception.

The group `m[0]` is a special case: it refers to the entire matched sequence. If the match was filled in by `std::regex_match`, this will always be the entire input string; if the match was filled in by `std::regex_search`, then this will be just the part of the string that matched the regex.

There are also two named groups: `m.prefix()` and `m.suffix()`. These refer to the sequences that were *not* part of the match--before the matched substring and after it, respectively. It is an invariant that if the match succeeded at all, then `m.prefix() + m[0] + m.suffix()` represents the entire input string.

All of these "group" objects are represented not by `std::string` objects--that would be too expensive--but by lightweight objects of type `std::sub_match<It>` (where `It` is either `std::string::const_iterator` or `const char *` as noted previously). Every `sub_match` object is implicitly convertible to `std::string`, and otherwise behaves a lot like a `std::string_view`: you can compare submatches against string literals, ask them for their lengths, and even output them to a C++ stream with `operator<<`, without ever converting them to `std::string`. The downside of this lightweight efficiency is the same downside we get every time we deal with iterators pointing into a container we may not own: we run the risk of *dangling iterators*:

```
    static std::regex rx("(left|right) ([0-9]+)");
    std::string line = "left 20";
    std::smatch m;
    std::regex_match(line, m, rx);
      // m[1] now holds iterators into line
```

Regular Expressions

```
line = "hello world";
  // reallocate line's underlying buffer
std::string oops = m[1];
  // this invokes undefined behavior because
  // of iterator invalidation
```

Looking at the preceding code snippet, you might worry that an implicit conversion (from, say, `const char *` to `std::string`) might cause iterator-invalidation bugs in harmless-looking code. Consider the following:

```
static std::regex rx("(left|right) ([0-9]+)");
std::smatch m;
std::regex_match("left 20", m, rx);
  // m[1] would hold iterators into a temporary
  // string, so they would ALREADY be invalid.
  // Fortunately this overload is deleted.
```

Fortunately, the standard library foresaw this lurking horror and evaded it by providing a special-case overload `regex_match(std::string&&, std::smatch&, const std::regex&)`, which is *explicitly deleted* (using the same `=delete` syntax you'd use to delete an unwanted special member function). This ensures that the preceding innocent-looking code will fail to compile, rather than being a source of iterator-invalidation bugs. Still, iterator invalidation bugs can happen, as in the previous example; to prevent them, you should treat `smatch` objects as extremely temporary, kind of like a `[&]` lambda that captures the world by reference. Once a `smatch` object has been filled in, don't touch anything else in the environment until you've extracted the parts of the `smatch` that you care about!

To summarize, a `smatch` or `cmatch` object offers the following methods:

- `m.ready()`: True if m has been filled in at all, in the time since its construction.
- `m.empty()`: True if m represents a failed match (that is, if it was most recently filled in by a failed `regex_match` or `regex_search`); false if m represents a successful match.
- `m.prefix()`, `m[0]`, `m.suffix()`: `sub_match` objects representing the unmatched prefix, matched, and unmatched suffix parts of the input string. (If m represents a failed match, then none of these are meaningful.)
- `m[k]`: A `sub_match` object representing the part of the input string matched by the *k*th capturing group. `m.str(k)` is a convenient shorthand for `m[k].str()`.
- `m.size()`: Zero if m represents a failed match; otherwise, one more than the number of capturing groups in the regex whose successful match is represented by m. Notice that `m.size()` always agrees with `operator[]`; the range of meaningful submatch objects is always `m[0]` through `m[m.size()-1]`.

- `m.begin()`, `m.end()`: Iterators enabling ranged for-loop syntax over a match object.

And a `sub_match` object offers the following methods:

- `sm.first`: The iterator to the beginning of the matched input substring.
- `sm.second`: The iterator to the end of the matched input substring.
- `sm.matched`: True if `sm` was involved in the successful match; false if `sm` was part of an optional branch that got bypassed. For example, if the regex was `(a)|(b)` and the input was `"a"`, we would have `m[1].matched && !m[2].matched`; whereas if the input were `"b"`, we would have `m[2].matched && !m[1].matched`.
- `sm.str()`: The matched input substring, pulled out and converted to `std::string`.
- `sm.length()`: The length of the matched input substring (`second - first`). Equivalent to `sm.str().length()`, but much faster.
- `sm == "foo"`: Comparison against `std::string`, `const char *`, or a single `char`. Equivalent to `sm.str() == "foo"`, but much faster. Unfortunately, the C++17 standard library does not provide any overload of `operator==` taking `std::string_view`.

Although you will likely never have a use for this in real code, it is possible to create a match or submatch object storing iterators into containers other than `std::string` or buffers of `char`. For example, here's our same function, but matching our regex against a `std::list<char>`—silly, but it works!

```
template<class Iter>
std::pair<std::string, std::string>
parse_command(Iter begin, Iter end)
{
   static std::regex rx("(left|right) ([0-9]+)");
   std::match_results<Iter> m;
   if (std::regex_match(begin, end, m, rx)) {
     return { m.str(1), m.str(2) };
   } else {
     throw "Unrecognized command!";
   }
}

void test() {
   char buf[] = "left 20";
   std::list<char> lst(buf, buf + 7);
```

```
      auto [dir, dist] = parse_command(lst.begin(), lst.end());
      assert(dir == "left" && dist == "20");
    }
```

Converting submatches to data values

Just to close the loop on parsing, here's an example of how we could parse string and integer values out of our submatches to actually move our robot:

```
    int main()
    {
      std::regex rx("(left|right) ([0-9]+)");
      int pos = 0;
      std::string line;
      while (std::getline(std::cin, line)) {
        try {
          std::smatch m;
          if (!std::regex_match(line, m, rx)) {
            throw std::runtime_error("Failed to lex");
          }
          int how_far = std::stoi(m.str(2));
          int direction = (m[1] == "left") ? -1 : 1;
          pos += how_far * direction;
          printf("Robot is now at %d.\n", pos);
        } catch (const std::exception& e) {
          puts(e.what());
          printf("Robot is still at %d.\n", pos);
        }
      }
    }
```

Any unrecognized or invalid string input is diagnosed either by our custom `"Failed to lex"` exception or by the `std::out_of_range` exception thrown by `std::stoi()`. If we were to add a check for integer overflow before modifying `pos`, we'd have a rock-solid input parser.

If we wanted to handle negative integers and case-insensitive directions, the following modifications would do the trick:

```
    int main()
    {
      std::regex rx("((left)|right) (-?[0-9]+)", std::regex::icase);
      int pos = 0;
      std::string line;
      while (std::getline(std::cin, line)) {
        try {
```

```
        std::smatch m;
        if (!std::regex_match(line, m, rx)) {
          throw std::runtime_error("Failed to lex");
        }
        int how_far = std::stoi(m.str(3));
        int direction = m[2].matched ? -1 : 1;
        pos += how_far * direction;
        printf("Robot is now at %d.\n", pos);
      } catch (const std::exception& e) {
        puts(e.what());
        printf("Robot is still at %d.\n", pos);
      }
    }
  }
}
```

Iterating over multiple matches

Consider the regex (?!\d)\w+, which matches a single C++ identifier. We already know how to use std::regex_match to tell whether an input string *is* a C++ identifier, and how to use std::regex_search to find the *first* C++ identifier in a given input line. But what if we want to find *all* the C++ identifiers in a given input line?

The fundamental idea here is to call std::regex_search in a loop. This gets complicated, though, because of the non-consuming "lookbehind" anchors such as ^ and \b. To implement a loop over std::regex_search correctly from scratch, we'd have to preserve the state of these anchors. std::regex_search (and std::regex_match for that matter) supports this use-case by providing flags of its own--flags which determine the *starting state* of the finite state machine for this particular matching operation. For our purposes, the only important flag is std::regex::match_prev_avail, which tells the library that the iterator begin, representing the start of the input, is not actually at the "beginning" of the input (that is, it might not match ^) and that if you want to know the previous character of the input for purposes of \b, it is safe to inspect begin[-1]:

```
auto get_all_matches(
  const char *begin, const char *end,
  const std::regex& rx,
  bool be_correct)
{
  auto flags = be_correct ?
    std::regex_constants::match_prev_avail :
    std::regex_constants::match_default;
  std::vector<std::string> result;
  std::cmatch m;
```

Regular Expressions

```
      std::regex_search(begin, end, m, rx);
      while (!m.empty()) {
        result.push_back(m[0]);
        begin = m[0].second;
        std::regex_search(begin, end, m, rx, flags);
      }
      return result;
    }

    void test() {
      char buf[] = "baby";
      std::regex rx("\\bb.");
        // get the first 2 letters of each word starting with "b"
      auto v = get_all_matches(buf, buf+4, rx, false);
      assert(v.size() == 2);
        // oops, "by" is considered to start on a word boundary!

      v = get_all_matches(buf, buf+4, rx, true);
      assert(v.size() == 1);
        // "by" is correctly seen as part of the word "baby"
    }
```

In the preceding example, when !be_correct, each regex_search invocation is treated independently, so there is no difference between searching for \bb. from the first letter of the word "by" or from the third letter of the word "baby". But when we pass match_prev_avail to the later invocations of regex_search, it takes a step back-- literally--to see whether the letter before "by" was a "word" letter or not. Since the preceding "a" is a word letter, the second regex_search correctly refuses to treat "by" as a match.

Using `regex_search` in a loop like this is easy... unless the given regex might match an empty string! If the regex ever returns a successful match m where `m[0].length() == 0`, then we'll have an infinite loop. So the inner loop of our `get_all_matches()` should really look more like this:

```
while (!m.empty()) {
  result.push_back(m[0]);
  begin = m[0].second;
  if (begin == end) break;
  if (m[0].length() == 0) ++begin;
  if (begin == end) break;
  std::regex_search(begin, end, m, rx, flags);
}
```

The standard library provides a "convenience" type called `std::regex_iterator` that will encapsulate the preceding code snippets' logic; using `regex_iterator` might conceivably save you some subtle bugs related to zero-length matches. Sadly, it won't save you any typing, and it slightly increases the chances of dangling-iterator pitfalls. `regex_iterator` is templated on its underlying iterator type in the same way as `match_results`, so if you're matching `std::string` input you want `std::sregex_iterator` and if you're matching on `const char *` input you want `std::cregex_iterator`. Here's the preceding example, recoded in terms of `sregex_iterator`:

```
auto get_all_matches(
  const char *begin, const char *end,
  const std::regex& rx)
{
  std::vector<std::string> result;
  using It = std::cregex_iterator;
  for (It it(begin, end, rx); it != It{}; ++it) {
    auto m = *it;
    result.push_back(m[0]);
  }
  return result;
}
```

Consider how this awkward for-loop might benefit from a helper class, along the lines of `streamer<T>` from the example near the end of Chapter 9, *Iostreams*.

You can also iterate over the submatches within each match, either manually or using a "convenience" library type. Manually, it would look something like this:

```
auto get_tokens(const char *begin, const char *end,
  const std::regex& rx)
{
  std::vector<std::string> result;
  using It = std::cregex_iterator;
  std::optional<std::csub_match> opt_suffix;
  for (It it(begin, end, rx); it != It{}; ++it) {
    auto m = *it;
    std::csub_match nonmatching_part = m.prefix();
    result.push_back(nonmatching_part);
    std::csub_match matching_part = m[0];
    result.push_back(matching_part);
    opt_suffix = m.suffix();
  }
  if (opt_suffix.has_value()) {
    result.push_back(opt_suffix.value());
  }
  return result;
}
```

Recall that `regex_iterator` is just a wrapper around `regex_search`, so `m.prefix()` in this case is guaranteed to hold an entire non-matching portion, all the way back to the end of the previous match. By alternately pushing back non-matching prefixes and matches, and finishing with a special case for the non-matching suffix, we split the input string into a vector of "words" alternating with "word separators." It's easy to modify this code to save only the "words" or only the "separators" if that's all you need; or even to save `m[1]` instead of `m[0]`, and so forth.

The library type `std::sregex_token_iterator` encapsulates all of this logic very directly, although its constructor interface is fairly confusing if you aren't already familiar with the preceding manual code. `sregex_token_iterator`'s constructor takes an input iterator-pair, a regex, and then a *vector of submatch indices*, where the index –1 is a special case meaning "prefixes (and also, suffix)."

```
auto get_tokens(const char *begin, const char *end,
  const std::regex& rx)
{
  std::vector<std::string> result;
  using TokIt = std::cregex_token_iterator;
  for (TokIt it(begin, end, rx, {-1, 0}); it != TokIt{}; ++it) {
    std::csub_match some_part = *it;
    result.push_back(some_part);
  }
```

```
        return result;
    }
```

If we change the array `{-1, 0}` to just `{0}`, then our resulting vector will contain only the pieces of the input string matching `rx`. If we change it to `{1, 2, 3}`, our loop will see only those submatches (`m[1]`, `m[2]`, and `m[3]`) in each match `m` of `rx`. Recall that because of the `|` operator, submatches can be bypassed, leaving `m[k].matched` false. `regex_token_iterator` does not skip those matches. For example:

```
std::string input = "abc123...456...";
std::vector<std::ssub_match> v;
std::regex rx("([0-9]+)|([a-z]+)");
using TokIt = std::sregex_token_iterator;
std::copy(
    TokIt(input.begin(), input.end(), rx, {1, 2}),
    TokIt(),
    std::back_inserter(v)
);
assert(!v[0].matched); assert(v[1] == "abc");
assert(v[2] == "123"); assert(!v[3].matched);
assert(v[4] == "456"); assert(!v[5].matched);
```

The most attractive use of `regex_token_iterator` might be to split a string into "words" at whitespace boundaries. Unfortunately it is not significantly easier to use--or to debug-- than old-school approaches such as `istream_iterator<string>` (see Chapter 9, *Iostreams*) or `strtok_r`.

Using regular expressions for string replacement

If you're coming from Perl, or if you often use the command-line utility `sed`, you probably think of regexes primarily as a way to *modify* strings--for example, "remove all substrings matching this regex," or "replace all instances of this word with another word." The C++ standard library does provide a sort of replace-by-regex functionality, under the name `std::regex_replace`. It's based on the JavaScript `String.prototype.replace` method, which means that it comes with its own idiosyncratic formatting mini-language.

Regular Expressions

`std::regex_replace(str, rx, "replacement")` returns a `std::string` constructed by searching through `str` for every substring matching the regex `rx` and replacing each such substring with the literal string `"replacement"`. For example:

```
std::string s = "apples and bananas";
std::string t = std::regex_replace(s, std::regex("a"), "e");
assert(t == "epples end benenes");
std::string u = std::regex_replace(s, std::regex("[ae]"), "u");
assert(u == "upplus und bununus");
```

However, if `"replacement"` contains any `'$'` characters, special things will happen!

- `"$&"` is replaced with the entire matching substring, `m[0]`. Both libstdc++ and libc++ support `"$0"` as a non-standard synonym for `"$&"`.
- `"$1"` is replaced with the first submatch, `m[1]`; `"$2"` is replaced with `m[2]`; and so on, all the way up to `"$99"`. There is no way to refer to the 100th submatch. `"$100"` represents "`m[10]` followed by a literal `'0'`." To express "`m[1]` followed by a literal `'0'`," write `"$010"`.
- `"$`"` (that's a backtick) is replaced with `m.prefix()`.
- `"$'"` (that's a single-quote) is replaced with `m.suffix()`.
- `"$$"` is replaced with a literal dollar sign.

Notice that `"$`"` and `"$'"` are far from symmetrical, because `m.prefix()` always refers to the part of the string between the end of the last match and the start of the current one, but `m.suffix()` always refers to the part of the string between the end of the current match and the *end of the string*! You'll never use either `"$`"` or `"$'"` in real code.

Here's an example of using `regex_replace` to remove all the instances of `std::` from a piece of code, or to change them all to `my::`:

```
auto s = "std::sort(std::begin(v), std::end(v))";
auto t = std::regex_replace(s, std::regex("\\bstd::(\\w+)"), "$1");
assert(t == "sort(begin(v), end(v))");
auto u = std::regex_replace(s, std::regex("\\bstd::(\\w+)"), "my::$1");
assert(u == "my::sort(my::begin(v), my::end(v))");
```

JavaScript's `String.prototype.replace` allows you to pass in an arbitrary function instead of a dollar-sign-studded format string. C++'s `regex_replace` doesn't support arbitrary functions yet, but it's easy to write your own version that does:

```
template<class F>
std::string regex_replace(std::string_view haystack,
    const std::regex& rx, const F& f)
```

```cpp
{
  std::string result;
  const char *begin = haystack.data();
  const char *end = begin + haystack.size();
  std::cmatch m, lastm;
  if (!std::regex_search(begin, end, m, rx)) {
    return std::string(haystack);
  }
  do {
    lastm = m;
    result.append(m.prefix());
    result.append(f(m));
    begin = m[0].second;
    begin += (begin != end && m[0].length() == 0);
    if (begin == end) break;
  } while (std::regex_search(begin, end, m, rx,
    std::regex_constants::match_prev_avail));
  result.append(lastm.suffix());
  return result;
}

void test()
{
  auto s = "std::sort(std::begin(v), std::end(v))";
  auto t = regex_replace(s, std::regex("\\bstd::(\\w+)"),
    [](auto&& m) {
      std::string result = m[1].str();
      std::transform(m[1].first, m[1].second,
        begin(result), ::toupper);
      return result;
    });
  assert(t == "SORT(BEGIN(v), END(v))");
}
```

With this improved `regex_replace` in hand, you can perform complicated operations such as "convert every identifier from `snake_case` to `CamelCase`" with ease.

This concludes our whirlwind tour of the facilities provided in C++'s `<regex>` header. The remainder of this chapter consists of a detailed introduction to the ECMAScript dialect of regex notation. I hope it will be useful to readers who haven't worked with regexes before, and that it will serve as a refresher and reference for those who have.

A primer on the ECMAScript regex grammar

The rules for reading and writing regexes in the ECMAScript dialect are simple. A regex is just a string of characters (such as `a[bc].d*e`), and you read it from left to right. Most characters represent only themselves, so that `cat` is a valid regex and matches only the literal string `"cat"`. The only characters that don't represent themselves--and thus the only way to build regexes that represent languages more interesting than `"cat"`--are the following punctuation characters:

```
^ $ \ . * + ? ( ) [ ] { } |
```

`\`--if you're using a regex to describe a set of strings involving punctuation characters, you can use a backslash to escape those special characters. For example, `\$42\.00` is a regex for the singleton language whose only member is the string `"$42.00"`. Perhaps confusingly, backslash is *also* used to turn some normal characters into special characters! n is a regex for the letter "n", but `\n` is a regex for the newline character. d is a regex for the letter "d", but `\d` is a regex equivalent to `[0-9]`.

The complete list of backslash characters recognized by C++'s regex grammar is:

- `\1`, `\2`, ... `\10`, ... for backreferences (to be avoided)
- `\b` for a word boundary and `\B` for `(?!\b)`
- `\d` for `[[:digit:]]` and `\D` for `[^[:digit:]]`
- `\s` for `[[:space:]]` and `\S` for `[^[:space:]]`
- `\w` for `[0-9A-Za-z_]` and `\W` for `[^0-9A-Za-z_]`
- `\cX` for various "control characters" (to be avoided)
- `\xXX` for hexadecimal, with the usual meaning
- `\u00XX` for Unicode, with the usual meaning
- `\0`, `\f`, `\n`, `\r`, `\t`, `\v` with their usual meanings

`.`--This special character represents "exactly one character," with almost no other requirements. For example, `a.c` is a valid regex and matches inputs such as `"aac"`, `"a!c"`, and `"a\0c"`. However, `.` will *never* match a newline or carriage-return character; and because C++ regexes work at the byte level, not the Unicode level, `.` will match any single byte (other than `'\\n'` and `'\\r'`) but will never match a sequence of multiple bytes even if they happen to make up a valid UTF-8 codepoint.

[]--A group of characters enclosed in square brackets represents "exactly one of this set," so that `c[aou]t` is a valid regex and matches the strings `"cat"`, `"cot"`, and `"cut"`. You can use square-bracket syntax to "escape" most characters; for example, `[$][.][*][+][?][(][)][[][{][}][|]` is a regex for the singleton language whose only member is the string `"$.*+?()[{}|"`. However, you cannot use brackets to escape], \, or ^.

[^]--A group of characters enclosed in square brackets with a leading ^ represents "exactly one, *not* of this set," so that `c[^aou]t` will match `"cbt"` or `"c^t"` but not `"cat"`. The ECMAScript dialect does not treat the trivial cases `[]` or `[^]` specially; `[]` means "exactly one character from the empty set" (which is to say, it never matches anything), and `[^]` means "exactly one character *not* from the empty set" (which is to say, it matches any single character--just like . but better, because it *will* match newline and carriage-return characters).

The `[]` syntax treats a couple more characters specially: If - appears inside square brackets anywhere except as the first or last character, it denotes a "range" with its left and right neighbors. So `ro[s-v]e` is a regex for the language whose members are the four strings `"rose"`, `"rote"`, `"roue"`, and `"rove"`. A few commonly useful ranges--the same ranges exposed via the `<ctype.h>` header--are built in using the syntax `[:foo:]` inside square brackets: `[[:digit:]]` is the same as `[0-9]`, `[[:upper:][:lower:]]` is the same as `[[:alpha:]]` is the same as `[A-Za-z]`, and so on.

There are also built-in syntaxes that look like `[[.x.]]` and `[[=x=]]`; they deal with locale-dependent comparisons and you will never have to use them. Merely be aware that if you ever need to include the character [inside a square-bracketed character class, it will be in your best interest to backslash-escape it: both `foo[=([;]` and `foo[(\[=;]` match the strings `"foo="`, `"foo("`, `"foo["`, and `"foo;"`, but `foo[([=;]` is an invalid regex and will throw an exception at runtime when you try to construct a `std::regex` object from it.

+--An expression or single character followed immediately by + matches the previous expression or character any positive number of times. For example, the regex `ba+` matches the strings `"ba"`, `"baa"`, `"baaa"`, and so on.

*--An expression or single character followed immediately by * matches the previous expression or character any number of times--even no times at all! So the regex `ba*` matches the strings `"ba"`, `"baa"`, and `"baaa"`, and also matches `"b"` alone.

?--An expression or single character followed immediately by ? matches the previous expression or character exactly zero or one times. For example, `coo?t` is a regex matching only `"cot"` and `"coot"`.

Regular Expressions

`{n}`--An expression or single character followed immediately by a curly-braced integer matches the previous expression or character exactly the number of times indicated. For example, `b(an){2}a` is a regex matching `"banana"`; `b(an){3}a` is a regex matching `"bananana"`.

`{m,n}`--When the curly-braced construct has the form of two integers *m* and *n* separated by a comma, the construct matches the previous expression or character anywhere from *m* to *n* times (inclusive). So `b(an){2,3}a` is a regex matching only the strings `"banana"` and `"bananana"`.

`{m,}`--Leaving *n* blank effectively makes it infinite; so `x{42,}` means "match x 42 or more times," and is equivalent to `x{42}x*`. The ECMAScript dialect does not allow leaving *m* blank.

`|`--Two regular expressions can be "glued together" with `|` to express the idea of *either-or*. For example, `cat|dog` is a regex matching only the strings `"cat"` and `"dog"`; and `(tor|shark)nado` matches either `"tornado"` or `"sharknado"`. The `|` operator has very low precedence in regexes, just as it does in C++ expressions.

`()`--Parentheses work just as in mathematics, to enclose a sub-expression that you want to bind tightly together and treat as a unit. For example, `ba*` means "the character b, and then zero or more instances of a; but `(ba)*` means "zero or more instances of ba." So the former matches `"b"`, `"ba"`, `"baa"`, and so on; but the version with parentheses matches `""`, `"ba"`, `"baba"`, and so on.

Parentheses also have a second purpose--they are used not just for *grouping* but also for *capturing* parts of a match for further processing. Each opening `(` in the regex generates another submatch in the resulting `std::smatch` object.

If you want to group some subexpression tightly together without generating a submatch, you can use a *non-capturing* group with the syntax `(?:foo)`:

```
std::string s = "abcde";
std::smatch m;
std::regex_match(s, m, std::regex("(a|b)*(.*)e"));
assert(m.size() == 3 && m[2] == "cd");
std::regex_match(s, m, std::regex("(?:a|b)*(.*)e"));
assert(m.size() == 2 && m[1] == "cd");
```

Non-capturing might be useful in some obscure context; but generally, it will be clearer to the reader if you just use regular capturing `()` and ignore the submatches you don't care about, as opposed to scattering `(?:)` around your codebase in an attempt to squelch all unused submatches. Unused submatches are very cheap, performance-wise.

Non-consuming constructs

`(?=foo)` matches the pattern `foo` against the input, and then "rewinds" so that none of the input is actually consumed. This is called "lookahead." So for example `c(?=a)(?=a)(?=a)at` matches `"cat"`; and `(?=.*[A-Za-z])(?=.*[0-9]).*` matches any string containing at least one alphabetic character and at least one digit.

`(?!foo)` is a "negative lookahead"; it looks ahead to match `foo` against the input, but then *rejects* the match if `foo` would have accepted, and *accepts* the match if `foo` would have rejected. So, for example, `(?!\d)\w+` matches any C++ identifier or keyword--that is, any sequence of alphanumeric characters that does *not* start with a digit. Notice that the first character must not match `\d` but is not consumed by the `(?!\d)` construct; it must still be accepted by `\w`. The similar-looking regex `[^0-9]\w+` would "erroneously" accept strings such as `"#xyzzy"` which are not valid identifiers.

Both `(?=)` and `(?!)` are not only non-consuming but also *non-capturing*, just like `(?:)`. But it is perfectly fine to write `(?=(foo))` to capture all or part of the "looked-ahead" portion.

`^` and `$`--A caret `^` on its own, outside any square brackets, matches only at the beginning of the string to be matched; and `$` matches only at the end. This is useful to "anchor" the regex to the beginning or end of the input string, in the context of `std::regex_search`. In `std::regex::multiline` regexes, `^` and `$` act as "lookbehind" and "lookahead" assertions respectively:

```
std::string s = "ab\ncd";
std::regex rx("^ab$[^]^cd$", std::regex::multiline);

assert(std::regex_match(s, rx));
```

Putting it all together, we might write the regex `foo[a-z_]+(\d|$)` to match "the letters `foo`, followed by one or more other letters and/or underscore; followed by either a digit or the end of the line."

If you need a deeper dive into regex syntax, consult `cppreference.com`. And if that's not enough--the best thing about C++'s copying the ECMAScript flavor of regexes is that any tutorial on JavaScript regexes will also be applicable to C++! You can even test out regular expressions in your browser's console. The only difference between C++ regexes and JavaScript regexes is that C++ supports the double-square-bracket syntax for character classes such as `[[:digit:]]`, `[[.x.]]`, and `[[=x=]]`, whereas JavaScript doesn't. JavaScript treats those regexes as equivalent to `[\[:digt]\]`, `[\[.x]\]`, and `[\[=x]\]` respectively.

Obscure ECMAScript features and pitfalls

Earlier in this chapter I mentioned a few features of `std::regex` that you would be better off to avoid, such as `std::regex::collate`, `std::regex::optimize`, and flags that change the dialect away from ECMAScript. The ECMAScript regex grammar itself contains a few obscure and avoid worthy features as well.

A backslash followed by one or more digits (other than `\0`) creates a *backreference*. The backreference `\1` matches "the same sequence of characters that was matched by my first capturing group"; so for example the regex `(cat|dog)\1` will match the strings `"catcat"` and `"dogdog"` but not `"catdog"`, and `(a*)(b*)c\2\1` will match `"aabbbcbbbaa"` but not `"aabbbcbbba"`. Backreferences can have subtly weird semantics, especially when combined with non-consuming constructs such as `(?=foo)`, and I recommend avoiding them when possible.

> **TIP** If you're having trouble with backreferences, the first thing to check is your backslash-escaping. Remember that `std::regex("\1")` is a regex matching ASCII control character number 1. What you meant to type was `std::regex("\\1")`.

Using backreferences takes you out of the world of *regular languages* and into the wider world of *context-sensitive languages*, which means that the library must trade in its extremely efficient finite-state-machine-based matching algorithm for more powerful but expensive and slow "backtracking" algorithms. This seems like another good reason to avoid backreferences unless they're absolutely necessary.

However, as of 2017, most vendors do not actually switch algorithms based on the *presence* of backreferences in a regex; they'll use the slower backtracking algorithm based on the *mere possibility* of backreferences in the ECMAScript regex dialect. And then, because no vendor wants to implement a whole second algorithm just for the backreference-less dialects `std::regex::awk` and `std::regex::extended`, they end up using the backtracking algorithm even for those dialects! Similarly, most vendors will implement `regex_match(s, rx)` in terms of `regex_match(s, m, rx)` and then throw out the expensively computed `m`, rather than using a potentially faster algorithm for `regex_match(s, rx)`. Optimizations like this might come to a library near you sometime in the next 10 years, but I wouldn't hold your breath waiting for them.

Another obscure quirk is that the *, +, and ? quantifiers are all *greedy* by default, meaning that, for example, (a*) will prefer to match as many a characters as it can. You can turn a greedy quantifier *non-greedy* by suffixing an extra ?; so for example (a*?) matches the *smallest* number of a characters it can. This makes no difference at all unless you're using capturing groups. Here's an example:

```
std::string s = "abcde";
std::smatch m;
std::regex_match(s, m, std::regex(".*([bcd].*)e"));
assert(m[1] == "d");
std::regex_match(s, m, std::regex(".*?([bcd].*)e"));
assert(m[1] == "bcd");
```

In the first case, .* greedily matches abc, leaving only d to be matched by the capturing group. In the second case, .*? non-greedily matches only a, leaving bcd for the capturing group. (In fact, .*? would have preferred to match the empty string; but it couldn't do that without the overall match being rejected.)

Notice that the syntax for non-greediness doesn't follow the "normal" rules of operator composition. From what we know of C++'s operator syntax, we'd expect that a+* would mean (a+)* (which it does) and a+? would mean (a+)? (which it doesn't). So, if you see consecutive punctuation characters in a regular expression, watch out--it may mean something different from what your intuition tells you!

Summary

Regular expressions (regexes) are a good way to *lex* out the pieces of an input string before parsing them. The default regex dialect in C++ is the same as in JavaScript. Use this to your advantage.

Prefer to avoid raw string literals in situations where an extra pair of parentheses could be confusing. When possible, limit the number of escaped backslashes in your regexes by using square brackets to escape special characters instead.

std::regex rx is basically immutable and represents a finite state machine. std::smatch m is mutable and holds information about a particular match within the haystack string. Submatch m[0] represents the whole matched substring; m[k] represents the *k*th capturing group.

`std::regex_match(s, m, rx)` matches the needle against the *entire* haystack string; `std::regex_search(s, m, rx)` looks for the needle *in* the haystack. Remember that the haystack goes first and the needle goes last, just like in JavaScript and Perl.

`std::regex_iterator`, `std::regex_token_iterator`, and `std::regex_replace` are relatively inconvenient "convenience" functions built on top of `regex_search`. Get comfortable with `regex_search` before worrying about these wrappers.

Beware of dangling-iterator bugs! Never modify or destroy a `regex` that is still referenced by `regex_iterator`; and never modify or destroy a `string` that is still referenced by `smatch`.

11
Random Numbers

In the previous chapter, you learned about regular expressions, a feature that has been part of the C++ standard library since C++11, but which is still little-known by many programmers. You saw that regular expressions are useful in two situations at the opposite ends of the C++ spectrum--in complex programs requiring bulletproof parsing of complicated input formats, and in trivial scripts where the important things are readability and speed of development.

Another library feature that lands squarely in both of these categories is *random number generation*. Many scripting programs require a little bit of randomness here and there, but C++ programmers have been taught for decades that the classic libc `rand()` function is passé. At the other end of the spectrum, `rand()` is spectacularly inappropriate, both for cryptography and for complicated numerical simulations. The C++11 `<random>` library, however, manages to hit all three of these targets.

In this chapter, we'll cover the following topics:

- The difference between truly random and pseudo-random number sequences
- The difference between a *generator* of random bits and a *distribution* that produces data values
- Three strategies to seed a random number generator
- Several standard library generators and distributions, and their use cases
- How to shuffle a deck of cards in C++17

Random numbers versus pseudo-random numbers

When talking about random numbers in the context of computer programming, we must be careful to distinguish between truly random numbers, which come from a physically non-deterministic source, and *pseudo-random* numbers, which come from an algorithm that deterministically produces a stream of "random-looking" numbers. Such an algorithm is called a **pseudo-random number generator** (**PRNG**). Every PRNG conceptually works the same way--it has some internal *state*, and it has some way for the user to ask for the *next output*. Every time we ask for the next output, the PRNG scrambles its internal state according to some deterministic algorithm and returns some piece of that state. Here's an example:

```
template<class T>
class SimplePRNG {
  uint32_t state = 1;
public:
  static constexpr T min() { return 0; }
  static constexpr T max() { return 0x7FFF; }

  T operator()() {
    state = state * 1103515245 + 12345;
    return (state >> 16) & 0x7FFF;
  }
};
```

This `SimplePRNG` class implements a *linear congruential generator*, which is likely very similar to your standard library's implementation of `rand()`. Notice that `SimplePRNG::operator()` produces integers in the `[0, 32767]` 15-bit range, but its internal `state` has a 32-bit range. This pattern is true in real-world PRNGs as well. For example, the standard Mersenne Twister algorithm keeps almost 20 kilobytes of state! Keeping so much internal state means that there are lots of bits to scramble, and only a small fraction of the PRNG's internal state leaks out at each generation. This makes it difficult for a human (or a computer) to predict the PRNG's next output, given only a few of the preceding outputs. The difficulty of predicting its outputs leads us to call this thing a *pseudo-random* number generator. If its output was full of obvious patterns and easy to predict, we'd probably call it a *non-random* number generator!

Despite its pseudo-random qualities, a PRNG's behavior is always perfectly *deterministic*; it follows exactly the algorithm it was coded to follow. If we take a program that uses a PRNG and run it several times in a row, we expect to get the exact same sequence of pseudo-random numbers each time. Its strict determinism leads us to call this thing a *pseudo-random number generator*.

Another aspect of *pseudo-random* number generators is that two generators running the exact same algorithm, but with tiny variations in their initial states, will rapidly magnify these variations, *diverge* from each other, and produce completely different-looking output sequences--just as two drops of water placed in slightly different spots on the back of your hand will run off in completely divergent directions. This means that if we want a different sequence of pseudo-random numbers each time we run our program, all we have to do is make sure that we use a different *initial state* for our PRNG. Setting a PRNG's initial state is called *seeding* the PRNG.

We have at least three strategies for seeding our PRNG:

- Using a seed supplied *from outside*--from the caller or end user. This is the most appropriate for anything that needs reproducibility, such as Monte Carlo simulations or anything that you'll unit test.
- Using a predictable but variable seed, such as the current timestamp. Prior to C++11, this was the most common strategy, because the C standard library provides a portable and convenient `time` function, but does not provide any portable source of truly random bits. Seeding based on something as predictable as `time` is not suitable for anything security-related. As of C++11, you shouldn't ever use this strategy.
- Using a *truly random* seed obtained directly from some platform-specific source of "truly random" bits.

Truly random bits are collected by the operating system based on all sorts of random events; a classic approach is for every system call to collect the low-order bits of the hardware cycle counter and XOR them into the operating system's *entropy pool*. A PRNG deep inside the kernel is periodically reseeded with bits from the entropy pool; the output sequence of that PRNG is exposed to application programmers. On Linux, the raw entropy pool is exposed as `/dev/random` and the PRNG's output sequence is exposed as `/dev/urandom`. Fortunately, you'll never need to deal with either of those devices directly; the C++ standard library has you covered. Read on.

Random Numbers

The problem with rand()

The old school C way of generating *random* numbers is to call `rand()`. The `rand()` function, which is still part of C++, takes no arguments and produces a single, uniformly distributed integer in the `[0, RAND_MAX]` range. The internal state can be *seeded* by calling the library function, `srand(seed_value)`.

The classic code to generate a *random* number in the `[0, x)` range hasn't changed since the 1980s, shown here:

```
#include <stdlib.h>

int randint0(int x) {
  return rand() % x;
}
```

However, this code has several problems. The first and most obvious problem is that it doesn't generate all *x* outputs with equal likelihood. Suppose, for the sake of argument, `rand()` returns a uniformly distributed value in the `[0, 32767]` range, then `randint0(10)` will return each value in the `[0, 7]` range one-3276th more often than it returns either 8 or 9.

The second problem is that `rand()` accesses global state; the same random number generator is shared by every thread in your C++ program. This isn't a thread-safety concern--`rand()` has been guaranteed to be thread-safe since C++11. However, it is a problem for performance (because each call to `rand()` must take a global mutex lock), and it is a problem for reproducibility (because if you use `rand()` from multiple threads concurrently, different runs of the program may yield different answers).

A third and related problem with the global-statefulness of `rand()` is that any function anywhere in the program can modify that state just by calling `rand()`. This makes it effectively impossible to use `rand()` in a unit-test-driven environment. Consider the following code snippet:

```
int heads(int n) {
  DEBUG_LOG("heads");
  int result = 0;
  for (int i = 0; i < n; ++i) {
    result += (rand() % 2);
  }
  return result;
}

void test_heads() {
```

```
    srand(17); // nail down the seed
    int result = heads(42);
    assert(result == 27);
}
```

Clearly, the unit test, `test_heads`, will break as soon as we start parallelizing our unit tests (because a call to `rand()` from some other thread will interfere with the delicate workings of this test). However, more subtly, it can also break simply because someone changed the implementation of `DEBUG_LOG` to add or remove a call to `rand()`! This kind of *spooky action at a distance* is a problem any time your architecture depends on global variables. We saw a similar danger with `std::pmr::get_default_resource()` in Chapter 8, *Allocators*. In every case, my strongly recommended remedy is the same--*Don't use global variables. Don't use global state.*

So, the C library has two problems--it provides no way to generate a truly uniform distribution of pseudo-random numbers, and it fundamentally depends on global variables. Let's see how the C++ standard library's `<random>` header fixed both of these problems.

Solving problems with `<random>`

There are two core concepts provided by the `<random>` header--the *generator* and the *distribution*. A *generator* (a class modeling the `UniformRandomBitGenerator` concept) encapsulates the internal state of a PRNG into a C++ object, and provides a next output member function in the form of the function-call operator, `operator()(void)`. A *distribution* (a class modeling `RandomNumberDistribution`) is a kind of filter you can place over the output of a generator so that instead of getting uniformly distributed random bits, as you do from `rand()`, you get actual data values distributed according to a specified mathematical distribution and constrained to a specific range, such as `rand() % n`, but more mathematically appropriate and vastly more flexible.

The `<random>` header contains a total of seven *generator* types and twenty *distribution* types. Most of them are templates taking lots of parameters. The majority of these generators are more historically interesting than practically useful, and the vast majority of these distributions are of interest only to mathematicians. So, in this chapter, we'll concentrate on just a few standard generators and distributions, each of which illustrates something interesting about the standard library.

Dealing with generators

Given any *generator* object g, you can perform the following operations on it:

- `g()`: This scrambles the internal state of the generator and yields its next output.
- `g.min()`: This tells you the smallest possible output of `g()` (typically 0).
- `g.max()`: This tells you the largest possible output of `g()`. That is, the range of possible outputs of `g()` is `g.min()` to `g.max()` inclusive.
- `g.discard(n)`: This effectively makes n calls to `g()` and discards the results. In a good library implementation, you'll pay for scrambling the generator's internal state n times, but save any cost associated with computing the next outputs from the state.

Truly random bits with std::random_device

The `std::random_device` is a *generator*. Its interface is incredibly simple; it's not even a class template, just a plain old class. Once you've constructed an instance of `std::random_device` using its default constructor, you can use its overloaded call operator to fetch values of type `unsigned int` that are uniformly distributed in the closed [rd.min(), rd.max()] range.

One caveat--`std::random_device` doesn't fully model the `UniformRandomBitGenerator` concept. Most importantly, it is neither copyable nor moveable. This isn't much of a problem in practice, because you generally don't keep a *truly* random generator around for very long. Instead, you'll use a very short-lived instance of `std::random_device` to generate a *seed* for a long-lived pseudo-random generator of some other type, like this:

```
std::random_device rd;
unsigned int seed = rd();
assert(rd.min() <= seed && seed <= rd.max());
```

Now let's look at the only pseudo-random generator you'll ever need to know.

Pseudo-random bits with std::mt19937

The only pseudo-random generator you'll ever need to know is called the *Mersenne Twister* algorithm. This algorithm has been known since 1997, and high-quality implementations in any programming language are easy to find. Technically speaking, the Mersenne Twister algorithm defines a whole family of related PRNGs--it's the algorithmic equivalent of a C++ template--but the most commonly used member of the family is known as **MT19937**. That string of digits might look like a timestamp, but it's not; it's the size in bits of the Twister's internal state. Because the Mersenne Twister's next output function scrambles its state so perfectly that it will eventually reach every possible state (but one) before looping back around to the beginning--the *period* of the MT19937 generator is $2^{19937}-1$. Compare this to our `SimplePRNG` from the beginning of this chapter, which has an internal state of only 32 bits and a period of 2^{31}. (Our `SimplePRNG` generator has 2^{32} possible internal states, but only half of them are reached before it loops around again. For example, `state=3` is not reachable from the initial `state=1`.)

Enough theory. Let's see the Mersenne Twister in action! The C++ class template corresponding to the Mersenne Twister *algorithm template* is `std::mersenne_twister_engine<...>`, but you won't use it directly; you'll use the convenience typedef `std::mt19937`, as shown here:

```
std::mt19937 g;
assert(g.min() == 0 && g.max() == 4294967295);

assert(g() == 3499211612);
assert(g() == 581869302);
assert(g() == 3890346734);
```

The default constructor for `std::mt19937` sets its internal state to a well-known standard value. This ensures that the output sequence you get from a default-constructed `mt19937` object will be identical across all platforms--as opposed to `rand()`, which tends to give different output sequences on different platforms.

To get a different output sequence, you need to provide a *seed* to the constructor of `std::mt19937`. There are two ways to do this in C++17--the tedious way and the simple way. The tedious way is to construct a truly random 19937-bit seed and copy it into the `std::mt19937` object via a *seed sequence,* as shown here:

```
std::random_device rd;

uint32_t numbers[624];
std::generate(numbers, std::end(numbers), std::ref(rd));
  // Generate initial state.

SeedSeq sseq(numbers, std::end(numbers));
  // Copy our state into a heap-allocated "seed sequence".

std::mt19937 g(sseq);
  // Initialize a mt19937 generator with our state.
```

Here, the `SeedSeq` type can be either `std::seed_seq` (a glorified `std::vector`; it uses heap allocation) or a properly handwritten "seed sequence" class, such as the following piece of code:

```
template<class It>
struct SeedSeq {
  It begin_;
  It end_;
public:
  SeedSeq(It begin, It end) : begin_(begin), end_(end) {}

  template<class It2>
  void generate(It2 b, It2 e) {
    assert((e - b) <= (end_ - begin_));
    std::copy(begin_, begin_ + (e - b), b);
  }
};
```

Of course, this is quite a bit of code to write just to construct a single PRNG object! (I told you, this was the *tedious* way.) The simple way, and the way you'll see being used in practice, is to seed MT19937 with a single, truly random *32-bit integer*, as follows:

```
std::random_device rd;

std::mt19937 g(rd());
  // 32 bits of randomness ought to be enough for anyone!
  // ...Right?
```

Beware! 32 is a much, much smaller number than 19937! This simple method of seeding is capable of producing only four billion different output sequences, *ever*; this means that if you run your program over and over with random seeds, you can expect to see some repetitions after only a few hundred thousand runs. (This is an application of the famous *Birthday Paradox*.) However, if this level of predictability is important to you, you should probably also be aware that the Mersenne Twister is *not cryptographically secure*. This means that even if you initialize it with a truly random 19937-bit seed sequence, a malicious attacker can reverse-engineer all 19937 bits of your original seed and predict every subsequent output with perfect accuracy after seeing only a few hundred terms of the output sequence. If you need a **cryptographically secure pseudo-random number generator (CSPRNG)**, you should be using something like AES-CTR or ISAAC, neither of which is provided by the C++ standard library. You should still wrap your CSPRNG implementation in a class modeling `UniformRandomBitGenerator` so that it can be used with standard algorithms, which we'll get to at the end of this chapter.

Filtering generator outputs with adaptors

We've mentioned that the raw output of a *generator* is usually filtered through a single *distribution* in order to convert the generator's raw bits into usable data values. Interestingly, it is also possible to send a generator's output through a *generator adaptor*, which can reformat the raw bits in various, perhaps useful ways. The standard library provides three adaptors--`std::discard_block_engine`, `std::shuffle_order_engine`, and `std::independent_bits_engine`. These adaptor types work just like the *container adaptors* (such as `std::stack`) we discussed in Chapter 4, *The Container Zoo*--they provide a certain interface but delegate most of their implementation details to some other class.

An instance of `std::discard_block_engine<Gen, p, r>` keeps an *underlying generator* of type `Gen`, and delegates all its operations to that underlying generator, except that `discard_block_engine::operator()` will return only the first `r` of every `p` outputs from the underlying generator. For example, consider the following example:

```
std::vector<uint32_t> raw(10), filtered(10);

std::discard_block_engine<std::mt19937, 3, 2> g2;
std::mt19937 g1 = g2.base();

std::generate(raw.begin(), raw.end(), g1);
std::generate(filtered.begin(), filtered.end(), g2);

assert(raw[0] == filtered[0]);
assert(raw[1] == filtered[1]);
  // raw[2] doesn't appear in filtered[]
```

```
    assert(raw[3] == filtered[2]);
    assert(raw[4] == filtered[3]);
      // raw[5] doesn't appear in filtered[]
```

Notice that a reference to the underlying generator can be retrieved via `g2.base()`. In the preceding example, `g1` is initialized as a copy of `g2.base()`; this explains how calling `g1()` doesn't affect the state of `g2`, and vice versa.

An instance of `std::shuffle_order_engine<Gen, k>` keeps a buffer of the last *k* outputs from its underlying generator, and an additional integer `Y`. Each call to `shuffle_order_engine::operator()` sets `Y = buffer[Y % k]`, then sets `buffer[Y] = base()()`. (The formula to compute the buffer index from `Y` is actually more complicated than a simple modulus, but it basically has the same effect.) Notably, `std::shuffle_order_engine` does *not* use `std::uniform_int_distribution` to map `Y` onto the `[0, k)` range. This doesn't affect the *randomness* of the generator's output--if the underlying generator is already pseudo-random, shuffling its outputs a little bit won't make them any more or less random, no matter what algorithm we use to do the shuffling. Therefore, the algorithm used by `shuffle_order_engine` was picked specifically for its historical interest--it is a building block for a classic algorithm described in Donald Knuth's *The Art of Computer Programming*:

```
    using knuth_b = std::shuffle_order_engine<
      std::linear_congruential_engine<
        uint_fast32_t, 16807, 0, 2147483647
      >,
      256
    >;
```

An instance of `std::independent_bits_engine<Gen, w, T>` keeps no state other than its underlying generator of type `Gen`. The `independent_bits_engine::operator()` function calls `base()()` just enough times to compute at least *w* random bits; then, it pastes together exactly *w* of those bits (via an algorithm of more historical than practical interest) and serves them up as an unsigned integer of type `T`. (It is an error if `T` is not an unsigned integer type, or if `T` has fewer than *w* bits.)

Here is an example of `independent_bits_engine` pasting together bits from multiple calls to `base()()`:

```
    std::independent_bits_engine<std::mt19937, 40, uint64_t> g2;
    std::mt19937 g1 = g2.base();

    assert(g1() == 0xd09'1bb5c);     // Take "1bb5c"...
    assert(g1() == 0x22a'e9ef6);     // and "e9ef6"...
    assert(g2() == 0x1bb5c'e9ef6);   // Paste and serve!
```

And here is an example of using `independent_bits_engine` to chop off all but the least significant digit from the output of `mt19937` (creating a *coin flipper* generator), and then, pasting together 32 of this generator's outputs to build back up to a 32-bit generator:

```
using coinflipper = std::independent_bits_engine<
    std::mt19937, 1, uint8_t>;

coinflipper onecoin;
std::array<int, 64> results;
std::generate(results.begin(), results.end(), onecoin);
assert((results == std::array<int, 64>{{
    0,0,0,1, 0,1,1,1, 0,1,1,1, 0,0,1,0,
    1,0,1,0, 1,1,1,1, 0,0,0,1, 0,1,0,1,
    1,0,0,1, 1,1,1,0, 0,0,1,0, 1,0,1,0,
    1,0,0,1, 0,0,0,0, 0,1,0,0, 1,1,0,0,
}}));

std::independent_bits_engine<coinflipper, 32, uint32_t> manycoins;
assert(manycoins() == 0x1772af15);
assert(manycoins() == 0x9e2a904c);
```

Notice that `independent_bits_engine` does *not* perform any complicated operation on the bits of its underlying generator; in particular, it assumes that its underlying generator has no bias. If the `WeightedCoin` generator has a bias toward even numbers. You'll see that bias show up in the output of `independent_bits_engine<WeightedCoin, w, T>` as well.

Despite our spending several pages talking about these generators, remember that there is no reason to use any of these obscure classes in your own code! If you need a PRNG, use `std::mt19937`; if you need a cryptographically secure PRNG, use something like AES-CTR, or ISAAC; and, if you need a relatively small number of true random bits, to seed your PRNG; use `std::random_device`. These are the only generators that you will ever use in practice.

Dealing with distributions

Now that we've seen how to generate random bits on demand, let's look at how to convert those random bits to numeric values matching a particular *distribution*. This two-step process--generate raw bits, and then format them into data values--is very similar to the two-step process of buffering and parsing we covered in Chapter 9, *Iostreams*. First, get the raw bits and bytes, then perform some kind of operation to convert those bits and bytes into typed data values.

Given any distribution object `dist`, you can perform the following operations on it:

- `dist(g)`: This yields the next output according to the appropriate mathematical distribution. It may require several calls to `g()`, or none at all, depending on the internal state of the `dist` object.
- `dist.reset()`: This clears the internal state of the `dist` object, if any. You'll never need to use this member function.
- `dist.min()` and `dist.max()`: These tell you the smallest and largest possible outputs of `dist(g)` for any random bit generator `g`. Generally, these values are either self-evident or meaningless; for example, `std::normal_distribution<float>().max()` is `INFINITY`.

Let's see a few distribution types in action.

Rolling dice with uniform_int_distribution

The `std::uniform_int_distribution` method is the simplest distribution type in the standard library. It performs the same operation we tried to perform with `randint0` earlier in this chapter--map a random unsigned integer into a given range--, but it does it without any bias. The simplest implementation of `uniform_int_distribution` looks something like this:

```
template<class Int>
class uniform_int_distribution {
  using UInt = std::make_unsigned_t<Int>;
  UInt m_min, m_max;
public:
  uniform_int_distribution(Int a, Int b) :
    m_min(a), m_max(b) {}

  template<class Gen>
  Int operator()(Gen& g) {
    UInt range = (m_max - m_min);
    assert(g.max() - g.min() >= range);
    while (true) {
      UInt r = g() - g.min();
      if (r <= range) {
        return Int(m_min + r);
      }
    }
  }
};
```

Random Numbers

The actual standard library implementation has to do something to get rid of that `assert`. Typically, they'll use something like `independent_bits_engine` to generate exactly `ceil(log2(range))` random bits at a time, minimizing the number of times the `while` loop needs to run.

As implied in the preceding example, `uniform_int_distribution` is stateless (although this is not *technically* guaranteed), and so the most common way to use it is to create a new distribution object every time you generate a number. So, we can implement our `randint0` function like this:

```
int randint0(int x) {
  static std::mt19937 g;
  return std::uniform_int_distribution<int>(0, x-1)(g);
}
```

Now will probably be a good time to remark on an oddity of the `<random>` facilities. As a general rule, any time you supply an *integral numeric range* to one of these functions or constructors, it is treated as a *closed* range. This is in stark contrast to how ranges usually work in C and C++; we even saw in Chapter 3, *The Iterator-Pair Algorithms*, how deviating from the *half-open range* rule was usually the sign of buggy code. However, in the case of C++'s random-number facilities, there is a new rule--*the closed range* rule. Why?

Well, the key advantage of the half-open range is that it can easily represent an *empty range*. On the other hand, half-open ranges cannot represent a *completely full range*, that is, a range that covers the entire domain. (We saw this difficulty pop up in Chapter 4, *The Container Zoo*, in the implementation of `std::list<T>::end()`.) Suppose we want to express the idea of a uniform distribution over the entire range of `long long`. We can't express that as the half-open range `[LLONG_MIN, LLONG_MAX+1)` because `LLONG_MAX+1` will overflow. However, we *can* express it as the closed range `[LLONG_MIN, LLONG_MAX]`--and so, that's what the `<random>` library's functions and classes (such as `uniform_int_distribution`) do. The `uniform_int_distribution<int>(0,6)` method is a distribution over the seven-number range `[0,6]`, and `uniform_int_distribution<int>(42,42)` is a perfectly valid distribution that invariably returns 42.

On the other hand, `std::uniform_real_distribution<double>(a, b)` *does* operate on a half-open range! The `std::uniform_real_distribution<double>(0, 1)` method yields values of type `double`, uniformly distributed in the `[0, 1)` range. In the floating-point domain, there's no problem with overflow--a half-open range of `[0, INFINITY)` is actually expressible, although, of course, there's no such thing as a *uniform distribution* over an infinite range. Floating-point also makes it difficult to say the difference between a half-open range and a closed range; for example, `std::uniform_real_distribution<float>(0, 1)(g)` can legitimately return `float(1.0)` any time it generates a random real number close enough to 1 that it rounds up about one in every 2^{25} results. (At press time, libc++ behaves as described here. GNU's libstdc++ applies a patch that makes close-to-1 real numbers round down instead of up so that the floating-point number just below 1.0 appears marginally more often than chance would predict.)

Generating populations with normal_distribution

The most useful example of a real-valued distribution is probably the *normal distribution*, also known as the **bell curve**. In the real world, normal distributions show up all over the place, particularly in the distribution of physical traits in a population. For example, a histogram of adult human heights will tend to look like a normal distribution--lots of individuals clustered around the average height, and others tailing off to each side. Flip this around, and it means that you might want to use a normal distribution to assign heights, weights, and so on, to the simulated individuals in a game.

The `std::normal_distribution<double>(m, sd)` method constructs an instance of `normal_distribution<double>` with mean (m) and standard deviation (sd). (These parameters default to m=0 and sd=1 if you don't provide them, so watch out for typos!) Here's an example of using `normal_distribution` to create a "population" of 10,000 normally distributed samples, and then verifying their distribution mathematically:

```
double mean = 161.8;
double stddev = 6.8;
std::normal_distribution<double> dist(mean, stddev);

  // Initialize our generator.
std::mt19937 g(std::random_device{}());

  // Fill a vector with 10,000 samples.
std::vector<double> v;
for (int i=0; i < 10000; ++i) {
  v.push_back( dist(g) );
}
```

```
std::sort(v.begin(), v.end());

  // Compare expectations with reality.
  auto square = [](auto x) { return x*x; };
  double mean_of_values = std::accumulate(
    v.begin(), v.end(), 0.0) / v.size();
  double mean_of_squares = std::inner_product(
    v.begin(), v.end(), v.begin(), 0.0) / v.size();
  double actual_stddev =
    std::sqrt(mean_of_squares - square(mean_of_values));
  printf("Expected mean and stddev: %g, %g\n", mean, stddev);
  printf("Actual mean and stddev: %g, %g\n",
         mean_of_values, actual_stddev);
```

Unlike the other distributions we've seen in this chapter (or will see), `std::normal_distribution` is stateful. While it is okay to construct a new instance of `std::normal_distribution` for each value you generate, if you do that, you're effectively halving the efficiency of your program. This is because the most popular algorithm to generate normally distributed values produces two independent values per step; `std::normal_distribution` can't give you both values at once, so it hangs onto one of them in a member variable to give it to you the next time you ask. The `dist.reset()` member function can be used to clear out this saved state, not that you'd ever want to do that.

Making weighted choices with discrete_distribution

The `std::discrete_distribution<int>(wbegin, wend)` method constructs a discrete, or weighted, distribution over the integers in the half-open `[0, wend - wbegin)` range. This is easiest to explain with the following example:

```
template<class Values, class Weights, class Gen>
auto weighted_choice(const Values& v, const Weights& w, Gen& g)
{
  auto dist = std::discrete_distribution<int>(
    std::begin(w), std::end(w));
  int index = dist(g);
  return v[index];
}

void test() {
  auto g = std::mt19937(std::random_device{}());
  std::vector<std::string> choices =
```

Random Numbers

```
      { "quick", "brown", "fox" };
    std::vector<int> weights = { 1, 7, 2 };
    std::string word = weighted_choice(choices, weights, g);
      // 7/10 of the time, we expect word=="brown".
}
```

The `std::discrete_distribution<int>` method makes its own internal copy of the weights you pass in, in a private member variable of type `std::vector<double>` (and as usual for `<random>`, it's not allocator-aware). You can get a copy of this vector by calling `dist.probabilities()` as follows:

```
int w[] = { 1, 0, 2, 1 };
std::discrete_distribution<int> dist(w, w+4);
std::vector<double> v = dist.probabilities();
assert((v == std::vector{ 0.25, 0.0, 0.50, 0.25 }));
```

You probably don't want to use `discrete_distribution` directly in your own code; at best, you'll want to encapsulate its use in something like the preceding `weighted_choice` function. However, if you need to avoid heap allocation or floating-point math, it might pay to use a simpler, non-allocating function, such as the following:

```
template<class Values, class Gen>
auto weighted_choice(
    const Values& v, const std::vector<int>& w,
    Gen& g)
{
  int sum = std::accumulate(w.begin(), w.end(), 0);
  int cutoff = std::uniform_int_distribution<int>(0, sum - 1)(g);
  auto vi = v.begin();
  auto wi = w.begin();
  while (cutoff > *wi) {
    cutoff -= *wi++;
    ++vi;
  }
  return *vi;
}
```

However, there's a reason the *default* library implementation of `discrete_distribution` does all its math as floating-point: it saves you from having to worry about integer overflow. The preceding code will have bad behavior if `sum` overflows the range of `int`.

Shuffling cards with std::shuffle

Let's close this chapter by looking at std::shuffle(a,b,g), the one standard algorithm that takes a random number generator as input. It's a *permutative algorithm* by the definitions of Chapter 3, *The Iterator Pair-Algorithms*--it takes a range of elements [a,b] and shuffles them around, preserving their values but not their positions.

The std::shuffle(a,b,g) method was introduced in C++11 to replace the older std::random_shuffle(a,b) algorithm. That older algorithm "randomly" shuffled the [a,b) range, but without specifying the source of the randomness; in practice, this meant that it would use the global C library's rand() with all its attendant problems. As soon as C++11 introduced a standardized way of talking about random number generators with <random>, it was time to get rid of the old rand() based random_shuffle; and, as of C++17, std::random_shuffle(a,b) is no longer part of the C++ standard library.

Here's how we can use C++11's std::shuffle to shuffle a deck of playing cards:

```
std::vector<int> deck(52);
std::iota(deck.begin(), deck.end(), 1);
  // deck now contains ints from 1 to 52.

std::mt19937 g(std::random_device{}());
std::shuffle(deck.begin(), deck.end(), g);
  // The deck is now randomly shuffled.
```

Recall that every *generator* in <random> is completely specified so that, for example, an instance of std::mt19937 seeded with a fixed value will produce exactly the same outputs on every platform. The same is *not* true of *distributions* such as uniform_real_distribution, nor is it true of the shuffle algorithm. Switching from libc++ to libstdc++, or even just upgrading your compiler, may cause changes in the behavior of your std::shuffle.

Notice that the preceding code snippet uses the "simple" method of seeding its Mersenne Twister, which means that it can only ever produce about 4×10^9 different shuffles--out of the 8×10^{67} ways, you can shuffle a deck of cards by hand! If you were shuffling cards for a real casino game, you'd certainly want to use the "tedious" method of seeding, described earlier in this chapter, or--simpler, if performance isn't a concern--just use std::random_device directly:

```
std::random_device rd;
std::shuffle(deck.begin(), deck.end(), rd);
  // The deck is now TRULY randomly shuffled.
```

Whatever generator and seeding method you use, you'll be able to plug it right into `std::shuffle`. This is the benefit of the standard library's composable approach to random number generation.

Summary

The standard library provides two random-number-related concepts--*generator* and *distribution*. Generators are stateful, must be seeded, and produce unsigned integer outputs (raw bits) via `operator()(void)`. The two important generator types are `std::random_device`, which produces truly random bits, and `std::mt19937`, which produces pseudo-random bits.

Distributions are *usually* stateless, and produce numeric data values via `operator()(Gen&)`. The most important distribution type for most programmers will be `std::uniform_int_distribution<int>(a,b)`, which produces integers in the closed range `[a,b]`. The standard library provides other distributions, such as `std::uniform_real_distribution`, `std::normal_distribution`, and `std::discrete_distribution`, as well as many arcane distributions useful to mathematicians and statisticians.

The one standard algorithm that uses randomness is `std::shuffle`, which replaces the old-style `std::random_shuffle`. Don't use `random_shuffle` in the new code.

Be aware that `std::mt19937` has exactly the same behavior on every platform, but the same is not true of any *distribution* type, nor of `std::shuffle`.

12 Filesystem

One of the biggest new features of C++17 is its `<filesystem>` library. This library, like many other major features of modern C++, originated in the Boost project. In 2015, it went into a standard technical specification to gather feedback, and finally, was merged into the C++17 standard with some changes based on that feedback.

In this chapter, you'll learn the following:

- How `<filesystem>` returns dynamically typed errors without throwing exceptions, and how you can too
- The format of a *path*, and the fundamentally incompatible positions of POSIX and Windows on the subject
- How to stat files and walk directories using portable C++17
- How to create, copy, rename, and remove files and directories
- How to fetch the free space of a filesystem

A note about namespaces

The standard C++17 filesystem facilities are all provided in a single header, `<filesystem>`, and everything in that header is placed in its own namespace: `namespace std::filesystem`. This follows the precedent set by C++11's `<chrono>` header with its `namespace std::chrono`. (This book omits a full treatment of `<chrono>`. Its interactions with `std::thread` and `std::timed_mutex` are covered briefly in Chapter 7, *Concurrency*.)

Filesystem

This namespacing strategy means that when you use the `<filesystem>` facilities, you'll be using identifiers such as `std::filesystem::directory_iterator` and `std::filesystem::temp_directory_path()`. These fully qualified names are quite unwieldy! But pulling the entire namespace into your current context with a `using` declaration is probably an overkill, especially, if you have to do it at file scope. We've all been taught over the past decade never to write `using namespace std`, and that advice won't change, no matter how deeply the standard library nests its namespaces. Consider the following code:

```
using namespace std::filesystem;

void foo(path p)
{
    remove(p); // What function is this?
}
```

A better solution for everyday purposes is to define a *namespace alias* at file scope (in a `.cc` file) or namespace scope (in a `.h` file). A namespace alias allows you to refer to an existing namespace by a new name, as seen in the following example:

```
namespace fs = std::filesystem;

void foo(fs::path p)
{
    fs::remove(p); // Much clearer!
}
```

In the remainder of this chapter, I will be using the namespace alias `fs` to refer to `namespace std::filesystem`. When I say `fs::path`, I mean `std::filesystem::path`. When I say `fs::remove`, I mean `std::filesystem::remove`.

Defining a namespace alias `fs` somewhere global has another pragmatic benefit as well. At press time, of all the major library vendors, only Microsoft Visual Studio claims to have implemented the C++17 `<filesystem>` header. However, the facilities of `<filesystem>` are very similar to those provided by libstdc++ and libc++ in `<experimental/filesystem>`, and by Boost in `<boost/filesystem.hpp>`. So, if you consistently refer to these facilities by a custom namespace alias, such as `fs`, you'll be able to switch from one vendor's implementation to another just by changing the target of that alias--a one-line change, as opposed to a massive and error-prone search-and-replace operation on your entire codebase. This can be seen in the following example:

```
#if USE_CXX17
  #include <filesystem>
  namespace fs = std::filesystem;
```

[340]

```
#elif USE_FILESYSTEM_TS
 #include <experimental/filesystem>
 namespace fs = std::experimental::filesystem;
#elif USE_BOOST
 #include <boost/filesystem.hpp>
 namespace fs = boost::filesystem;
#endif
```

A very long note on error-reporting

C++ has a love-hate relationship with error-reporting. By "error-reporting" in this context, I mean "what to do, when you can't do what you were asked". The classical, typical, and still the best-practice way to report this kind of "disappointment" in C++ is to throw an exception. We have seen in the previous chapters that, sometimes, throwing an exception is the *only* sensible thing to do, because there is no way to return to your caller. For example, if your task was to construct an object, and construction fails, you cannot return; when a constructor fails, the only same course of action is to throw. However, we have *also* seen (in Chapter 9, *Iostreams*) that C++'s own `<iostream>` library does not take this sane course of action! If the construction of a `std::fstream` object fails (because the named file cannot be opened), you will get an exception; you'll get a fully constructed `fstream` object where `f.fail() && !f.is_open()`.

The reason we gave in Chapter 9, *Iostreams*, for the "bad" behavior of `fstream` was the *relatively high likelihood* that the named file will not be openable. Throwing an exception every time a file can't be opened is uncomfortably close to using exceptions for control flow, which we have been taught--properly--to avoid. So, rather than force the programmer to write `try` and `catch` blocks everywhere, the library returns as if the operation had succeeded, but allows the user to check (with a normal `if`, not a `catch`) whether the operation really did succeed or not.

That is, we can avoid writing this cumbersome code:

```
try {
  f.open("hello.txt");
  // Opening succeeded.
} catch (const std::ios_base::failure&) {
  // Opening failed.
}
```

Instead, we can simply write this:

```
f.open("hello.txt");
if (f.is_open()) {
  // Opening succeeded.
} else {
  // Opening failed.
}
```

The iostreams approach works pretty well when the result of the operation is described by a heavyweight object (such as an `fstream`) which has a natural *failed* state, or where such a *failed* state can be added during the design stage. However, it has some downsides as well, and it flatly cannot be used if there is no heavyweight type involved. We saw this scenario at the end of Chapter 9, *Iostreams*, when we looked at ways of parsing integers from strings. If we don't expect failure, or don't mind the performance hit of "using exceptions for control flow," then we use `std::stoi`:

```
// Exception-throwing approach.
try {
  int i = std::stoi(s);
  // Parsing succeeded.
} catch (...) {
  // Parsing failed.
}
```

If we need portability to C++03, we use `strtol`, which reports errors via the thread-local global variable `errno`, as seen in this code:

```
char *endptr = nullptr;
errno = 0;
long i = strtol(s, &endptr, 10);
if (endptr != s && !errno) {
  // Parsing succeeded.
} else {
  // Parsing failed.
}
```

And in bleeding-edge C++17 style, we use `std::from_chars`, which returns a lightweight struct containing the end-of-string pointer and a value of the strong enum type `std::errc` indicating success or failure, as follows:

```
int i = 0;
auto [ptr, ec] = std::from_chars(s, end(s), i);
if (ec != std::errc{}) {
  // Parsing succeeded.
} else {
  // Parsing failed.
}
```

The `<filesystem>` library needs approximately the same capacity for error-reporting as `std::from_chars`. Pretty much any operation you can perform on your filesystem might fail due to the actions of other processes running on the system; so, throwing an exception on every failure (á là `std::stoi`) seems uncomfortably close to using exceptions for control flow. But threading an "error result" like `ec` through your entire codebase can also be tedious and (no pun intended) error-prone. So, the standard library decided to have its cake and eat it too by providing *two interfaces* to almost every function in the `<filesystem>` header!

For example, the following are the two `<filesystem>` functions for determining the size of a file on disk:

```
uintmax_t file_size(const fs::path& p);

uintmax_t file_size(const fs::path& p,
    std::error_code& ec) noexcept;
```

Both the preceding functions take an `fs::path` (which we'll discuss more further in the chapter), and return a `uintmax_t` telling the size of the named file in bytes. But what if the file doesn't exist, or it exists, but the current user-account doesn't have permission to query its size? Then, the first overload will simply *throw an exception* of type `fs::filesystem_error`, indicating what went wrong. But the second overload will never throw (in fact, it's marked `noexcept`). Instead, it takes an out-parameter of type `std::error_code`, which the library will fill in with an indication of what went wrong (or clear, if nothing went wrong at all).

Comparing the signatures of `fs::file_size` and `std::from_chars`, you might notice that `from_chars` deals in `std::errc`, and `file_size` deals in `std::error_code`. These two types, while related, are not the same! To understand the difference--and the entire design of the non-throwing `<filesystem>` API--we'll have to take a quick detour into another part of the C++11 standard library.

Using <system_error>

The difference between the error-reporting mechanisms of `std::from_chars` and `fs::file_size` is a difference in their intrinsic complexity. `from_chars` can fail in exactly two ways-- either the given string had no initial string of digits at all, else there were so *many* digits that it would cause an overflow to read them all. In the former case, a classic (but inefficient and, generally, dangerous) way to report the error would be to set `errno` to `EINVAL` (and return some useless value such as 0). In the latter case, a classic approach would be to set `errno` to `ERANGE` (and return some useless value). This is more or less (but rather less than more) the approach taken by `strtol`.

The salient point is that with `from_chars`, there are exactly two things that can possibly *ever* go wrong, and they are completely describable by the single set of error codes provided by POSIX `<errno.h>`. So, in order to bring the 1980's `strtol` into the twenty-first century, all we need to fix is to make it return its error code directly to the caller rather than indirectly, via the thread-local `errno`. And so, that's all the standard library did. The classic POSIX `<errno.h>` values are still provided as macros via `<cerrno>`, but as of C++11, they're also provided via a strongly typed enumeration in `<system_error>`, as shown in the following code:

```
namespace std {
  enum class errc {
    // implicitly, "0" means "no error"
    operation_not_permitted = EPERM,
    no_such_file_or_directory = ENOENT,
    no_such_process = ESRCH,
    // ...
    value_too_large = EOVERFLOW
  };
} // namespace std
```

`std::from_chars` reports errors by returning a struct (`struct from_chars_result`) containing a member variable of type `enum std::errc`, which will be either 0 for *no error*, or one of the two possible error-indicating values.

Now, what about `fs::file_size`? The set of possible errors encountered by `file_size` is much much larger--in fact, when you think of the number of operating systems in existence, and the number of different filesystems supported by each, and the fact that some filesystems (such as NFS) are distributed over *networks* of various types, the set of possible errors seems an awful lot like an *open set*. It might be possible to boil them all down onto the seventy-eight standard `sys::errc` enumerators (one for each POSIX `errno` value except `EDQUOT`, `EMULTIHOP`, and `ESTALE`), but that would lose a lot of information. Heck, at least one of the missing POSIX enumerators (`ESTALE`) is a legitimate failure mode of `fs::file_size`! And, of course, your underlying filesystem might want to report its own filesystem-specific errors; for example, while there is a standard POSIX error code for *name too long*, there is no POSIX error code for *name contains disallowed character* (for reasons we'll see in the next major section of this chapter). A filesystem might want to report exactly that error without worrying that `fs::file_size` was going to squash it down onto some fixed enumeration type.

The essential issue here is that the errors reported by `fs::file_size` might not all come from the same *domain*, and therefore, they cannot be represented by a single fixed-in-stone *type* (for example, `std::errc`). C++ exception-handling solves this problem elegantly; it is fine and natural for different levels of the program to throw different types of exceptions. If the lowest level of a program throws `myfs::DisallowedCharacterInName`, the topmost level can catch it--either by name, by base class, or by .... If we follow the general rule that everything thrown in a program should derive from `std::exception`, then any `catch` block will be able to use `e.what()` so that at least the user gets some vaguely human-readable indication of the problem, no matter what the problem was.

The standard library *reifies* the idea of multiple error domains into the base class `std::error_category`, as seen in the following code:

```
namespace std {

class error_category {
public:
  virtual const char *name() const noexcept = 0;
  virtual std::string message(int err) const = 0;

  // other virtual methods not shown

  bool operator==(const std::error_category& rhs) const {
    return this == &rhs;
  }
};

} // namespace std
```

Filesystem

`error_category` behaves a lot like `memory_resource` from Chapter 8, *Allocators*; it defines a classically polymorphic interface, and certain kinds of libraries are expected to subclass it. With `memory_resource`, we saw that some subclasses are global singletons, and some aren't. With `error_category`, *each* subclass *must* be a global singleton, or it's not going to work.

To make memory resources useful, the library gives us *containers* (see Chapter 4, *The Container Zoo*). At the most basic level, a container is a pointer representing some allocated memory, plus a handle to the *memory resource* that knows how to deallocate that pointer. (Recall that a handle to a memory resource is called an *allocator*.)

To make the `error_category` subclasses useful, the library gives us `std::error_code`. At the most basic level (which is the *only* level, in this case), an `error_code` is an `int` representing an error enumerator plus a handle to the `error_category` that knows how to interpret that enumerator. It looks like this:

```
namespace std {

class error_code {
  const std::error_category *m_cat;
  int m_err;
public:
  const auto& category() const { return m_cat; }
  int value() const { return m_err; }
  std::string message() const { return m_cat->message(m_err); }
  explicit operator bool() const { return m_err != 0; }

  // other convenience methods not shown
};

} // namespace std
```

So, to create a finicky filesystem library subsystem, we could write the following:

```
namespace FinickyFS {

enum class Error : int {
  success = 0,
  forbidden_character = 1,
  forbidden_word = 2,
  too_many_characters = 3,
};

struct ErrorCategory : std::error_category
{
  const char *name() const noexcept override {
```

```
      return "finicky filesystem";
    }

    std::string message(int err) const override {
      switch (err) {
        case 0: return "Success";
        case 1: return "Invalid filename";
        case 2: return "Bad word in filename";
        case 3: return "Filename too long";
      }
      throw Unreachable();
    }

    static ErrorCategory& instance() {
      static ErrorCategory instance;
      return instance;
    }
  };

  std::error_code make_error_code(Error err) noexcept
  {
    return std::error_code(int(err), ErrorCategory::instance());
  }

} // namespace FinickyFS
```

This preceding code defines a new error domain, the `FinickyFS::Error` domain, reified as `FinickyFS::ErrorCategory::instance()`. It allows us to create objects of type `std::error_code` via expressions such as `make_error_code(FinickyFS::Error::forbidden_word)`.

> **TIP**
> Notice that **argument-dependent lookup** (ADL) will find the correct overload of `make_error_code` without any help from us. `make_error_code` is a customization point in exactly the same way as `swap`: just define a function with that name in your enum's namespace, and it will work without any additional effort.

```
// An error fits comfortably in a statically typed
// and value-semantic std::error_code object...
std::error_code ec =
  make_error_code(FinickyFS::Error::forbidden_word);

// ...Yet its "what-string" remains just as
// accessible as if it were a dynamically typed
// exception!
assert(ec.message() == "Bad word in filename");
```

[347]

Filesystem

We now have a way to pass `FinickyFS::Error` codes losslessly through the system--by wrapping them inside trivially copyable `std::error_code` objects, and getting the original error back out at the topmost level. When I put it that way, it sounds almost like magic--like exception handling without exceptions! But as we've just seen, it's very simple to implement.

Error codes and error conditions

Notice that `FinickyFS::Error` is not implicitly convertible to `std::error_code`; in the last example, we used the syntax `make_error_code(FinickyFS::Error::forbidden_word)` to construct our initial `error_code` object. We can make `FinickyFS::Error` more convenient for the programmer if we tell `<system_error>` to enable implicit conversions from `FinickyFS::Error` to `std::error_code`, as follows:

```
namespace std {
template<>
struct is_error_code_enum<::FinickyFS::Error> : true_type {};
} // namespace std
```

Be careful when reopening namespace `std`--remember that you must be outside any other namespace when you do it! Otherwise, you'll be creating a nested namespace such as namespace `FinickyFS::std`. In this particular case, if you get it wrong, the compiler will helpfully error out when you try to specialize the non-existent `FinickyFS::std::is_error_code_enum`. As long as you only ever reopen namespace `std` in order to specialize templates (and as long as you don't mess up the template-specialization syntax), you won't have to worry too much about anything *quietly* failing.

Once you've specialized `std::is_error_code_enum` for your enum type, the library takes care of the rest, as seen in this code:

```
class error_code {
  // ...
  template<
    class E,
    class = enable_if_t<is_error_code_enum_v<E>>
  >
  error_code(E err) noexcept {
    *this = make_error_code(err);
  }
};
```

[348]

The implicit conversion seen in the previous code enables convenient syntax such as direct comparisons via ==, but because each std::error_code object carries its domain along with it, comparisons are strongly typed. Value-equality for the error_code objects depends not only on their *integer value*, but also the *address* of their associated error-category singletons.

```
std::error_code ec = FinickyFS::Error::forbidden_character;

// Comparisons are strongly typed.
assert(ec == FinickyFS::Error::forbidden_character);
assert(ec != std::io_errc::stream);
```

Specializing is_error_code_enum<X> is helpful if you're often going to be assigning X to variables of type std::error_code, or returning it from functions that return std::error_code. In other words, it's useful if your type X really does represent *the source of an error*--the throwing side of the equation, so to speak. But what about the catching side? Suppose you notice that you've written this function, and several more like it:

```
bool is_malformed_name(std::error_code ec) {
  return (
    ec == FinickyFS::Error::forbidden_character ||
    ec == FinickyFS::Error::forbidden_word ||
    ec == std::errc::illegal_byte_sequence);
}
```

The preceding function defines a *unary predicate* over the entire universe of error codes; it returns true for any error code associated with the concept of malformed names as far as our FinickyFS library is concerned. We can just drop this function straight into our library as FinickyFS::is_malformed_name()--and, in fact, that's the approach I personally recommend--but the standard library also provides another possible approach. You can define not an error_code, but an error_condition, as follows:

```
namespace FinickyFS {

enum class Condition : int {
  success = 0,
  malformed_name = 1,
};

struct ConditionCategory : std::error_category {
  const char *name() const noexcept override {
    return "finicky filesystem";
  }
  std::string message(int cond) const override {
    switch (cond) {
      case 0: return "Success";
```

[349]

```
          case 1: return "Malformed name";
        }
        throw Unreachable();
      }
      bool equivalent(const std::error_code& ec, int cond) const
      noexcept override {
        switch (cond) {
          case 0: return !ec;
          case 1: return is_malformed_name(ec);
        }
        throw Unreachable();
      }
      static ConditionCategory& instance() {
        static ConditionCategory instance;
        return instance;
      }
    };
    std::error_condition make_error_condition(Condition cond) noexcept
    {
      return std::error_condition(int(cond),
      ConditionCategory::instance());
    }

    } // namespace FinickyFS

    namespace std {
    template<>
    struct is_error_condition_enum<::FinickyFS::Condition> : true_type
    {};
    } // namespace std
```

Once you've done this, you can get the effect of calling `FinickyFS::is_malformed_name(ec)` **by writing the comparison** (`ec == FinickyFS::Condition::malformed_name`)**, like this:**

```
        std::error_code ec = FinickyFS::Error::forbidden_word;

        // RHS is implicitly converted to error_code
        assert(ec == FinickyFS::Error::forbidden_word);

        // RHS is implicitly converted to error_condition
        assert(ec == FinickyFS::Condition::malformed_name);
```

However, because we did not provide a function `make_error_code(FinickyFS::Condition)`, there will be no easy way to construct a `std::error_code}` object holding one of these conditions. This is appropriate; condition enums are for testing against on the catching side, not for converting to `error_code` on the throwing side.

The standard library provides two code enum types (`std::future_errc` and `std::io_errc`), and one condition enum type (`std::errc`). That's right--the POSIX error enum `std::errc` actually enumerates *conditions*, not *codes*! This means that if you're trying to stuff POSIX error codes into a `std::error_code` object, you're doing it wrong; they are *conditions*, which means they're for *testing against* on the catching side, not for throwing. Sadly, the standard library gets this wrong in at least two ways. First, as we've seen, `std::from_chars` does throw a value of type `std::errc` (which is doubly inconvenient; it would be more consistent to throw a `std::error_code`). Second, the function `std::make_error_code(std::errc)` exists, cluttering up the semantic space, when really only `std::make_error_condition(std::errc)` should (and does) exist.

Throwing errors with std::system_error

So far, we've considered `std::error_code`, a nifty non-throwing alternative to C++ exception-handling. But sometimes, you need to mix non-throwing and throwing libraries at different levels of the system. The standard library has your back--for one-half of the problem, anyway. `std::system_error` is a concrete exception type derived from `std::runtime_error`, which has just enough storage for a single `error_code`. So, if you are writing a library API which is throw-based, not `error_code`-based, and you receive an `error_code` indicating failure from a lower level of the system, it is perfectly appropriate to wrap that `error_code` in a `system_error` object, and `throw` it upward.

```
// The lower level is error_code-based.
uintmax_t file_size(const fs::path& p,
    std::error_code& ec) noexcept;

// My level is throw-based.
uintmax_t file_size(const fs::path& p)
{
  std::error_code ec;
  uintmax_t size = file_size(p, ec);
  if (ec) {
    throw std::system_error(ec);
  }
  return size;
}
```

Filesystem

In the opposite case--where you've written your library API to be non-throwing, but you make calls into lower levels that might throw--the standard library provides, basically, no help. But you can write an `error_code` unwrapper fairly easily yourself:

```cpp
// The lower level is throw-based.
uintmax_t file_size(const fs::path& p);

// My level is error_code-based.
uintmax_t file_size(const fs::path& p,
    std::error_code& ec) noexcept
{
  uintmax_t size = -1;
  try {
    size = file_size(p);
  } catch (...) {
    ec = current_exception_to_error_code();
  }
  return size;
}
```

The preceding code snippet calls `current_exception_to_error_code()`, which is a non-standard function you can write yourself. I recommend something along these lines:

```cpp
namespace detail {

enum Error : int {
    success = 0,
    bad_alloc_thrown = 1,
    unknown_exception_thrown = 2,
};
struct ErrorCategory : std::error_category {
    const char *name() const noexcept override;
    std::string message(int err) const override;
    static ErrorCategory& instance();
};
std::error_code make_error_code(Error err) noexcept {
    return std::error_code(int(err), ErrorCategory::instance());
}

} // namespace detail

std::error_code current_exception_to_error_code()
{
    try {
        throw;
    } catch (const std::system_error& e) {
        // also catches std::ios_base::failure
        // and fs::filesystem_error
```

[352]

```
            return e.code();
    } catch (const std::future_error& e) {
        // catches the oddball
        return e.code();
    } catch (const std::bad_alloc&) {
        // bad_alloc is often of special interest
        return detail::bad_alloc_thrown;
    } catch (...) {
        return detail::unknown_exception_thrown;
    }
}
```

This concludes our digression into the confusing world of `<system_error>`. We now return you to your regularly scheduled `<filesystem>`, already in progress.

Filesystems and paths

In Chapter 9, *Iostreams*, we discussed the POSIX concept of file descriptors. A file descriptor represents a source or sink of data which can be targeted by `read` and/or `write`; often, but not always, it corresponds to a file on disk. (Recall that file descriptor number 1 refers to `stdout`, which is usually connected to the human user's screen. File descriptors can also refer to network sockets, devices such as `/dev/random`, and so on.)

Furthermore, POSIX file descriptors, `<stdio.h>`, and `<iostream>` are all concerned, specifically, with the *contents* of a file on disk (or wherever)--the sequence of bytes that makes up the *contents* of the file. A file in the *filesystem* sense has many more salient attributes that are not exposed by the file-reading-and-writing APIs. We cannot use the APIs of Chapter 9, *Iostreams*, to determine the ownership of a file, or its last-modified date; nor can we determine the number of files in a given directory. The purpose of `<filesystem>` is to allow our C++ programs to interact with these *filesystem* attributes in a portable, cross-platform way.

Filesystem

Let's begin again. What is a filesystem? A filesystem is an abstract mapping from *paths* to *files*, by means of *directory entries*. Perhaps a diagram will help, if you take it with a large grain of salt:

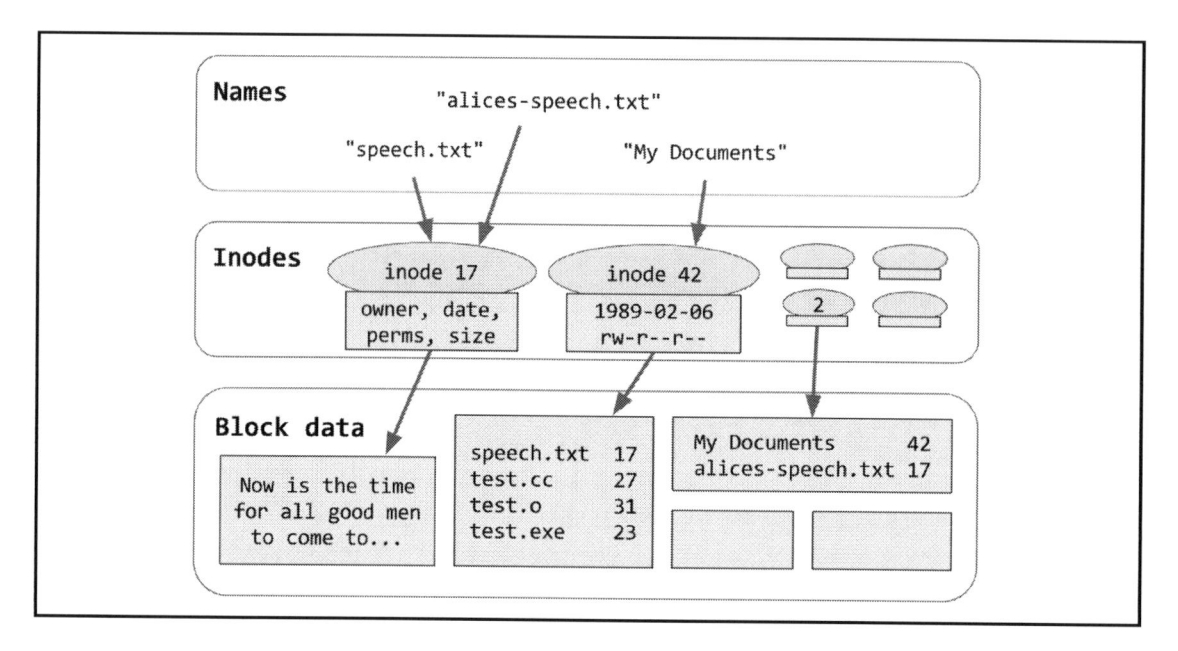

```
Names
                "alices-speech.txt"
    "speech.txt"         "My Documents"

Inodes
    inode 17          inode 42
    owner, date,      1989-02-06              2
    perms, size       rw-r--r--

Block data
                    speech.txt  17     My Documents       42
    Now is the time test.cc     27     alices-speech.txt  17
    for all good men test.o     31
    to come to...   test.exe    23
```

At the top of the preceding diagram, we have the somewhat abstract world of "names." We have a mapping from those names (such as speech.txt) onto concrete structures that POSIX calls *inodes*. The term "inode" is not used by the C++ standard--it uses the generic term "file"--but I will try to use the term inode when I want to be precise. Each inode contains a full set of attributes describing a single file on disk: its owner, its date of last modification, its *type*, and so on. Most importantly, the inode also tells exactly how big the file is, and gives a pointer to its actual contents (similarly to how a std::vector or std::list holds a pointer to *its* contents). The exact representation of inodes and blocks on disk depends on what kind of filesystem you're running; names of some common filesystems include ext4 (common on Linux), HFS+ (on OS X), and NTFS (on Windows).

Notice that a few of the blocks in that diagram hold data that is just a tabular mapping of *names* to *inode numbers*. This brings us full circle! A *directory* is just an inode with a certain *type*, whose contents are a tabular mapping of names to inode numbers. Each filesystem has one special well-known inode called its *root directory*.

Suppose that the inode labeled "2" in our diagram is the *root directory*. Then we can unambiguously identify the file containing "Now is the time..." by a path of names that leads from the root directory down to that file. For example, `/My Documents/speech.txt` is such a path: starting from the root directory, `My Documents` maps to inode 42, which is a directory where `speech.txt` maps to inode 17, which is a normal file whose contents on disk are "Now is the time...". We use slashes to compose these individual names into a single path, and we put a single slash on the front to indicate that we're starting from the root directory. (In Windows, each partition or drive has a separate root directory. So, instead of writing just `/My Documents/speech.txt`, we might write `c:/My Documents/speech.txt` to indicate that we're starting from drive C's root directory.)

Alternatively, "`/alices-speech.txt`" is a path leading straight from the root directory to inode 17. We say that these two paths ("`/My Documents/speech.txt`" and "`/alices-speech.txt`") are both *hard-links* for the same underlying inode, which is to say, the same underlying *file*. Some filesystems (such as the FAT filesystem used by many USB sticks) do not support having multiple hard links to the same file. When multiple hard links *are* supported, the filesystem must count the number of references to each inode so that it knows when it's safe to delete and free up an inode--in a procedure exactly analogous to the `shared_ptr` reference-counting we saw in Chapter 6, *Smart Pointers*.

When we ask a library function such as `open` or `fopen` to "open a file," this is the process it's going through deep down in the innards of the filesystem. It takes the filename you gave it and treats it as a *path*--splits it up at the slashes, and descends into the directory structure of the filesystem until it finally reaches the inode of the file you asked for (or until it hits a dead end). Notice that once we have reached the inode, there is no longer any sense in asking "What is the name of this file?", as it has at least as many names as there are hard-links to it.

Representing paths in C++

Throughout Chapter 9, *Iostreams*, every function that expected a "filename" (that is, a path) as a parameter was happy to take that path as a simple const char *. But in the `<filesystem>` library, we're going to complicate that picture, all because of Windows.

All POSIX filesystems store names (like `speech.txt`) as simple raw byte strings. The only rules in POSIX are that your names can't contain '`\0`', and your names can't contain '`/`' (because that's the character we're going to split on). On POSIX, "`\xC1.h`" is a perfectly valid filename, despite the fact that it is *not* valid UTF-8 and *not* valid ASCII, and the way it'll display on your screen when you `ls .` is completely dependent on your current locale and codepage. After all, it's just a string of three bytes, none of which are '`/`'.

Filesystem

On the other hand, Window's native file APIs, such as `CreateFileW`, always store names as UTF-16. This means that, by definition, paths in Windows are always valid Unicode strings. This is a major philosophical difference between POSIX and NTFS! Let me say it again, slowly: In POSIX, file names are *strings of bytes*. In Windows, file names are *strings of Unicode characters*.

If you follow the general principle from Chapter 9, *Iostreams* that everything in the world should be encoded with UTF-8, then the difference between POSIX and Windows will be manageable--maybe, even negligible. But if you are ever required to debug problems with strangely named files on one or the other system, keep in mind: In POSIX, filenames are strings of bytes. In Windows, filenames are strings of characters.

Since Windows APIs expect UTF-16 strings (`std::u16string`) and POSIX APIs expect byte strings (`std::string`), neither representation is exactly appropriate for a cross-platform library. So, `<filesystem>` invents a new type: `fs::path`. (Recall that we're using our namespace alias throughout this chapter. That's `std::filesystem::path` in reality.) `fs::path` looks something like this:

```
class path {
public:
  using value_type = std::conditional_t<
    IsWindows, wchar_t, char
  >;
  using string_type = std::basic_string<value_type>;

  const auto& native() const { return m_path; }
  operator string_type() const { return m_path; }
  auto c_str() const { return m_path.c_str(); }

  // many constructors and accessors omitted
private:
  string_type m_path;
};
```

Notice that `fs::path::value_type` is `wchar_t` in Windows, even though C++11's UTF-16 character type `char16_t` would be more appropriate. This is just an artifact of the library's historical roots in Boost, which dates back to before C++11. In this chapter, whenever we talk about `wchar_t`, you can assume we're talking about UTF-16, and vice versa.

To write portable code, pay attention to the return type of any function you use to convert an `fs::path` to a string. For example, notice that the return type of `path.c_str()` is not the const char *--it's const value_type *!

```
fs::path p("/foo/bar");

const fs::path::value_type *a = p.c_str();
    // Portable, for whatever that's worth.

const char *b = p.c_str();
    // OK on POSIX; compilation error on Windows.

std::string s = p.u8string();
const char *c = s.c_str();
    // OK on both POSIX and Windows.
    // Performs 16-to-8 conversion on Windows.
```

The preceding example, case `c`, is guaranteed to compile, but its behavior differs on the two platforms: in POSIX platforms, it'll give you the raw byte-string you want, and in Windows, it'll expensively convert `path.native()` from UTF-16 to UTF-8 (which is exactly what you asked for--but your program might be faster if you found a way to avoid asking).

`fs::path` has a templated constructor that can construct a `path` from just about any argument. The argument can be a sequence of any character type (`char`, `wchar_t`, `char16_t`, or `char32_t`), and that sequence can be expressed as a pointer to a null-terminated string, an *iterator* to a null-terminated string, a `basic_string`, a `basic_string_view`, or an iterator-pair. As usual, I mention this huge variety of overloads not because you'll want to use any of them beyond the basics, but so that you'll know how to avoid them.

The standard also provides the free function `fs::u8path("path")`, which is just a synonym for `fs::path("path")`, but might serve as a reminder that the string you're passing in is supposed to be UTF-8-encoded. I recommend ignoring `u8path`.

This all might sound scarier than it is. Bear in mind that if you stick to ASCII filenames, you won't need to worry about encoding issues; and if you remember to avoid the "native" accessor methods, `path.native()` and `path.c_str()`, and avoid the implicit conversion to `fs::path::string_type`, then you won't have to worry too much about portability.

Filesystem

Operations on paths

Once we have a path object, we can query it for many useful combinations of its slash-separated components. In the following code snippet, each identifier x (except path itself) represents the return value of the member function path.x():

```
assert(root_path == root_name / root_directory);
assert(path == root_name / root_directory / relative_path);
assert(path == root_path / relative_path);

assert(path == parent_path / filename);
assert(filename == stem + extension);

assert(is_absolute == !is_relative);
if (IsWindows) {
  assert(is_relative == (root_name.empty() ||
root_directory.empty()));
} else {
  assert(is_relative == (root_name.empty() &&
root_directory.empty()));
}
```

So, for example, given the path p = "c:/foo/hello.txt", we have p.root_name() == "c:", p.root_directory() == "/", p.relative_path() == "foo/hello.txt", p.stem() == "hello", and p.extension() == ".txt". At least, that's what we'd have in Windows! Notice that in Windows, an absolute path requires both a root name and a root directory (neither "c:foo/hello.txt" nor "/foo/hello.txt" is an absolute path), whereas, in POSIX, where root names don't exist, an absolute path requires only a root directory ("/foo/hello.txt" is an absolute path, and "c:foo/hello.txt" is a relative path that starts with the funny-looking directory name "c:foo").

In the last code snippet, we use operator/ to concatenate paths. fs::path supports both operator/ and operator/= for this purpose, and they do almost exactly what you'd expect--concatenate two pieces of a path with a slash in between them. If you want to concatenate pieces of a path without adding that slash, use operator+=. Unfortunately, the C++17 standard library is missing operator+ for paths, but it's easy to add as a free function, as follows:

```
static fs::path operator+(fs::path a, const fs::path& b)
{
  a += b;
  return a;
}
```

Paths also support concatenation with and without slashes under the confusing member-function names `path.concat("foo")` (without slash) and `path.append("foo")` (with slash). Beware that this is exactly backwards from what you'd expect! Therefore, I strongly advise never to use the named member functions; always use the operators (perhaps including your custom-defined `operator+` as described in the preceding code).

The last potentially confusing thing about `fs::path` is that it provides `begin` and `end` methods, just like `std::string`. But unlike `std::string`, the unit of iteration is not the single character--the unit of iteration is the *name*! This is seen in the following example:

```
fs::path p = "/foo/bar/baz.txt";
std::vector<fs::path> v(p.begin(), p.end());
assert((v == std::vector<fs::path>{
  "/", "foo", "bar", "baz.txt"
}));
```

You'll never have a reason to iterate over an absolute `fs::path` in real code. Iterating over `p.relative_path().parent_path()`--where every iterated element is guaranteed to be a directory name--might have some value in unusual circumstances.

Statting files with directory_entry

> **TIP**
> Beware! `directory_entry` is the most bleeding-edge part of the C++17 `<filesystem>` library. What I am about to describe is neither implemented by Boost, nor by `<experimental/filesystem>`.

Retrieving a file's metadata from its inode is done by querying an object of type `fs::directory_entry`. If you're familiar with the POSIX approach to retrieving metadata, imagine that a `fs::directory_entry` contains a member of type `fs::path` and a member of type `std::optional<struct stat>`. Calling `entry.refresh()` is, basically, the same thing as calling the POSIX function `stat()`; and calling any `accessor` method, such as `entry.file_size()`, will implicitly call `stat()` if and only if the optional member is still disengaged. Merely constructing an instance of `fs::directory_entry` won't query the filesystem; the library waits until you ask a specific question before it acts. Asking a specific question, such as `entry.file_size()`, may cause the library to query the filesystem, or (if the optional member is already engaged) it might just use the cached value from the last time it queried.

```
fs::path p = "/tmp/foo/bar.txt";
fs::directory_entry entry(p);
```

Filesystem

```
            // Here, we still have not touched the filesystem.

    while (!entry.exists()) {
       std::cout << entry.path() << " does not exist yet\n";
       std::this_thread::sleep_for(100ms);
       entry.refresh();
         // Without refresh(), this would loop forever.
    }
       // If the file is deleted right now, the following
       // line might print stale cached values, or it
       // might try to refresh the cache and throw.
    std::cout << entry.path() << " has size "
            << entry.file_size() << "\n";
```

An older way to accomplish the same goal is to use `fs::status("path")` or `fs::symlink_status("path")` to retrieve an instance of the class `fs::file_status`, and then to pull information out of the `file_status` object via cumbersome operations such as `status.type() == fs::file_type::directory`. I recommend you not try to use `fs::file_status`; prefer to use `entry.is_directory()` and so on. For the masochistic, you can still retrieve a `fs::file_status` instance directly from a `directory_entry`: `entry.status()` is the equivalent of `fs::status(entry.path())`, and `entry.symlink_status()` is the equivalent of `fs::symlink_status(entry.path())`, which, in turn, is a slightly faster equivalent of `fs::status(entry.is_symlink() ? fs::read_symlink(entry.path()) : entry.path())`.

Incidentally, the free function `fs::equivalent(p, q)` can tell you if two paths are both hard-linked to the same inode; and `entry.hard_link_count()` can tell you the total number of hard-links to this particular inode. (The only way to determine the *names* of those hard-links is to walk the entire filesystem; and even then, your current user account might not have the permission to stat those paths.)

Walking directories with directory_iterator

A `fs::directory_iterator` is just what it says on the tin. An object of this type lets you walk the contents of a single directory, entry by entry:

```
           fs::path p = fs::current_path();
             // List the current directory.
           for (fs::directory_entry entry : fs::directory_iterator(p)) {
              std::cout << entry.path().string() << ": "
                << entry.file_size() << " bytes\n";
           }
```

Incidentally, notice the use of `entry.path().string()` in the preceding code. This is required, because `operator<<` acts extremely bizarrely on path objects--it always outputs as if you'd written `std::quoted(path.string())`. If you want the path itself, with no extra quotes, you always have to convert to `std::string` before outputting. (Similarly, `std::cin >> path` won't work to get a path from the user, but that's less obnoxious, since you should never use `operator>>` anyway. See Chapters 9, *Iostreams*, and Chapter 10, *Regular Expressions*, for more information on lexing and parsing input from the user.)

Recursive directory walking

To recurse down a whole directory tree, in the style of Python's `os.walk()`, you can use this recursive function modeled on the previous code snippet:

```
template<class F>
void walk_down(const fs::path& p, const F& callback)
{
  for (auto entry : fs::directory_iterator(p)) {
    if (entry.is_directory()) {
      walk_down(entry.path(), callback);
    } else {
      callback(entry);
    }
  }
}
```

Or, you can simply use a `fs::recursive_directory_iterator`:

```
template<class F>
void walk_down(const fs::path& p, const F& callback)
{
  for (auto entry : fs::recursive_directory_iterator(p)) {
    callback(entry);
  }
}
```

The constructor of `fs::recursive_directory_iterator` can take an extra argument of type `fs::directory_options`, which modifies the exact nature of the recursion. For example, you can pass `fs::directory_options::follow_directory_symlink` to follow symlinks, although this is a good way to wind up in an infinite loop if a malicious user creates a symlink pointing back to its own parent directory.

Modifying the filesystem

Most of the `<filesystem>` header's facilities are concerned with examining the filesystem, not modifying it. But there are several gems hidden in the rubble. Many of these functions seem designed to make the effects of the classic POSIX command-line utilities available in portable C++:

- `fs::copy_file(old_path, new_path)` : Copy the file at `old_path` to a new file (that is, a new inode) at `new_path`, as if by `cp -n`. Error if `new_path` already exists.
- `fs::copy_file(old_path, new_path, fs::copy_options::overwrite_existing)`: Copy `old_path` to `new_path`. Overwrite `new_path` if possible. Error if `new_path` exists and is not a regular file, or if it's the same as `old_path`.
- `fs::copy_file(old_path, new_path, fs::copy_options::update_existing)`: Copy `old_path` to `new_path`. Overwrite `new_path` if and only if it's older than the file at `old_path`.
- `fs::copy(old_path, new_path, fs::copy_options::recursive | fs::copy_options::copy_symlinks)`: Copy an entire directory from `old_path` to `new_path` as if by `cp -R`.
- `fs::create_directory(new_path)`: Create a directory as if by `mkdir`.
- `fs::create_directories(new_path)`: Create a directory as if by `mkdir -p`.
- `fs::create_directory(new_path, old_path)` (notice the reversal of the arguments!): Create a directory, but copy its attributes from those of the directory at `old_path`.
- `fs::create_symlink(old_path, new_path)`: Create a symlink from `new_path` to `old_path`.
- `fs::remove(path)`: Remove a file or an empty directory as if by `rm`.
- `fs::remove_all(path)`: Remove a file or directory as if by `rm -r`.
- `fs::rename(old_path, new_path)`: Rename a file or directory as if by `mv`.
- `fs::resize_file(path, new_size)`: Extend (with zeroes) or truncate a regular file.

Reporting disk usage

Speaking of classic command-line utilities, one final thing we might want to do with a filesystem is ask how full it is. This is the domain of the command-line utility `df -h` or the POSIX library function `statvfs`. In C++17, we can do it with `fs::space("path")`, which returns (by value) a struct of type `fs::space_info`:

```
struct space_info {
    uintmax_t capacity;
    uintmax_t free;
    uintmax_t available;
};
```

Each of these fields is measured in bytes, and we should have `available <= free <= capacity`. The distinction between `available` and `free` has to do with user limits: On some filesystems, a portion of the free space might be reserved for the root user, and on others, there might be per-user-account disk quotas.

Summary

Use namespace aliases to save typing, and to allow dropping in alternative implementations
of a library namespace, such as Boost.

`std::error_code` provides a very neat way to pass integer error codes up the stack without exception handling; consider using it if you work in a domain where exception handling is frowned upon. (In which case, that is likely *all* you will be able to take away from this particular chapter! The `<filesystem>` library provides both throwing and non-throwing APIs; however, both APIs use the heap-allocating (and, potentially, throwing `fs::path` as a vocabulary type. The only reason to use the non-throwing API is if it eliminates a case of "using exceptions for control flow.)

`std::error_condition` provides only syntactic sugar for "catching" error codes; avoid it like the plague.

A `path` consists of a `root_name`, a `root_directory`, and a `relative_path`; the last of these is made up of *names* separated by slashes. To POSIX, a *name* is a string of raw bytes; to Windows, a *name* is a string of Unicode characters. The `fs::path` type attempts to use the appropriate kind of string for each platform. To avoid portability problems, beware of `path.c_str()` and implicit conversions to `fs::path::string_type`.

Directories store mappings from *names* to *inodes* (which the C++ standard just calls "files"). In C++, you can loop over an `fs::directory_iterator` to retrieve `fs::directory_entry` objects; methods on the `fs::directory_entry` allow you to query the corresponding inode. Restatting an inode is as simple as calling `entry.refresh()`.

`<filesystem>` provides a whole zoo of free functions for creating, copying, renaming, removing, and resizing files and directories, and one last function to get the total capacity of the filesystem.

Much of what was discussed in this chapter (the `<filesystem>` parts, at least) is bleeding-edge C++17 that, as of press time, has not been implemented by any compiler vendor. Use such new features with caution.

Index

<

\<random\> header 325
\<system_error\>
  used, for error reporting 344

A

adaptor
  generator outputs, filtering 329
  std::priority_queue<T> 97
algebraic types 116
algorithm
  used, for affecting object lifetime 55
allocator-aware container
  creating 240
allocator
  about 111, 217
  concepts 218
  different allocators, propagating 249
  interfaces 218
  propagating, with scoped_allocator_adaptor 246
  with memory 111
argument-dependent lookup (ADL) 347
arrays
  managing, with std::unique_ptr<T[]> 151

B

backslash-escaping 297
bell curve 334
bucket lists 110
buffering
  versus formatting 255

C

C++11 116
C++
  finally keyword 149
  I/O, trouble with 254
  paths, representing 355
classically polymorphic functions 8
concrete monomorphic functions 8
const iterators 19
container
  associating, to single memory resource 235
cryptographically secure pseudo-random number generator (CSPRNG) 329
Curiously Recurring Template Pattern (CRTP) 162
custom thread pool
  building 207
  performance, improving 212

D

data
  shunting, with std::copy 44
deprecated std::iterator 31
directories
  exploring, with directory_iterator 360
  recursive directory, exploring 361
directory_entry
  files, statting with 359
discriminated union 121
disk usage
  reporting 363
distributions
  dealing with 331
  discrete_distribution 335
  normal_distribution 334
  std::shuffle 337
  uniform_int_distribution 332

E

ECMAScript regex grammar
  about 314
  features 318

    non-consuming constructs 317
    pitfalls 318
error-reporting
    about 341
    error codes 348
    error conditions 348
    errors, throwing with std::system_error 351
    with <system_error> 344

F

fancy pointers
    metadata, carrying 230
files
    statting, with directory_entry 359
filesystem
    about 353
    modifying 362
finally keyword 149
formatting
    versus buffering 255
futures
    promises 193
    std::future 198

G

generators
    dealing with 326
    g() 326
    g.discard(n) 326
    g.max() 326
    g.min() 326
    output, filtering with adaptors 329
    std::mt19937 327
    std::random_device 326
generic programming
    with templates 10

H

hashes
    about 108
    bucket lists 110
    load factor 110
    std::unordered_map<K, V> 108
    std::unordered_set<T> 108
headers 37

heap allocation, problems
    heap corruption, via pointer arithmetic 144
    memory leaks 144
    use-after-free 144
heap
    about 63
    defining, with memory_resource 219
heapsort 63

I

I/O
    trouble with 254
initialization
    delaying, with std::optional 127
input iterators 25
input
    line or word, reading 291
integer indices
    problem 15
iostreams
    formatting, with ostringstream 282
    hierarchy 270
    locales 283
    manipulators 275
    sticky-manipulator problem, solving 280
    wrappers 278
iterators
    categories 22
    implementing, with standard library 28
    input iterators 25
    output iterators 25
    range, defining 21

L

lexing 295
load factor 110
locales 283
locks
    deadlock 178
    lock leaks 178
    use-outside-of-lock 178

M

make_variant 125
manipulators

   used, for formatting iostreams 275
matches
   multiple matches, iterating over 307
memory management
   with std::unique_ptr<T> 145
memory resource
   handling, with allocator 217
memory_resource
   heap, defining 219
merges 66
mergesort 66
Mersenne Twister algorithm 327
multiset
   about 104
   elements, moving 105
mutex
   about 175
   associating, with controlled data 181
   special-purpose mutex types 185

N

named classes 121
namespaces 339
non-consuming constructs 317
non-noexcept move constructors
   pitfalls 89
normal_distribution 334
nullable handles
   holding, with weak_ptr 156
numbers
   converting, to strings 284
   strings, converting 287

O

object ownership 76
object-oriented (OO) programming 8
observer_ptr<T>
   used, for denoting un-special-ness 163
ostringstream
   used, for formatting iostreams 282
output iterators 25

P

partitioning algorithm 58
paths
   about 353
   operations, performing 358
   representing, in C++ 355
permutation 56, 62
permutative algorithm
   std::sort 56
pointers
   using 17
polymorphic class types
   versus std::any 134
pool resource
   allocating from 224
   synchronized pool resource 225
   unsynchronized pool resource 225
POSIX API
   using 256
POSIX file descriptor
   lseek(fd, offset, SEEK_CUR) 258
   lseek(fd, offset, SEEK_END) 258
   lseek(fd, offset, SEEK_SET) 258
   read(fd, buffer, count) 258
   write(fd, buffer, count) 258
printf
   used, for formatting 267
pseudo-random number generator (PRNG) 322
pseudo-random numbers
   versus random numbers 322

R

rand() function
   problem 324
random numbers
   versus pseudo-random numbers 322
read-only range algorithms 38
recursive directory
   exploring 361
reference counting
   with std::shared_ptr<T> 152
reference types
   tagging, with reference_wrapper 115
regular expressions (regexes)
   about 295, 296
   backslash-escaping 297
   matching 301
   reifying, into std::regex objects 299

searching 301
  submatches, converting to data values 306
  submatches, extracting out of match 302
  used, for string replacement 311
Resource Allocation Is Initialization (RAII) 77
reversing algorithm 58
rotation 62

S

scoped_allocator_adaptor
  used, for propagating allocator 246
set 104
single memory resource
  container, associating to 235
smart pointers
  features 145
  origins 143
snprintf
  used, for formatting 267
sorted array
  deleting, with std::remove_if 69
  inserting, with std::lower_bound 67
  searching, with std::lower_bound 67
special-purpose mutex
  read-write lock, downgrading 188
  read-write lock, upgrading 188
  types 185
  waiting, for condition 189
standard allocator types
  default memory resource, setting 238
  using 237
standard allocator
  features 226
  metadata, carrying with fancy pointers 230
standard C API
  buffering 262
  formatting, with printf 267
  formatting, with snprintf 267
  using 260
standard library
  iterators, implementing with 28
standard memory resources
  allocating, from pool resource 224
  using 222
Standard Template Library (STL) 12

std::any
  copyability 137
  for infinite alternatives 132
  versus polymorphic class types 134
std::array<T, N> 78
std::atomic<T>
  complicated operations, performing 173
  for bigger types 175
  used, for thread-safe accesses 171
std::copy
  used, for shunting data 44
std::deque<T> 91
std::enable_shared_from_this 159
std::forward_list<T> 95
std::function 138
  allocation 140
  copyability 140
std::list<T>
  about 92
  examples 93
std::lower_bound
  used, for inserting in sorted array 67
  used, for searching in sorted array 67
std::map<K, V> 99
std::move algorithm
  implementing 47
std::move_iterator algorithm
  implementing 47
std::mt19937 327
std::multimap<K, V> 104
std::multiset<T> 104
std::mutex
  locks, handling 178
  using 175
std::optional
  initialization, delaying 127
std::priority_queue<T> 97
std::queue<T> 96
std::random_device 326
std::regex objects
  regular expressions, reifying into 299
std::remove_if
  used, for deleting from sorted array 69
std::set<T> 99
std::shared_ptr<T>

considerations 163
  Curiously Recurring Template Pattern (CRTP) 162
  double-manage, avoiding 155
  for reference counting 152
  nullable handles, holding with weak_ptr 156
std::shuffle 337
std::sort 56
std::stack<T> 96
std::string 114
std::system_error
  used, for throwing error 351
std::transform algorithm
  used, for complicated copying 51
std::tuple
  about 117
  named classes 121
  tuple values, manipulating 120
std::unique_ptr<T>
  deletion callback, customizing 150
  used, for automatically managing memory 145
  used, instead of finally keyword 149
std::unordered_map<K, V> 108
std::unordered_set<T> 108
std::variant
  alternatives, expressing 121
  make_variant 125
  value semantics 125
  variants, visiting 123
std::vector<T>
  about 81
  erasing 86
  inserting 86
  non-noexcept move constructors, pitfalls 89
  resizing 83
  vector<bool>, pitfalls 88
streambuf 271
streams 271
string replacement
  with regular expressions 311
strings
  converting, to numbers 287
  numbers, converting to 284
swapping algorithm 58

T

tasks
  packaging 197
templates
  used, for generic programming 10
threads
  current thread, identifying 202
  exhaustion 205
  handling 201
  individual threads, identifying 202
  std::async, using 205
transparent comparators 103
trees
  std::map<K, V> 99
  std::set<T> 99
transparent comparators 103
type erasure
  about 135
  std::any 137
  std::function 138

U

uniform_int_distribution 332

V

value semantics 125
variant
  using 131
vector<bool>
  pitfalls 88
vocabulary type
  about 113
volatile keyword
  problem with 168

W

weak_ptr
  nullable handles, holding 156
Windows Subsystem for Linux (WSL) 256
wrappers
  used, for formatting iostreams 278
write-only range algorithms
  implementing 53

Made in the USA
San Bernardino, CA
20 August 2019